Pathways to Scientific Teaching

EDITED BY:

Diane Ebert-May
Michigan State University

Janet Hodder
University of Oregon

 Sinauer Associates, Inc. Publishers
Sunderland, Massachusetts

About the Cover:

Active learning in a large lecture course at Michigan State University. Photograph by Kurt Stepnitz, MSU University Relations.

Pathways to Scientific Teaching
Sinauer Associates, Sunderland MA
©2008 The Ecological Society of America

Address editorial correspondence and orders to:
Sinauer Associates, 23 Plumtree Road, Sunderland, MA 01375 U.S.A.
FAX: 413-549-1118
Email: publish@sinauer.com
Internet: www.sinauer.com

Library of Congress Cataloging-in-Publication Data

Pathways to scientific teaching / edited by Diane Ebert-May, Janet Hodder.
     p. cm.
 Includes bibliographical references and index.
 ISBN 978-0-87893-222-1 (hardcover : alk. paper)
 1. Ecology—Study and teaching—United States. 2. Biology—Study and teaching—United States. 3. Science—Study and teaching—United States. 4. Science teachers—Training of—United States. I. Ebert-May, Diane, 1949- II. Hodder, Janet, 1954-

QH541.2.P38 2008
577.071—dc22

                         2007046165

Printed in China
6 5 4 3 2 1

To Audrey Champagne who mentored and Henry Hooper who believed
DE-M

To Miss Knight, Chip Wray, and Bob Terwilliger, who showed me new ways to learn
JH

Contents

Chapter 4

Students: Reading Science 80

Chapter 5

Faculty and Students: Assessing Multiple Ways 104

Chapter 6

Students: Preparing Homework for Class 136

Chapter 7

Faculty: Moving from Assessment to Research 170

Chapter 8

Faculty: A Community of Researchers 204

Foreword

Designing a course is hard work—what to cover, course requirements, and so on. But designing a course to meet the needs of a diverse student population in a way that really connects teaching with learning is even harder. Like many new instructors, I came to this insight the hard way. I began my career as an assistant professor in 1993. My first days teaching in a lecture hall that held 450 students were a shock—both to me and to the students, many of whom came from small towns in Montana with populations smaller than that of the lecture hall when every seat was filled. For me, and many of the students who arrived in that lecture room, the setting was daunting. We all had a lot to learn about education.

No one questions the goal of better connecting teaching with learning. The problem is that few faculty members at colleges and universities have had formal training in how to teach. What is the result? We teach like we were taught—faculty lecture and students regurgitate. In this model, courses are, by default, more about teaching than about learning, and it should come as no great wonder that many students in lecture courses vote with their feet—they choose a coffee house instead of the lecture hall. And after listening to myself lecture in class after class, I began to wonder what could be done to better engage these students. As a new professor, I knew how to develop collaborations with other plant physiological ecologists to build my research program. But how did one go about developing a network of colleagues to grow as a teacher? The answer came in 1994 at an annual meeting of the Ecological Society of America, where a small network of individuals had gathered to talk about teaching science. Diane Ebert-May, who also taught biology in a large lecture format, was at this meeting, and she and I decided to try to make our courses more student-centered. In particular, we promised to share our insights with each other on what seemed to work well and what didn't as we began experimenting with our teaching. Thus was born our teaching and learning community. Over the next several years, we tried new pedagogical strategies—once Diane even called me mid-lecture to clarify an instruction on a classroom experiment I had designed. Teaching these large classes (and the smaller ones too) became much more fun, and we saw changes in how our students responded. A most noticeable change was that students came to class and they participated! Soon we began trying to document these changes to make our teaching more evidence-based.

Three years later, in 1997, Diane and I met in Diane's sunroom on a bright snowy day in Flagstaff, AZ, to talk about our shared experiences teaching biology, and to imagine what teaching would look like if we approached it more like we approach our scientific scholarship. We marveled at the firewall of sorts between our lives as teachers and our lives as scientific researchers. While we and other faculty easily establish collaborative communities for our research, teaching is often a solitary endeavor where we close the door to our classroom and do the best we can—faculty typically teach the way they were taught. Diane and I also were inspired by a passage written by Bruce Alberts stating that "scientists should be no more willing to fly blind in their teaching than they are in scientific research, where no new investigation is begun without an extensive examination of what is already known."[1] With wine in hand, we envisioned a community of faculty who would use research to inform their classroom teaching and who would mentor one another. If there wasn't a ready-

---

[1] National Research Council. 1997. *Science Teaching Reconsidered*. Washington DC: National Academies Press.

made group of teaching collaborators on one's own campus, we imagined one could turn to a virtual community of teaching collaborators, much like we had done with each other over the years. Luckily for all of us, Diane Ebert-May and Jan Hodder turned this vision into a reality with the FIRST (Faculty Institutes for Reforming Science Teaching) Program, funded by the NSF. What they learned is collected in the pages of this book.

Ten years have passed from the time when we sipped wine on that cold day and brainstormed about a teaching "collaboratorium" of sorts. And what amazing progress! Since then, scores of faculty from dozens of campuses across the U.S.A. have participated in FIRST training. And through their efforts they are beginning to change the conversation in substantive ways at small and large colleges and universities about how we teach. Over this same period, we have also seen a revolution in our understanding of how people learn.[2] Indeed, if we take the time to look, research has taught us a lot about how to connect teaching and learning. Bruce Alberts was right!

So it really is a privilege and honor to introduce *Pathways to Scientific Teaching*, a book that brings to life engaging examples, doable assessment tips, and practical approaches—all woven together with stories of scientific discovery and the voices of faculty who have used these approaches in their classrooms. The faculty we meet in this book have struggled to focus their courses on student learning outcomes—what these should be, a process to get there, and the evidence to let the faculty and students know they made it. Indeed, as much as this book is about how to teach, it is also about finding a community of teaching collaborators.

How have the people we meet in this book connected teaching with learning? One way is with the good stories that come from cutting-edge research that leads to discoveries. Another is by treating their teaching the way they treat their research—as an enterprise that depends on evidence for evaluating the efficacy of a treatment. In the case of teaching, this means carefully examining the extent to which we can really connect *how* we are teaching (our pedagogical strategies) to student learning. This volume provides a roadmap of how to make even the largest lecture class more engaging, interactive, and, ultimately, focused on the learners. Through this volume, the reader will see that the first step down this road is to ask ourselves *what do we want our students to know and be able to do?* The next step is to put together a plan in which our teaching strategies, course content, and assessment plan are tightly connected to the thinking skills and conceptual understanding we hope to help our students develop.

This book helps advance the agenda for truly connecting teaching with learning by making our approach to teaching more scientific and reminding us we all have a role to play beyond making our classes more student-focused. But to spread and sustain the approaches described in this book, we also have a role to play in how teaching is valued on our campuses. We cannot forget to advocate for and raise the value of this kind of teaching and learning within our institutions, especially when decisions for promotion and tenure are being made. Truly, the future of the *Pathway to Scientific Teaching* depends on it.

---

[2] Bransford JD, Brown AL, Cocking RR (eds.). 2000. *How People Learn: Brain, Mind, Experience, and School.* Washington DC: National Academies Press.

Carol Brewer
Associate Dean and Professor of Biology
University of Montana

Acknowledgments

Our pathway towards writing this book began in 1998 with the establishment of a national network of faculty who participated in Faculty Institutes for Reforming Science Teaching (FIRST), generously supported by the National Science Foundation for the past nine years. During this time, more than 170 faculty at 49 universities and colleges throughout the United States provided inspiration, ideas, and a sincere commitment to students that helped shape the direction of this book. We especially thank those in the FIRST project who contributed as authors to the Pathways articles: Janet Batzli, Terry Derting, Christopher Finelli, Evelyn Gaiser, Debra Linton, Tammy Long, Douglas Luckie, Suzanne Koptur, Amanda McConney, George Middendorf, Linda Nagel, Courtney Richmond, Kristen Rosenfeld, Everett Weber, and Kathy Williams. Their creative application of scientific teaching is the backbone of the book. The Pathways series was based on the scientific articles in this book—we are grateful to the authors. Their enthusiasm for the project underlined the importance of scientists engaging students in genuine learning of their disciplines. The manuscript benefited from the thoughtful reviews of scientist-teachers—Jean Tsao, George Middendorf, Nancy Stamp, and Rich Boone. Sue Silver at the Ecological Society of America was a wonderful editor to work with, month after month, and Andy Sinauer supported and encouraged the vision of this book. Finally, our students deserve special thanks for their willingness to break tradition and experiment with scientific learning and, hopefully, reap the benefits.

Diane Ebert-May
East Lansing, Michigan

Janet Hodder
Charleston, Oregon
September 2007

esa *Ecological Society of America*

The Ecological Society of America is the country's primary professional organization of ecologists and environmental scientists, with over 10,000 members in the United States and around the world.

Since its founding in 1915, ESA has promoted the responsible application of ecological principles to the solution of environmental problems through ESA reports, journals, research, and expert testimony to Congress.

Membership Benefits include:

- Networking opportunities and contacts with over 10,000 professional ecologists worldwide, through the online ESA Membership Directory, through Section and Chapter activities, and at the Annual Meeting and other conferences.

- Free print and online subscription to *Frontiers in Ecology and the Environment*, a world-class journal of interdisciplinary science for scientists, educators, resource managers, and policy-makers.

- Advance notification of employment opportunities.

- Substantial cost savings on registration for the Ecological Society of America's Annual Meeting, which draws 3000–4000 attendees from around the world.

- Discounts on subscriptions to the Society's well-respected and highly cited scientific journals—*Ecology*, *Ecological Monographs*, and *Ecological Applications*—which provide the latest peer-reviewed research worldwide.

- Representation in the policy arena; ESA ensures that ecological science informs national policy decisions, and works to garner federal support for ecological research.

- Opportunity to join the regional chapters or discipline-related sections.

- A professional Certification Program for ecologists; ESA maintains a List of Certified Ecologists.

- National and international media attention through press releases of papers published in ESA's four high-impact journals help to convey important ecological research to the general public.

For more information on these and other membership benefits, please visit www.esa.org/member_services, or contact ESA's membership department at membership@esa.org or 202-833-8773.

Pathways to
Scientific Teaching

Introduction

Does This Sound Familiar to You?

I went to a workshop on active learning in undergraduate science courses and was inspired to try clickers in my course the following term. My first attempt at innovation was a disaster! The technology failed and the students were just as frustrated as I, so I went back to my comfort zone—straight lecture. Yet, throughout the semester I remained dissatisfied with my students' performance in the course. The following year I made a second attempt at active learning by coteaching an introductory course with a colleague who swears by active learning and has evidence that it works.

All we did the first day was focus on the students—their names, their peers, their expectations for the course, and their concerns about how to succeed in a large lecture course. Within the first 5 minutes of class it was obvious to me that students were the center of attention. Students formed groups and talked to each other about expectations for the group. Students thought about and wrote about their learning goals. For homework, students were required to complete an investigation of the course website that included answering questions about the syllabus and other information on the site and submitted their responses via MSU's classroom management system (Angel, which is like Blackboard or Web CT). I get it. Students were actively engaged in learning from the minute they stepped into the classroom. On day one we set the standards and facilitated their role in the course.

OK, so how do I sustain this learner-centered course? How do I plan and organize all of the details that go into meaningful active learning? Is there a daily pattern to follow? Can I really do this on my own, or do I need graduate and undergraduate students in class with me? And what about coverage of material? How will I ever cover everything? Will students learn science? Or is it just a touchy, feely hug fest every day?

Reflection by Jean Tsao, Assistant Professor, Department of Fisheries and Wildlife Department and Large Animal Clinical Sciences, Michigan State University

Although active-learning methods are available throughout the literature and the internet, in this book we move beyond the "activity" and its implementation. Our broader intent is to help faculty develop a vision of what an active-learning classroom looks like, sounds like, and feels like. We use the principles of *scientific teaching* to provide instructional models for faculty to see how student learning takes place through the process of scientific discovery (Handelsman et al. 2004). Simply defined, the "goal of scientific teaching is to make teaching more scientific" (Handelsman et al. 2007, p. 1). When implemented in a classroom, we see students actively engaged in the thinking, creativity, rigor, and experimentation we associate with the practice of science—in much the same way we see students learn when they are in the field and in laboratories.

Scientific teaching uses instructional methods that work for a diverse population of students and requires that teaching focus on student learning outcomes. This means that faculty need to determine what their students should know and be able to do—before they begin the process of designing or restructuring a course. Faculty face three challenges when changing their courses: (1) determining the goals and objectives of the course, (2) designing instructional methods, and (3) assessing the effectiveness of those methods on student learning. Although it seems overwhelming at first, there is a vast body of research about how students learn that provides a solid foundation to guide our actions. In this book we will help faculty face these challenges by providing pathways to construct models of active learning that are derived from what they do best—science. Faculty will see that it is second nature for them to think about teaching in the same way they think about science, and students will move beyond memorization towards genuine understanding.

The theoretical framework that underlies this book and the principles of scientific teaching is constructivism—a theory about how people learn. The essence of constructivist theory is that people use their existing knowledge to build new mental frameworks (Bransford et al. 1999). But people construct meaningful understanding only when they confront their own naïve conceptions and are forced to reorient their thinking (Ausubel 2000). By promoting active-learning methods shown to improve learning by students from diverse populations, scientific teaching embraces the principles of constructivism. Students in an active-learning classroom do more than listen to lecture and take notes; they work with collaborative groups to solve problems, construct hypotheses, collect and analyze data, and evaluate outcomes. In class, just as in the research laboratory, students actively engage in scientific practices that develop higher-order thinking skills and improve critical reasoning abilities. Consequently, the students' conceptual framework is accessed so they can incorporate new information. In addition to increasing substantive opportunities for students to learn actively and construct a meaningful understanding of science, scientific teaching relies heavily on the use of assessment data to drive instructional decisions and provide feedback to both students and faculty. In this approach, students are fully engaged as partners in the learning process, not as passive recipients.

Practically, each article in this book is an instructional unit that models a way to use scientific teaching to create an active-learning classroom. Assessment is the arbiter of each unit and will provide evidence to both instructors and students about how well the learning goals are accomplished.

Overview

Pathways to Scientific Teaching is based on series of two-page articles published in *Frontiers in Ecology and the Environment* from August 2004 to June 2006 that illustrated effective instructional methods to help students gain conceptual understanding in ecology. This book is neither a set of recipes for active learning, nor is it an example of how to build a course. Rather, it is a collection of units based on the philosophy of scientific teaching that includes pedagogical principles and methods reported to help students improve their higher-level thinking abilities.

Each unit was written using a backward design framework (Wiggins and McTighe 1998). First, the instructor determines what the students should know and be able to do—learning goals. Next, the instructor determines the acceptable evidence that indicates students are achieving the goals, and designs the assessments that will measure their progression. Finally, the instructor plans the active-learning activities.

Chapter Design

Each chapter contains science papers, as originally published in *Frontiers in Ecology and the Environment*, followed by the associated *Pathways* articles, published back-to-back in the same issue, which use the science papers in a variety of ways to assist student learning. Although the original *Pathways* articles are tied to specific science papers, each is easily adapted to use with different papers or readings from a variety of sources. The student and faculty goals are transferable to any scientific content.

Application

The activities in each article take place during one or two class periods and are designed for large enrollment courses (>75–100 students), but are easily scaled down to smaller enrollments. Many units include student work outside of class time. Importantly, each unit includes learning goals for students, teaching goals for faculty, and formative and summative assessments to measure learning outcomes.

Flow of the Book

Chapter 1 describes the critical first day of an undergraduate course using a scientific teaching model. Student buy-in to an active-learning community is key to the success of a course, and what instructors do on the first day of class sets the tone. This chapter differs from the others since no articles are associated with it. Rather, it spells out concrete ways of building a community with large numbers of students on the most important day of the course. Then Chapters 2–6 illustrate how to sustain that community in the classroom. Chapter 2 describes how to organize the flow of an individual active-learning class, beginning on day two and continuing throughout the semester. Students appreciate organization in courses and quickly learn the patterns; it frees them to think. Chapter 3 shows how students "do science" in large lecture settings and illustrates the kinds of assessments that provide evidence about student outcomes from these activities. Guiding student groups through questions and problems that demand critical analysis during class provides both the teacher and students feedback about students' thinking. As students experience the process of science they begin to see what they know and what they need to know. Chapter 4 describes ways to read scientific literature that help students address what they need to know about a topic. All of the units demonstrate different forms of assessment, and Chapter 5 specifically models multiple forms of assessment to determine how well students understand concepts and to detect issues the instructor may need to address. Scientific teaching demands that students are prepared when they come to class, so Chapter 6 provides examples of directed homework that focuses students on class preparation and holds them accountable. Finally, for evidence of whether scientific teaching "works," we need frameworks for conducting research about student learning that ultimately convince us that our time and effort to create meaningful innovations in courses actually improves student learning; Chapter 7 provides an introduction to these frameworks. Chapter 8 emphasizes the importance of building a community of scholars as we define and make public the scholarship of teaching and learning.

Chapter 1

The First Day of Class— The Most Important

How motivated, empowered, and confident are students when they walk into a science course with 250 (or more) other students? Often students' expectations are limited to taking notes on lectures, reading assigned text chapters, and struggling through exams in a subject that is often perceived by them as more challenging than many of their other courses. Students readily assume the role of passive participant because they are not called upon to do anything else. In an active, learner-centered classroom, a shift occurs from the instructor, as the primary deliverer of information and controller of grades, towards students, as active participants in the learning process. Maryellen Weimer (2002) eloquently describes how theories of education and social change (Freire 1993) inspired her to give students in her courses some control over those learning processes that directly affected them. Within a short period of time, she saw a change in students' motivation, confidence, and enthusiasm for learning. If scientific teaching is a pathway to move us toward learner-centered instruction and the reallocation of power—from teacher as sole authority in the classroom to a balance of power with students—we must begin by building the classroom community.

Students Arrive—What Happens?

As students enter the large lecture hall they pick up one blank file folder and one Mr. Sketch™ "smelly marker" (non-toxic and fun to smell), which are in boxes on tables with "please take one" signs. As soon as class starts, I welcome students and make certain they are in the right course, and then say to them, "Although this is a large course, I am going to learn all of your names and you will have the opportunity to learn each others' names. In this class, our names are impor-

tant." Few faculty challenge the value of calling students by name, yet in large classes the majority of students remain anonymous, as it is difficult for an instructor to remember names they do not use regularly. Some faculty use photographs of their students to help them recall the names. Another effective method that decreases anonymity, increases personal interactions, and engages students immediately is the use of folders to associate students' names with faces.

Next, I give the following list of instructions in rapid succession to immediately engage students and get them thinking about themselves:

1. In the middle of the folder, print in large letters with the marker, your first name (or whatever you would like to be called in this course).

2. Next, in the upper right hand corner, write down where you were born. If you don't remember where you were born, write the coolest place on Earth you would like to have been born.

3. In the upper left hand corner, write your major or what you hope to study at this university.

4. Now think positive thoughts about yourself; in the bottom left hand corner, write down an adjective your very best friend would use to describe you.

5. Continue to think positive thoughts about yourself; in the bottom right hand corner, write an adjective your parents would use to describe you.

At this point, I ask everyone in the class to hold up their folder so I can see their names, and I walk around pronouncing some, particularly the phonetically challenging ones. Then, I ask who thinks they were born farthest from East Lansing, MI; a little geography and acknowledgement of diversity is the intention here. The class begins to take on the personality of the students—it is all about them.

Forming Cooperative Groups

In a large class, I let students form groups randomly. I ask them to form groups of four (three or five works, but I prefer four) and move around to situate themselves so they can talk with each other. Students introduce themselves and exchange information about each other—including emails and phone numbers. The sounds of active learning erupt. As the groups form, I walk around and learn more about the students from their folders and just by listening. Once the groups are established, I ask students to create a name for their group, and each individual writes the group name on the folder tab. Students are engaged in this process.

Folder Use and Management of Class

At the end of class, each group puts their folders in a separate hanging file in plastic file boxes. My undergraduate teaching assistant makes labels with each group's name and organizes the groups in the boxes alphabetically. I put the boxes on two-wheel carts and take them to class each time, as I teach in a building 15 minutes away from my office. Students pick up their folders before class begins.

After the first day of class, I do look at students' perceptions of how their best friend and parents would describe them. This is based on a thoughtful strategy developed by Robin Wright (Wright and Boggs 2002), in which she goes into much more detail about forming groups based on Myers-Briggs personality traits. As new individuals join the course, I assign them to groups, and the members help the new person fill out the folder. Groups are finally stabilized by the end of the official course-add period.

In class, students raise folders rather than hands to be called upon. If the classroom is structured with tables in fairly steep tiers rather than fixed seats with the movable writing arms, students can hang their folders over the edge so the names are visible to both the instructor and them. One key to learning names is using them without fail to call on students. I also use the folders to pass back exams and homework. Once

students complete the initial introduction to one another, we turn to their next set of responsibilities in the community.

Student Expectations for the Community

On the first day, I also ask students to provide their expectations for our social code of conduct in the large classroom. How we function together in this environment is important to everyone's learning. First everyone thinks about their expectations individually, and then I call on students by name to give their list of desired behaviors, and record them on the overhead or visualizer. Without fail, students address issues concerning cell phones, side conversations, changes in the syllabus, starting and ending class on time, respecting each other, and more. During the following class meeting, all of the expectations are projected from the notes and students use their clickers (personal response systems) to accept or reject their course code of conduct. The reaction is striking when they see solidarity in their vote to accept—and the balance of power in terms of social conduct begins to emerge.

Student Expectations for their Group

Now in class we turn to the value of working as a member of a cooperative group (Johnson et al. 1978; Johnson et al. 1998; Springer et al. 1999). I explicitly address how working as a member of a cooperative group is an effective and efficient method of learning science or any subject. Interacting with other people is a natural way for humans to learn, but each person must construct her/his own knowledge in the process. I encourage students to work and study together both in and out of class meetings. The written materials they produce as homework assignments, in-class activities, and projects are outcomes of these interactions, and a means of assessing their personal understanding. Then I ask groups to discuss and develop a document of expectations for their group in terms of individual accountability and group responsibility; and think about how the group will function effectively. In addition, what are the consequences if an individual does not meet the expectations of the group in terms of quantity and quality of work? One person records the document for the group on carbonless paper (i.e., 8.5" × 11" pads purchased for the course from local bookstores). Once the group members agree with the document, all members sign it. One copy is turned in and the carbon copy remains with the group. I read these documents (or a subsample) and each is recorded as present and filed. During the semester, if issues develop within groups regarding quality and quantity of work, we refer to this document before action is taken. The major problem that arises is nonparticipation by a group member, and the agreed upon consequences by the group are implemented if they so choose.

Student Learning Goals

I ask students to reflect on their personal learning goals for the course: What do they expect to learn and be able to do upon successful completion? They write these on their carbonless paper and turn in a copy. Before the next class, I quickly summarize the learning goals and plot a histogram that shows the relative numbers of students supporting each goal. Again, I post these on the course website and refer to them at the beginning of the next class. I compare the course goals on the syllabus to the goals students articulated for the course, and together we discuss our shared expectations for the course in a whole-class discussion. If appropriate, I modify the course goals on the syllabus, further demonstrating the shared balance of power and responsibility of the students.

Do all of this on day one? Perhaps you run out of time and must continue the following day. Whatever the case, the investment in building a learner-centered community on day one will result in a foundation for the remainder of the course.

Academic Integrity and Responsible Conduct

Fully integrated with students' expectations for the community and their groups is honesty about their intellectual work. In the website homework for the first day, students must read the academic integrity and responsible conduct section of the course webpage. During the next class meeting, groups address the scenario in Panel 1, which is projected from the notes.

I call on several groups to report and I record their comments on the overhead. This often leads to a lively discussion that results in the instructor clearly articulating the standards for the class.

PANEL 1
Scenario: Academic Integrity and Responsible Conduct

The homework assignment is an individual assignment, but groups are encouraged to discuss the assignment. After discussion, each individual writes an interpretation of data about increasing carbon dioxide in the atmosphere. Your group is composed of four people, and three of you meet to discuss the assignment. Each of you writes it up individually after the discussion. One hour before class, the fourth person in the group shows up and does not have the assignment. This person asks for your work so she/he can use it to do her/his individual assignment. Cooperative groups are guided by the following standards: individual accountability and group responsibility. In this case,

1. What are the responsibilities and consequences for the individual who was asked for the assignment?

2. What are the responsibilities and consequences for the individual who requested the assignment from a group member?

3. Discuss in your groups.

4. Select one person to report out to the class.

Faculty: Organizing the Flow of Class

Overview

You and your students are energized by the first day and ready to move on to day two. But then you ask, "Is there a routine I can establish to sustain me throughout the semester day in and day out?" To plan the sequence of an active-learning class for the long haul, we use a backward design approach (Wiggins and McTighe 1998). The stages in the backward design process involve thinking about what we want students to know and do as an outcome (goal) of the class, determining the acceptable evidence (assessment) that students have achieved the goals, and then planning the learning experiences and instruction (activities) to help students accomplish the goals. Backward design invokes a different starting point than just determining a list of concepts to "cover" in a class period. Since research indicates that "coverage" does not directly correlate with learning, students should "uncover" knowledge via active learning, during which they mentally engage with information to transform, organize, and reorganize their existing knowledge (Etkina et al. 2005). Once the goals and assessments are determined for class meeting periods, the learning experiences and instruction are designed so that all students can construct understanding themselves (Fosnot 1996; Bransford et al. 2000).

The two articles in this chapter illustrate how a learning cycle (Lawson et al. 1989; BSCS 1993) is an instructional model that helps to structure a class so that students actively acquire and retain knowledge. The learning cycle is described in a variety of forms throughout the literature, but all cycles basically include three instructional phases: engaging students to determine prior knowledge, students exploring the concept, and students explaining and elaborating the concepts learned. Reminder—*students* are actively doing the learning cycle that the instructor designed. The teaching challenge for faculty on a daily basis is creating an engagement question and exploration activity that enables students to build conceptual understanding about the topic. Accountability of individual students and their groups is critical in all stages of the cycle; so, quizzes, minute papers (Angelo Cross 1993), and use of clickers (electronic response systems) (Handelsman et al. 2007) help motivate students to critically reflect on their learning.

Rising atmospheric CO_2 and carbon sequestration in forests

Peter A Beedlow, David T Tingey, Donald L Phillips, William E Hogsett, and David M Olszyk

Rising CO_2 concentrations in the atmosphere could alter Earth's climate system, but it is thought that higher concentrations may improve plant growth through a process known as the "fertilization effect". Forests are an important part of the planet's carbon cycle, and sequester a substantial amount of the CO_2 released into the atmosphere by human activities. Many people believe that the amount of carbon sequestered by forests will increase as CO_2 concentrations rise. However, an increasing body of research suggests that the fertilization effect is limited by nutrients and air pollution, in addition to the well documented limitations posed by temperature and precipitation. This review suggests that existing forests are not likely to increase sequestration as atmospheric CO_2 increases. It is imperative, therefore, that we manage forests to maximize carbon retention in above- and belowground biomass and conserve soil carbon.

Front Ecol Environ 2004; 2(6): 315–322

Atmospheric CO_2 is an environmental paradox. It is an essential component in photosynthesis and thus essential for life, yet its increasing concentration in the atmosphere threatens to alter Earth's climate. Fossil fuel burning and changing land use since the onset of the Industrial Era have caused a steady rise in atmospheric CO_2 (Figure 1). While there is general agreement among scientists that the climate system is changing as a result of increasing atmospheric concentrations of CO_2 and other greenhouse gases, the degree to which temperature and precipitation patterns will change is uncertain. Nevertheless, strategies to remove CO_2 from the atmosphere are a focus of global change research and international treaty negotiations.

Terrestrial ecosystems are important in the Earth's carbon (C) balance and, potentially, in offsetting anthropogenic emissions of CO_2 (Figure 2). The biosphere (land and ocean) absorbs about half of the roughly 6 petagrams (Pg; 10^{15} grams) of C emitted annually from human activities (Schimel *et al*. 2001). On land, the largest C sink (1.3–2.9 Pg of C per year) is in the northern hemisphere (Houghton 2003), although substantial interannual variability exists (Schimel *et al*. 2001). As of the early 1990s, the temperate forests of the northern hemisphere have been thought to be a net sink of 0.6 to 0.7 Pg of C per year, based on forest inventories (Goodale *et al*. 2002). There is uncertainty, however, regarding the sources and sinks in the terrestrial biosphere (Houghton 2003). Moreover, it is not known whether present sequestration rates can be sustained, in view of the limits to forest regrowth and nutrient availability (Scholes and Noble 2001; Schimel *et al*. 2001).

Understanding the response of forest vegetation, associated soils, and soil organisms to elevated atmospheric CO_2 is central to determining the capacity of forested ecosystems to sequester anthropogenic CO_2. While reforestation and afforestation can clearly increase C sequestration (Prentice *et al*. 2001), it is not certain that rising atmospheric CO_2 will increase sequestration in existing forests. Here, we address how nitrogen (N) availability, air pollution, and C processing in forest ecosystems may limit sequestration in existing forests and associated soils with rising levels of atmospheric CO_2.

In a nutshell:

- An increase in carbon (C) sequestration by forests due to the fertilization effect is not likely to happen, because of limiting factors, including soil nitrogen and air pollution
- Long-term C sequestration in forest soils is dependent on soil type and characteristics, and is therfore unlikely to increase as a result of rising atmospheric CO_2
- Maximum C retention and conservation should be goals of forest management, in order to increase and retain long-term C pools
- Soil types that sequester substantial amounts of carbon should be identified and protected

■ Where does the C go?

CO_2 enters the plant through stomata, the small pores in leaves through which CO_2, water vapor, and other gases are exchanged with the atmosphere. Within the leaf, CO_2 reacts with the rubisco enzyme complex, forming carbohydrates that are used to make various plant tissues and form storage pools (Figure 3). Some of the C assimilated in plants is released as CO_2 to the atmosphere through respiration. C is transferred to the soil by root exudates, root death, litter fall (leaves, twigs, and branches), and coarse woody debris (larger branches and trunks). Over time, litter and coarse woody debris on the forest floor and dead roots within the soil decompose via the soil food

US Environmental Protection Agency, 200 SW 35th Street, Corvallis, OR 97333

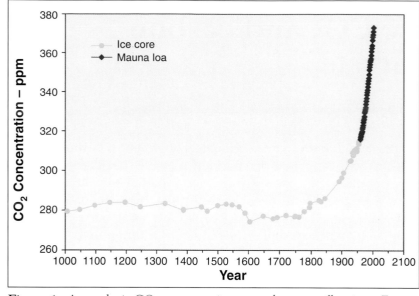

Figure 1. *Atmospheric CO_2 concentrations over the past millennium. From a pre-industrial level of approximately 280 ppm in the atmosphere, CO_2 concentrations have risen to over 370 ppm in the year 2000. By the end of the 21st century – depending on future industrial trends – concentrations are projected to reach 540 to 970 ppm (Prentice et al. 2001). (Data sources: Etheridge et al. 1998; Keeling et al. 2004.)*

chain and are converted into soil organic matter. Decomposition releases most of the C to the atmosphere as CO_2, but a small portion is sequestered.

Not all tree growth is equally suited for long-term C sequestration in biomass (Figure 3). Deciduous trees hold

their leaves for 1 year while conifers can hold needles for as long as 8 or more years. Fine roots live for days or years, depending on the species (Matamala *et al.* 2003). In contrast, tree trunks, large branches, and large roots, which remain on the tree for several decades or centuries, are the primary sites of C sequestration. As branches fall and trees die, decomposition releases CO_2 to the atmosphere (Harmon *et al.* 1990). When trees are harvested, some of the biomass is left to decompose; a portion is converted into manufactured forest products such as buildings, furniture, and paper items. Forest products have a carbon-storage half-life ranging from only 4 years for items made of paper to 65 years for building materials and furniture (Pussinen *et al.* 1997), times similar to those found in leaf litter and branch decomposition. To increase C sequestration in trees the amount of C allocated to trunks and large branches must be increased or the trees must live longer; C that is allocated to leaves and fine roots is recycled to the atmosphere too quickly to be an effective C sink.

Most of the annual C accumulation in growing forested ecosystems is found in trees and forest-floor litter; only a small portion enters the underlying mineral soil (Hooker and Compton 2003). Soil C compounds can be classified based on turnover time (Trumbore 1997): the "active" (or "fast") pool turns over in days to a year, the "intermediate" pool turns over in years to decades, and turnover in the "passive" (or "slow") pool takes more than a century. The active pool consists of easily decomposed litter and fine roots. The intermediate pool is a mixture of compounds with varying turnover times, but in many soils this pool contains the most C (Trumbore 1997). The passive pool – most important to long-term C sequestration – is composed of persistent organic compounds, such as humus, and accumulates very slowly.

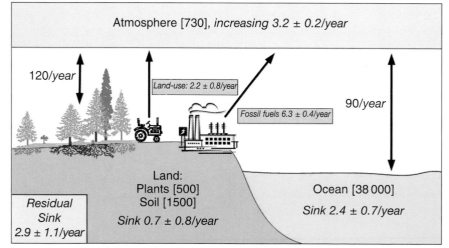

Figure 2. *The global C cycle. The global C cycle is represented showing the C pools (in brackets), atmospheric exchanges (double-headed arrows), anthropogenic emissions (arrows), and sinks (in italics). All units are in Pg C (1 Pg = 10^{15} grams = one billion metric tons) and fluxes in Pg C per year. The indicated C pools are annual averages over the 1980s. Atmospheric C is increasing by approximately 0.44% per year. To balance the global budget a residual sink for 2.9 Pg of C is needed; this represents C that is not accounted for – missing C (Houghton 2003). In contrast to the static view conveyed here, the C system is dynamic and coupled to the climate system on seasonal, interannual, and decadal timescales. (Data sources: pools and exchanges from Prentice et al. 2001; anthropogenic emissions and sinks from Houghton 2003.)*

■ Will elevated CO_2 increase forest C sequestration?

The most obvious way to increase C sequestration is to increase forest growth. Elevated atmospheric CO_2 concentrations increase photosynthesis in C3 plants – the photosynthetic type that includes most forest tree species – by increasing CO_2 uptake (Norby *et al.* 1999). This increase is a result of molecular competition within leaves for binding sites on the rubisco molecule shifting to increase carboxylation and decrease oxygenation. Tree productivity should therefore increase if other growth factors such as nutrients, water, or temperature are not limiting. Theoretically, elevated CO_2 will enhance photosynthesis and decrease the need for plants to open their stomates as widely as they do at lower CO_2 concentrations, allowing them to conserve water (Schäfer *et al.* 2002). This CO_2-induced increase in primary productivity and water use efficiency is commonly known as the "fertilization effect". It is often assumed that forested ecosystems will increase C sequestration rates with rising concentrations of atmospheric CO_2. Indeed, this assumption is the basis for projecting future C fluxes with most state-of-the-art global vegetation models (Cramer *et al.* 2001).

Evidence is now emerging that this fertilization effect is variable and often limited by environmental factors. In most experiments, elevated CO_2 increases photosynthesis (at least initially), but the long-term effect on ecosystem productivity is unclear. Early results from an open-air CO_2 enrichment experiment in a young North Carolina forest showed increased ecosystem net primary productivity during the first 2 years of exposure (DeLucia *et al.* 1999), but later findings indicate that this productivity declined with time (Finzi *et al.* 2002). Trees in Italy that are near springs emitting high CO_2 concentrations grow no faster than their counterparts away from the springs (Tognetti *et al.* 2000). Although elevated CO_2 may increase the C assimilation rate, it does not necessarily mean that growth will be increased, as other limiting factors come into play, particularly in natural ecosystems (Norby *et al.* 1999; Hungate *et al.* 2003).

There are a number of factors that could diminish the effect of CO_2 fertilization on forest growth. Clearly, increasing temperature and drought can reduce growth, but perhaps more importantly, changing climatic patterns can affect net ecosystem productivity (Knapp *et al.* 2002). There is a mounting body of evidence, however, for limitations beyond temperature and precipitation. These involve: (1) the potential for N availability to restrict the ability of forests to sustain CO_2-induced increases in growth; (2) the effects of regional air pollution – N deposition and tropospheric ozone – on C sequestration; and (3) the reallocation of C in forests as a result of rising atmospheric CO_2 with potential effects on C sequestration.

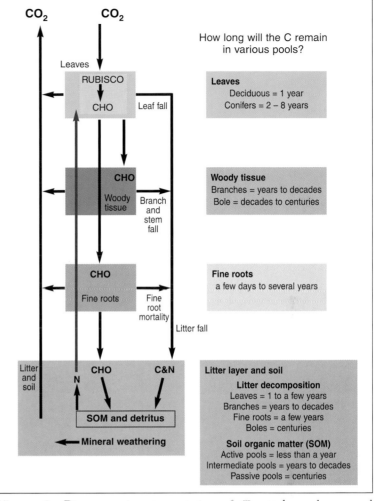

Figure 3. *Diagrammatic representation of C uptake, release, and retention time in forested ecosystems. CHO represents the movement of photosynthates between plants, soils, and the atmosphere.*

■ Nitrogen availability

At the cellular level, enzymes are required to convert atmospheric CO_2 into carbohydrates. They are also required for plant growth and maintenance. To produce enzymes, plants must have adequate N. In fact, most of the N in leaves is found in enzymes, especially rubisco, which facilitate uptake of CO_2 during photosynthesis.

Mineral weathering, along with mineralizing litter and soil organic matter, form the soil pools of N and other essential nutrients which are taken up by fine roots and associated mycorrhizae and moved throughout the plant (Figure 3). Although the amount of N in different tissues may vary, it is essential for sustained plant growth (Finzi *et al.* 2002). If the soil N is deficient, growth is limited. Consequently, plants will increase growth in response to increasing levels of atmospheric CO_2 only if there is a sustained increase in nutrient use efficiency or there is continuing supply of N (Finzi *et al.* 2002). The increased N supply can be met by: (1) N reallocated from within the plant; (2) increased mineralization in the litter and soil; (3) fertilizers; and (4) air pollution (N deposition).

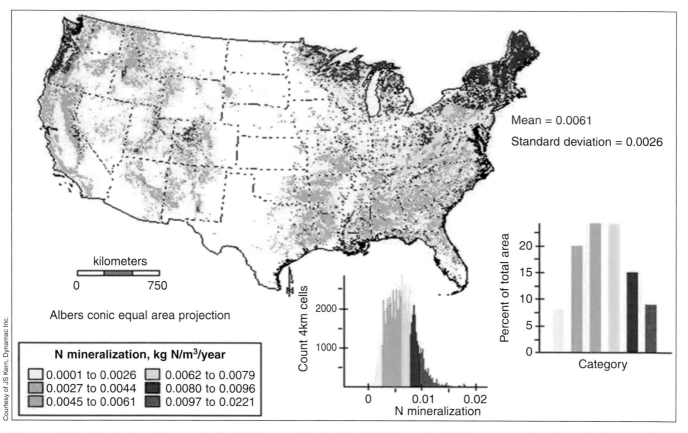

Figure 4. *The distribution of mineralizable N in forested lands of the US. Mineralizable N represents the N in soils that is available to plants. Notice that forest soils containing the highest levels of N occupy less than 10% of the total, and that soils relatively rich in N are found in the northern regions.*

At the ecosystem level, soil N availability can limit the CO_2 fertilization effect and rising atmospheric CO_2 can alter decomposition and N mineralization and fixation, thus changing N availability in the soil (McGuire *et al.* 1995). A long-term study in a North Carolina pine forest failed to find increased N mineralization with elevated CO_2 exposure (Finzi *et al.* 2002). Increased C storage, if it occurs with rising atmospheric CO_2, places an additional demand on available N. As organic matter contains N, storing more C requires removing some N from the actively cycling pool and sequestering it, along with the C, in wood, leaves, litter, and soil. Litter and soil are both rather high in N, creating a continuing demand for it and other nutrients.

Modeling studies support the concept of N limitation and show that the observed increase and subsequent slowing of plant growth in response to elevated CO_2 is a consequence of nutrient limitation (Pan *et al.*1998). Applying a biogeochemical model to forest stands in the western Cascade Mountains of the Pacific Northwest, McKane *et al.* (1997) suggest that soil N is a primary constraint on the ability of those forests to sequester C. In 100-year model runs, elevated atmospheric CO_2 and temperature raised total ecosystem C storage by less than 10% for a N-poor site versus 25% for a N-rich site. Vegetation models that account for N limitation also predict much less C sequestration under future climate scenarios than do models that assume N is always sufficient (Pan *et al.*1998; Hungate *et al.* 2003).

The availability of N varies between and within forested regions. Consequently, the CO_2 fertilization potential for particular forest stands will also vary. For example, in forested lands of the US (Figure 4), the distribution of N not only varies from region to region, but the land area with the most N that can be mineralized (ie the most available N) is less than 10% of the total. In areas where N is deficient, C sequestration is not likely to increase with rising levels of CO_2.

■ Regional air pollution

Fossil fuel combustion and intensive agriculture have increased atmospheric inputs of nitrate (NO_3^-) and ammonium (NH_4^+) to forests, grasslands, and cultivated lands (Figure 5). Such anthropogenic deposition of N on N-poor soils could relieve limitations on forested land, which would allow CO_2-induced growth stimulation. Model simulations suggest that N deposition in temperate forests of eastern North America and Europe allows for up to 25% of the C sequestration in these forests (Townsend *et al.* 1996). However, results from tracer studies using N isotopes in temperate forests in the US and Europe show the C sequestration resulting from growth stimulation by N deposition to be less than 10%, if only woody tissues, which have longer turnover times, are considered (Nadelhoffer *et al.* 1999).

While soil N is important for forest growth, N deposition appears to play only a minimal role in increasing C sequestration when compared to the negative effects of air pollution. In fact, N deposition could lead to forest decline if available N exceeds the capacity of plants to use it; N compounds can bond with calcium and magnesium ions in soil, which can then be leached from the ecosystem, thereby limiting plant growth (Nosengo 2003). Although rising CO_2 and N deposition may have increased forest growth over the past several decades, the magnitude of these increases has been considerably reduced by concurrent increases in air pollution – primarily tropospheric ozone (Ollinger *et al.* 2002).

In the US, vast areas of forests are potentially impacted to varying degrees by tropospheric, or ground-level ozone pollution (Hogsett *et al.* 1997; Figure 6). On a global scale, damaging ozone concentrations (defined as >60 ppb) occur over 29% of the world's temperate and sub-polar forests and are predicted to affect 60% of these forests by 2100 (Fowler *et al.* 1999).

Ozone is formed in sunlight by the reactions of volatile organic compounds and nitrogen oxide air pollutants. Global warming could exacerbate risks to forests from ozone, because hot weather and high atmospheric pressure promote its formation. Moreover, increased fossil fuel use will probably increase the production of ozone-forming air pollutants.

In trees, ozone reduces CO_2 assimilation and alters C allocation (Andersen 2003). It causes foliage to die and drop prematurely, which reduces the amount of C available for growth and sequestration. In some cases, the stimulatory effect of CO_2 on forest productivity is reduced by more than 20% by ozone pollution (Tingey *et al.* 2001; Ollinger *et al.* 2002; Karnosky *et al.* 2003). In addition, the interacting effects of CO_2 and ozone can alter the susceptibility of plants to pest damage and diseases (Percy *et al.* 2002).

Ozone not only reduces C sequestration in trees; it also inhibits sequestration in soils. In a field experiment, the passive soil C pool was decreased by 5% when exposed to CO_2 and ozone combined compared to elevated CO_2 over 4 years of exposure (Loya *et al.* 2003).

■ Carbon reallocation

It appears unlikely that rising CO_2 will cause a sustained increase in C sequestration, because of limitations such as N availability and ozone. However, if rising CO_2 could increase the allocation of C into long-term storage pools in wood or mineral soil, it would increase sequestration even without a sustained increase in plant growth. If C is reallocated, in order to have much influence on sequestration it must result in trees that live substantially longer or are substantially larger than they would have been without being exposed to elevated CO_2.

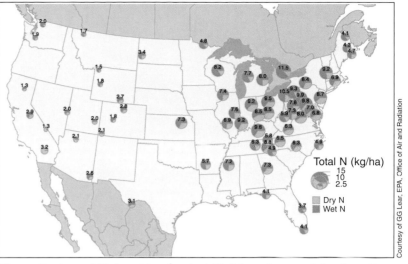

Figure 5. *Annual N deposition for the US. Map of wet and dry deposition, which illustrates the extent and magnitude of deposition. The size of the circles corresponds to the relative magnitude of deposition and the color represents the form (wet versus dry), with the total amount shown as kilograms per hectare. The eastern part of the US has deposition values 2–3 times greater than the western section.*

If rising CO_2 increased wood density or tissue C content, sequestration would increase. Yet, observed effects of elevated CO_2 on wood density range from no effect (Calfapietra *et al.* 2003) to a small increase that diminished with exposure time (Telewski *et al.* 1999), suggesting that increases in wood density will not create a major C sink.

If rising CO_2 increases plant size, more C would be sequestered. Experimental studies show that if water and nutrients are adequate, elevated CO_2 does initially increase plant growth, but the CO_2 benefit decreases with time. Nevertheless, the initial advantage of increased growth may be maintained even though increased net ecosystem productivity tapers off, if larger trees could gain a competitive advantage that would prevail throughout their lifetime (Calfapietra *et al.* 2003). The unanswered question is whether tree stands will ultimately have more volume of wood than stands growing at that same site without the benefit of elevated CO_2, or if the stand volume will be unchanged but concentrated in fewer, larger trees. It is not clear that rising CO_2 will permit plants at specific sites to grow larger than they would otherwise, given the availability of other resources.

Increasing the duration of leaves and roots, or tree life spans could also increase C sequestration. However, elevated CO_2 has been shown to decrease needle longevity (Schäfer *et al.* 2002) and to increase C allocation to foliar nonstructural carbohydrates, leaves, and fine roots, which are rapidly respired without adding to sequestration (Norby *et al.* 2003; Olszyk *et al.* 2003). In loblolly pine (*Pinus taeda*), elevated CO_2 reduced the age of maturity while cone and seed production increased (LaDeau and Clark 2001); accelerated maturation may shorten life span, resulting in faster C turnover, but not necessarily

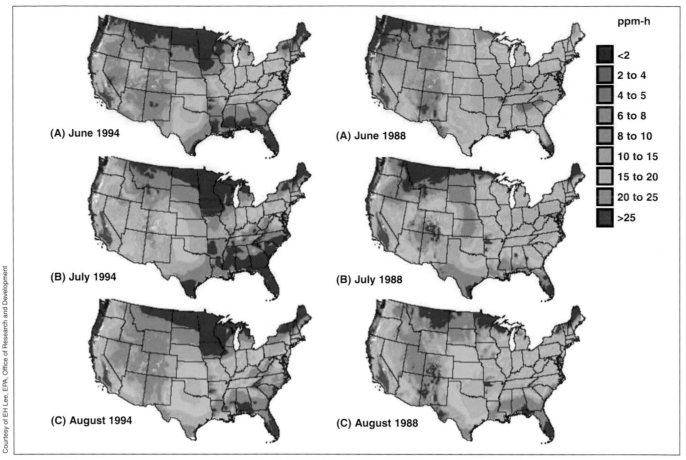

Figure 6. Monthly ozone exposures expressed as SUMO6 across the US, illustrating the monthly and year-to-year variability depending on temperature and emissions. Ozone concentrations peaked during the record high temperatures and drought of 1988 throughout the eastern half of the US. More typical conditions prevailed during 1994. SUMO6 is the sum of all hourly ozone concentrations between 7 am and 7 pm that are equal to, or exceed, 60 ppb over a 3-month growing season. Exposures were spatially interpolated to relate ozone concentrations to elevation, temperature, and geographical coordinates following the procedure of Hogsett et al. (1997).

more biomass. Accelerated maturation is compounded by the fact that the ability of forests to sequester C decreases with time (Finzi *et al.* 2002).

Climate, topography, soil parent material, time, and organisms determine the amount of C in soils (Johnson 1995). Elevated CO_2 only directly affects the organisms in this relationship. To increase C sequestration in soil, elevated CO_2 must increase C pools with turnover times of decades and centuries. C in the active pool is lost too quickly. The passive soil C pool, which contains persistent organic material such as humus, is obviously important to sequestration, but intermediate pools – those that turn over on decadal time periods – can also be important. Alternatively, sequestered C can be maintained by reducing the loss of passive C through management practices that minimize erosion and oxidation of C compounds in soils (Johnson 1995).

Evidence that rising CO_2 will increase C sequestration in soil is generally lacking. Although elevated CO_2 can increase net primary production, the additional C is either allocated to fine root production, which is rapidly turned over, or is respired directly by soil organisms. Elevated CO_2

has been shown to have little or no effect on passive soil organic matter (Schlesinger and Lichter 2001). In fact, the amount of passive soil organic matter is more dependent on soil characteristics, such as soil maturity and mineralogy, than on vegetation production (Trumbore 1997; Hagedorn *et al.* 2003).

Experimentally elevated CO_2 levels have not resulted in long-term increases in litter (Schäfer *et al.* 2002; Norby *et al.* 2003) or soil organic matter production (Schlesinger and Lichter 2001). Elevated CO_2 stimulated fine root production in deciduous forest species, which in turn increased soil respiration as the C was cycled through short-term pools without adding to the C present (King *et al.* 2001; Norby *et al.* 2002). Elevated CO_2 did not stimulate more fine root production or allocation of C to fine roots in Douglas fir (Olszyk *et al.* 2003), although C allocation was shifted belowground (Hobbie *et al.* 2004). Similar findings were reported for a loblolly pine forest exposed to elevated CO_2 (Schlesinger and Lichter 2001). Hobbie *et al.* (2004) hypothesize that the additional C assimilated by plants exposed to elevated CO_2 was used by the belowground biota with no movement of C into long-term storage. This is supported by reported changes to belowground food chains due to elevated CO_2 (Fransson *et al.* 2001).

Model simulations suggest that higher N availability may increase litter quality and subsequent C sequestration (McMurtrie *et al.* 2000). There is no clear evidence of that happening in the field, however. Elevated CO_2 increased C to N and lignin to N ratios in tissues while decreasing decomposition rates in some C3 plants, but not in C4 plants (Ball 1997). In a survey of six species from alpine, temperate grassland, and tropical forest ecosystems, Hirschel *et al.* (1997) concluded that elevated CO_2 did not affect litter quality or decomposition rates. Similarly, elevated CO_2 experiments show no effect on mineralization or the availability of N for plant growth (Zak *et al.* 2003).

■ Conclusions

Changes in climatic conditions, growing season length, precipitation, cloud cover, and temperature have contributed to increases in global net primary production over the past two decades (Nemani *et al.* 2003), suggesting that terrestrial ecosystems are sequestering more C. Nevertheless, the fertilization effect of rising atmospheric CO_2 does not appear to be an important factor in the increased sequestration. Land-use changes, particularly the regrowth of forests on land previously used for agriculture, have played a major role (Schimel *et al.* 2001); in general, recovery from historic land use may be the dominant current terrestrial sink for C (Caspersen *et al.* 2000).

There is little experimental evidence to suggest that either rising atmospheric CO_2 or N deposition will contribute to sustained stimulation of C sequestration in forests or associated soils. Nutrient limitations in unmanaged forests are likely to constrain tree response to rising CO_2, while increased soil respiration seems to be balancing the increased input of C to soil (Schlesinger and Lichter 2001).

As rising CO_2 is not expected to stimulate C sequestration in forests, it is imperative that the C in these ecosystems be conserved. Forested landscapes should be managed to maximize C accumulation and retention in trunks and large branches. Soils accumulate C very slowly, and the passive C pool is largely a function of soil characteristics. Particularly important is protecting soil C, including the litter layer, during and following logging activities, especially in forest types that hold high levels of soil C, such as those in cool climates and bog and swamp woodlands (Johnson and Kern 2003).

Regionally, elevated tropospheric ozone is already reducing C sequestration in forests. Ozone not only reduces sequestration in natural forests, but also affects reforestation and afforestation projects. Consequently, it is important to reduce the extent and magnitude of exposures.

Managing forested ecosystems to maximize C sequestration and retention will require a detailed knowledge of past, present, and future land use, and how those practices affect carbon sources and sinks at regional scales. Social, political, and economic effects on C sequestration must be quantified and any ensuing conflicts with C conservation resolved before effective sequestration strategies for forests can be developed.

Promoting terrestrial sinks will certainly help lower atmospheric CO_2 concentrations, but some perspective is warranted. Even if all of the C that was lost from the land due to human activities over the last 250 years could be returned, it would only lower atmospheric C concentrations by about 70 parts per million (ppm) from projected concentrations of 500–950 ppm by 2100 (Scholes and Noble 2001). This amounts to only a 7–14% reduction. Avoiding additional loss of land C is therefore critical.

■ Acknowledgements

We thank JG Carter, RK Dixon, MT Little, and AM Solomon for their thoughtful comments. We also thank JS Kern, EH Lee, and GG Lear for the maps. This work was funded by the US Environmental Protection Agency (EPA) and approved for publication after EPA review. Approval does not signify that the contents reflect the views of the agency, and the mention of trade names or commercial products does not imply endorsement.

■ References

Andersen CP. 2003. Source–sink balance and carbon allocation below ground in plants exposed to ozone. *New Phytol* **157**: 213–28.

Ball AS. 1997. Microbial decomposition at elevated CO_2 levels: effect of litter quality. *Glob Change Biol* **3**: 379–86.

Calfapietra C, Gielen B, Sabatti M, *et al.* 2003. Do above-ground growth dynamics of poplar change with time under CO_2 enrichment? *New Phytol* **160**: 305–18.

Caspersen JP, Pacala SW, Jenkins JC, *et al.* 2000. Contributions of land-use history to carbon accumulation in U.S. forests. *Science* **290**: 1148–51.

Cramer WA, Bondeau A, Woodward FI, *et al.* 2001. Global response of terrestrial ecosystem structure and function to CO_2 and climate change. *Glob Change Biol* **7**: 357–73.

DeLucia EH, Hamilton JG, Naidu SL, *et al.* 1999. Net primary production of a forest ecosystem with experimental CO_2 enrichment. *Science* **284**: 1177–79.

Etheridge DM, Steele LP, Langenfelds RJ, *et al.* 1998. Historical CO_2 records from the Law Dome DE08, DE08-2, and DSS ice cores. In: Trends: a compendium of data on global change. Oak Ridge, TN: Carbon Dioxide Information Analysis Center, Oak Ridge National Laboratory, US Department of Energy.

Finzi AC, DeLucia EH, Hamilton JG, *et al.* 2002. The nitrogen budget of a pine forest under free air CO_2 enrichment. *Oecologia* **132**: 567–78.

Fowler D, Cape JN, Coyle M, *et al.* 1999. The global exposure of forests to air pollutants. *Water Air Soil Poll* **116**: 5–32.

Fransson PMA, Taylor AFS, and Finlay RD. 2001. Elevated atmospheric CO_2 alters root symbiont community structure in forest trees. *New Phytol* **152**: 431–42.

Goodale CL, Apps MJ, Birdsey RA, *et al.* 2002. Forest carbon sinks in the northern hemisphere. *Ecol Appl* **12**: 891–99.

Hagedorn F, Spinnler D, Bundt M, *et al.* 2003. The input and fate of new C in two forest soils under elevated CO_2. *Glob Change Biol* **9**: 862–72.

Harmon ME, Ferrell WK, and Franklin JF. 1990. Effects on carbon storage of conversion of old-growth forests to young forests. *Science* **247**: 699–702.

Hirschel G, Körner C, and Arnone JA. 1997. Will rising atmospheric CO_2 affect leaf litter quality and in situ decomposition rates in native plant communities? *Oecologia* **110**: 387–92.

Hobbie EA, Johnson MG, Rygiewicz PT, *et al*. 2004. Isotopic estimates of new carbon inputs into litter and soils in a four-year climate change experiment with Douglas-fir. *Plant Soil* **259**: 331–43.

Hogsett WE, Weber JE, Tingey DT, *et al*. 1997. Environmental auditing: an approach for characterizing tropospheric ozone risk to forests. *Environ Manage* **21**: 105–20.

Hooker TD and Compton JE. 2003. Forest ecosystem carbon and nitrogen accumulation during the first century after agricultural abandonment. *Ecol Appl* **13**: 299–313.

Houghton RA. 2003. Why are estimates of the terrestrial carbon balance so different? *Glob Change Biol* **9**: 500–09.

Hungate BA, Dukes JS, Shaw MR, *et al*. 2003. Nitrogen and climate change. *Science* **302**: 1512–13.

Johnson MG. 1995. The role of soil management in sequestering soil carbon. In: Lal R, Kimble J, Levine E, and Stewart BA (Eds). Soil management and greenhouse effect. Boca Raton, FL: CRC Press.

Johnson MG and Kern JS. 2003. Quantifying the organic carbon held in forested soils of the United States and Puerto Rico. In: Kimble JM, Heath LS, Birdsey RA, and Lal R (Eds). The potential of U.S. forests soils to sequester carbon and mitigate the greenhouse effect. Boca Raton, FL: CRC Press.

Karnosky DF, Zak DR, Pregitzer KS, *et al*. 2003. Tropospheric O_3 moderates responses of temperate hardwood forests to elevated CO_2: a synthesis of molecular to ecosystem results from the Aspen FACE project. *Funct Ecol* **17**: 289–304.

Keeling CD and Whorf TP. 2004. Atmospheric CO_2 records from sites in the SIO air sampling network. In: Trends: a compendium of data on global change. Oak Ridge, TN: Carbon Dioxide Information Analysis Center, Oak Ridge National Laboratory, US Department of Energy.

King JS, Pregitzer KS, Zak DR, *et al*. 2001. Fine-root biomass and fluxes of soil carbon in young stands of paper birch and trembling aspen as affected by elevated atmospheric CO_2 and tropospheric O_3. *Oecologia* **128**: 237–50.

Knapp AK, Fay PA, Blair JM, *et al*. 2002. Rainfall variability, carbon cycling, and plant species diversity in a mesic grassland. *Science* **298**: 2202–05.

LaDeau SL and Clark JS. 2001. Rising CO_2 levels and the fecundity of forest trees. *Science* **292**: 95–98.

Loya WM, Pregitzer KS, Karberg NJ, *et al*. 2003. Reduction of soil carbon formation by tropospheric ozone under increased carbon dioxide levels. *Nature* **425**: 705–07.

Matamala R, Gonzàlez-Meler M, Jastrow JD, *et al*. 2003. Impacts of fine root turnover on forest NPP and soil C sequestration potential. *Science* **302**: 1385–87.

McKane RB, Tingey DT, Beedlow PA, *et al*. 1997. Spatial and temporal scaling of CO_2 and temperature effects on Pacific Northwest forest ecosystems. *Am Assoc Adv Sci Pacific Div Abstracts* **16**: 56.

McGuire AD, Melillo JM, and Joyce LA. 1995. The role of nitrogen in the response of forest net primary production to elevated atmospheric carbon dioxide. *Ann Rev Ecol Syst* **26**: 473–503.

McMurtrie RE, Dewar RC, Medlyn BE, *et al*. 2000. Effects of elevated [CO_2] on forest growth and carbon storage: a modeling analysis of the consequences of changes in litter quality/quantity and root exudation. *Plant Soil* **224**: 135–52.

Nadelhoffer KJ, Emmett BA, Gundersen P, *et al*. 1999. Nitrogen deposition makes a minor contribution to carbon sequestration in temperate forests. *Nature* **398**: 145–48.

Nemani RR, Keeling CD, Hashimoto H, *et al*. 2003. Climate-driven increases in global terrestrial net primary productivity. *Science* **300**: 1560–63.

Norby RJ, Hanson PJ, O'Neill EG, *et al*. 2002. Net primary productivity of a CO_2-enriched deciduous forest and the implications for carbon storage. *Ecol Appl* **12**: 1261–66.

Norby RJ, Sholtis JD, Gunderson CA, *et al*. 2003. Leaf dynamics of a deciduous forest canopy: no response to elevated CO_2. *Oecologia* **136**: 574–84.

Norby RJ, Wullschleger SD, Gunderson CA, *et al*. 1999. Tree responses to rising CO_2 in field experiments: implications for the future forest. *Plant Cell Environ* **22**: 683–714.

Nosengo N. 2003. Fertilized to death. *Nature* **425**: 894–95.

Ollinger SV, Aber JD, Reich PB, and Freuder RJ. 2002. Interactive effects of nitrogen deposition, tropospheric ozone, elevated CO_2 and land use history on the carbon dynamics of northern hardwood forests. *Glob Change Biol* **8**: 545–62.

Olszyk DM, Johnson MG, Tingey DT, *et al*. 2003. Whole-seedling biomass allocation, leaf area, and tissue chemistry for Douglas-fir exposed to elevated CO_2 and temperature for 4 years. *Can J For Res* **33**: 269–78.

Pan Y, Melillo JM, McGuire AD, *et al*. 1998. Modeled responses of terrestrial ecosystems to elevated atmospheric CO_2: a comparison of simulations by the biogeochemistry models of the Vegetation/Ecosystem Modeling and Analysis Project (VEMAP). *Oecologia* **114**: 389–404.

Percy KE, Awmack CS, Lindroth RL, *et al*. 2002. Altered performance of forest pests under atmospheres enriched by CO_2 and O_3. *Nature* **420**: 403–07.

Prentice IC, Farquhar GD, Fasham MJR, *et al*. 2001. The carbon cycle and atmospheric carbon dioxide. In: Houghton JT, Ding Y, Griggs DJ, *et al*. (Eds). Climate Change 2001: The Scientific Basis. Contribution of Working Group I to the Third Assessment Report of the Intergovernmental Panel on Climate Change, p 183–237. Cambridge, UK: Cambridge University Press.

Pussinen A, Karjalainen T, Kellomäki S, *et al*. 1997. Potential contribution of the forest sector to carbon sequestration in Finland. *Biomass and Bioenergy* **13**: 377–87.

Schäfer KVR, Oren R, Lai C, *et al*. 2002. Hydrologic balance in an intact temperate forest ecosystem under ambient and elevated atmospheric CO_2 concentration. *Glob Change Biol* **8**: 895–911.

Schimel DS, House JI, Hibbard KA, *et al*. 2001. Recent patterns and mechanisms of carbon exchange by terrestrial ecosystems. *Nature* **414**: 169–72.

Schlesinger WH and J Lichter. 2001. Limited carbon storage in soil and litter of experimental forest plots under increased atmospheric CO_2. *Nature* **411**: 466–69.

Scholes RJ and Noble IR. 2001. Storing carbon on land. *Science* **294**: 1012–13.

Telewski FW, Swanson RT, Strain BR, *et al*. 1999. Wood properties and ring width responses to long-term atmospheric CO_2 enrichment in field-grown loblolly pine (*Pinus taeda L.*). *Plant Cell Environ* **22**: 213–19.

Tingey DT, Laurence JA, Weber JA, *et al*. 2001. Elevated CO_2 and temperature alter the response of *Pinus ponderosa* to ozone: a simulation analysis. *Ecol Appl* **11**: 1412–24.

Tognetti R, Cherubini P, and Innes JL. 2000. Comparative stem-growth rates of Mediterranean trees under background and naturally enhanced ambient CO_2 concentrations. *New Phytol* **146**: 59–74.

Townsend AR, Braswell BH, Holland EA, *et al*. 1996. Spatial and temporal patterns in terrestrial carbon storage due to deposition of fossil fuel nitrogen. *Ecol Appl* **6**: 806–14.

Trumbore SE. 1997. Potential responses of soil organic carbon to global environmental change. *Proc Natl Acad Sci* **94**: 8284–91.

Zak DR, Holmes WE, Finzi AC, *et al*. 2003. Soil nitrogen cycling under elevated CO_2: a synthesis of forest FACE experiments. *Ecol Appl* **13**: 1508–14.

Climate change: confronting student ideas

Diane Ebert-May[1], Kathy Williams[2], Doug Luckie[1], and Janet Hodder[3]

Students bring prior knowledge about science to our courses, yet sometimes their information is inaccurate. The Beedlow et al. article in this issue (p 315–322) provides a foundation for addressing several incomplete, naïve, or erroneous ideas that have been identified in students' thinking about the carbon cycle (Carlsson 2002; Ebert-May et al. 2003), what scientists know about the relationship between plant growth and rising atmospheric CO_2 concentrations, and the relationship between carbon and nitrogen cycles.

The scientific teaching approach for this article involves three components: learning goals, instructional strategies that are inquiry-driven and student-centered, and assessment (ie obtaining data that measure student achievement of learning goals). The learning goals are based on the question: "What do students need to know to demonstrate a genuine understanding of the carbon cycle and its relation to global climate change?" The instructional strategy chosen for this example is based on the *learning cycle*, an instructional model that enables students to address misconceptions and develop more accurate understanding (Posner et al. 1982; Kennedy 2004). In this case, students actively confront their current ideas about global warming by exploring the question "Where does the carbon go?" (a section in Beedlow et al. 2004) and ultimately come to a deeper understanding of the carbon cycle. Assessments probe students' understanding and misconceptions before, during, and after instruction, to evaluate the effectiveness of teaching and learning.

■ Learning goals

In this example, students will:
- Predict how the carbon cycle responds to elevated atmospheric CO_2
- Explain the pathways and processes involved in the movement of carbon
- Illustrate how nitrogen limits plant growth in response to elevated CO_2
- Determine if elevated CO_2 could increase forest carbon sequestration
- Use scientific methods to predict the effect of human activity on climate change

Further goals that are relevant to the course can be included.

■ Instructional strategy

The *learning cycle* is a teaching model, based on cognitive psychology research, which shows that people learn best by interactively constructing understanding (Bransford et al. 1999). This approach has several phases. First, students are engaged with a question or activity probing prior knowledge and focusing their thinking. Then they explore and share their ideas or concepts, after which the instructor explains scientific concepts and processes to bring order to the students' explorations.

Engagement (*last 10 minutes of prior class*): With this article we use pop culture to engage students in thinking critically about the science of climate change, as portrayed in a current disaster film (*The Day After Tomorrow*) and by doing so, build understanding about the carbon cycle. Engage students as the preceding class ends by assigning Beedlow et al. as homework and announcing: "Next class we will discuss climate change and *"where the carbon goes"* based on this paper". Also, show a 30-second trailer for the movie *The Day After Tomorrow* (www.thedayaftertomorrow.com) and ask students who saw the movie to describe major scientific points on climate change that it addresses.

Explain that before the next class you need to learn what they currently understand about carbon cycling, and administer a two-question quiz (Panel 1). Collect the responses, without providing correct answers; instead, ask students to consider as they read how elevated CO_2 might influence the ultimate outcome of *The Day After Tomorrow* (Peplow 2004). In addition, ask students to draw a simple model of a forest ecosystem, using arrows to indicate carbon and nitrogen flow, and to bring two copies (one to turn in and one to use in class). Announce a graded quiz on the reading at the start of the next class.

Exploration (*15 minutes at the beginning of class*): Administer the same quiz (Panel 1) as class starts and collect individual responses for assessment. Using the same quiz after the assignment holds students accountable for reading, and assesses changes in misconceptions held before and after reading. Results help direct the exploration and explanation phases of instruction.

After the quiz, have students explain their responses to their neighbor ("Think/Pair/Share" in Johnson et al. 1998). Walk around, listening to students. After 5 minutes of discussion, call on students to create a list of answers and justifications on the overhead or board. We predict you will still hear some of the misconceptions listed in Panel 2. In this phase, students wrestle with prior and new ideas to gain understanding (Posner et al. 1982; Bransford et al. 1999). This exploration helps delimit the explanation phase of instruction.

Explanation (*30 minutes*): Explain the basic elements of the carbon cycle required to understand relationships between the carbon cycle and global climate change. Lectures, as explanation, can help clarify students' thinking when ongoing feedback is provided (McKeachie 2002). For example, ask students to identify the incorrect reasoning in the misconceptions presented in the quiz,

[1]*Michigan State University*, [2]*San Diego State University*, [3]*University of Oregon*

Panel 1. Quiz *(Pre-test)*

This example pre-test is designed to check students' prior knowledge before any instructional intervention. It can be conducted with paper and pencil or electronic scoring devices, but should be short and relevant to the *Where does the carbon go?* section in Beedlow *et al.* Accurate conceptions are noted as "answers" and the incorrect choices represent known student misconceptions

(1) The majority of actual weight (biomass) gained by plants as they grow comes from which of the following substances: [answer b]
    a. organic substances in soil that are taken up by plant roots.
    b. carbon dioxide in the air that enters through leaf stomata.
    c. minerals dissolved in water taken up by plant roots.
    d. energy from the sun captured by leaves.
    e. carbon from decomposed leaf litter in soil.

(2) What are the different pathways that a carbon atom can take once it is inside a plant? Choose all that are correct. [answer a, b, c, d]
    a. It can exit the plant as CO_2.
    b. It can become part of the plant cell walls, protein, fat, DNA.
    c. It can be consumed by an insect feeding on the plant and become part of the insect's body.
    d. It can exit the soil as CO_2 as plant tissue decomposes.

Results from this quiz will allow you to prepare your lecture using students' prior knowledge. Save these data for future reference and to share with others.

explaining how someone might think they were correct. Since research indicates the attention span of most students is 10–15 minutes in a lecture setting (Johnson *et al.* 1998), the instructor can augment student explanations when necessary, rather than lecturing at length.

Have small groups of students use their forest ecosystem models to predict how carbon in various pools (ie oceans, atmosphere, plants, detritus; Figure 2, Beedlow *et al.*) would change with increasing atmospheric CO_2. Challenge students to write predictions based on specific questions such as: (1) How will changes in atmospheric CO_2 alter photorespiration rates? and (2) Under what conditions does elevated CO_2 increase forest carbon sequestration (storage)? Ask them to include scientific reasoning to support their predictions. Ask a few groups to explain their model predictions to

Panel 2. Common misconceptions held by undergraduates about the carbon cycle

Misconceptions are linked to pages in Beedlow *et al.* (2004) for explanations

(1) Global warming will make all parts of the earth warmer
(2) Increased atmospheric CO_2 will always increase productivity (p 317)
(3) Carbon moves through different pools at the same rate (Figure 3)
(4) The largest pools of carbon are on land and in living organisms (Figure 2).
(5) Photosynthesis provides energy for uptake of carbon and nutrients through plant roots (Figure 3; p 317)
(6) Plants get their biomass from nutrients in the soil (p 315–316)
(7) Soil respiration means the soil is respiring rather than the organisms living in the soil (p 315–316)
(8) Plant cells do not undergo respiration; only animal cells respire (p 315)

the class. This provides an opportunity for the instructor to dispel persistent misconceptions.

■ Assessment

As class ends, assess students' progress in achieving the defined learning goals (5-10 minutes). Use a quick writing assignment (eg "minute paper", Angelo and Cross 1993) to further probe students' understanding. You might ask one of the following: (1) Predict whether increased CO_2 will increase plant growth, giving one or two supporting reasons; (2) List three locations where you might find C atoms from CO_2 taken up by plants. Briefly describe one forest management practice that could affect carbon storage or release; (3) Describe two factors that might limit forest carbon sequestration; (4) What is the scientific evidence that humans either do or do not influence climate change? By asking these questions before, during, and after the learning cycle, we can assess how many, and perhaps why, students still have misconceptions about the carbon cycle.

■ Summary

Beedlow *et al.* provides a rich conceptual background and synthesis of interrelations of the carbon and nitrogen cycles and the effects of air pollution on carbon sequestration. The instructional potential of this paper is broad and how it is used depends on the learning goals for your students. Clearly, this example will be interpreted and implemented differently by faculty with diverse teaching and disciplinary expertise.

■ Acknowledgements

We thank the National Science Foundation for the project "Faculty Institutes for Reforming Science Teaching" FIRST (DUE 0088847) and the CCLI "Ecology curriculum reform: Integrating innovative teaching and global change technology" (DUE 9952816). We appreciate helpful comments from reviewers.

■ References

Angelo TA and Cross KP. 1993. Classroom assessment techniques: a handbook for college teachers, 2nd ed. San Francisco: Jossey-Bass.

Bransford JD, *et al.* (Eds). 1999. How people learn: brain, mind, experience, and school. Washington DC: National Academy Press

Carlsson B. 2002. Ecological understanding 1: ways of experiencing photosynthesis. *Int J Sci Edu* **24**: 681–99.

Ebert-May, *et al.* 2003. Disciplinary research strategies for assessment of learning. *Bioscience* **53**: 1221–28.

Johnson DW, *et al.* 1998. Active learning: cooperation in the college classroom. Edina, MN: Iteraction Book Company.

Kennedy D. 2004. Climate change and climate science. *Science* **304**: 1565.

McKeachie WJ 2002. Teaching tips: strategies, research, and theory for college and university teachers, 11th ed. Lexington, MA: Heath and Co.

Peplow M. 12 May 2004. Disaster movie makes waves: but could the climate crash "the day after tomorrow"? Nature Science Update. www.nature.com/nsu/040510/040510-6.html. Viewed June 2004.

Posner GH, *et al.* 1982. Accommodation of a scientific conception: toward a theory of conceptual changes. *Sci Educ* **66**: 211–27.

The rising tide of ocean diseases: unsolved problems and research priorities

Drew Harvell[1], Richard Aronson[2], Nancy Baron[3], Joseph Connell[4], Andrew Dobson[5], Steve Ellner[1], Leah Gerber[6], Kiho Kim[7], Armand Kuris[4], Hamish McCallum[8], Kevin Lafferty[4, 9], Bruce McKay[10], James Porter[11], Mercedes Pascual[12], Garriett Smith[13], Katherine Sutherland[11], Jessica Ward[1]

New studies have detected a rising number of reports of diseases in marine organisms such as corals, molluscs, turtles, mammals, and echinoderms over the past three decades. Despite the increasing disease load, microbiological, molecular, and theoretical tools for managing disease in the world's oceans are underdeveloped. Review of the new developments in the study of these diseases identifies five major unsolved problems and priorities for future research: (1) detecting origins and reservoirs for marine diseases and tracing the flow of some new pathogens from land to sea; (2) documenting the longevity and host range of infectious stages; (3) evaluating the effect of greater taxonomic diversity of marine relative to terrestrial hosts and pathogens; (4) pinpointing the facilitating role of anthropogenic agents as incubators and conveyors of marine pathogens; (5) adapting epidemiological models to analysis of marine disease.

Front Ecol Environ 2004; 2(7): 375–382

Infectious diseases have recently caused substantial community- and ecosystem-wide impacts in marine communities. A long-spined sea urchin disease virtually eradicated urchins from the Caribbean and facilitated a coral to algal shift on many reefs (Hughes *et al.* 1994). Coral diseases, such as white band (Figure 1), white plague, white pox, and aspergillosis (Figure 2), have caused major changes in Caribbean reef community structure (Aronson and Precht 2001; Weil and Smith 2003; Kim and Harvell 2004). Populations of marine mammals such as seals, otters, and sea lions (Figure 3) have been heavily impacted by diseases (Kim *et al.* 2004), yet the community and ecosystem consequences of these mass mortalities is unknown. These acute and chronic disease events have

caused serious economic losses in terms of declining fisheries revenue and ecosystem damage. Recent examples of economically destructive infectious diseases include coral diseases in the Caribbean, abalone disease in California, herpes and leptospirosis in California sea lions, lobster disease and salmon virus in Maine, and oyster protozoans in Maryland and Texas.

A 2-year effort by the Marine Disease Working Group at the National Center for Ecological Analysis and Synthesis (MDWG-NCEAS) to evaluate key issues in marine diseases focused on three problems: (1) whether disease impacts are increasing in the ocean; (2) whether current modeling and management approaches for terrestrial organisms are adequate for marine situations; and (3) developing case studies of new statistical and modeling approaches to manage marine organisms that are under disease threat. Both the impacts and prevalence of marine diseases were unusually high in recent decades, but lack of adequate baseline data makes this challenging to quantify (Harvell *et al.* 1999, 2002). Because of the logistical difficulties in conducting marine research and monitoring, many marine mortality events probably go undetected or are poorly understood. Often, the specific cause of the disease outbreak, whether an infectious agent (such as viruses, bacteria, fungi, protozoans, and macroparasites such as helminthes and nematodes) or non-infectious agent, has not even been identified. In addition, activities that scientists predict will increase disease occurrence are on the rise (Lafferty *et al.* in press). For example, ocean aquaculture increased two-fold from 1996–1998 (Pew Oceans Commission 2003); the quantities of ballast water from shipping has increased; the rate of new invertebrate introductions to the marine environment has risen; many marine fisheries are collapsing; and global temperatures

---

In a nutshell:

- An increasing incidence of disease has been detected in marine organisms such as corals, molluscs, marine mammals, turtles, and echinoderms, over the past three decades
- Spread rates appear faster in some marine epidemics than in terrestrial ones
- Controls applied for terrestrial outbreaks (quarantine, culling, vaccination) are not yet used in the ocean
- Some marine pathogens originate on land, then flow downstream into oceans
- Marine disease can alter populations and cause major changes in marine communities

---

[1]*Cornell University (cdh5@cornell.edu);* [2]*Dauphin Island Marine Lab;* [3]*COMPASS;* [4]*University California Santa Barbara;* [5]*Princeton University, Princeton, NJ;* [6]*Arizona State University, Tempe, AZ;* [7]*American University;* [8]*University of Queensland, Australia;* [9]*USGS;* [10]*Seaweb;* [11]*University of Georgia;* [12]*University of Michigan;* [13]*University of South Carolina*

Courtesy of W Precht

Figure 1. *Caribbean elkhorn coral (Acropora palmate) infected with white band disease.*

are expected to increase. Each of these activities has the potential to substantially accelerate the transmission rate of new pathogens and some will also make the hosts more susceptible.

Quantitative analysis of the scientific literature of the past three decades indicates a large increase in the number of reports about marine diseases in corals, turtles, molluscs, marine mammals, and echinoderms (Ward and Lafferty 2004; Figure 4). Lack of baseline data for marine organism diseases makes quantifying the magnitude of this increase difficult, but Ward and Lafferty's (2004) comprehensive, carefully designed quantitative study is the best estimate so far. They used literature reports as a proxy for actual events, and tested the reliability with known disease events, such as rabies outbreaks. Other groups of marine organisms, including crustaceans, seagrasses, and marine fishes, showed no proportionate increase in disease reports. Fish disease actually decreased over 30 years in agreement with expectations based on declining stocks. This literature analysis provides a quantitative basis for earlier inferences that impacts from disease are higher in the oceans of today than in the past, with the important caveat that only some taxa show a clear increase.

The MDWG concludes that the perceived burgeoning of marine disease outbreaks is real for some marine taxa, but is undetectable or not present in others (Harvell *et al.* 1999; Hayes *et al.* 2001). Corals have clearly experienced increased impacts from bleaching and disease over the past 30 years (Ward and Lafferty 2004; Figure 4). In Florida, coral cover is being lost at an escalating rate (Porter *et al.* 2001; Patterson *et al.* 2004), apparently linked to diseases such as white band (Figure 1) and aspergillosis (Figure 2), and to declining water quality.

Globally, coral disease is widespread, with many new syndromes being discovered, such as those affecting plating corals of Palau (Figure 5). Thus far, the Caribbean appears to be a hot spot for disease syndromes and outbreaks (Weil and Smith 2003).

Another reliable baseline also suggests that the current high levels of damage from coral disease are unusual. *Acropora cervicornis* was the dominant coral on many Caribbean reefs until it was virtually eradicated by disease. The signature of this species loss, which has not occurred in the previous 3800 years, is readily detectable in recent cores (Aronson and Precht 2001).

Epidemiological models for the analysis of human disease were developed early in the 20th century (Kermack and McKendrick 1927) and were more recently adapted by Anderson and May (1979) for the study of human disease and terrestrial wildlife. Examples of new management decisions or approaches originating from modeling studies, include the decision to vaccinate dogs but not lions for distemper to slow a distemper epidemic among Serengeti lions (Packer *et al.* 1999), the damping of red grouse cycles by controlling trichostrongylid worms (Hudson *et al.* 1998), and mapping the spread of rabies in raccoons (Smith *et al.* 2002). Adapting these models to the analysis of marine diseases requires an appreciation of the fundamental differences between marine and terrestrial systems and outbreaks, in particular the greater host and pathogen diversity in the ocean, the fact that transmission dynamics and spread rates may be higher in marine systems than in terrestrial systems, and that hosts in the ocean are predominantly invertebrates with short-lived, localized immunity dynamics. Management strategies, such as population viability assessments and decisions about the size and networking of marine reserves, may be dependent on the role of disease (Lafferty and Gerber 2002; McCallum *et al.* unpublished).

■ **Problems and priorities**

To better address the lack of information and tools for marine disease, we highlight five unsolved problems and priorities for future work.

The origins and spread of most marine diseases are poorly known

Important diseases of marine organisms can originate from aquaculture. Recent examples include infectious salmon anemia (ISA), which spread from farmed to wild populations and from Norway to Canada and Maine over several years (Ritchie *et al.* 2001; Murray *et al.* 2002); white spot syndrome virus, which affects wild and cultured penaeid

Figure 2. *(a) Caribbean seafans (Gorgonia ventalina) infected with Aspergillus and (b) Sea fan skeletons killed by aspergillosis.*

shrimp and spread to the Americas from Asia in 1995 (Jory and Dixon 1999); and Taura syndrome virus of white shrimp (*Penaeus vannamei*), which began to spread to North America from Ecuador in 1992 (Overstreet *et al.* 1999). There are currently no accurate estimates of the magnitude of the spillover problem for other possible pathogens, but aquaculture is a likely source of new pathogens entering wild populations in the ocean.

Ballast water is also an important potential source of pathogens that has yet to be investigated. Given the hundreds of new invertebrates and unknown numbers of microorganisms and potential pathogens introduced in ballast water, this is an urgent priority for future research.

Data on pathogen spread in the ocean are limited, but the few cases in which information is available indicate that disease may spread at least as rapidly as any terrestrial epidemic (McCallum *et al.* 2003). For example, a herpes epidemic in pilchards spread along the Australian coastline at approximately 10 000 km per year (Murray *et al.* 2001), a bacterial infection in long-spined urchins in the Caribbean in the mid 1980s spread at 3000–4800 km per year (Lessios 1988), and morbillivirus infection in seals spread at 3000 km per year (Heide-Jorgensen *et al.* 1992). In terrestrial environments, only the epizootics of myxomatosis and calicivirus in Australian rabbits and the virus-vectored West Nile virus in North American birds have rates of spread in excess of 1000 km per year. Although the data are still too limited to conclude whether spread rates are really different in marine and terrestrial ecosystems, it is clear that they are extremely rapid in the ocean and in some cases may well exceed those on land.

The most likely explanation for this relatively rapid spread is the lack of barriers to dispersal in some parts of the ocean and the potential for long-term survival of pathogens outside the host. Whether these rates are the rule is uncertain; despite the impression that marine systems are quite open, studies of gene flow indicate that some marine systems are functionally more closed than

they appear (McCallum *et al.* 2003). The findings suggest that pathogens may pose a particularly severe problem in the ocean.

Not only is spread rate in the ocean rarely measured, information on the modes of marine disease transmission is also lacking. Many terrestrial epidemics propagate via flying insect vectors, but vectored transmission in the ocean is poorly documented. One of the few known examples is a coral predator, the fireworm, that transmits *Vibrio shiloi*, the bacterium responsible for infectious coral bleaching (Figure 6; Sussman *et al.* 2003). Long-range dispersal of some marine parasites with complex life cycles occurs where migratory sea birds are the definitive hosts. Pathogen interchange between terrestrial and marine environments seems to be predominantly from land to ocean (usually via rivers), although little is known about the actual rates of pathogen exchange. For example, the

Figure 3. *Sea lion with aborted pup. The probable cause was beta herpes virus.*

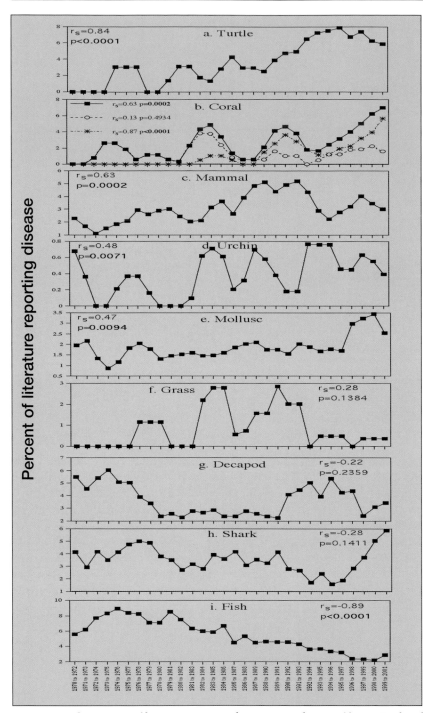

Figure 4. *Thirty years of literature reports about marine diseases (from Ward and Lafferty 2004). Data for each taxon are the proportion of papers reporting disease studies for each group, normalized for total literature in each group, and plotted as 3-year running means. In each of the five taxa shown, the proportion of the literature about disease increased from 1970 to 2001. Diseases of other taxa reported in Ward and Lafferty (2004), such as fish and crustaceans, did not increase significantly over the same time interval.*

et al. 2002; Cole *et al.* 2002). Developing evidence suggests that two coral diseases, aspergillosis and serratiosis, also originated in terrestrial ecosystems (Patterson *et al.* 2002; Garrison *et al.* 2003). Seal distemper in Lake Baikal appears to have originated from dogs, while the origins of a different strain of marine phocine distemper is still not verified (Harvell *et al.* 1999). Although not all marine diseases necessarily originate on land, it is important to understand that some do and others, like acanthocephalan infestations in sea otters, are affected by their host food base, which is sensitive to terrestrial influences.

The immediate research priority to ameliorate this problem is to develop molecular and microbiological diagnostics that can identify and track particular pathogen types, to trace origins and the spread of marine pathogens.

Infectious stages and host range

It is possible that some microorganisms can persist longer in marine than terrestrial conditions. Although most terrestrial bacteria do not survive for long in the marine environment, there are exceptions. Enteric bacteria are well adapted for increased salinities, but are susceptible to bacteriophage and bacteriovores like *Bdellovibrio* species. Bacteria that do not form spores can remain dormant in saltwater sediments for long periods and are resuspended when sediments are disturbed (Heidelberg *et al.* 2002). Spore-forming bacteria and fungi can remain viable for thousands of years and can be transported over tremendous distances (Moir and Smith 1990). Viruses of terrestrial origin may make up a substantial proportion of the microbial plankton (Griffin *et al.* 1999; Wommack *et al.* 1999). The survival of terrestrial microbes in estuarine environments and along shorelines can have a great impact. For example, runoff from land containing non-marine species (particularly human-associated species such as members of the Enterobacteriaceae) has necessitated the closure of beaches for extended periods of time (days to weeks), even after the primary input has subsided (Haile *et al.* 1999). Viable spores of normal soil fungi, including *Aspergillus sydowii*, which infects gorgonian corals (Figure 2) have been found in open oceanic waters and trenches.

An environmental reservoir is a habitat in which a

parasite *Toxoplasma gondii*, which infects otters in Southern California, is considered an emergent disease from land because only domestic cats are known to shed infective oocysts. Otters sampled near freshwater runoff are three times more likely to be seropositive for *T gondii* than otters that live distant from freshwater runoff (Miller

pathogen survives in a viable form without its primary host. These reservoirs may be biotic, such as a secondary host in which there is no pathogenic relationship, or an alternate abiotic habitat in which the pathogen can either persist or multiply. A pathogen with an environmental reservoir has the potential to kill every member of a host species, because it is not limited by host density. Examples of such abiotic reservoirs are brackish water, estuarine sediment (for cholera), and soil. For aspergillosis in corals, airborne dust has been suggested as a reservoir (Garrison *et al.* 2003). Crevices in reefs appear to be reservoirs for black band disease of corals (Kuta and Richardson 2002), and some of the normal gut microbiota in humans or seagulls are possibly pathogenic to certain coral species (Patterson *et al.* 2002).

In addition to having environmental reservoirs, many marine pathogens have wide host ranges, allowing them to be unusually destructive. For example, coral disease outbreaks caused by generalist pathogens include black band disease, reported on 42 species from 21 genera, white plague types I and II, collectively known to infect 22 species and 16 genera (Weil and Smith 2003; Green and Bruckner 2000), and *Porites* pox, which affects at least 10 species of Philippine *Porites* (Raymundo *et al.* 2002). From a conservation perspective, pathogens with a wide host range are of particular concern (Lafferty and Gerber 2002); those infecting large host populations are responsible for virtually all recent disease outbreaks in endangered species (see Dobson and Foufopoulos 2001).

This problem could be mitigated by developing rapid response capability to identify, study, and manage disease outbreaks as they occur.

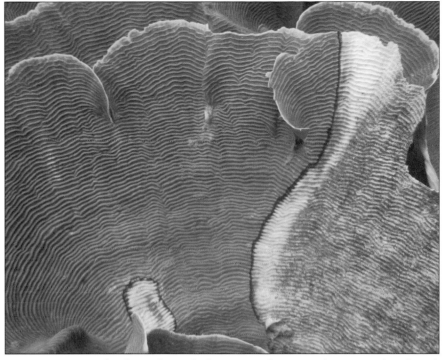

Figure 5. *Recently detected coral diseases: Palauan* Pachyceris *infected with unknown red band infection.*

hosts, should facilitate epidemic spread of relatively virulent pathogens. This occurs among clonal terrestrial plants and where genetic variation has been restricted, such as in farmed animals and plants. The unusual colonial biology and short-lived immunity dynamics of these hosts requires modifications to the modeling framework developed by Anderson and May (1979).

Microbial diversity is also higher in marine environments, although numbers are severely underestimated because many marine microorganisms cannot be cultured. In addition, new bacterial pathogens, such as coral white plague (*Aurantimonas*), are being discovered in entirely new genera (Denner *et al.* 2003).

Research priorities here should include the development of better molecular diagnostics.

Taxonomic diversity of hosts and pathogens

Of the 34 animal phyla, only nine occur on land (Schubel and Butman 2000), making the potential for diverse host–parasite interactions in marine environments greater than in terrestrial ones. In addition to the greater diversity of host phyla, more classes of organisms are involved in parasitic relationships in marine environments (McCallum *et al.* unpublished) and hosts in the ocean include groups such as coral that have no terrestrial counterpart. Among animals, modular, clonal life forms, like corals and sponges are more common in marine environments. As hosts, modular and other clonal species may permit a build-up of more virulent disease strains, because their genetic homogeneity, coupled with the relatively rapid evolution of pathogens compared to

Anthropogenic agents and pathogens

The interaction of disease-resistance mechanisms with environmental stressors is reviewed briefly for corals in Mullen *et al.* (2004), and for other marine animals in Kim *et al.* (2004). Chemical contaminants, especially polychlorinated biphenyls (PCBs), DDTs, and organometals, can bioaccumulate up the food chain and are found in the tissues of marine mammals. The effects of these contaminants on endocrine function, immune competence, and carcinogenesis are well documented in laboratory rodents. Adrenal hyperplasia with associated pathology in Baltic seals has been attributed to exposure to high levels of PCBs. Both cellular and humoral immunity were reduced in harbor seals fed herring from the Baltic sea compared to immune responses in seals fed less contami-

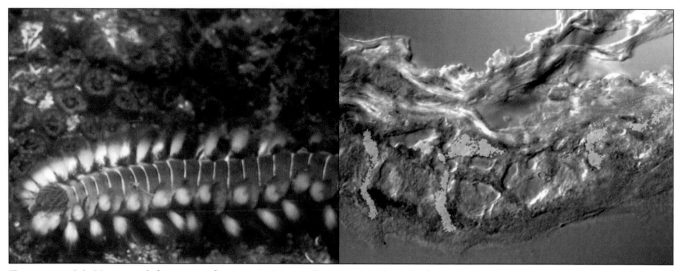

Figure 6. *(a) Vectors of disease in the ocean.* Hermodice carunculata *feeding on* Oculina *(Sussman* et al. *2003). (b) Photomicrograph of* Hermodice *gut stained with FISH probe specific for* Vibrio shiloi, *the pathogen causing coral bleaching (Sussman* et al. *2003).*

nated Atlantic fish. Severity of phocine distemper in experimentally infected harbor seals was greater in animals fed diets with higher levels of PCBs (Harder *et al.* 1992). Contaminants have also been associated with high prevalences of *Leptospira* and calicivirus infections in California sea lions demonstrating premature parturition (Gilmartin *et al.* 1976). Experimental exposure of oysters to tributyl tin increased infection intensity and mortality.

Eutrophication due to runoff of nutrient or organic materials may also cause an increase in the abundance of diseased organisms. The best examples are for non-infectious microorganisms, such as harmful algal blooms. *Pfiesteria* outbreaks in North Carolina estuaries correlate with increasing eutrophication of these environments. The 2002 "blackwater" event in Florida Bay, which killed 70% of the scleractinian corals and all of the clionid sponges in long-term benthic transects on coral reefs within the Bay, occurred during a red tide event (*Karenia brevis*), driven by elevated nutrient conditions in the bay (Porter pers comm).

Coral reefs, especially the elkhorn coral, *Acropora palmata* (Figure 1), grow in oligotrophic waters, and it is hypothesized that newly elevated nutrient conditions in the Florida Keys may have contributed to the outbreak of a fecal enteric microbe that traditionally grows under such conditions (Patterson *et al.* 2002). Disease severity caused by seafan aspergillosis (Figure 2) sometimes correlates with lower water quality conditions, including elevated nitrogen concentrations and turbidity (Kim and Harvell 2002), but aspergillosis also occurs at pristine sites which are low in anthropogenic inputs. Aspergillotic lesions grow at a greater rate when nitrate levels are elevated (Bruno *et al.* 2003). Kuta and Richardson (2002) detected significantly higher nitrite concentrations at sites with black band disease (BBD) than at control sites without BBD in the Florida Keys, but the authors emphasize how difficult the relationship between disease and water quality has been to detect on coral reefs.

A better understanding of environmental facilitators of disease and host immunity should be another research priority.

Epidemiological models

Epidemiological models developed for the study of human disease have not yet been successfully applied to ocean wildlife or management in the ocean. Adapting such models to marine organisms requires understanding fundamental differences between marine and terrestrial systems and outbreaks, including the fact that transmission dynamics and spread rates may be greater in the relatively more open ocean. Hosts in the ocean are predominantly invertebrates with short-lived immunity, so human-based models with lifetime immunity may be inappropriate. Different environmental facilitators may be predictive of marine epizootics than those on land. Initial disease modeling in marine protected areas suggests some very different patterns than on land (McCallum *et al.* unpublished).

A further research priority is to develop forecasting models for outbreaks with environmental or climate sensitivity. These could be modeled after crop disease and coral bleaching forecasts.

■ Conclusions

Measures to prevent and manage marine diseases could be as varied as the organisms and pathogens involved. Remediation strategies for infectious diseases in humans and wildlife include vaccination, antibiotic therapy, quarantine, culling, and the development of resistant transgenics. Each of these are currently ineffective (vaccination, quarantine, culling, antibiotics) or prohibitively expensive (transgenics) in marine ecosystems. The most practical immediate remediation for many marine communities is to reduce pathogen inputs (especially from land) and synergistic stressors, such as warm temperatures and eutrophic waters. Reducing such inputs requires knowing the source of new marine pathogens – research should focus on identifying sources and reducing inputs, while at the same time developing control measures. Immunological strategies, such as vaccination or breeding of resistant strains, may be effective for marine vertebrates, as long as the specific pathogen is known. Marine invertebrate hosts also have cellular and antimicrobial responses to pathogens that could perhaps be enhanced through breeding or engineering. Implementing these approaches may be a decade away, although some breeding programs have already been successful in oysters.

Consideration of what is known about current marine diseases and what sorts of approaches have been useful on land, for both humans and wildlife, suggest the following five research priorities: (1) Develop molecular and microbiological diagnostics and capability to identify and track particular pathogen types to trace origins and spread of marine pathogens; (2) Develop rapid response capability to identify, monitor, and manage disease outbreaks as they occur; (3) Document longevity and host range of infectious stages; (4) Pinpoint the facilitating role of environment in disease outbreaks; and (5) Develop forecasting models for outbreaks that are sensitive to environmental or climatic factors.

■ Acknowledgements

This work was conducted as part of the Marine Disease Working Group organized by D Harvell and supported by the National Center for Ecological Analysis and Synthesis, a Center funded by NSF, the University of California, and the Santa Barbara campus. The work was initiated while Harvell was a sabbatical fellow at NCEAS and written at the Whitely Center of Friday Harbor Laboratories. Special thanks to Patty Debenham at Seaweb for her insights and to Harvell's lab group at Cornell for comments.

■ References

Anderson RM and May R. 1979. Population dynamics of infectious disease. *Nature* **280**: 361.

Amos K and Thomas JA. 2002 Disease interactions between wild and cultured fish: observations learned from the Pacific Northwest. *Bull Eur Fish Pathol* **22**: 95–102.

Aronson RB and Precht WF. 2001. White band disease and the changing face of Caribbean coral reefs. *Hydrobiologia* **460**: 24–38.

Bruno JF, Petes LE, Harvell CD, and Hettinger A. 2003. Nutrient enrichment can increase the severity of coral diseases. *Ecol Lett* **6**: 1056–61.

Cole RA, Lindsay D, Howe DK, et al. 2002. Biological and molecular characterizations of *Toxoplasma gondii* strains obtained from southern sea otters (*Enhydra lutris nereis*). *J Parasitol* **3**: 526–30

Denner EBM, Smith G, Busse H-J, et al. 2003. Characterisation of the bacterial pathogen, WP1, the causative agent of Plague type II disease of Caribbean scleractinian corals: description of *Aurantimonas coralicida*. *Int J Syst Evol Micr* **53**: 1115–22.

Dobson A and Foufopolous J. 2001. Emerging infectious pathogens of wildlife. *Philos T Roy Soc B* **1411**: 1001–12.

Ford SE. 1996. Range extension by the oyster parasite *Perkinsus marinus* into the Northeastern United States: response to climate change? *J Shellfish Res* **15**: 45–56.

Garrison VH, Shinn EA, Foreman WT, et al. 2003. African and Asian dust: from Desert soils to coral reefs. *BioScience* **5**: 469–80.

Gilmartin WG, DeLong RL, Smith AW, et al. 1976. Premature parturition of the Callifornia sealion. *J Wildlife Dis* **12**: 104–15.

Green E and Bruckner AW. 2000. The significance of coral disease epizootiology for coral reef conservation. *Biol Conserv* **96**: 347–61.

Griffin DW, Gibson CJ, Lipp EK, et al. 1999. Detection of viral pathogens by reverse transcriptase PCR and of microbial indicators by standard methods in the canals of the Florida Keys. *Appl Environ Microb* **65**: 4118–25.

Haile R, Witte J, Gold M, et al. 1999. The health effects of swimming in ocean water contaminated by storm drain runoff. *Epidemiology* **10**: 355–63.

Harder TC, Wilhus T, Leibold W, and Liess B. 1992. Investigations on the course and outcome of phocine distemper virus infection in harbor seals (*Phoca vitulina*) exposed to polychlorinated biphenyls. *J Vet Med B* **39**: 19–31.

Harvell CD, Kim K, Burkholder JM, et al. 1999. Emerging marine diseases – climate links and anthropogenic factors. *Science* **285**: 1505–10.

Harvell CD, Mitchell C, Ward J, et al. 2002. Climate warming and disease risks for terrestrial and marine biota. *Science* **296**: 2158–62.

Harvell CD, Mullen K, and Peters E. Coral resistance to disease. In: Rosenberg E (Ed). Coral health and disease. Tel Aviv, Israel: Tel Aviv Press. In press.

Hasson KW, Lightner DV, and Mari J. 1999. The geographic distribution of Taura Syndrome Virus (TSV) in the Americas: determination by histopathology and in situ hybridization using TSV-specific cDNA probes. *Aquaculture* **171**: 1–2.

Hayes ML, Bonaventura J, Mitchell TP, et al. 2001. How are climate and marine biological outbreaks functionally related? *Hydrobiologia* **460**: 213–20.

Heidelberg JF, Heidelberg KB, and Colwell RR. 2002. Seasonality of Chesapeake Bay bacterioplankton species. *Appl Environ Microb* **68**: 5488–97.

Herbst LH. 1994. Fibropapillomatosis of marine turtles. *Annu Rev Fish Dis* **4**: 389–425.

Heide-Jorgensen MP, Harkonen T, Dietz R, and Thompson PM. 1992. Retrospective of the 1988 European seal epizootic. *Dis Aquat Organ* **13**: 37–62.

Hoegh-Guldberg O. 1999. Climate change, coral bleaching and the future of the world's coral reefs. *Mar Freshwater Res* **8**: 839–66.

Hudson PJ, Dobson AP, and Newborn D. 1998. Prevention of population cycles by parasite removal. *Science* **282**: 2256–58.

Hughes T. 1994. Catastrophes, phase shifts, and large scale degradation of a Caribbean coral reef. *Science* **265**: 1547–51.

Jolles A, Sullivan P, Alker AP, and Harvell CD. 2002. Disease transmission in sea fans: inferring process from spatial pattern. *Ecology* **9**: 2373–78.

Jones JB, Hyatt AD, Hine PM, et al. 1997. Special topic review: Australasian pilchard mortalities. *World J Microb Biot* **13**: 383–92.

Jory DE and Dixon HM. 1999. Shrimp whitespot virus in the western hemisphere. *Aquacult Mag* **25**: 83–91.

Kermack WO and McKendrick WG. 1927. A contribution to the mathematical theory of epidemics. *P Roy Soc Lond A* **115**: 700–21.

Kim K and Harvell CD. 2002. Aspergillosis of sea fan corals: disease dynamics in the Florida Keys, USA. In: Porter J and Porter K (Eds). Linkages between ecosystems in the South Florida hydroscapes. Boca Raton, FL: CRC.

Kim, K. and Harvell, C.D. 2004. The rise and fall of a seven year seafan-fungal epizootic. *Am Nat.* in press.

Kim K, Dobson A, Gulland FMD, and Harvell CD. 2004. Disease and the conservation of marine diversity. In: Norse E and Crowder L (Eds). Conservation of marine ecosystems. Washington DC: Island Press.

Kuta KG and Richardson LL. 2002. Ecological aspects of black band disease of corals: relationships between disease incidence and environmental factors. *Coral Reefs* **21**: 393–98.

Lafferty KD and Gerber L. 2002. Good medicine for conservation biology: the intersection of epidemiology and conservation theory. *Conserv Biol* **16**: 593–604.

Lafferty K, Porter J, and Ford S. Are diseases increasing in the ocean? *Ann Rev Ecol Evol Sys.* In press.

Lessios HA, Robertson DR, and Cubit JD. 1984. Spread of *Diadema antillarum* mass mortality through the Caribbean. *Science* **226**: 335–37.

Lessios HA. 1988. Mass mortality of *Diadema antillarum* in the Caribbean: what have we learned? *Annu Rev Ecol Syst* **19**: 371–93.

McCallum H, Harvell CD, Dobson A. 2003. Rates of spread of marine pathogens. *Ecol Lett* **12**: 1062–67.

McCallum H, Gerber LR, and Jani A. Does infectious disease influence the efficacy of marine protected areas? A theoretical framework. In preparation.

Miller MA, Gardner IA, Krueder C, *et al.* 2002. Coastal freshwater runoff is a risk factor for Toxoplasma gondii infection of southern sea otters (*Enhydra lutris nereis*). *Int J Parasitol* **32**: 997–1006.

Moir A and Smith DA. 1990. The genetics of bacterial spore germination. *Annu Rev Microbiol* **44**: 531–54.

Mullen K, Peters E, and Harvell CD. 2004. Coral resistance to disease. In: Rosenberg E (Ed). Coral health and disease. Berlin: Springer-Verlag Press.

Murray AG, O'Callaghan M, and Jones B. 2002. Simple models of massive epidemics of herpesvirus in Australian (and New Zealand) pilchards. *Environ Int* **27**: 243–48.

Overstreet RM, Lightner DV, Hasson KW. 1999. Susceptibility to Taura syndrome virus of some penaeid shrimp species native to the Gulf of Mexico and the southeastern United States. *J Invertebr Pathol* **2**: 165–76.

Packer C, Altizer S, Appel M, *et al.* 1999. Viruses of the Serengeti: patterns of infection and mortality in African lions. *J Anim Ecol* **68**: 1161–78.

Patterson KL, Porter JW, Ritchie KB, *et al.* 2002. The etiology of White Pox, a lethal disease of the Caribbean elkhorn coral, *Acropora palmate*. *P Natl Acad Sci USA* **13**: 8725–30.

Patterson KL, Porter JW, Torres C. 2004. Disease and immunity in Caribbean and Indo-Pacific zooxanthellate corals. *Mar Ecol Progr Ser* **266**: 273–302.

Porter JW, Dustan JP, Japp WC, *et al.* 2001. Patterns of spread of coral disease in the Florida Keys. *Hydrobiologia* **460**: 1–24.

Palumbi SR, Gaines S, and Warner R. 2003. New technology in development of marine reserves. *Front Ecol Environ* **2**: 73–79.

Pew Oceans Commission. 2003. America's living oceans: charting a course for sea change. A report to the nation. Arlington, VA: Pew Oceans Commission.

Raymundo LJ, Harvell CD, and Reynolds T. 2002. *Porites* ulcerative white spot disease: description, prevalence, and host range of a new coral disease affecting Indo-Pacific reefs. *Dis Aquat Organ*. In press.

Rice TD, Williams HN, and Turny BF. 1998. Susceptibility of bacteria in estuarine environments to autochthonous bdellovibrios. *Microb Ecol* **35**: 256–64.

Ritchie RJ, Cook M, Melville K, *et al.* 2001. Identification of infectious salmon anemia virus in atlantic salmon from Nova Scotia: evidence for functional strain differences. *Dis Aquat Organ* **44**: 171–78.

Schubel JR and Butman CA. 2000. Keeping a finger on the pulse of marine biodiversity: how healthy is it? In: Raven PH and Williams T (Eds). Nature and human society: the quest for a sustainable future. Washington DC: National Academy Press.

Smith DL, Lucey B, Waller LA, *et al.* 2002. Predicting the spatial dynamics of rabies epidemics on heterogeneous landscapes. *P Natl Acad Sci USA* **99**: 3668–72.

Sussman M, Loya Y, Fine M, and Rosenberg E. 2003. The marine fireworm *Hermodice carunculata* is a winter reservoir and spring–summer vector for the coral-bleaching pathogen *Vibrio shiloi*. *Environ Microb* **5**: 250–55.

Ward JR and Lafferty K. 2004. The elusive baseline of marine disease: are marine diseases in ocean ecosystems increasing? *PLoS Biol* **2**: 0542–47.

Weil E and Smith G. 2003. Scleractinian and octocoral disease Caribbean-wide. In: Kasim MK, Moosa, Soemodihardjo S, *et al.*(Eds). Proceedings of the Ninth International Coral Reef Symposium: 23–27 Oct 2000: Bali, Indonesia.

Wilcox RM and Fuhrman JA. 1994. Bacterial viruses in coastal seawater: lytic rather than lysogenic production. *Mar Ecol Prog Ser* **114**: 35–45.

Wommack KE, Ravel J, Hill RT, *et al.* 1999. Population dynamics of Chesapeake Bay virioplankton: total community analysis by pulsed-field gel electrophoresis. *Appl Environ Microbiol* **65**: 231–40.

Marine pathology: revealing the ocean's etiology to earthbound students

Janet Hodder[1], Diane Ebert-May[2]*, Kathy Williams[3], and Doug Luckie[2]

Students, especially those from the inland parts of a country, tend to have a "terrestrial-centric" view of Earth. For some, exploration of marine ecosystems may occur only during holidays or while watching the Discovery channel. The idea that oceans have pathogens that cause devastating diseases in a variety of organisms is less familiar to students than human diseases and medical treatments.

Harvell et al. (see pages 375–382) provide an excellent resource to help students bridge familiar topics in science with the unfamiliar. This review points out how little we know about diseases in the ocean and exemplifies the nature of science by discussing the process of investigating complex questions and showing that a lot of information is uncertain and awaits further exploration. Here we present a way to use this reading for a single class meeting, but this segment of instruction does not stand alone. It would fit well after a section on disease, viruses, immunology, or biogeochemical cycles.

■ Learning goals

In this example, teams of students will:
- Demonstrate understanding of the scientific process by constructing hypotheses and a means of testing them.
- Compare and contrast diseases in marine and terrestrial ecosystems.
- Illustrate why knowledge of ocean diseases is incomplete and uncertain.

Instructional strategy (50 minute period): We again use the learning cycle to provide students with opportunities to interactively engage with the material to construct better understanding (BSCS 1993; Bransford et al. 1999; Ebert-May et al. 2004).

Engagement (last ten minutes of prior class): At the end of class, introduce the Harvell et al. paper as homework. To provide context, show figures from the paper with brief explanations about hosts and their pathogens, as well as how transmission occurs. Use the graphs in Figure 4 to show disease increases in recent times. Challenge the class by asking them to predict why diseases in the oceans are increasing. Ask students to think individually for 30 seconds, and then turn to their neighbor to discuss for 2 minutes. Select 2–3 pairs to report orally, record their predictions on an overhead, and provide feedback.

To learn about your students' prior knowledge ask them to answer this question:
How is testing and determining treatment for a serious viral infection like Severe Acute Respiratory Syndrome (SARS) carried out within the human population? Students write their responses on carbonless paper[1], turn in their answers and pick up their homework assignment (Panel 1) on the way out of class, or access it on the class website.

Next class period
After students have submitted their homework, ask them to form groups of four by disease topic. This process can be facilitated in larger classes by providing a list of all the diseases mentioned in the paper and assigning sections of the classroom for each disease topic on an overhead prepared beforehand. When the groups have formed, ask students to form two pairs within each group to compare findings for 2 minutes; with pairs, everyone has a chance to talk.

Panel 1. Homework

Read the Harvell et al. paper "The rising tide of ocean diseases..."

- Choose one marine disease discussed and use information from the paper, library resources, the Internet, and textbooks to briefly explain the following:

  a. Symptons of the disease
  b. Pathogens causing the illness, including how they are transmitted
  c. Anthropogenic factors influencing the disease
  d. Known or potential treatments
  e. Three ways this marine disease is similar to human disease caused by a similar pathogen

- Take notes, to be used in class, on your findings. Use your carbonless paper notebook so you can turn in one copy while keeping another for yourself.

Grading ideas: assign one point per correct item or grade quickly with + or –. Notes: no need to make comments because students have a copy and will work with the material in class.

---

[1]Carbonless paper is a laboratory research pad in 8.5" x 11" format, quad or line ruled, available at campus bookstores. It provides students with a record of what they do in class and eliminates the need to return papers to large numbers of students. For writing that is graded, individual student's points are posted on the web, and the next day in class, faculty show anonymous examples of "exemplary" and "needs improvement" that students can compare to their answer and discuss if appropriate.

---

[1]University of Oregon, [2]*Michigan State University, (ebertmay@msu.edu) and [3]San Diego State University
For the introduction to the Pathways to Scientific Teaching series, see Front Ecol Environ 2004; **2(6)**: 323

Courtesy of E Weil

Porites sp from Palau is affected by an unidentified disease syndrome causing blue spots surrounded by darker halos.

Exploration *(25 minutes)*: The entire team of four begins the exploration by designing a research study to investigate "their" disease. Instruct each group to create a draft plan, on their carbonless paper, to treat the disease they are discussing, based on the following points:

• Define the problem: what is known and unknown about the disease?
• Develop one testable hypothesis that would provide information to increase our knowledge about this disease
• Design a method to test the hypothesis.
• Predict results that would support or refute your hypothesis.

Walk around and listen to student discussions; respond to questions by offering suggestions without giving solutions. After 10 minutes, give them a 5-minute warning to finish the assignment. At that time, select 2–3 groups to report out and provide them with a transparency and pen to show their draft plan to the class. After each report, ask the group to respond to one or two questions from the class or yourself. Ask groups to submit a copy of their draft plans (you collect the original, they keep the copy of the carbonless paper).

Explanation *(25 minutes)*: Explain the biological concepts students need to know to reinforce their understanding of the Harvell *et al.* paper. Focus on comparing and contrasting the major qualitative differences between marine and terrestrial environments that can influence the outcome of a disease. Supplement your explanations with information from McCallum *et al.* (2004). As an exercise in the middle of your lecture ask the students to look at the Harvell *et al.* paper again. Assign each fifth of the class one of the five unsolved problems in the paper and ask them to count how many times the section indicates "we don't know" as an illustration of how much remains to be learnt about the ocean and disease. After students report out and you record

the numbers, ask them to write one plausible reason for this lack of knowledge. Again, select two or three individuals to share their thinking with the class, record their ideas, synthesize and discuss. Then continue to compare marine to terrestrial systems, for example:

• Types of pathogens and their transmission and persistence
• Taxonomic diversity and life history differences of major phyla
• Environmental stressors
• Application of human or terrestrial models in ocean disease situations.

Assessment *(10–15 minutes of the next class period)*: Inform students that at the beginning of the next class you will provide a scenario from the Harvell et al. paper from which each individual (or group) will write a second hypothesis and the experimental approach (not to be confused with protocol) they would use to test this. This assessment reminds students that much is still to be learnt about ocean disease and their hypothetical experiment could potentially contribute to that knowledge. An exemplary response would include a relevant reason for the investigation (biological rationale) and a hypothesis with an independent variable (what is manipulated) and a dependent variable (what is measured), the organism or system, and the predicted direction of the results using the appropriate comparison. Alternatively, a multiple choice question presenting possible hypotheses about the scenario (only one of which included all of the above components) or a conceptual multiple choice question that assessed students' ability to compare diseases in marine and terrestrial environments are useful, depending on the learning goals one wants to emphasize most.

■ Acknowledgements

We thank the National Science Foundation for their long-term support of the FIRST project, Faculty Institutes for Reforming Science Teaching (DUE 0088847) and Drew Harvell.

■ References

Bransford JD, Brown AL and Cocking RR. (Eds). 1999. How people learn: brain, mind, experience, and school. Washington DC: National Academy Press.

[BSCS] Biological Sciences Curriculum Study. 1993. Developing biological literacy. Colorado Springs, CO: Biological Sciences Curriculum Study.

Ebert-May D, Williams K, Luckie D, and Hodder J. 2004. Climate change: confronting student ideas. *Front Ecol Environ* **2**: 324–25.

Harvell, Aronson R, Baron N, et al. 2004. The rising tide of ocean diseases: unsolved problems and research priorities. *Front Ecol Environ* **2**: 375–382

McCallum HI, Kuris A, Harvell CD, et al. Does terrestrial epidemiology apply to marine systems? *Trends Ecol Evol* (In press)

Chapter **3**

Students: Doing Science

Overview

How can I engage students in scientific activities in these large-enrollment courses? Although the principles of scientific teaching are imbedded in the practice of science in the field or laboratory, the challenge of doing this with large numbers of students in a lecture hall is daunting. While some activities are difficult or impossible to do in this environment, we can actively engage students in science by parsing activities into smaller chunks. For example, students can solve problems, analyze data, interpret evidence, make models, and evaluate arguments in their groups in class. The key in a large course is to break down problems into small, doable parts over several class meetings, but then be certain to guide students towards connecting the components of the problem together. This truly models what scientists do and gives students the opportunity to practice the elements of science in class.

One of the major concerns of faculty and students about problem-oriented, learner-centered activities in class is individual student accountability as well as responsibility within their groups. The power of groups to foster learning is well documented (Johnson et al. 1978; Springer et al. 1999). The dynamics of cooperative teams' interactions are critical. Several publications report ideas for implementing successful cooperative learning and addressing issues such as group formation, heterogeneity within groups, timing of activities, and motivation (Mazur 1996; Beichner et al. 1999; Smith et al. 2005; Handelsman et al. 2007). The articles in this chapter model how student groups can do science in large lecture settings, and provide examples of different types of assessments of learning outcomes.

Generality in ecology: testing North American grassland rules in South African savannas

Alan K Knapp[1], Melinda D Smith[2,3], Scott L Collins[4], Nick Zambatis[5], Mike Peel[6], Sarah Emery[7], Jeremy Wojdak[7], M Claire Horner-Devine[8], Harry Biggs[5], Judith Kruger[5], and Sandy J Andelman[2]

Ecology has emerged as a global science, and there is a pressing need to identify ecological rules – general principles that will improve its predictive capability for scientists and its usefulness for managers and policy makers. Ideally, the generality and limits of these ecological rules should be assessed using extensive, coordinated experiments that ensure consistency in design and comparability of data. To improve the design of these large-scale efforts, existing data should be used to test prospective ecological rules and to identify their limits and contingencies. As an example of this approach, we describe prospective rules for grassland responses to fire and rainfall gradients, identified from long-term studies of North American grasslands and tested with existing data from long-term experiments in South African savanna grasslands. Analyses indicated consistent effects of fire on the abundance of the dominant (grasses) and subdominant (forbs) flora on both continents, but no common response of grass or forb abundance across a rainfall gradient. Such analyses can inform future research designs to refine and more explicitly test ecological rules.

Front Ecol Environ 2004; 2(9): 483–491

Progress in ecology has resulted from testing specific predictions derived from hypotheses (the hypothetico-deductive model) and through the synthesis of accumulated results into general patterns and underlying mechanisms (Pickett *et al.* 1994). The ultimate goal for ecology, like all sciences, is the refinement of knowledge into theories and laws that are predictive and able to

---

In a nutshell:

- Proposing ecological rules and testing their limits is necessary for ecology to become a more predictive science
- Rules enabling forecasts of community and ecosystem responses to key drivers would be valuable to managers and policy makers
- Prospective rules that predict responses to fire frequency and rainfall gradients, based on long-term studies in North American grasslands, were tested in South African savanna grasslands, using existing data from ongoing, long-term experiments
- Analyses indicated consistent effects of fire on the abundance of grasses and forbs in both grasslands and savannas, but not consistent responses of forbs to rainfall gradients
- Synthetic analyses of existing data can provide insight into the general applicability of proposed rules, identify contingencies and data needs, and guide future research

---

[1]*Department of Biology, Colorado State University, Ft Collins, CO 80523 (aknapp@lamar.colostate.edu)*; [2]*National Center for Ecological Analysis and Synthesis, University of California-Santa Barbara*; [3]*Department of Ecology and Evolutionary Biology, Yale University*; [4]*Department of Biology, University of New Mexico*; [5]*South African National Parks, South Africa*; [6]*ARC Range and Forage Institute, South Africa*; [7]*WK Kellogg Biological Station, Michigan State University*; [8]*Department of Biological Sciences, Stanford University*

withstand repeated tests (Murray 2001). In laboratory-based sciences, the ability to precisely and independently repeat experiments, a key step in the scientific method, is facilitated by the rigorous control of experimental conditions. In ecological experiments, particularly those conducted in the field, the background environment is always changing; genetic composition and variability among the study organisms are seldom constant, and both organism behaviors and ecosystem states are derived from an often unknown past. All of these factors reduce the likelihood that repeated experiments will yield similar results. An unfortunate outcome is the perception that ecological systems are idiosyncratic and have limited predictability.

Two comments from the literature illustrate the inherent challenges of ecological studies. Over 20 years ago, while conducting experiments in the field, plant ecophysiologist Melvin T Tyree (1983) noted that "progress was rather slow because weather conditions could not be arranged to meet experimental requirements". Later CAS Hall (1988) lamented that "if physicists had to model electrons that behaved differently when they were hungry, they would probably be not much ahead of ecologists…".

Such challenges are perhaps responsible for the restrained pace of synthesis, the combining of results from numerous studies into coherent generalities, and consequently the slow development of widely accepted laws in ecology. Indeed, the existence and generality of laws for ecological systems has long been debated (McIntosh 1985; Lawton 1999; Berryman 2003; Colyvan and Ginzburg 2003), and some have argued that it is fruitless to seek laws because of the complexity of these systems (McIntosh 1985; Peters 1991). To some extent, this debate reflects different definitions and expectations of sci-

Figure 1. *Intensive study of ecosystems and experimental manipulation of the drivers that structure them can lead to the formation of rules that have predictive value at hierarchical levels ranging from the organism to the ecosystem. For example, the long-term study of fire on experimental watersheds at the Konza Prairie LTER site has led to a series of predictive rules for this mesic grassland (Knapp et al. 1998), but the generality of these rules is unknown. Determining how well rules apply in other systems and identifying those contingencies or exceptions that lead to alternative responses is an important step towards ecology becoming a more predictive science.*

entists. Scientific laws can be defined as conditional statements of relationship or causation, or as statements of process that always hold within defined limits (Pickett *et al.* 1994). Because this definition suggests that laws are immutable, it may be too restrictive for many ecological systems. We suggest an important, albeit subtle, distinction, namely that ecologists seek rules rather than laws. Rules still reflect the notion of generality and conditional probability, but they place less restrictive boundaries on expectations (Lawton 1999). Rules, after all, are made to be broken.

Most ecologists would agree that ecological rules exist, at least as defined by Lawton (1999) as "general principles that underpin and create patterns", and ecologists have certainly made progress in testing general ecological processes and phenomena in multiple ecosystems (eg Pickett and White 1985; Brown *et al.* 2001; Loreau *et al.* 2001; Rees *et al.* 2001; Enquist *et al.* 2003). However, despite a wealth of comparative studies, ecological rules and their predictive limits are seldom explicitly examined (Figure 1). This may be because ecologists are wary of the uncertainties associated with field experiments and they know, as Lawton cautioned, that some level of contingency (exceptions related to history or other events) must almost always temper them. Nonetheless, distilling generalizations from an ever-increasing body of detailed ecological data, formulating prospective rules that govern ecological systems, and explicitly testing them are essential steps for making ecology a more predictive science (Figure 2).

Only a few ecological rules have been formally proposed that apply to both multiple taxa and systems (eg Rosenzweig 1995; Ritchie and Olff 1999; Reynolds 2002; Turchin 2001; Enquist *et al.* 2003; Berryman 2003). Some of these span orders of magnitude in scale, and are products of the emerging field of macroecology (Brown 1995). Despite their promise, such rules are often questioned on a variety of grounds (ie Murray 2001; Coomes *et al.* 2003; Harte 2004; Cyr and Walker 2004). Indeed, Simberloff (2004) recently conceded that the discipline of community ecology has no general rules in the sense that physics does, but instead has only "fuzzy generalizations". He suggested, as did Lawton, that this occurs in part because the basic units of community ecology – species – are more numerous, diverse, and complex than the basic particles of physics. Thus, ecological rules may need to focus on a different set of ecological units, such as metabolic pathways, functional traits, or biomass. In this regard, we concur with Cooper's (1998) arguments that there are many potential ecological rules (causal, theoretical, and phenomenological) that may have strong predictive capabilities, when their boundaries or limits are correctly identified. This perspective is consistent with a broader definition of ecological rules, modified from Lincoln *et al.* (1990), as generalizations or statements that predict the occurrence of a particular ecological phenomenon, if certain conditions are met. Thus, rules describe how ecological systems will behave within certain boundaries (Berryman 2003), and allow for predictions within these constraints. Indeed, general rules pertaining to the ways in which terrestrial ecosystems recover from disturbances were proposed long ago (Odum 1969), though many are yet to be formally tested.

Generalizations that could be applied to ecological patterns and processes, and their underpinning rules, based on the key factors that drive and constrain communities and ecosystems, would certainly be valuable in forecasting the responses of biomes to global change (Dynesius *et al.* 2004). They would also help land managers and policy makers, who are grappling with resource and conservation issues in a rapidly changing world. The most robust rules – either empirically or theoretically derived – should be able to withstand the test of time, and will therefore probably be generated from the long-term study of ecological systems (eg the Hubbard Brook Experimental Forest; Bormann and Likens 1979; Figure 1). However, for ecological science to advance, it is critical to test predictions from rules in systems other than those used to develop them. Clearly, if the drivers responsible for the structure and dynamics of particular ecosystems have been correctly identified and are mechanistically understood, ecological rules should have predictive value in other, similar systems. Testing rules in other ecosystems provides a means of assessing their generality, as well as detecting important contingent factors (Dynesius *et al.* 2004; Figure 2).

How might an assessment of general ecological responses, their underpinning ecological rules, and their contingencies, best be accomplished? Currently, there are two general methods. The first is the standard comparative approach (eg Grime 2001), in which observations and mechanistic experiments designed to elucidate key traits of organisms or ecosystem drivers can be used to generate prospective rules and test predictions derived from them. The preferred approach for identifying general responses, formulating rules, and testing them includes coordinated experiments designed for synthesis prior to initiating the research (Hector *et al.* 1999; Webster *et al.* 2003). This "*a priori*" approach ensures consistency in the implementation of treatments, and commonality in the way data are collected. However, the relevant time scales for the manifestation of many ecological processes and patterns can exceed 5–10 years (Callahan 1984; Brown *et al.* 2001), making such experiments expensive and their outcomes less than timely.

An alternative to an *a priori* approach is *post hoc* (after the fact) synthesis, which involves combining existing results from a collective body of research designed to elucidate specific ecological processes or phenomena. Traditional literature reviews are qualitative examples of this type of approach. More recently, meta-analyses of results from studies that focus on a specific manipulation (such as responses to elevated CO_2; Jablonski *et al.* 2002) or specific ecological relationships (Waide *et al.* 1999) have permitted more quantitative analyses. Formal rules can be created and their limits tested with either *post hoc* or *a priori* approaches (Figure 2).

An additional and complementary *post hoc* approach involves the analysis and synthesis of raw data, rather than results, from past studies. What distinguishes this kind of approach is that data can be used from studies that were not necessarily focused on similar ecological questions. Previous analyses may not even be of interest – a fundamental departure from traditional literature

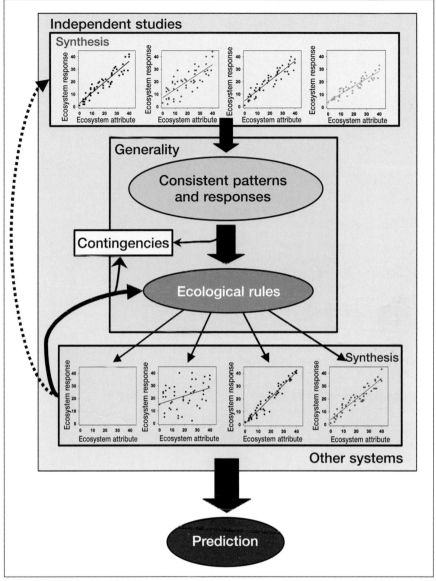

Figure 2. *Framework describing the iterative process of formulating ecological rules. The syntheses of research results from independent studies (top) may be planned a priori from coordinated research programs or result from the post hoc analysis of disparate studies. After consistencies in pattern and process are idealized, with potential contingent factors noted, these prospective rules can be explicitly tested in other systems. This may be accomplished with new research or through the continued analysis and synthesis of existing data and results. Through the synthesis of these assessments (dotted line), formal ecological rules can be articulated and predictions become more robust. Throughout the process, the identification of contingent factors will modify and ultimately define the predictive limits (ie the domain) of these rules. Contingent factors themselves can also serve as foci for additional research, further advancing ecological understanding.*

reviews and meta-analyses. Instead, formerly disparate datasets are combined and made comparable, so that new questions can be addressed. In this way, we can take advantage of the abundant data that currently exist, not to mine them for patterns (Burnham and Anderson 2002), but rather to test new predictions. This approach also avoids the publication and investigator bias that plagues meta-analyses (Tomkins and Kotiaho 2004). Of course

---

Panel 1. Comparison of key attributes of *a priori* (planned) synthesis of ecological data versus *post hoc* (after the fact) synthesis of existing data from disparate studies

Identifying general ecological patterns and processes, and their underpinning rules, is best accomplished through synthesis planned initially as part of the study. However, *post hoc* synthesis of data has several advantages, including low cost and timeliness; results can also be valuable in guiding new research.

Attributes of *a priori* synthesis:

(1) Experiments are motivated by common questions/hypotheses, with only minor subsequent modifications. Final synthetic analyses explicitly address these questions

(2) Core experiments/studies share a common design and sites are selected to maximize the usefulness and generality of results

(3) Rare or unplanned events during the course of study often improve understanding because of the common experimental design and structure

(4) Datasets are collected consistently and are comparable temporally and spatially

(5) Context (spatial and temporal) for interpretation is predetermined and remains consistent

(6) Cost is substantial, particularly if long-term data are needed – includes data collection and synthetic analyses

Attributes of *post hoc* synthesis:

(1) Questions/hypotheses are exploratory and will probably be altered substantially, depending on data availability and quality

(2) Experiments/studies are variable in their design and study sites can be diverse

(3) Unusual events inevitably affect some studies but not others and thus add uncertainty

(4) Data are variable in quality and temporal and spatial dimensions and units

(5) Context for interpretation will probably decrease (spatially and temporally) as data limitations are identified

(6) Cost is minimal – limited to synthetic analyses

---

are maintained across replicate watersheds to address a number of questions regarding ecological patterns and processes in grasslands (Knapp *et al.* 1998; Figure 1). Consistent with the LTER paradigm, numerous response variables are measured spatially across treatment and landscape gradients and temporally across years in which the climate varies naturally. Small-scale plot studies and short-term experiments complement long-term studies to elucidate specific ecological interactions.

Based on data from several of these studies, Collins *et al.* (1998) assessed the interactive roles of fire and large herbivores in determining the productivity and community composition of the Kansas site. They showed that the cumulative effects of frequent fire – increased productivity and biomass of the dominant grasses, but reduced plant species richness – were mediated by grazing. Large herbivores enhanced plant species richness in frequently burned areas through reductions in the biomass of the dominant grasses. A mechanistic link to grass canopy (biomass) removal was made possible by combining results from complementary plot-level mowing experiments, in which similar response variables were measured (Collins *et al.* 1998). Combining data from distinct fire, grazing, and mowing experiments to understand controls on community composition was made possible by an experimental design that facilitated *a priori* synthesis of results (Panel 1).

there are limitations to this, and any *post hoc* approach, but new analyses of data can provide substantial ecological insight, generate new hypotheses, and improve future experiments, particularly if these data were collected over long time periods.

■ *A priori* versus *post hoc* synthesis

Through experience with both *a priori* and *post hoc* syntheses of ecological data we have identified important strengths and weaknesses for each approach (Panel 1). Two brief examples of each type of synthesis are provided, each using results from long-term ecological research (LTER) sites to illustrate the differences. We focus on examples based on long-term studies because this is where *post hoc* synthesis has the greatest value, when compared to the initiation of new research. We then propose basic rules for ecosystem structure derived from studies of temperate grasslands in North America and test them in South African sub-tropical savanna grasslands.

LTER sites are excellent examples of research programs designed for synthetic analyses and the development of ecological rules for specific biomes because of the breadth of data collected from the level of the individual organism to the entire ecosystem, and because all programs have a unifying, site-based perspective (Callahan 1984). At the Konza Prairie LTER site, a mesic grassland in northeastern Kansas, long-term manipulations of key drivers (fire and grazing)

The LTER program also provides an example of *post hoc* synthetic analyses (Knapp and Smith 2001). In this case, aboveground net primary production (ANPP) data, collected for a variety of different site-specific purposes at all LTER sites, were combined to test hypotheses about continental-scale patterns and controls of ANPP, and inter-annual variability in productivity. Due to differences in the quality and temporal extent of ANPP data collected between sites, the original questions were revised and the context and scope of the analysis was altered. As a result, just a subset of the data was used. Similar alteration in scope as a result of data limitations is common in *post hoc* analyses (Panel 1). Nonetheless, *post hoc* analyses of these data proved valuable, indicating that although mean annual rainfall was strongly related to mean ANPP across sites, inter-annual variability in rainfall was not related to temporal variability in ANPP. Instead, a more complex model that included the ability of producers to respond to variation in resources was developed to explain these patterns.

Figure 3. (a) Upland view of an experimental watershed on the Konza Prairie Biological Station in northeastern Kansas. Konza Prairie was one of the original six LTER sites and is dominated by C_4 grasses; the abundance of C_3 woody species is dependent on fire frequency (Knapp et al. 1998). (b) View of an experimental burn plot (EBP) near Satara, Kruger National Park, South Africa. This 7-ha plot, part of an experiment ongoing for > 50 years, is frequently burned and is also dominated by C_4 grasses, with widely dispersed C_3 shrubs and trees.

In both examples, new understanding of ecological patterns and processes emerged from synthetic analyses of data. However, the process of understanding differed. Although *a priori* synthesis most closely resembles a traditional scientific approach and *post hoc* synthesis clearly has greater limitations, using existing data in such analyses adds value to both completed and ongoing studies, and may be valuable in identifying knowledge and data gaps.

■ Searching for ecological generality in grasslands and savannas

Results from either *a priori* or *post hoc* syntheses can directly lead to the generation of ecological rules. However, a key step towards increasing predictability in ecology is to apply rules derived from one system to another (Figure 2). The goal is to generate a broader understanding of each system, and also of general ecological rules. If the rules apply across systems, we can hypothesize that mechanisms driving patterns in one system operate similarly in others, and we can then design experiments to test this hypothesis. If the rules do not apply, we can investigate which assumptions in one system are violated in the other, or in other words, identify

important contingencies. In either case, new knowledge and understanding are derived about each system, research decisions can be prioritized, new cross-site experiments can be initiated, and the process of synthesis can begin anew.

To illustrate this process and the *post hoc* synthesis of data rather than results, we summarize our experiences from a recent working group held at the National Center for Ecological Analysis and Synthesis (Santa Barbara, CA), in which long-term data were analyzed to test three proposed ecological rules concerning key drivers (fire, grazing, and moisture availability) of grassland plant community structure (Panel 2). These rules are based on well-known patterns and responses observed in North American grasslands. The long-term datasets analyzed to generate them were from grassland LTER sites in Kansas and New Mexico. To test the generality of the rules in a savanna grassland ecosystem, we used data from a long-term (over 50 year) fire experiment (Biggs *et al.* 2003) in Kruger National Park (KNP) in the Republic of South Africa, and two long-term monitoring programs in, and adjacent to, the KNP (Table 1; Figure 3). The savanna grasslands of South Africa share many attributes with these North American grasslands: C_4 graminoid dominance, common or co-

Table 1. Description and locations of long-term studies included in analyses of fire, grazing, and precipitation drivers in the savanna grasslands of North America (NA) and South Africa (SA)

Site	Location	PPT	Biome type	Treatments	Dates of data	# plots	Published description
Konza LTER	Kansas, NA	834	Mesic grassland, temperate	Experimental fire, grazing	1984–2000	660	Collins 1992
Sevilleta LTER	New Mexico NA	250	Xeric grassland, temperate	Experimental grazing	1989–2002	Transects (400 m)	Ryerson and Parmenter 2001
Experimental burn plots	KNP, SA	495, 551,653	Savanna, subtropical	Experimental fire, natural grazing	1998, 2001	32	Biggs *et al.* 2003
Veld Condition Analysis	KNP, SA	499 (465–700)	Savanna, subtropical	Natural fire and grazing	1989–1999	533	Kennedy *et al.* 2003
Game reserves	Adjacent to KNP, SA	547 (411–690)	Savanna, subtropical	Managed fire, grazing	1989–2001	544	Peel *et al.* 2004

KNP = Kruger National Park; PPT = annual precipitation (in mm; multiple values or ranges provided when plots were arrayed over large areas).

that their effects could be assessed in a full factorial design. In contrast, in the South African studies, fire was imposed by natural, prescribed, and experimental means at various intervals, and grazers were present at all times. This did not allow for the separation of fire and grazing effects, but only for their combined effect at high versus low fire frequency.

After the North American data were transformed from species-level resolution to growth form categories to reflect attributes of the South African data, the patterns and the prospective rules were reassessed to ensure that they were still supported by the North American grassland datasets. This also allowed us to determine the amount of information lost due to data transformation. Converting data from species-level resolution to growth form categories did not alter predictions regarding the impact of fire and grazing on grass dominance and forb abundance at the Konza LTER site (Figure 4). Moreover, growth form abundance was significantly related to community richness (Figure 4), suggesting that this taxonomically coarse metric has predictive power for the emergent property of diversity. Thus, little information was lost by focusing on growth form abundance, and the link between key drivers (fire and herbivory) and community richness was maintained.

Because of differences in the imposed fire regimes at the North American and South African sites, and the presence of herbivores at all savanna sites, only high (fire

dominant C_3 woody plants, fire, grazing by large herbivores and extreme climatic variability (drought) as key drivers of ecosystem structure and function (Scholes and Walker 1993; Bond *et al.* 2003). It is important to note that these long-term studies in South Africa were not designed to elucidate a specific ecological phenomenon, nor were they intended for broad comparative analyses. Rather, they were designed to focus on local management issues (Biggs *et al.* 2003).

We assembled datasets from these five long-term studies and compiled key data attributes (temporal, spatial, taxonomic resolution of sampling). This process allowed us to identify a common basis from which analysis could proceed. Initial barriers to synthesis included differences in taxonomic resolution of the datasets. Although all plant species were identified in North American studies, most of the South African sampling was less detailed. For example, as the resource of interest from a management perspective, only the grass and tree species were identified and the remaining species were categorized by growth form (graminoids, forbs, and, in some cases, smaller woody plants). Size of plots and sampling methodology also varied. Analysis of community richness was therefore not possible. Instead, all data had to be transformed to a common response variable that could still be related to plant community richness or diversity. In this case, we used relative grass and forb abundance. A third barrier involved key differences in the ways in which fire and grazing occurred at each site. At Konza Prairie, fire was imposed at fixed intervals and grazing treatments occurred independently, so

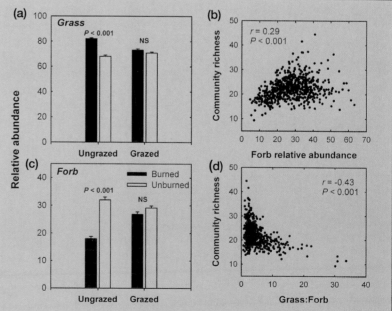

Figure 4. (a and c) Effect of long-term (>15 years) frequent burning (annual spring fire) versus protection from fire (unburned) on the relative abundance of graminoids (primarily C_4 grasses) and forbs (C_3 dicots) in mesic grassland at the Konza Prairie LTER site. Sites were either grazed by native herbivores (Bos bison) or protected from these grazers. (b and d) Relationship between plant community species richness and forb abundance, or the ratio of grass:forb abundance across all fire and grazing treatments. Statistical significance is indicated in each panel; NS = not significant.

every 1 or 2 years) versus low fire frequency categories in the presence of grazers could be assessed. Re-analysis of Konza LTER data with these fire frequencies as a main effect indicated that frequent fire led to reductions in forb abundance, regardless of ungulate presence (Figure 5). The influence of grazing could therefore be removed from the first rule (Panel 2). When the South African datasets were analyzed, similar patterns emerged, indicating that the effects of fire were consistent in grassland and savanna ecosystems across broad ranges of grazing intensity and types of large ungulates (Figure 5). Although frequent fire enhanced graminoid dominance and reduced forb abundance in both systems, it is important to note that the link between forb abundance and community diversity evident in North American grasslands remains to be evaluated in South African savannas (Fynn *et al.* 2004; Uys *et al.* 2004).

When contrasting xeric and mesic LTER grassland sites in North America, a positive relationship between forb abundance and precipitation has been described in the literature (Weaver 1954; Panel 2) and this pattern is observed today (Figure 6). In contrast to the strong support for a consistent fire effect on grass/forb abundance, such a relationship was not evident in the South African sites (Figure 6). In North America, relative abundance of forbs was more than two-fold higher in mesic (Konza) as opposed to xeric (Sevilleta) grasslands without grazers, each representing the endpoints of a central US grassland precipitation gradient. The addition of large ungulates weakened this relationship, but the pattern was still evident (Figure 6). Across South African sites, no underlying pattern of forb abundance and precipitation was detected. Although the range of precipitation levels was less in South Africa, the lack of even a trend in the relationship between forb abundance and precipitation suggests that this pattern cannot be generalized to subtropical savannas. This may be because South African savannas differ markedly from North American grasslands in large herbivore diversity (much greater in South Africa; McNaughton and Georiadis 1986; du Toit 2003) and evolutionary history (South African savannas are much older; Owen-Smith and Cumming 1993). Either may influence plant community–herbivore relationships. Nonetheless, these results suggest that needed insight could result from manipulating grazers in these savannas in ways comparable to North American grassland studies.

These examples of synthetic analyses of existing data identify additional key considerations of *post hoc* synthesis. These include some drawbacks (eg the need to alter the scope and type of questions being addressed whenever data limitations are identified), but there are benefits. Such activities may spur re-analysis of data and provide new insight. In this case, data from Konza had not been analyzed by growth form to determine if the effect of fire frequency on plant community composition was sufficiently robust

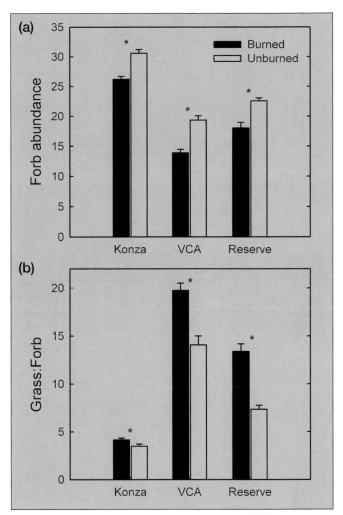

Figure 5. (a) Response of forb abundance and (b) the ratio of grass:forb abundance to long-term fire frequency (burned = fires annually or biannually, unburned = fires occurring less than once in 8 years) at a mesic grassland in North America (Konza Prairie) and two savanna grasslands, one in South Africa's Kruger National Park (KNP; VCA = Veld Condition Analysis) and the other adjacent to KNP (Reserve = sites managed as game reserves). Grazing intensity was variable within each site. Standard errors are shown with each bar and statistical significance is indicated by an *. Data from the experimental burn plots in Kruger could not be included due to inadequate replicates of main treatments.

to be detected regardless of grazing intensity. From a regional perspective, this level of analysis may be particularly valuable, since grazing pressures and fire frequency are quite variable in the Great Plains grasslands. Knowledge of the broad impacts of potential shifts in fire regimes on forb abundance, community richness, and biodiversity in grasslands and savannas has clear conservation implications. Finally, although using data from different studies may not allow for the kind of rigorous, quantitative tests of rules that *a priori* synthesis can offer, qualitative (directional) tests are possible, and these can yield insights and provide direction for future research.

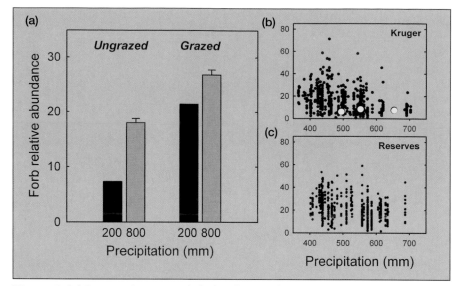

Figure 6. (a) *Pattern of increasing forb abundance with increasing annual precipitation, as exhibited by the comparison of relative forb abundance at two LTER grassland sites in North America (dark bars = the arid Sevilleta LTER site in New Mexico; gray bars = the mesic Konza Prairie LTER site in Kansas). Also shown is the increase in relative forb abundance with grazing, which tempers the effect of precipitation. (b and c) Lack of a relationship between forb relative abundance and precipitation in savanna grasslands of South Africa, based on data from three long-term studies. Kruger (KNP) data are from the Veld Condition Analysis study (dark circles) and the experimental burning plots study (yellow circles). Reserves data are from sites adjacent to KNP managed as game reserves.*

■ Conclusions

In the past, the discipline of ecology has been dominated by detailed, short-term studies at a single (local) spatial scale (McIntosh 1985). Most ecological research today is still of short duration and narrowly focused. This occurs despite recognition that our understanding of ecological processes, and how they shape the patterns and dynamics of complex biological systems, can be limited by our failure to consider the effects of history, contingent factors, and regional and global drivers. This, in turn, compromises our ability to generalize across multiple spatial and temporal scales (Lawton 1999; May 1999; Thompson *et al.* 2001). With the global nature of new ecological drivers, such as climate warming and species invasions, and the expectations imposed on policy makers and managers to respond to these environmental challenges, we need to identify general patterns and ecological rules that apply broadly. We also need to test their limits (Figure 2) in order to identify potential contingent factors that result in exceptions to the rules. This is particularly important given that financial resources will never be sufficient to support the study of complex ecological phenomena in all ecosystems worldwide. Clearly, other approaches must be adopted.

Fundamental ecological laws that span multiple taxonomic levels, biomes, or ecological hierarchies, though elusive, should still be sought (Murray 2001; Enquist *et al.* 2003). However, through the careful selection of key ecological attributes or processes, we should accept Lawton's implicit challenge to develop formalized "ecological rules" where possible. Such rules can and should be developed for grasslands, forests, lakes, and other systems, as tools for improving scientific understanding and natural resource management. Ultimately, ecological rules should be tested with research programs specifically designed for this purpose, but an initial, cost-effective step is to more fully utilize the diverse and numerous datasets available from studies around the world. The Ecological Society of America's *Ecological Archives* is one repository for such data. This information may prove invaluable in the search for generality in ecological patterns and processes and for testing specific predictions in other systems. At a minimum, their synthesis adds value to the original research by prompting novel re-analysis and informing research designs for future studies that include *a priori* synthesis.

■ Acknowledgements

This work was supported by the National Science Foundation's Long-term Ecological Research Program, the Knowledge Network for Biocomplexity project (NSF Grant #DEB 99–80154) and the National Center for Ecological Analysis and Synthesis (NSF Grant #DEB–0072909) at the University of California, Santa Barbara.

■ References

Berryman AA. 2003. On principles, laws and theory in population ecology. *Oikos* **103**: 695–701.

Biggs R, Biggs HC, Dunne T, *et al.* 2003. What is the design of the Experimental Burning Plot (EBP) trial in the Kruger National Park? *Koedoe* **46**: 1–15.

Bond WJ, Midgley GF, and Woodward FI. 2003. What controls South African vegetation – climate or fire? *S Af J Bot* **69**: 79–91.

Bormann FH and Likens GE. 1979. Pattern and process in a forested ecosystem. New York, NY: Springer-Verlag.

Brown JH. 1995. Macroecology. Chicago, IL: The University of Chicago Press.

Brown JH, Whitham TG, Morgan Ernest SK, and Gehring CA. 2001. Complex species interactions and the dynamics of ecological systems: long-term experiments. *Science* **293**: 643–50.

Burnham KP and Anderson DR. 2002. Model selection and multimodel inference: a practical information–theoretic approach. New York, NY: Springer-Verlag.

Callahan JT. 1984. Long-term ecological research. *BioScience* **34**: 363–67.

Collins SL. 1992. Fire frequency and community heterogeneity in tallgrass prairie vegetation. *Ecology* **73**: 2001–06.

Collins SL, Knapp AK, Briggs JM, *et al.* 1998. Modulation of diversity by grazing and mowing in native tallgrass prairie. *Science* **280**: 745–47.

Colyvan M and Ginzburg LR. 2003. Laws of nature and laws of ecology. *Oikos* **101**: 649–53.

Coomes DA, Duncan RP, Allen RB, and Truscott J. 2003. Disturbances prevent stem size-density distributions in natural forests from following scaling relationships. *Ecol Lett* **6**: 980–89.

Cooper G. 1998. Generalizations in ecology: a philosophical taxonomy. *Biol Philos* **13**: 555–86.

Cyr H and Walker SC. 2004. An illusion of mechanistic understanding. *Ecology* **85**: 1802–04.

du Toit JT. 2003. Large herbivores and savanna heterogeneity. In: duToit JT, Rogers KH, and Biggs HC (Eds). The Kruger experience: ecology and management of savanna heterogeneity. Washington DC: Island Press.

Dynesius M, Jansson R, Hohansson ME, and Nilsson C. 2004. Intercontinental similarities in riparian-plant diversity and sensitivity to river regulation. *Ecol Appl* **14**: 173–91.

Enquist BJ, Economo EP, Huxman TE, *et al.* 2003. Scaling metabolism from organisms to ecosystems. *Nature* **423**: 639–42.

Fynn RWS, Morris CD, and Edwards TJ. 2004. Effect of burning and mowing on grass and forb diversity in a long-term grassland experiment. *Appl Veg Sci* **7**: 1–10.

Grime JP. 2001. Plant strategies, vegetation processes and ecosystem properties. New York, NY: John Wiley and Sons.

Hall CAS. 1988. An assessment of several of the historically most influential theoretical models used in ecology and of the data provided in their support. *Ecol Model* **43**: 5–31.

Harte J. 2004. The value of null theories in ecology. *Ecology* **85**: 1792–94.

Hector A, Schmid B, Beierkuhnlein C, *et al.* 1999. Plant diversity and productivity experiments in European grasslands. *Science* **286**: 1123–27.

Jablonski LM, Wang X, and Curtis PS. 2002. Plant reproduction under elevated CO_2 conditions: a meta-analysis of reports on 79 crop and wild species. *New Phytol* **156**: 9–26.

Kennedy AD, Biggs H, and Zambatis N. 2003. Relationship between grass species richness and ecosystem stability in Kruger National Park, South Africa. *Afric J Ecol* **41**: 131–40.

Knapp AK, Briggs JM, Hartnett DC, and Collins SL. 1998. Grassland dynamics: long-term ecological research in tallgrass prairie. New York, NY: Oxford University Press.

Knapp AK, Blair JM, Briggs JM, Collins SL, *et al.* 1999. The keystone role of bison in North American tallgrass prairie. *BioScience* **49**: 39–50.

Knapp AK and Smith MD. 2001. Variation among biomes in temporal dynamics of aboveground primary production. *Science* **291**: 481–84.

Lawton JH. 1999. Are there general laws in ecology? *Oikos* **84**: 177–92.

Lincoln RJ, Boxshall GA, and Clark PF. 1990. A dictionary of ecology, evolution and systematics. Cambridge, UK: Cambridge University Press.

Loreau M, Naeem S, Inchausti P, *et al.* 2001. Biodiversity and ecosystem functioning: current knowledge and future challenges. *Science* **294**: 804–08.

May RM. 1999. Unanswered questions in ecology. *Phil Trans Royal Soc Lond B* **354**: 1951–59.

McIntosh RP. 1985. The background of ecology. Cambridge, UK: Cambridge University Press.

McNaughton SJ and Georiadis NJ. 1986. Ecology of African grazing and browsing mammals. *Annu Rev Ecol Syst* **17**: 39–65.

Murray BG. 2001. Are ecological and evolutionary theories scientific? *Biol Rev* **76**: 255–89.

Odum EP. 1969. The strategy of ecosystem development. *Science* **164**: 262–70.

Owen-Smith RN and Cumming DHM. 1993. Comparative foraging strategies of grazing ungulates in African savanna grasslands. In: Proceedings of the XVII International Grasslands Congress, New Zealand Grasslands Association, Palmerston North, New Zealand.

Peel M, Davies R, and Hurt R. 2004. The value and costs of wildlife and wildlife-based activities in the eastern lowveld savanna, South Africa. In: Lawes M, Eeley H, Shackleton C, and Geach B (Eds.) Indigenous forests and woodland in South Africa. Pietermaritzburg, South Africa: University of Kwazulu Natal Press.

Peters RH. 1991. A critique for ecology. Cambridge, UK: Cambridge University Press.

Pickett STA, Kolasa J, and Jones CG. 1994. Ecological understanding: the nature of theory and the theory of nature. New York: Academic Press.

Pickett STA and White PS. 1985. The ecology of natural disturbance and patch dynamics. New York: Academic Press.

Rees M, Condit R, Crawley M, *et al.* 2001. Long-term studies of vegetation dynamics. *Science* **293**: 650–55.

Risser PG, Birney EC, Blocker HD, *et al.* 1981. The true prairie ecosystem. Stroudsburg, PA: Hutchinson Ross Publishing. Co.

Ritchie ME and Olff H. Spatial scaling laws yield a synthetic theory of biodiversity. *Nature* **400**: 557–60.

Rosenzweig ML. 1995. Species diversity in space and time. Cambridge, UK: Cambridge University Press.

Ryerson DE and Parmenter RR. 2001. Vegetation change following removal of keystone herbivores from desert grasslands in New Mexico. *J Veg Sci* **12**: 167–80.

Scholes RJ, and Walker BH. 1993. An African savanna: synthesis of the Nylsvley Study. Cambridge, UK: Cambridge University Press.

Simberloff D. 2004. Community ecology: is it time to move on? *Am Nat* **163**: 787–99.

Thompson JN, Reichman OJ, Morin PJ, *et al.* 2001. Frontiers of ecology. *BioScience* **51**: 15–24.

Tomkins JL and Kotiaho JS. 2004. Publication bias in meta-analysis: seeing the wood for the trees. *Oikos* **104**: 194–96.

Turchin P. 2001. Does population ecology have general laws? *Oikos* **94**: 17–26.

Tyree MT. 1983. Maple sap uptake, exudation, and pressure changes correlated with freezing exotherms and thawing endotherms. *Pl Physiol* **73**: 277–85.

Uys RG, Bond WJ, and Everson TM. 2004. The effect of different fire regimes on plant diversity in southern African grasslands. *Biol Conserv* **118**: 489–99.

Waide RB, Willig MR, Steiner CF, *et al.* 1999. The relationship between productivity and species richness. *Ann Rev Ecol Sys* **30**: 257–300.

Weaver JE. 1954. North American prairie. Lincoln, NE: Johnsen Publishing Co.

Webster JR, Mulholland PJ, Tank JL, *et al.* 2003. Factors affecting ammonium uptake in streams – an inter-biome perspective. *Freshwat Biol* **48**: 1329–52.

Practicing scientific inquiry: what are the rules?

Diane Ebert-May[1], Kathy S Williams[2], Everett P Weber[1], Janet Hodder[3], Douglas Luckie[1]

Ecologists attempt to establish general principles from a vast range of organizational, spatial, and temporal scales (Belovsky *et al.* 2004). The process of developing generalities in ecology involves two approaches often not addressed in introductory science courses – inductive and deductive. One way of thinking about this is to consider the inductive approach as examining particular cases and deriving general conclusions or rules from them, and the deductive approach as using generalities to make specific predictions that can then be tested. In this issue of *Frontiers*, Knapp *et al.* (pp 483–91) underline the need for general principles or "rules" in ecology, and research that tests the predictive limits of those rules. The rules illustrated in this article are based on long-term studies from the Konza prairie and Sevilleta Long-Term Ecological Research (LTER) sites. Existing data from savanna grasslands in South Africa are used to test rules derived from Konza studies of grassland responses to fire.

■ Learning goal

Two general principles that underpin scientific teaching in this series of articles are that (1) students acquire deeper understanding by actively constructing knowledge and (2) successful assessments demonstrate students' abilities to use their knowledge. In Hodder *et al.* (2004), students used a guided-inquiry approach to define a problem, construct hypotheses, and design a method to test a hypothesis. In Williams *et al.* (2004), students applied the process of science to explore general principles about plant invasions. In this article, students will use *open-ended inquiry* to understand that the process of science is more than a rote series of steps (NRC 2000). Rather, it is an iterative process that uses both inductive and deductive reasoning to design experiments that generate new data, and to synthesize existing data. Both types of reasoning are means by which we identify patterns, construct arguments or rules to explain them, develop and test predictions about their causes and nature, and ultimately refine or possibly modify the rules. The assessments help students understand the varied processes of science and investigate how generalities in ecology arise and how they can change. Thus, a major outcome is for students to realize that ecological systems are complex and that their hypothesis may not hold true for all systems. Their conception that science is learned as a series of facts is challenged by this inquiry.

■ Instructional design

Many datasets are available to help instructors achieve these outcomes (LTER: www.lternet.edu/data; ESA: http://tiee.ecoed.net; GLOBE: www.globe.gov). Here the LTER data are used as the basis for an open-ended inquiry. Students will engage in the processes of science as they search for patterns and predict causal effects about the influence of precipitation and temperature on net primary productivity in different biomes.

This instruction is designed for a large enrollment introductory course and begins as homework by teams of two to four students. Knapp *et al.* is assigned as reading (particularly the first section). Each team selects two LTER sites from the LTER Net Primary Productivity database (http://intranet.lternet.edu/cgi-bin/anpp.pl) and searches for patterns that describe the effect of precipitation and temperature on primary productivity (Knapp and Smith 2001). Approximately 25 years of data are available for import, for plotting graphs (Panel 1). Open-ended inquiries will have multiple results, depending on the questions students ask and the analytical approaches used.

■ Homework

Teams are asked to:

- Describe the pattern they observed and propose a rule (for example, as temperature increases, primary production decreases).
- Support it with two graphs or models based on the data.
- Test the rule by comparing the figures from their LTER sites to those constructed using data from one or two different LTER sites.
- Use what they know about biomes and ecophysiology from the course resources, and interpret the results.
- Ask: "Is the rule supported?". If it is not supported, propose one or two reasons that could explain why not; if it is supported, propose one or two other factors that were not measured or included in the database that might alter the patterns detected by students.

Ask students to submit their results before class (one response per group, via email or internet). The instructor selects two or three rules or predictions that were not supported.

■ Classwork

In class, the instructor presents two or three of the unsupported rules (using overheads, PowerPoint, or the Web,

[1]*Michigan State University*, [2]*San Diego State University*, [3]*University of Oregon*

with rules and figures that do and do not fit). Teams select one example and derive a new rule or causal relation that could be tested next.

After their group discussion, individuals write up their new rule or prediction, with supporting reasons, and turn it in. Then the instructor can call on some groups to show their new rules and others can suggest ways to test them. The instructor can use that time to clear up any errors in logic, discuss variability in the data, and assure students that "messy" data are not to be feared or discarded. Rather, those inconsistencies help us better understand how natural systems work. Students seldom have opportunities like this, to rethink and adjust a rule so they can test it again, as happens in scientific processes.

■ Assessment

An instructor can use the following questions to develop a rubric (see www.flaguide.org/cat/rubrics/rubrics7.php) to assess students' understanding of the processes of inquiry and ecological concepts:

How do students conduct the process of inquiry?
Are the data represented accurately in graphs? (eg Are the dependent and independent variables correctly illustrated?)

What do students learn?
How well do students answer "why" questions about ecological concepts through the accurate and logical interpretation of patterns and supporting evidence from their inquiry?

After students attempt to derive new rules in class, to what degree has the activity enhanced their understanding of controls on net primary productivity and how those controls vary among different biomes?

■ Final note

Knapp *et al.* conclude that proposing and testing rules or general principles in complex systems can inform future research in ecology. Similarly, engaging students in open-ended inquiry and assessing their ability to use processes of science is a method to test rules and predictions about how students learn science. This too, informs future research in education.

By completing this inquiry, students will see that hypotheses are built on observations of different types – even from other peoples' datasets. This will also demonstrate how several interpretations can come from the same data and that some may be better supported than others. Students often think that a goal of science is to support hypotheses and predictions in ways that lead to formal principles and theories. This activity will allow students to see that refuting, rather than just supporting, hypotheses can lead to a more complete understanding of how the world works. Ultimately, this inquiry can

demonstrate how the complexities of biotic and physical interactions make it so difficult to come up with major principles of ecology.

■ Acknowledgements

We thank the National Science Foundation for their long-term support of the Faculty Institutes for Reforming Science Teaching (FIRST) project (DUE 0088847) and the CCLI "Ecology curriculum reform: Integrating innovative teaching and global change technology" DUE-9952816, Alan Knapp and Sonia Ortega.

■ References

Belovsky GE, Botkin DB, Crowl TA, *et al.* 2004. Ten suggestions to strengthen the science of Ecology. *Bioscience* **54**: 345–51.

Hodder J, Ebert-May D, Williams K, and Luckie D. 2004. Marine pathology: revealing the ocean's etiology to earthbound students. *Front Ecol Environ* **2**: 383–84.

Knapp AK and Smith MD. 2001. Variation among biomes in temporal dynamics of aboveground primary production. *Science* **291**: 481–84.

NRC (National Research Council). 2000. Inquiry and the National Science Education Standards. Washington DC: National Academy Press.

Williams KS, Ebert-May D, Luckie D, *et al.* 2004. Novel assessments: detecting success in student learning. *Front Ecol Environ* **2**: 444–45.

Divided culture: integrating agriculture and conservation biology

John E Banks

Production agriculture, with its implied ecosystem simplification, pesticide and fertilizer use, and emphasis on yield, often appears to be at odds with conservation biology. From a farmer's perspective, the weight conservation biology places on wildlife may seem overly idealistic and naive, detached from economic and sociopolitical reality. In fact, these endeavors are two sides of the same coin, with a shared heritage in decades of population and community ecological theory and experimentation. Better integration of the two disciplines requires acknowledging their various goals and working to produce mutually beneficial outcomes. The best examples of this type of integrated approach result from careful implementation of sustainable agriculture practices that support biological conservation efforts via habitat amelioration or restructuring. Successful integrated approaches take into account both the environmental and economic costs of different farming schemes and compensate farmers for the costs they incur by implementing environmentally friendly farming strategies. Drawing primarily from examples in insect population dynamics, this paper highlights some innovative programs that are leading the way towards a more holistic integration.

Front Ecol Environ 2004; 2(10): 537–545

For a conservation biologist, the word "agriculture" conjures up images of slashed and burned landscapes, drifting pesticides, and genetic anomalies that threaten the natural world on many fronts. From a farmer's point of view, conservation biologists can appear to live in a dream world, where the indiscriminate protection of species receives priority over all else, including economics and livelihood considerations. Agricultural production and conservation biology often appear to have diametrically opposing goals and methodologies, pitting food production against the preservation of biological diversity. Yet scratching the surface of these simplistic stereotypes reveals that the two endeavors have some remarkable similarities, so that recent efforts worldwide have made real progress in integrating them.

> ## In a nutshell:
> - Agriculture and conservation biology seem opposed in their goals and approaches yet share a common ecological heritage
> - Communication and cooperation between the two fields are vital for achieving mutual benefits
> - More holistic approaches that incorporate a landscape perspective, economics, pesticide use, and the results of empirical and theoretical work should be applied at the interface of agriculture and conservation biology research
> - Innovative research and incentive programs worldwide point the way towards better integration of conservation and agriculture

Environmental Science, Interdisciplinary Arts and Sciences, University of Washington, 1900 Commerce Street, Tacoma, WA 98402 (banksj@u.washington.edu)

Scientific publications on agricultural research in the US as early as the mid-19th century clearly recognized the potential benefits of full integration of agriculture and conservation efforts: "If forests, in their primitive state, supply food to birds and insects, or afford shelter to larger animals or reptiles, in a civilized country [they] may be expected to abound more or less wherever there are trees and shrubs to supply them with food and shelter" (Anonymous 1842).

Unfortunately, until only a few decades ago, scientists seem to have strayed from this holistic perspective. For most of the 20th century, relatively few agricultural research projects explicitly focused on the incorporation of non-farmland resources into croplands, except in cases that might strictly benefit agricultural production. Until recently, government agencies in the US (eg the Soil Conservation Service – now the USDA Natural Resources Conservation Service) were more concerned with conservation as a means of minimizing erosion and its effects on public works projects than on preserving biodiversity. For their part, conservation biologists, frequently under pressure to produce timely responses to crises, have often overlooked the fact that agricultural ecosystems represent a sizable proportion of global terrestrial landscapes (eg over 50% of the European Union landscape and close to 70% of Denmark and Bangladesh), and have largely failed to incorporate them into research and policy-setting activities. Despite these differences in focus, a close look at the ecological basis for many aspects of agriculture and biological conservation reveals striking similarities. Both disciplines are concerned with managing natural resources based on societal mandates: agriculture focus-

Figure 1. *Non-crop deterrents to herbivores and resources for beneficial insects are often incorporated into small commercial farms, such as this organic farm on the western slope of Colorado.*

es on production food and fiber crops, whereas conservation efforts generally focus on the maintenance of biological diversity. Both of these endeavors require a deep understanding of population dynamics, community ecology, and the effects of spatial scale and disturbance on biotic communities. Fortunately, scientists and practitioners alike have recently been making progress in recognizing these similarities, and have integrated them in creative and innovative ways.

This paper explores some of the similarities and differences in the perspectives of these two disciplines, and describes some examples that are paving the way to integration. Because insect population dynamics studies abound in both agricultural and conservation biology research, these studies will be used to illustrate comparisons between the two fields.

■ A shared heritage: experiments and theory

Habitat heterogeneity

Much of what we know about how populations and communities of plants and animals interact stems from experiments conducted in agricultural settings, which are relatively simple and easy to manipulate. Work exploring how habitat diversity (or heterogeneity) may influence resident organisms has generated insights that are especially valuable to both agriculture and conservation biology. Root's (1973) early field experiments in fleabeetle–collard systems have stimulated much empirical and theoretical work to test the idea that diversified planting schemes may thwart insect herbivores seeking to

colonize and invade host plants. Building on earlier ecological work (eg Elton 1927), Root and others demonstrated that more diverse environments may attract a broader array of predators and parasitoids, enhancing prey control and fostering biodiversity (Root 1973; Andow 1991). In the three decades following Root's pioneering insect work, there has been much ado about vegetation diversity and spatial arrangements of vegetation and other resources in applied agriculture. Results from these studies have been embraced by conservation biologists, especially as applied to reserve design and habitat fragmentation (Quinn and Harrison 1988).

A subdiscipline of earlier biological control work, conservation biological control (CBC), has flourished over the past several decades (van den Bosch and Telford 1964; Barbosa 1998). Fueled by increasing awareness of the dangers that alien biological control agents may pose to native non-target species, CBC research is aimed at encouraging native predators and parasitoids of pests species in and around farmlands, usually by manipulating habitat or resources that are important to these organisms (Landis *et al.* 2000). Ornamentals and other non-crop plants are often actively sown into crop areas to provide pollen, nectar, and alternative prey for predators and parasitoids (Figure 1). Manipulating habitat effectively is no easy task; some changes may result in increased pest problems due to predator–predator interference or the inadvertent creation of additional resources for pests (Snyder *et al.* in press). Historically, most CBC studies have focused primarily on the benefits to agricultural production, with little concern for community or regional biodiversity conservation. However, a large body of work conducted over the past 10 years emphasizes the need for a larger, landscape perspective in integrating agricultural pest control and biodiversity considerations (Kruess and Tscharntke 1994; Marino and Landis 1996; Thies and Tscharntke 1999; Östman *et al.* 2001). Recent studies have focused on identifying the benefits of CBC to biodiversity conservation (see Landis *et al.* 2000); more support for this type of work is necessary to generate innovative solutions that address both agriculture and conservation concerns.

■ Metapopulation theory

Many of the quantitative analytical tools commonly employed by ecologists in modern conservation studies were developed with agricultural pest control in mind. Metapopulation theory, which considers species' survival from the perspective of groups of populations, each with their own individual internal dynamics but linked by dispersal, has frequently been used to analyze the viability of rare or endangered species (Gilpin and Hanski 1991) such as the northern spotted owl. This framework was originally formulated for a very different purpose, namely to improve upon ways of eradicating insect pests in agriculture (Levins 1969). This shared heritage, which highlights other influential factors common to the two fields, such as dispersal and resource dynamics, could be used to greater advantage. Although in temperate agroecosystems, insect pest populations often fluctuate in synchrony and therefore do not lend themselves to metapopulation analysis, metapopulation theory has been successfully applied in agroecological studies (eg Landis and Menalled 1998; Hietala-Koivu et al. 2004). Similarly, island biogeographic approaches, famously used in a variety of conservation settings (Quinn and Harrison 1998) rarely receive serious consideration in agroecological circles, although some classic works have outlined applications for herbivorous insects (eg Janzen 1968). The application of theory to agriculture has been most powerful when it inspires direct field tests. For instance, Murdoch et al. (1996) disrupted insect dispersal in an elegant field experiment designed to test whether or not stable scale insect–parasitoid interactions were driven by metapopulation dynamics. There is clearly a need for agroecology research to embrace such theory-based approaches, much in the way that conservation biology has adopted the use of matrix modeling and viability analyses to combat extinction crises.

■ Habitat fragmentation, loss, and spatial scale

The habitat alterations associated with agricultural production often have devastating effects on plant and animal populations, and in some cases a cascade of further effects stems from socioeconomic factors. A poignant example lies in tropical fruit and vegetable production. After rainforests are replaced by monocultures, changes in world markets or pathogen outbreaks may result in displaced workers who have little alternative but to clear further forestlands in order to subsistence farm (see Vandermeer and Perfecto 1995).

Apart from these more complex human–environment interactions, combating the combined effects of habitat loss and fragmentation poses tremendous challenges. Recent research suggests that while habitat loss often accounts for most of the detrimental effects on biodiversity (Schmiegelow and Monkkonen 2002), the spatial configuration and relative abundance of small and large remnant patches may greatly influence biodiversity and biological control (Kruess and Tscharntke 1994). The details of habitat degradation and loss may be especially critical in understanding declines in pollinator biodiversity across a broad range of taxa (Kremen and Ricketts 2000). For instance, the presence of forest fragments has recently

been identified as crucial for bolstering pollination and subsequent yield in Brazilian coffee agroecosystems (De Marco and Coelho 2004). At issue are taxon-specific habitat requirements and dispersal abilities, which differ even among the members of the same class of organisms. For example, aphids and beetles respond differently to fragmentation of host plants (Kareiva 1987; Banks 1998), and butterflies and beetles respond differently to habitat fragmentation than their respective parasitoids (Kruess and Tscharntke 1994). These and other examples underscore the need to identify and prioritize conservation of particular taxa in landscapes that are mosaics of agricultural and natural areas.

In recent years, the spatial scale at which experiments are conducted has also received much attention in ecological circles (Tilman and Kareiva 1998), yet it is still rare for experiments in both agroecology and conservation biology to explicitly incorporate scale as a treatment factor (but see Marino and Landis 1996; Roland and Taylor 1997; Banks 1998). Recent surveys of how increased vegetation diversity in agroecosystems affects insect pest populations indicate that answers vary with the spatial scale of experimental plots (Bommarco and Banks 2003). This is not surprising; spatial scale critically impacts the dispersal abilities of organisms in a species-specific way, something that conservation biologists have been aware of for a long time (Doak et al. 1992). Given the sensitivity of species interactions to scale, from parasitoid releases to set-aside conservation policies, we need a better understanding of how spatial scale interacts with both biotic and abiotic processes.

■ Agricultural lands as habitat

Anyone familiar with tropical ecosystems is aware of the degree to which natural vegetation encroaches upon tropical agricultural habitats (Figure 2). Recent work suggests that agricultural areas in the tropics, often in a mosaic of rainforest fragments, may be important to the conservation of species ranging from mammals to insects (Ricketts et al. 2001; Daily et al. 2003). Similar attention has been paid to temperate agricultural landscapes as bird habitat; several studies – including analyses of set-asides established by England's Common Agricultural Policy – have indicated that non-crop vegetation structure may greatly influence the suitability of such habitats for wildlife (Firbank et al. 2003). Because it is often prohibitively expensive to eradicate weeds, farmers in the tropics often tolerate weeds or other "volunteer" crop species in their fields. An inadvertent benefit of this, which low-input or organic farmers in temperate regions also enjoy, is that planned or unplanned increases in vegetation diversity can lead to increases in beneficial species and reduced chemical inputs (Figure 3).

Conservation biologists have heralded the biodiversity increase associated with lower intensity farming as a step in the right direction (Figure 4) – but which species rep-

Figure 2. *A rainforest fragment adjacent to a farm in rural Costa Rica. Encroaching natural vegetation can influence agricultural production; interchanges between agricultural areas and nearby non-crop areas can be important to both agriculture and conservation.*

resent the right kind of biodiversity? While conservation biologists have been focusing on the importance of functional biodiversity rather than "biodiversity for biodiversity's sake" for years (see Kareiva and Levin 2003), there is still a tendency within agricultural circles to focus on biodiversity strictly in terms of crop production benefits. Recent work on the threat of invasive species illustrates this difference in perspective. For instance, long-term studies documenting beetle species composition following the introduction of the seven spotted ladybird beetle (*Coccinella septempunctata*) have revealed a decline in native ladybird beetle species in temperate areas in the northern US (Elliott *et al.* 1996). This decline, however, seems to have been offset by a matching overall increase in ladybird beetle abundance (compensated in part by invasive *C septempunctata*), with little loss in predation on aphid prey in agricultural systems. As a result, the invading ladybird beetle has been the subject of little concern for farmers; indeed, *C septempunctata* was introduced for the very purpose of controlling aphid pests, and seems to be doing its job. Why should growers be concerned about a slight decline in native biota associated with its introduction?

One answer comes from the fact that native fauna, both predators and prey, have had a chance to coevolve with their community in a way that introduced organisms (eg imported biological control agents) may not have had. Evidence suggests that native ladybird beetles, for instance, may be more attuned to fluctuations in prey density than their alien counterparts (Evans 2004), increasing their potential for better biological control. In agroecosystem predator–prey relationships, mismatches between native and non-native species are common, for the simple

reason that many of our agricultural predators and pests (and crops) were themselves imported from elsewhere. A further complication is the artificial annual cycle imposed on agroecosystem communities by harvest timing and markets. Predators, especially those introduced from elsewhere (as in classical biological control scenarios), are often asynchronous with their insect prey in annual cropping systems (Wissinger 1997); the prey cycle with the annual resource, whereas the predators may be cycling on a longer time scale. Furthermore, when subject to disturbances such as pesticide use, predators and other non-target organisms often fare worse than target species, in part due to longer generation times and lower reproductive rates (Stark *et al.* 2004). These effects, which are due to co-evolutionary forces and differences in life history strategies, provide a clear argument for the preservation of native species, in both managed and natural settings.

Recent work also suggests that native biodiversity may play a critical role in so-called "ecosystem services" (Daily 1997). In this case, there is a quantifiable link between the loss of biodiversity (in both natural and managed communities) and the sustainability of normal, healthy ecosystem functioning – something that is often not apparent until well after the loss of biodiversity. Similar "farm services" are provided by the agroecosystem biodiversity (Naylor and Ehrlich 1997), though we are yet to fully understand the extent that native biota play in agroecosystem regulation and function.

■ Integrated pest management: selective pesticides and cultural controls

Agriculture has run afoul of efforts in biological conservation through the continued widespread use of chemical pesticides. Agricultural inputs have been implicated in a series of both public and environmental health threats in recent years, including endocrine disruption in humans and wildlife (Solomon and Schettler 2000). The rise in environmental consciousness following the publication of Rachel Carson's book, *Silent Spring*, in 1962 has led to a rich legacy of studies that explored various aspects of sustainable agricultural systems, with an eye towards balancing the maintenance of pest control and biological integrity (Altieri 1995, 2004). This positive focus on sustainable agroecosystems has been accompanied by a tendency within agroecological research to ignore the "elephant in the room" – the fact that pesticide use is still widespread in the US. Despite the passage of the 1996 Food Quality Protection Act (FQPA) by Congress, which mandates that the Environmental Protection Agency

Figure 3. *Planned versus unplanned biodiversity: (a) a banana and coffee diculture in western Costa Rica, and (b) a "monoculture" of plantains, with a large number of volunteer plant species. Both planned and unplanned vegetation diversity can play an important role in fostering a diversity of species important both to agriculture and to ecosystem functioning.*

(EPA) reevaluate nearly 10 000 specific uses of pesticides, growers still rely heavily on chemical controls to regulate insect pests.

An alternative to chemical controls that is nicely aligned with biological conservation is the use of increased vegetation diversity to reduce insect pest populations. This approach allows for the incorporation of more plant species, some of which are important to bird and small mammal populations, into agroecosystems. This technique is thought to reduce colonization of pest insects by making it more difficult for them to find their host plants in a matrix of vegetation, and also to bolster natural enemy populations drawn to the wide array of resources (eg pollen, nectar, alternate prey) associated with increased plant diversity (Root 1973). While greater vegetation diversity can be an effective means of pest control, it is by no means a panacea; surveys and meta-analyses indicate that only in a simple majority of cases, increased vegetation diversity in croplands reduces herbivore pressure (Andow 1991; Tonhasca and Byrne 1994). Furthermore, these results are highly dependent on mitigating factors such as the spatial scale of the crop resources, a highly variable factor in agricultural settings (Bommarco and Banks 2003). The inconsistency of vegetation diversity as a pest control technique, coupled with mechanized harvesting, has made it difficult for farmers to

rely solely on cultural controls for combating insect outbreaks. Although integrated pest management has been widely used as a strategy for increasing sustainability in commercial farms, research exploring combinations of pesticide use with other forms of pest control such as cultural control (eg intercropping) appears to be declining in agroecology research. A brief survey of *Agriculture, Ecosystems, and Environment* (Elsevier), an international journal devoted to exploring the interface between agricultural and environmental issues, reveals that only 7% of the research articles in a recent volume (2003; Volume 95) explored the effects of pesticide use in their studies. This compares to 44% in a comparable number of articles from 20 years ago (1983; Volumes 9 and 10). This decline in studies incorporating pesticide use with other forms of sustainable farming strategies may simply reflect changes in the agroecology landscape; recent research focuses more on topics such as new technologies (eg GIS) and farming innovations in steeplands in remote tropical areas – but nonetheless it is a surprising trend. The loss of many traditional pesticides resulting from the FQPAs mandated EPA action has precipitated the development of a suite of new selective pesticides (eg imidacloprid) that growers are rapidly incorporating into their pest-management regimes. Real progress in implementing more sustainable farming in the US will require a shift from large-scale,

Figure 4. *Large amounts of natural vegetation in and around agricultural areas can increase the abundance and diversity of species, such as this orb spider, that are beneficial to agriculture – but are they functionally important in a larger sense?*

chemical controls as a bridge between organic and conventional farming.

■ Genetically modified organisms: déjà vu?

A discussion of the interface between agriculture and conservation would be incomplete without considering the impact that genetically modified organisms (GMOs) will likely have in both areas. Touted more than a decade ago as a means of potentially decreasing the use of herbicides and pesticides, increasing yields, and creating crops adapted to marginal habitats that would reduce pressure to convert other habitat for agriculture (OTA 1991), GM crops are now being seriously evaluated in terms of overall effects on agroecosystem communities (see Firbank 2003 and other articles in the same volume).

As noted in a recent editorial in this journal (Silver 2003), the results from a series of trials conducted in the UK indicate that the environmental benefits stemming from the use of genetically modified crops may not be as great as originally purported. At the same time, a recent debate over the potential for GM crops to negatively affect nymphalid butterflies and other non-target organisms has now subsided as a slate of recent field studies illustrate that such threats are minimal (Koch *et al.* 2003). Lessons learned from these and other GMO introductions have inspired greater vigilance worldwide, as the specter of increasing numbers of GMOs released into the natural landscape looms large on the horizon. In particular, concerns remain about transgene escape into non-cultivated wildlands and widespread resistance to endotoxins and herbicides (Hails 2002).

Conservation biologists have good reason to fret over these potentially devastating environmental impacts, as they conduct what is arguably one of the largest uncontrolled experiments ever conducted in field community ecology. Growers and conservation biologists have different stakes in this experiment: growers are concerned about frittering away a potentially powerful technology, whereas conservation biologists are struggling to predict how widespread deployment of transgenes such as Bt endotoxin will affect the natural environment. Both camps would benefit from more discussion and interaction, as the ultimate goal is to increase the sustainability of food production while also increasing environmental protection through decreased inputs. A positive sign is the recent establishment of policies recommending 20% non-trans-

heavy-input farming to medium-scale farming that incorporates nature-mimicking processes. A transition period will be necessary, during which farmers will rely on the continued use of increasingly selective pesticides and other inputs. The challenge that faces both conservationist biologists and growers is maximizing yields while minimizing environmental impacts.

Research integrating natural vegetation in croplands and limited selective pesticide sprays illustrates how farmers may be able to decrease pesticide use and still maintain adequate pest control. Lee *et al.* (2001) demonstrated that non-crop vegetation strips within farming areas might prove useful for offsetting the negative effects of insecticide sprays on predatory carabid beetles. Banks and Stark (2004) conducted a field experiment in which aphids in plots of broccoli surrounded by either weedy margins or bare ground were sprayed with pesticide or surfactant alone. Even exposure to a small amount (one-eighth of the recommended field application rate) of the selective pesticide imidacloprid yielded a major reduction in aphid pest densities (Figure 5). Furthermore, increased vegetation diversity acted synergistically with selective pesticide sprays, with pest densities in weedy plots dropping by only 4% when no pesticide was sprayed, but down by 40% on average 4 days after pesticide spraying (skew lines in Figure 5). These kinds of results highlight the need for further experiments combining cultural and genic plants in transgenic fields aimed at slowing insect resistance to Bt.

■ Getting it right: interdisciplinary approaches

Arguably, the best chances for bolstering both conservation and agriculture lie in gathering information across several scales: at the local level, understanding values and motives for stakeholders; at the landscape level, understanding biotic and abiotic forces and cycles; and at the national and international levels, understanding how policies and incentives play out at the other scales. Over seven decades after Weaver's (1927) early article in *Ecology*, considering Midwestern agriculture in the context of the prairie ecosystem, a proliferation of articles and books highlighting the need to render farming efforts more harmonious with the natural environment offer more holistic approaches to integrating agriculture and conservation (eg Landis and Menalled 1998; Thies and Tscharntke 1999; Östman *et al.* 2001; Jackson and Jackson 2002). Innovative programs that demonstrate a shift in focus from a single species to landscape and regional conservation efforts are springing up worldwide. In Australia, a recent comprehensive terrestrial conservation plan was the result of a cooperative effort to assess what it would take, in terms of economics, stakeholder involvement, and public policy to launch a concerted nationwide effort aimed at maintaining and restoring biodiversity to critical regions (NLWRA 2002). It will require integrating agricultural production and biodiversity conservation efforts; in some regions (eg Western Australia), historical land-clearing practices and cumulative salinization have rendered conservation progress extremely unlikely. In regions where yields and farming profit margins are low, government incentives will probably be needed to offset the economic disincentives perceived by farmers (NLWRA 2002). This sort of analysis, comprehensive in both scope and perspective, is a step in the right direction. The challenge remains to involve farmers (who manage about 60% of Australia's land) and to make them feel they have a vested interest in the conservation outcomes (NLWRA 2002).

Elsewhere, researchers from universities, governments, and non-profit agencies are experimenting with similar support systems for more conservation-oriented farming. In the neotropics, much recent research has documented the benefits of shade-grown coffee for arthropod, bird, and mammal conservation (see Somarriba *et al.* 2004). Shade grown certification programs sponsored by the Audubon Society and others have provided economic support for further conversion from sun to shade-grown coffee, as have suggestions from recent research that shade-grown coffee actually tastes better (Roubik 2002).

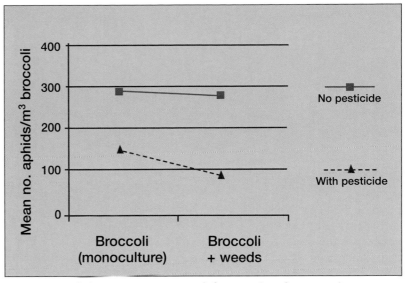

Figure 5. *Aphid response to increased diversity (weedy margins) treatments 4 days after selective pesticide application (see Banks and Stark 2004 for details). Skewed lines indicate that the effects of increased vegetation diversity are stronger in conjunction with pesticide use.*

In the US, the Nature Conservancy has been working with farmers in central California to increase on-farm resources for migratory birds. Using combinations of conservation tillage, sheep grazing, and flooding to control weeds, managers of Staten Island in San Joaquin County have seen marked increases in sandhill cranes and other wildlife (Ivey *et al.* 2003). Site managers have also made subtle changes in ditch structure and in the timing of waterfowl hunting access and harvesting in order to optimize shared use among humans and wildlife while maintaining agricultural profitability (Ivey *et al.* 2003).

In the European Union, a key aspect of more than a decade of programs aimed at encouraging farmers to be more environmentally friendly has been financial support for participants. Such strategies have resulted, for instance, in more than 10% of arable land in England being taken out of production to support wildlife – a program that has been particularly effective in providing habitat for breeding birds (Firbank *et al.* 2003). Critical to the success of such programs is the willingness to compensate participating farmers for potential losses due to habitat and farming practice modifications aimed at fostering wildlife in agricultural lands. Successful national and multi-national cooperative efforts have been moving towards a more progressive model of accounting that tries to incorporate the real costs of environmental degradation due to farming. This innovative approach is similar to recent exemplary corporate models incorporating real environmental costs into business and industry settings (eg Hawken *et al.* 1999), and continued success will require extensive cooperation among parties with very different worldviews. Early assessments of the efficacy of the EU programs are mixed and have generated substantial controversy (Kleijn *et al.* 2001), but the existence of such programs suggests we can be more confident about our abilities to bridge any remaining gaps between conservation and agriculture.

■ Conclusions

Differences in perspective between agriculture and conservation may appear large and irreconcilable at times. However, holistic, multi-scale, interdisciplinary approaches offer the most hope for better aligning the efforts and goals of these two disciplines. Current work bringing a landscape perspective to biological control and conservation in agricultural habitats is forging new alliances among researchers and practitioners from both disciplines. In both agroecological and biological conservation research, it is imperative that we continue to draw upon a shared ecological heritage and deliberately incorporate issues such as habitat heterogeneity, spatial scale, pesticide use, and the anticipated effects of GMOs into field and theoretical investigations. Furthermore, incorporating natural vegetation, mimicking natural systems, integrating community needs and addressing economic issues are all critical elements of mutually beneficial solutions.

■ Acknowledgments

Thanks to G Chang, M Marvier, B Snyder, and D Landis for helpful comments and suggestions. The Helen Riaboff Whiteley Center at Friday Harbor Laboratories on San Juan Island provided lodging and resources during the preparation of this article.

■ References

Altieri MA. 1995. Agroecology: the science of sustainable agriculture. Boulder, CO: Westview Press,.

Altieri MA. 2004. Linking ecologists and traditional farmers in the search for sustainable agriculture. *Front Ecol Environ* **2**: 35–42.

Andow D. 1991. Vegetational diversity and arthropod population response. *Annu Rev Entomol* **36**: 561–86.

Anonymous. 1842. Trees and shrubs: considered with reference to their importance in the economy of nature, and to man. *Am Agric* **1**: 18–20.

Banks JE. 1998. The scale of landscape fragmentation influences herbivore response to vegetation heterogeneity. *Oecologia* **117**: 236–46.

Banks JE and Stark JD. 2004. Aphid response to vegetation diversity and insecticide application. *Agr Ecosyst Environ* **103**: 595–99.

Barbosa P. 1998. Conservation biological control. New York, NY: Academic Press.

Bommarco R and Banks JE. 2003. Scale as modifier in vegetation diversity experiments: effects on herbivores and predators. *Oikos* **102**: 440–48.

Daily GC. 1997. Nature's services: societal dependence on natural ecosystems. Washington, DC: Island Press.

Daily GC, Ceballos G, Pachecho J, *et al.* 2003. Country biogeography of neotropical mammals: conservation opportunities in agricultural landscapes of Costa Rica. *Conserv Biol* **17**: 1814–26.

De Marco P and Coelho F. 2004. Services performed by the ecosystem: forest remnants influence agricultural cultures' pollination and production. *Biodivers Conserv* **13**: 1245–55.

Doak D, Marino P, and Kareiva P. 1992. Spatial scale mediates the influence of habitat fragmentation on dispersal success: implications for conservation. *Theor Popul Biol* **41**: 315–36.

Elliott N, Kieckhefer R, and Kauffmann W. 1996. Effects of an invading coccinellid on native coccinellids in an agricultural landscape. *Oecologia* **105**: 537–44.

Elton C. 1927. Animal ecology. London, UK: Sidgwick and Jackson.

Evans EW. 2004. Habitat displacement of North American ladybirds by an introduced species. *Ecology* **85**: 637–47.

Firbank LG. 2003. Introduction to the farm scale evaluations of spring-sown genetically modified crops. *Philos T Roy Soc B* **358**: 1777–78.

Firbank LG, Smart SM, Crabb J, *et al.* 2003. Agronomic and ecological costs and benefits of set-aside in England. *Agr Ecosyst Environ* **95**: 73–85.

Gilpin M and Hanski I. 1991. Metapopulation dynamics: empirical and theoretical investigations. New York, NY: Academic Press.

Hails RS. 2002. Assessing the risks associated with new agricultural practices. *Nature* **418**: 685–88.

Hawken P, Lovins A, and Lovins LH. 1999. Natural capitalism: creating the next industrial revolution. Boston, MA: Little, Brown and Co.

Hietala-Koivu R, Järvenpää T, and Helenius J. 2004. Value of semi-natural areas as biodiversity indicators in agricultural landscapes. *Agr Ecosys Environ* **101**: 9–19.

Ivey GL, Herziger CP, and Gause M. 2003. Farming for wildlife: an overview of agricultural operations at Staten Island, San Joaquin County, California. Galt, CA: The Nature Conservancy.

Jackson DL and Jackson LL. 2002. The farm as natural habitat: reconnecting food systems with ecosystems. Washington DC Island Press.

Janzen DH. 1968. Host plants as islands in evolutionary and contemporary time. *Am Nat* **102**: 592–95.

Kareiva P and Levin S. 2003. The importance of species: perspectives on expendability and triage. Princeton, NJ: Princeton University Press.

Kareiva PM. 1987. Habitat fragmentation and the stability of predator–prey interactions. *Nature* **326**: 388–90.

Kleijn D, Berendse F, Smit R, and Gilissen N. 2001. Agri-environment schemes do not effectively protect biodiversity in Dutch agricultural landscapes. *Nature* **413**: 723–25.

Koch RL, Hutchison WD, and Venette RC. 2003. Survival of monarch butterfly, *Danaus plexippus* (Nymphalidae), larvae on milkweed near Bt cornfields. *J Lepid Soc* **57**: 92–99.

Kremen C and Ricketts T. 2000. Global perspectives on pollination disruptions. *Conserv Biol* **14**: 1226–28.

Kruess A and Tscharntke T. 1994. Habitat fragmentation, species loss, and biological control. *Science* **264**: 1581–84.

Landis DA and Menalled FD. 1998. Ecological considerations in the conservation of effective parasitoid communities in agricultural systems. In: Barbosa P (Ed). Conservation biological control. San Diego, CA: Academic Press.

Landis DA, Wratten SD, and Gurr GM. 2000. Habitat management to conserve natural enemies of arthropod pests in agriculture. *Annu Rev Entomol* **45**: 175–201.

Lee JC, Menalled FD, and Landis DA. 2001. Refuge habitats modify impact of insecticide disturbance on Carabid beetle communities. *J Appl Ecol* **38**: 472–83.

Levins R. 1969. Some demographic and genetic consequences of environmental heterogeneity for biological control. *B Entomol Soc Am* **15**: 237–40.

Marino PC and Landis DA. 1996. Effect of landscape structure on parasitoid diversity and parasitism in agroecosystems. *Ecol Appl* **6**: 276–84.

Murdoch W, Swarbuck S, Luck R, *et al.* 1996. Refuge dynamics and metapopulation dynamics: an experimental test. *Am Nat* **134**: 288–310.

NLWRA (National Land and Water Resources Audit). 2002.

Australian Terrestrial Biodiversity Assessment: http://audit.ea. gov.au/ANRA/vegetation/docs/biodiversity/bio_assess_contents.cfm Viewed 2 November 2004

Naylor RL and Ehrlich PR. 1997. Natural pest control services and agriculture. In Daily GC (Ed). Nature's services: societal dependence on natural ecosystems. Washington DC: Island Press.

OTA (US Congress Office of Technological Assessment). 1991. Biotechnology in a global economy, OTA-BA-494. Washington DC: US Government Printing Office.

Östman Ö, Ekbom, B, Bengtsson J, and Weibull A-C. 2001. Landscape complexity and farming practice influence the condition of polyphagous carabid beetles. *Ecol Appl* **11**: 480–88.

Quinn JF and Harrison SP. 1988. Effects of habitat fragmentation and isolation on species richness: evidence from biogeographic patterns. *Oecologia* **75**: 132–40.

Ricketts TH, Daily GC, Ehrlich PR, and Fay JP. 2001. Countryside biogeography of moths in a fragmented landscape: biodiversity in native and agricultural habitats. *Conserv Biol* **15**: 378–88.

Roland J and Taylor PD. 1997. Insect parasitoid species respond to forest structure at different spatial scales. *Nature* **386**: 710–13.

Root RB. 1973. Organization of a plant–arthropod association in simple and diverse habitats: the fauna of collards (*Brassica oleracca*). *Ecol Monogr* **43**: 95–124.

Roubik DW. 2002. The values of bees to the coffee harvest. *Nature* **417**: 708.

Schmiegelow FKA and Monkkonen M. 2002. Habitat loss and fragmentation in dynamic landscapes: avian perspectives from the boreal forest. *Ecol Appl* **12**: 375–89.

Silver S. 2003. Crop of contention. *Front Ecol Environ* **1**: 511.

Snyder WE, Change GC, and Prasad RP. Conservation biological control: biodiversity influences the effectiveness of predators.

In: Barbosa P and Castellanos I (Eds). Ecology of predator–prey interactions. London, UK: Oxford University Press. In press.

Solomon GM and Schettler T. 2000. Environment and health: 6. Endocrine disruption and potential human health implications. *Can Med Assoc J* **163**: 1471–76.

Somarriba E, Harvey CA, Samper M, *et al*. 2004. Biodiversity conservation in neotropical coffee (*Coffea arabica*) plantations. In: Schroth G, da Fonseca GAB, Harvey CA, *et al.* (Eds). Agroforestry and biodiversity conservation in tropical landscapes. Washington DC: Island Press.

Stark JD, Banks JE, and Vargas R. 2004. How risky is risk assessment? The role that life history strategies play in susceptibility of species to pesticides and other toxicants. *P Natl Acad Sci USA* **101**: 732–36.

Thies C and Tscharntke T. 1999. Landscape structure and biological control in agroecosystems. *Science* **285**: 893–95.

Tilman DF and Kareiva PM. 1998. Spatial ecology. Princeton, NJ: Princeton University Press.

Tonhasca Jr A and Byrne DA. 1994. The effects of crop diversification on herbivorous insects: a meta-analysis approach. *Ecol Entomol* **19**: 239–44.

Van den Bosch R and Telford AD. 1964. Environmental modification and biological control. In: Debach P (Ed). Biological control of insect pests and weeds. New York, NY: Reinhold.

Vandermeer J and Perfecto I. 1995. Breakfast of biodiversity: the truth about rainforest destruction. Oakland, CA: The Institute for Food and Development Policy.

Weaver JE. 1927. Some ecological aspects of agriculture in the prairie. *Ecology* **8**: 1–17.

Wissinger SA. 1997. Cyclic colonization in predictably ephemeral habitats: a template for biological control in annual crop systems. *Biol Control* **10**: 4–15.

Ecological controversy: analysis to synthesis

Kathy S Williams[1], Diane Ebert-May[2], Douglas Luckie[2], and Janet Hodder[3]

The article by John Banks (see pp 537–545) in this issue of *Frontiers* outlines innovative programs worldwide that integrate the seemingly opposed goals of agriculture and conservation biology to produce mutually beneficial outcomes. This ecological conflict and subsequent movement towards integration provides an opportunity for students to actively learn science by structuring arguments for both sides of an issue, then synthesizing and integrating the best evidence and reasoning into a position statement. The intellectual skill of challenging the thinking of others by developing arguments is highly desirable in undergraduates (Conley 2003). By practicing critical analysis of arguments, students can move toward higher levels of reasoning (Toulmin 1958).

A common concern of instructors is "giving up" lecture time to implement student-centered activities during class. In part, this is based on the poorly supported assumption that students learn best through lecture (Posner *et al.* 1982; Bransford *et al.* 1999). However, research shows that students construct understanding better by interacting and processing information in small groups (Johnson *et al.* 1996; Springer *et al.* 1999). Nevertheless, the challenges of implementing small group experiences in large classes are not trivial, nor is ensuring student accountability for participation. Here we use a structured controversy based on Banks' paper to help students understand a complex ecological problem, and provide instructors with multiple forms of assessment to determine if the controversy "works" (ie helps students achieve the goals).

■ Goals for students

- Write a group position statement that synthesizes arguments and evaluates evidence about whether or not integrating agriculture and conservation biology effectively contribute to sustainable ecosystems.
- Integrate concepts of habitat diversity, insect population dynamics, biological control, pesticides, genetically modified (GM) organisms, and spatial scale into the argument.
- Assess the complexity of ecosystem management and difficulties in evaluating alternative approaches.
- Improve capacity to work as a member of a productive, collaborative group.

■ Goals for faculty

- Implement a structured controversy as a learning strategy in a large class.
- Evaluate the benefits of using structured controversy by (a) asking formative questions to determine students' assumptions and attitudes, and (b) analyzing their abilities to understand and synthesize information on the topic.

■ Instructional design – structured controversy

In a large (or small) class setting, the instructor engages students with a relevant current issue, then guides groups of four students, subdivided into pairs, through the process of controversy and resolution. In this example, all groups address the following issue: Both agriculture and conservation biology stakeholders are concerned with managing natural resources, despite conflicting goals of food production versus maintenance of biological diversity.

Assumption: Agricultural productivity is essential, while preserving natural sustainable systems is also seen as beneficial.

The class is challenged to weigh three perspectives proposed in this paper:
(a) Chemical versus biological controls of agricultural pests
(b) Managing planting for diverse versus simple (monoculture crop) planting systems
(c) Use of GM versus horticultural cultivars of crops

Students are responsible for reading the paper and understanding all three perspectives. Each group is assigned one perspective for further study (either a, b, or c). Both pairs of students within teams research both sides of their perspective using the Banks paper and additional materials (eg Zycherman and Taylor 2004 provide resources for a GM plant controversy). Each pair prepares a one-page persuasive argument that advocates and refutes both sides of their perspective, and concludes with a position statement for one side, derived from the most convincing ecological evidence. Consequently, students synthesize evidence and construct arguments, and then, working collaboratively, elucidate a knowledgeable position about the conflict between food production and maintenance of biological diversity.

In class, groups reconvene and are assigned randomly to argue one side of their position, and discuss the evidence supporting that position. Each group prepares a 2-minute oral presentation and selects a speaker to present it to the class. The structured controversy begins and the instructor selects groups to present well-supported arguments about the issues to their peers. Students are encouraged to ask questions and take notes during the discussion.

■ Assessment

The questions in Panel 1 are formative assessments, designed to inform the instructor and class about student positions before, during, and after the controversy exercise. Instructors collect students' responses to the

[1]*San Diego State University,* [2]*Michigan State University,* [3]*University of Oregon*

questions using personal response systems ("clickers") if available, or bubble sheets.

Next, have students imagine they are members of a panel of ecologists reviewing three proposals from companies who want to develop large-scale agricultural systems in previously uncultivated lands along a river in central Mexico, or in a local region, if appropriate. The three proposals differ only in their methods of insect pest control, use of GM plants, and planting patterns. Rank the following three proposals based on which will preserve and sustain local ecosystem functions most to least:

(a) This agricultural plan uses biological controls, GMOs, and diverse planting patterns.
(b) This agricultural plan uses chemical controls, GMOs, and diverse/heterogeneous planting patterns.
(c) This agricultural plan uses biological controls, selective breeding, and simple/homogeneous planting patterns.

Alternatively, these examples could be replaced by combinations generated by students. Either approach would address the goal of helping students understand the complexity of ecosystem management and difficulties in evaluating alternative approaches.

Finally, students demonstrate their ability to synthesize the arguments and evaluate positions by explaining *why* they think their first choice is better than the second and third, in terms of habitat diversity, insect population dynamics, biological control, pesticides, GM organisms, and spatial scale. A rubric distributed before class will guide student responses and assist instructors with evaluation (see Web Panel 2 for an example).

Ask students to close by recommending three features of the natural systems at risk that should be monitored to measure success if their first choice was implemented. The effectiveness of group interactions can be assessed by asking students to evaluate what they gained from working collaboratively on the controversy.

■ Analysis and discussion

Although most instructors consider it important to assess the effectiveness of active-learning instructional approaches, it is not easy to design assessments and analyze data that test their efficacy. The questions to ask about this activity include:

- Did active learning enhance students' understanding of the ecological concepts embedded in the controversy?
- Did students' thinking change during the course of the activity?
- How do students respond to subsequent exam questions related to the learning goals of the activity?
- How well did the cooperative groups function?

To answer these questions, two types of assessment are used: (1) self-report data about students' thinking about issues before, during, and after the activity, and students'

Panel 1. Formative assessments

Instructors assess students three times (before homework, beginning of class, after class controversy), by asking them to respond to each of the statements below with: (5) strongly agree, (4) agree, (3) neutral, (2) disagree, (1) strongly disagree.

1a. Use of chemical pesticides and fertilizers is the best way to control agricultural pests and increase productivity.
1b. Use of biological controls on pests maintains biodiversity of native pollinators and parasites and decreases productivity.
2a. Large-scale monocultures (eg corn or wheat) lead to the greatest agricultural productivity.
2b. Diversified planting practices (mixed crops) help preserve natural ecosystems.
3a. Planting GM species of crops is an effective way to reduce pest losses and increase crop yields.
3b. Planting commonly used horticultural varieties will have little effect on native insect species but will decrease crop yields.

Then ask students, as informed biologists, to decide which perspective from each pair above (1, 2, and 3) they would recommend for commercial agriculture to preserve the functioning of natural systems. Support each choice with one ecological reason.

---

assessment of their group interactions, and (2) direct data from students' analysis and synthesis of issues and application to a real world scenario. Critical evaluation of the data will enable instructors to explain not only *what* students know, but also *how* they learn. Ultimately, these results will inform future class sessions and generate additional questions and research about the effect of active learning on student understanding.

■ Acknowledgements

We thank J Banks, G Middendorf, and Janet Batzli for their insightful comments, and the National Science Foundation for their long-term support of the FIRST project, Faculty Institutes for Reforming Science Teaching (DUE 0088847) and the CCLI Ecology Curriculum Reform: Integrating Innovative Teaching and Global Change Technology (DUE-9952816).

■ References

Bransford JD, Brown AL, and Cocking RR. 1999. How people learn: brain, mind, experience, and school. Washington DC: National Academy Press.

Conley D. 2003. Understanding university success. Report: Association of American Universities and Pew Charitable Trusts. Eugene, OR: Center for Educational Policy Research.

Johnson DW, Johnson R, and Smith K. 1996. Academic controversy: enriching college instruction through intellectual conflict. ASHE-ERIC Higher Education Report 25(3). Washington DC.

Posner GJ, Strike KA, Hewson PW, and Gertzog WA. 1982. Accommodation of a scientific conception: toward a theory of conceptual change. *Sci Educ* **66**: 211–27.

Springer L, Stanne ME, and Donovan S. 1999. Effects of small-group learning on undergraduates in science, mathematics, engineering, and technology: a meta-analysis. *Rev Educ Res* **69**: 21–51.

Toulmin S. 1958. The uses of argument. Cambridge, UK: Cambridge University Press.

Zycherman D and Taylor J. 2004. What are the ecological impacts of plant biotechnology? Teaching Issues and Experiments in Ecology, Volume 2: Issues Figure Set #1 [online]. http://tiee.ecoed.net/vol/v2/issues/figure_sets/biotech/abstract.html. Viewed 8 November 2004.

The effects of atrazine and temperature on turtle hatchling size and sex ratios

Emily J Willingham

Temperature influences some hormone-governed developmental processes, as do environmental contaminants known as endocrine-disrupting compounds. Although many vertebrates exhibit developmental sensitivity to temperature or contaminants, little research has focused on the potential interaction of these two external influences during development. Here, embryos of the red-eared slider turtle (*Trachemys scripta elegans*) are used to model the potential interaction of increased temperature and the herbicide atrazine. The atrazine level selected (0.5 parts per billion) was based on common environmental concentrations and is within the range of federally approved drinking-water levels. Sex ratio was the endpoint of population effect in this study, with an increase in females construed as an effect of either temperature, atrazine, or the two together. Mass, carapace length and width, and plastron length were also assessed as endpoints of individual effects of exposure. Results show that increased temperature or atrazine alone do not affect sex ratio, but that the two interact to significantly increase the female fraction. Plastron length, carapace length and width, and mass were higher in atrazine-exposed turtles kept at the lower temperature, a result with fitness implications.

Front Ecol Environ 2005; 3(6): 309–313

Temperature and endocrine-disrupting contaminants may interact as developmental factors. In vertebrates, temperature can affect hormone-governed developmental pathways, including those involved in sex development (Chardard *et al.* 1995; Crews 1996; Hayes 1998), behavior (Rhen and Crews 2000), and metamorphosis (Hayes 1998). Production or activity of steroid hormones is the inferred endpoint of these temperature-induced pathways (Crews 1996). The implication is that changes in temperature alter developmental hormone levels or activity, which in turn affect sex and other parameters. Small temperature changes can cause important changes in organisms; in some reptiles, a 4 °C difference in incubation temperature can shift nest sex ratio from 100% male to 100% female (Crews 1996). Developmental temperature also influences other parameters in reptiles, including growth rate and mass (Tousignant and Crews 1995; Du and Ji 2003).

Many contaminants disrupt the same pathways during vertebrate development, often mimicking or blocking natural steroid hormone activity, typically at very low (parts per billion [ppb]) concentrations (Crisp *et al.* 1998). Exposure to these low doses can result in the same outcome as exposure to increased temperature (Willingham and Crews 2000).

Research shows that small temperature increases can augment the effect of a single low dose of natural steroid during development (Crews 1996), raising the question of whether temperature can interact with contaminants

that mimic steroids. The aim of the current research was to investigate whether a low, environmentally relevant dose of the commonly used herbicide atrazine interacts with increasing temperature to exert significant effects on sex development and other parameters in a temperature-sensitive species.

The species used to model these exposure effects in this study is the red-eared slider turtle, *Trachemys scripta elegans* (Figure 1), a species with temperature-dependent sex determination. Lower incubation temperatures (< 29.4 °C) produce a male-biased sex ratio in this species, while higher temperatures increase the female fraction; 31 °C results in 100% females. Estrogen exposure has the same effect as high temperature (ie more females) (Wibbels *et al.* 1994), and application of endocrine-disrupting contaminants produces the same result (Willingham and Crews 1999). The sensitive period for sex determination by exposure to temperature, estrogens, or contaminants is the middle third of development.

■ Materials and methods

Turtle eggs were purchased commercially (Kliebert Alligator and Turtle Farm, Hammond, LA) and transported to the laboratory. The eggs had all been laid on the same day and were maintained at 29.4 °C for 12 days, until brought to the lab. Eggs were maintained all together at room temperature for a week until embryos were at approximately stage 17 of development (Greenbaum 2002), as confirmed by three independent researchers. We selected 105 viable eggs from an initial group of 2000. The eggs were placed randomly into trays containing 1:1 vermiculite:water and incubated at one of two tempera-

Department of Biology, Texas State University, San Marcos, TX 78666; current address: Center for the Study and Treatment of Hypospadias, Department of Urology, University of California-San Francisco, San Francisco, CA 94122 (ewillingham@urol.ucsf.edu)

Figure 1. *Red-eared slider turtle* (Trachemys scripta elegans).

of ethanol was applied to the eggshell. Incubation continued to hatching; temperatures were monitored daily with the use of the incubator digital reading and an in-incubator thermometer, and egg groups were shifted daily to avoid any positional effects. Turtles hatched at stage 26 (Greenbaum 2002).

On the day of hatching (emergence from the eggshell), mass (0.1 g) was taken, and carapace width and length and plastron length (0.01 mm) were measured, using digital calipers. Carapace measurements were straightline, minimum (notch-to-notch) measurements. Hatchlings were then sacrificed by rapid decapitation and gonadal sex assessed using parameters described previously (Wibbels *et al.* 1994): Briefly, ovaries are long, thin, white, transparent, and not vascularized. Testes are short and round, opaque, and yellowish, and show evidence of seminiferous tubules. Presence or absence of oviducts was also noted. In this species, ovotestes are extremely rare (circa 1:20 000; pers observ) and have a characteristic baseball-bat shape; none were observed.

Two-by-two contingency table sex ratio data were analyzed using Fisher's exact one-tailed tests. One-tailed tests were applied because of the a priori assumption that atrazine would be estrogenic (Hayes *et al.* 2002). Version 2 of JMP (SAS Institute, Cary, NC) for PC was used for all statistical procedures. Length and width data were first analyzed by ANOVA for overall effects of single variables or interaction of variables; if a significant effect was found, further analysis between groups was performed (either ANOVA, student's t-tests, or nonparametric Wilcoxon).

■ Results

As expected, we obtained a male-biased sex ratio at the 26 °C temperature, and a circa 50:50 ratio at the 29.2 °C temperature (Figure 2). No significant differences in sex ratio or other parameters were found between the vehicle and temperature control groups, and these groups were combined as "temperature" for analysis, as has been done previously in similar work (Rhen *et al.*, 1999; Willingham *et al.* 1999; Willingham 2001). Neither the 0.5 ppb dose of atrazine nor the increased temperature alone significantly altered the female fraction (Figure 2). However, increased temperature combined with atrazine did significantly increase the female fraction compared to the 26 °C group (P = 0.03) (Figure 2).

Table 1 shows the results of a series of effects analyses performed for each of the following: mass, carapace length and width, and plastron length. For each, a P value is given. Where a P value of 0.1 or less resulted for all groups combined, further statistical analyses compared group to group (Figure 3a–d).

An analysis of temperature-by-treatment interaction on

tures, either 26 °C or 29.2 °C. The supplier had placed the eggs in small containers in groups of 15–20; these containers were arrayed on a lab bench, and one egg from each was serially placed into a given incubation tray to avoid clutch effects. In addition, at the time of treatment, eggs were again shuffled around among the incubation trays. Because eggs were initially kept at 29.4 °C by the supplier, we anticipated a male-biased sex ratio, rather than 100% males. The 29.2 °C temperature is known to yield mixed-sex ratios in the absence of any other manipulation.

Eggs were not weighed or marked to enable linkage of initial egg mass and individual hatchlings. Such an approach had been attempted previously, using grouped eggs for uniform incubation, but turtles tend to emerge from the eggs in groups, making identification of the originating egg problematic. Placing eggs individually into separate containers would have introduced incubation variables involving the containers, location in the incubator, incubation materials, and humidity, any of which could conceivably have confounded our results. In addition, we did not have the opportunity to take the mass of the eggs on the day of laying at the commercial supplier. For these reasons, we did not attempt to link initial egg mass and individual hatchlings.

Eggs were placed in desktop incubators (Brinsea, Titusville, FL), and randomized again into one of three possible treatment groups per temperature: temperature control (no treatment), ethanol (vehicle) control, or atrazine-treated. Treatment with atrazine involved applying 5 μL of ethanol containing 5 ng/10-g egg (0.5 ppb) of atrazine (special preparation, Accustandard) to the eggshell using a pipettor (Wibbels *et al.* 1994). The atrazine dose was based on federal limits of allowable levels in drinking water. In the vehicle control group, 5 μL

mass revealed a significant effect ($F = 6.9$; df = 1; $P = 0.0098$); further investigation disclosed an effect of atrazine on mass at 26 °C (ANOVA, $F = 5.3$; df = 1, 49; $P = 0.0252$) (Figure 3a). Univariate ANOVA was used because a Shapiro–Wilks test indicated that the atrazine-treated and control groups had a normal distribution ($P = 0.18$). No other significant effects on mass, including sex and sex interaction with treatment, were observed (Table 1).

For carapace length, the same analyses were performed. The 26 °C–Atr population was not normally distributed and, again, the nonparametric Wilcoxon rank sums analysis was used to compare this group with the 26 °C group.

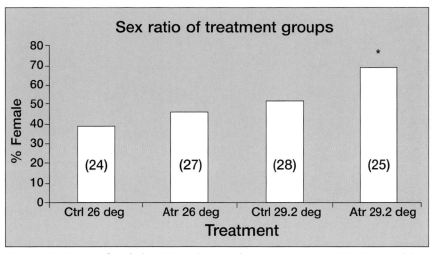

Figure 2. *Percent female hatchlings from each treatment group. N given in ( ) in bars. Asterisk indicates significant difference in female ratio versus 26 °C.*

The comparison of 26 °C and 26 °C–Atr groups showed a significant effect of atrazine on carapace length ($X^2 = 6.23$; df = 1; $P = 0.012$) (Figure 3c).

An effects analysis of temperature-by-treatment interaction on carapace width resulted in further investigation ($F = 3.53$; df = 1; $P = 0.06$). A Shapiro–Wilks test for normal distribution indicated that neither the 26 °C nor the 26 °C–Atr populations were normally distributed; thus, a Wilcoxon rank sums nonparametric test was performed. Results indicated a significant difference in carapace width between the two groups ($X^2 = 5.45$; df = 1; $P = 0.0197$) (Figure 3b). Also observed was a potential effect of temperature on carapace width ($P = 0.0720$); however, ANOVA analysis of the 26 °C vs. 29.2 °C hatchlings did not warrant a conclusion of a significant effect ($P = 0.066$).

An analysis of temperature-by-treatment interaction on plastron length revealed a significant effect ($F = 8.2$; df = 1; $P = 0.005$). Both the 26 °C and 26 °C–Atr groups were normally distributed; further investigation showed an effect of atrazine on plastron length at 26 °C (ANOVA, $F = 10.35$; df = 1, 49; $P = 0.0023$) (Figure 3d). A potential temperature-based effect on plastron length was identified in the effects analysis ($P = 0.0068$; Table 1); however, this effect of temperature is attributable to the 26 °C hatchlings that were exposed to atrazine.

■ Discussion

The results imply that atrazine, temperature, and temperature and atrazine together, exert endocrine influences and interact with each other. The stepwise increase in the female fraction as temperature is increased, when atrazine is added, and in the presence of both, directly reflects the stepwise response to increased temperature or exogenously applied estrogens in this species (Crews 1996). With the assumption that temperature and/or atrazine indicate an endocrine signal or dose, each graph in Figure 3 exhibits an inverted U-shaped dose response to an endocrine signal that is increasing as a result of temperature or exogenous atrazine, or both. This type of curve is common in endocrine-disruptor studies (Welshons *et al.* 2003).

Endocrine endpoints under the influence of developmental temperature include gonadal sex in some fish (eg Conover and Heins 1987) and in amphibians (eg Chardard *et al.* 1995) and many reptiles (Janzen and Paukstis 1991), including all crocodilians and some turtles. Other such endpoints include growth rate (Rhen and Lang 1999) and behaviors (Rhen and Crews 2000). All of these parameters can influence individual fitness and thus population success. Sex ratios directly relate to population-level effects.

Atrazine is known to disrupt endocrine-governed developmental processes (Hayes *et al.* 2002). Some low-dose contaminants have also been shown to affect fitness parameters, including mass and growth rate, in red-eared slider turtles (Willingham 2002) and also to reverse sex in this species (Willingham and Crews 1999).

In spite of the established influence of temperature or hormone/hormone mimics on development in vertebrates, to my knowledge no work has been published on

Table 1. Effects analyses for mass, carapace length, carapace width, and plastron length (*P* values)							
Effect tested	Temp	Atrazine	Sex	Temp x atr	Temp x sex	Atr x sex	Temp x atr x sex
Mass	0.6817	0.5292	0.2787	0.0098	0.2799	0.5831	0.1996
Carapace length	0.1593	0.5154	0.7668	0.0616	0.6193	0.4539	0.2363
Carapace width	0.0720	0.2574	0.9257	0.0631	0.2396	0.9152	0.2818
Plastron length	0.0068	0.2214	0.7947	0.0050	0.4416	0.9066	0.8101

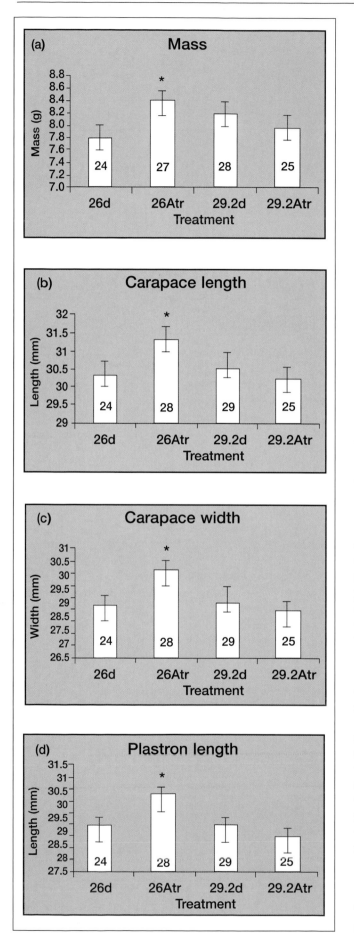

Figure 3. (a) Mass, (b) carapace length, (c) carapace width, and (d) plastron length of hatchlings from each treatment group. Asterisk indicates a significant (P < 0.05) difference in the parameter compared to the 26 °C group. The population size for each group is given inside the bars.

the potential for a hormone mimic such as atrazine to interact with temperature. The current work demonstrates for the first time that increased temperature alters the effects of an endocrine disruptor, with consequences at the population level.

Also, atrazine alters the expected size/mass of a hatchling to resemble that obtained at a mid-range temperature, with implications for individual fitness. A low, environmentally relevant dose of atrazine resulted in a significant increase in plastron length in turtles incubated at 26 °C. The 26 °C atrazine-exposed turtles were no different from the 29.2 °C groups in mass or carapace width or length. Thus, at a low temperature, atrazine produced the same result as the mid-range, higher temperature alone, namely bigger turtles. Size at hatching has been implicated as a fitness factor in reptiles, including turtles (Rhen and Lang 1999). Some research indicates that mid-range incubation temperatures may reduce fitness (Janzen 1995).

Atrazine may not have increased size or mass at 29.2 °C because hatchlings reached the limits of the species reaction norms for size or mass at that temperature. Research examining the effect of temperature from the high end of the incubation spectrum in this species indicates that that is the case (Willingham 2004).

The fact that we did not assess initial egg mass in the context of the hatchling size parameters leaves open the alternative explanation that initial egg mass was larger among the eggs in the atrazine-treated group and thus produced larger hatchlings. However, eggs were selected and placed in groups with uniformity in mind. In addition, atrazine at 26 °C had an effect on mass that is similar to that obtained with increased temperature (to 29.2 °C) in this study and in another study (Willingham 2004), an outcome that might be predicted if atrazine has estrogen-like effects (as per Hayes *et al.* 2002) and estrogen is also the endpoint of increased temperature.

It is possible that temperature and compounds such as atrazine, which interacted in this study, interact in other species that are influenced by developmental temperature. Although the current work used the turtle as a model for exposure, in a natural setting embryos would be exposed via contaminants in the yolk derived from the mother (eg Heinz *et al.* 1991) and would therefore be exposed from a much earlier period and more persistently.

■ **Acknowledgments**

The author acknowledges C Byerly for animal care and data collection assistance.

■ References

Chardard D, Desvages G, Pieau C, and Dournon C. 1995. Aromatase activity in larval gonads of *Pleurodeles waltl* (Urodele Amphibia) during normal sex differentiation and during sex reversal by thermal treatment. *Gen Comp Endocrinol* **99**: 100–7.

Conover DO and Heins SW. 1987. The environmental and genetic components of sex ratio in *Menidia menidia* (Piacea: Atherinidae). *Copeia* **1987**: 732–47.

Crews D. 1996. Temperature-dependent sex determination: the interplay of steroid hormones and temperature. *Zool Sci* **13**: 1–13.

Crisp TM, Clegg ED, Cooper RL, *et al.* 1998. Environmental endocrine disruption: an effects assessment analysis. *Environ Health Perspect* (Suppl) **106**: 11–56.

Du W-G and Ji X. 2003. The effects of incubation thermal environments on size, locomotor performance and early growth of hatchling soft-shelled turtles, *Pelodiscus sinensis*. *J Thermal Biol* **28**: 279–86.

Greenbaum E. 2002. A standardized series of embryonic stages for the emydid turtle *Trachemys scripta*. *Can J Zool* **80**: 1350–70.

Hayes TB. 1998. Sex determination and primary sex differentiation in amphibians. *J Exp Zool*. **281**: 373–99.

Hayes T, Chan R, and Licht PJ. 1993. Interactions of temperature and steroids on larval growth, development, and metamorphosis in a toad (*Bufo boreas*). *J Exp Zool* **266**: 206–15.

Hayes TB, Collins A, Lee M, *et al.* 2002. Hermaphroditic, demasculinized frogs after exposure to the herbicide atrazine at low ecologically relevant doses. *Proc Nat Acad Sci* **99**: 5476–80.

Heinz GH, Percival HF, and Jennings ML. 1991. Contaminants in American alligator eggs from Lake Apopka, Lake Griffin, and Lake Okeechobee, Florida. *Environ Mon Assess* **16**: 277–85.

Janzen FJ. 1995. Experimental evidence for the evolutionary significance of temperature-dependent sex determination. *Evolution* **49**: 864–73.

Janzen FJ and Paukstis GL. 1991. Environmental sex determination in reptiles: ecology, evolution, and experimental design. *Quart Rev Biol* **66**: 149–79.

Rhen T and Crews D. 2000. Organization and activation of sexual and agonistic behavior in the leopard gecko, *Eublepharis macularius*. *Neuroendocrinology* **71**: 252–61.

Rhen T and Lang J. 1999. Temperature during embryonic and juvenile development influences growth in hatchling snapping turtles, *Chelydra serpentina*. *J Therm Biol* **24**: 33–41.

Rhen T, Willingham EJ, Sakata JT, *et al.* 1999. Incubation temperature influences sex-steroid levels in juvenile red-eared slider turtles, *Trachemys scripta*, a species with temperature-dependent sex determination. *Biol Reprod* **61**: 1275–80.

Tousignant A and Crews D. 1995. Incubation temperature and gonadal sex affect growth and physiology in the leopard gecko (*Eublepharis macularius*), a lizard with temperature-dependent sex determination. *J Morphol* **224**: 159–70

Welshons WV, Thayer KA, Judy BM, *et al.* 2003. Large effects from small exposures. I. Mechanisms for endocrine disrupting chemicals with estrogenic activity. *Environ Health Persp* **111**: 994–1006.

Wibbels T, Bull JJ, and Crews D. 1994. Temperature-dependent sex determination: a mechanistic approach. *J Exp Zool* **270**: 71–78.

Willingham EJ. 2002. Embryonic exposure to low-dose pesticides: effects on fitness parameters in the hatchling red-eared slider turtle. *J Toxicol Environ Health* **64**: 257–72.

Willingham EJ. 2004. Different incubation temperatures result in differences in mass in female red-eared slider turtle hatchlings. *J Thermal Biol* **30**: 61–64.

Willingham EJ and Crews D. 1999. Sex reversal effects of environmentally relevant xenobiotic concentrations on the red-eared slider turtle, a species with temperature-dependent sex determination. *Gen Comp Endocrinol* **113**: 429–35.

Willingham EJ and Crews D. 2000. The red-eared slider turtle: an animal model for the study of low doses and mixtures. *Amer Zool* **40**: 421–29.

Willingham EJ, Rhen T, Sakata JT, and Crews D. 1999. Embryonic treatment with xenobiotics disrupts sex-steroid profiles in hatchling red-eared slider turtles, *Trachemys scripta*. *Environ Health Persp* **108**: 329–32.

Determining confidence: sex and statistics

Terry L Derting[1], Diane Ebert-May[2], Janet Hodder[3], and Everett P Weber[2]

In this article we demonstrate the use of a primary research paper as an assessment tool, helping to determine how well students understand a biological concept and their ability to interpret statistics. The article by Willingham (p 309–313) investigates the effects of temperature in conjunction with endocrine disrupting chemicals (EDCs) on sex determination in turtles. We have designed instruction and assessments on the subject of sex determination, a topic that is conceptually uncomplicated for most students, and statistical analyses which present them with some challenges. We have made the assumption that students have learned about mechanisms of sex determination among animal taxa, know how to develop and test hypotheses, and have a basic understanding of natural selection and fitness.

Student goals

- Apply understanding of sex determination to the consequences of altered sex ratios in animal populations.
- Demonstrate understanding of statistical testing and skills in interpreting data used in a research paper.

Instructor goals

- Use primary literature as a source of information about biological topics and as an assessment tool.
- Implement an active learning strategy to help students understand the concept of statistical testing and significance.

Engage – content

Begin the class with a question for students to discuss in their groups: "In some coastal areas, well-meaning individuals dig up eggs laid by sea turtles on beaches and re-bury them further inland where the eggs are better protected. What impact(s) do you think this has on the sexual development of these turtles?"

After selected groups report out, the instructor summarizes the discussion, adding information about sex determination and EDCs. The topic of EDCs is of interest to students, as the mechanisms and ubiquity of the effects are easily understood and are of personal relevance. Although controversy exists regarding the links between endocrine disruptors and negative impacts on human health, it is evident that these compounds are present on a global scale, with high levels occurring in the blood or body fats of humans and wildlife. This introduction leads to an exploration of the use of statistics in these types of studies.

[1]Murray State University, [2]Michigan State University, [3]University of Oregon

Explore – statistics and data

Two objectives guide students' exploration of statistics: (1) connect data interpretation and confidence level with statistical testing, and (2) connect statistical analyses of data with support or rejection of hypotheses.

The instructor polls the class, using computer-based personal response systems, "clickers" (Brewer 2004), or hand-held cards to provide real-time displays of responses to questions like the following, using five choices (eg 100%, 95–85%, 75–65%, 55–45%, < 40%):

"What level of confidence does an engineer need to have in a new material for building bridges for public use before the bridges are actually built with that material?" Students usually say 100%. After a discussion that perfection is never possible, groups of students decide what level of confidence they think is acceptable for these and similar items. These types of questions lead naturally to a discussion of the effects of sample size and data variability on confidence in results.

Sample size and confidence levels

Students then discuss the following scenario to explore determination of sample size:

"Suppose you are the head of a drug-testing team. You have a pool of 10 000 people on whom to test the drug. What sample size of people will you use – 10, 100, or 1000? You may assume that one individual by chance alone responds unpredictably to the drug. Explain your answer in terms of your confidence that the drug effects on all individuals measured are truly representative of the drug."

In groups, students calculate the impact of one anomalous outcome within a sample of 10, 100, or 1000 and relate their solutions to thinking about sample size and confidence levels. Why would they/would they not use a smaller or larger sample size? Students report out answers.

P-values

The next hurdle for students is in understanding what P-values mean in relation to hypothesis testing. Most students view hypotheses as absolutes – ie right or wrong – and have difficulty understanding statistical significance. The instructor builds on the previous activity by explaining the meaning of a P-value and that 0.05, which is equivalent to a 95% confidence level, is a value traditionally used to indicate actual rather than chance effects of treatments if the null hypothesis is true.

Explain – analysis

Students work in groups to explore the concept of statistical significance using P-values. Groups work with one of two datasets, representing the occurrence of cricket frogs by gonadal sex in relation to time period and/or geographic region (Figures 1a, b). Students interpret the data and consider the results in terms of corresponding *P*-values and hypothesis testing.

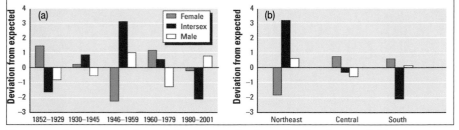

Figure 1. *Deviations of observed from expected values of cricket frog sex (a) by time period and (b) by region. Reproduced from Reeder* et al. *(2005) by permission from Environmental Health Perspectives.*

Problem

Reeder *et al.* (2005) studied museum specimens of cricket frogs, looking for relationships between EDC use, population declines, and the occurrence of intersexuality. Specimens were examined from three regions, each differing in human population density and land use, over five time periods which differed in relation to EDC use. After explaining the purpose of the studies, groups write a null hypothesis(es) based on the study and proceed as follows:

Group 1 (Figure 1a)

- Decide whether EDCs have primarily a feminizing or masculinizing effect on cricket frogs, justifying the answer in terms of the data.
- Explain what the authors mean by: "The proportion of specimens in each gonadal sex class differed significantly among the time periods of collection (*P* < 0.001)".

Group 2 (Figure 1b)

- Explain what the authors mean by: "The proportion of specimens in each gonadal sex class differed significantly among the geographical regions (*P* < 0.001)".
- Provide an ecological explanation for the statement, "In the 1990s, very few museum specimens of cricket frogs were available from regions that previously had the most elevated intersex rates".

The instructor picks groups to present their responses. Students are asked whether they think the results support or fail to support their group's stated hypothesis and to rate their confidence (strong, average, weak) in their response.

In a minute paper (Angelo and Cross 1993), students explain: (1) how *P*-values relate to confidence, and (2) why they stated that the results support or fail to support their group's stated hypothesis, justifying their answer in terms of the probability that the results occurred by chance alone.

■ Active homework – summative assessment

Willingham's paper is read for homework and questions are used to assess students' understanding of sex determination and the use of statistics. The instructor can evaluate all or several of the questions and should post one response that meets the highest level criteria for all questions. Questions can also be used in quizzes.

Content questions

- Explain the physiological mechanism whereby atrazine (and/or temperature) alters the sex of turtles.

- Explain two ways in which the shift in sex ratio between the control group and the atrazine–warm temperature group (see Figure 1 in Willingham paper) might influence a population.
- In what ways would population impacts differ if the effect of the treatments was an increase in the proportion of males, rather than females, in a population?
- What is meant by: "Size at hatching has been implicated as a fitness factor in reptiles, including turtles"?

Statistical questions

- Explain how the statistical results support or fail to support the hypothesis. In your explanation, show your understanding of the meaning of a *P*-value and confidence level.
- How would your confidence change if Willingham used a *P*-value of 0.1 instead of 0.05 to determine statistical differences among measurements of the experimental groups? Explain.
- What is the importance of statistical analyses in reaching conclusions based on evidence?

■ Final note

The answers to the homework questions provide an assessment of students' ability to apply the understanding gained in this class. The next steps will depend on how the instructor processes the answers and what is learned from these answers. The following class period may be a time to reinforce the content or statistical ideas that students found difficult.

■ Acknowledgements

We thank the National Science Foundation for their long-term support of the FIRST project, Faculty Institutes for Reforming Science Teaching (DUE 0088847). All Pathways papers are peer reviewed.

■ References

Angelo TA and Cross KP. 1993. Classroom assessment techniques. San Francisco, CA: Jossey-Bass.

Brewer CA. 2004. Near real-time assessment of student learning and understanding in biology courses. *Bioscience.* **54**: 1034–39.

Reeder AL, Ruiz MO, Pessier A, *et al.* 2005. Intersexuality and the cricket frog decline: historic and geographic trends. *Environ Health Perspec* **113**: 261–65. (http://ehp.niehs.nih.gov/members/2004/7276/7276.html).

A call to ecologists: measuring, analyzing, and managing ecosystem services

Claire Kremen[1] and Richard S Ostfeld[2]

Humans depend on ecosystem services, yet our ecological understanding of them is quite limited. In the classic example, when New York City decided to protect the Catskill Watershed rather than build an expensive water filtration plant, planners reasoned that the protection plan would be the cheaper option, even if they underestimated the area required by half. Such reasoning reflects our inability to predict how to manage lands to provide ecosystem services of sufficient quantity and quality. Human domination of the biosphere is rapidly altering the capacity of ecosystems to provide a variety of essential services; we therefore need to develop a better understanding of their ecological underpinnings, and to integrate this knowledge into a socioeconomic context to develop better policies and plans to manage them. We present a three-part research agenda to create the knowledge base necessary to accomplish this goal.

Front Ecol Environ 2005; 3(10): 540–548

Human domination of the biosphere is rapidly altering the composition, structure, and function of ecosystems (Vitousek et al. 1997), often eroding their capacity to provide services critical to human survival (Palmer et al. 2004). Ecosystem services are ecological functions that sustain and improve human life (Daily 1997). A recent classification of ecosystem services divides them into four categories: provisioning services, regulating services, supporting services, and cultural services (Millenium Ecosystem Assessment 2003). Provisioning services provide goods like food, fuel, and timber. Regulating services include climate and flood control. Supporting services include pollination, population control, soil formation, and other basic ecological properties upon which biodiversity and other ecosystem functions or services depend. Cultural services provide humans with recreational, spiritual, and aesthetic values. These four types of services both support and depend on

biodiversity (Figure 1), yet ecological understanding of most ecosystem services remains rudimentary, impeding progress in identifying targets for conservation and management (Balmford et al. 2003; Palmer et al. 2004; Robertson and Swinton 2005). Previous work has categorized ecosystem services, identified methods for economic valuation, mapped the supply and demand for services, assessed threats, and estimated economic values (Daily et al. 2000; Heal 2000; Millennium Ecosystem Assessment 2003; Turner et al. 2003; Biggs et al. 2004), but has not quantified the underlying role of biodiversity in providing these services. In contrast, studies on the role of diversity in determining ecosystem function are numerous, but often examine communities whose structures differ markedly from those providing services in real landscapes (Diaz et al. 2003; Symstad et al. 2003). Moreover, such studies have generally been restricted to a small set of ecosystem processes (Schwartz et al. 2000). Both of these approaches – descriptive, socioeconomic analyses of ecosystem services and experimental studies of how biodiversity affects ecosystem function – are necessary, but neither is sufficient to assess how biodiversity loss affects the current and future abilities of ecosystems to provide crucial services, or to devise appropriate management strategies (Kremen 2005). Given forecasts of global declines in provision of ecosystem services (Millenium Ecosystem Assessment 2003), it is critical to develop and implement a mechanistic research agenda and to integrate it with socioeconomic work on ecosystem services in order to devise the best management and policy tools for their conservation and sustainable use (Figure 2; Folke et al. 1996).

In a nutshell:

- Provision of ecosystem services by native biota is both undervalued and understudied
- To correct this, ecologists need to measure the contributions of individual ecosystem service providers, determine what affects their ability to provide services, and measure the scale over which providers and services operate
- We use this approach to describe crop pollination by wild bees and dilution of Lyme disease risk by vertebrates, showing how rapidly these two services decline with diminishing diversity
- This ambitious approach requires tremendous resources; first, ecologists must gain support from decision makers and the public

[1]Department of Environmental Science, Policy and Management, University of California, Berkeley, CA 94720-3114 (ckremen@nature.berkeley.edu); [2]Institute of Ecosystem Studies, 65 Sharon Turnpike, Millbrook, NY 12545

■ The ecology of ecosystem services

To manage ecosystem services in a changing world, we need to know how human activities affect the key species

Figure 1. (a) *Provisioning services: in Madagascar, people living near the rainforest rely on over 35 species of wild rainforest plants simply to build their homes, and use over 100 other species for various basic necessities (Kremen et al. 1998). (b) Supporting services: parasitoids help to control herbivorous insects (parasitized sphingid moth larva in Costa Rica). (c) Regulating services: forests surrounding rivers provide flood control and can help to justify conservation (the Namorana River in Ranomafana National Park, SE Madagascar). (d) Cultural services: the helmet vanga (*Euryceros prevostii*) is a rare, endemic species that attracts bird-watchers and tourists to Masoala National Park, Madagascar.*

or functional groups that provide these services, and the spatial and temporal scales of both disturbance and recovery. How do real-world changes in communities affect the magnitude and stability of ecosystem services? A comprehensive research program to define the "ecology of an ecosystem service" would include: (1) identifying the species or other entities that are key "ecosystem service providers" and measuring their functional contributions; (2) assessing the key environmental factors that influence the ability of these species to provide services; and (3) measuring the spatiotemporal scale over which providers and services operate (Kremen 2005). Only a few services are being investigated in such a complete manner (see Case studies section), and there are no cases in which multiple services are considered, to allow development of a systems approach (T Ricketts pers comm). A broader application of this approach will help not only in planning sustainable management of ecosystem services, but also in elucidating under what circumstances managing for ecosystem services can also provide incentives for

conserving biodiversity (Balvanera *et al.* 2001), not only in protected areas, but in broader landscapes that include primarily human land use (Folke *et al.* 1996).

■ Diversity–ecosystem function

Most diversity–ecosystem function research has focused on the role of species richness in influencing function, but ecosystem functioning also depends on the identities, densities, biomasses, and interactions of populations of contributing species within a community, as well as the aggregate abundance and spatial and temporal variation of these attributes (Diaz *et al.* 2003; Symstad *et al.* 2003; Kremen 2005). The predominant experimental approach has been to construct synthetic, experimental communities that are species-poor, have artificial abundance distributions, and concentrate on several ecosystem functions within a single class of ecosystem services ("supporting services" such as plant productivity; Schwartz *et al.* 2000; Loreau *et al.* 2001). To manage ecosystem services, we

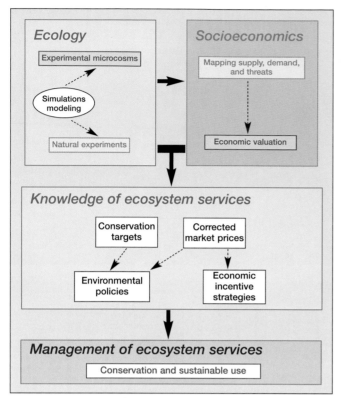

Figure 2. *Conceptual framework illustrating how greater ecological knowledge, in combination with socioeconomic knowledge, is needed to manage ecosystem services for sustainable use (Limburg and Folke 1999). Blue boxes: areas of greater current knowledge; orange boxes: poorly known (arrows indicate desired or existing linkages); white boxes: desired outcomes.*

need to understand how realistic changes in all of these aspects of community structure, acting singly or together, affect the magnitude and the stability of the ecosystem service over space and time. Ecological communities are capable of behaving in qualitatively different ways when species are lost. In some cases the provision of ecosystem services might be highly resilient, for instance if remaining species compensate for lost species, with little or no net loss in function (Schindler 1990). In others, however, species loss is accompanied by a marked loss of overall functioning (Larsen *et al.* 2005). What is responsible for these differences?

Compensation may occur through the portfolio effect (statistical averaging; Tilman *et al.* 1998); density compensation (Solan *et al.* 2004); response diversity (differential response of species to disturbance; Walker *et al.* 1999); or functional compensation (in which the efficiencies of individual ecosystem service providers change in response to changing community composition). Some studies suggest that more diverse communities are more resistant or resilient to environmental change due to such compensatory responses (Tilman *et al.* 1998; Walker *et al.* 1999). These different compensatory mechanisms may be interrelated and difficult to disentangle (Tilman *et al.* 1998) and too few studies have yet been conducted to ascertain how often each of these mechanisms operates, under what

conditions, and in what types of communities. In contrast, several studies have underscored the inability of ecological communities to compensate functionally for species loss (Larsen *et al.* 2005). Determining how often and under what conditions compensatory mechanisms occur is a promising and important area for future work.

Some patterns are beginning to emerge concerning community changes that lead to rapid loss of function, although much work remains to be done. Natural communities lose species (disassemble) in non-random fashion, with some species being prone to extirpation while others are quite robust. Communities in which disassembly is non-random often lose function more rapidly than do experimental communities in which a random order of species removal is imposed (eg Petchey and Gaston 2002; Jonsson and Malmqvist 2003; Ostfeld and LoGiudice 2003; Solan *et al.* 2004; Zavaleta and Hulvey 2004; Larsen *et al.* 2005). The rapid functional loss that can accompany non-random extinction order can occur via two mechanisms. In some cases, the species that contribute the most to function are also the most sensitive to disturbance (Larsen *et al.* 2005). In other cases, non-random extinction sequences lead to the loss of entire functional groups (Petchey and Gaston 2002; Zavaleta and Hulvey 2004), eliminating the complementarity between groups that is thought to enhance function through niche differentiation (Loreau *et al.* 2001) or facilitation (Cardinale *et al.* 2003), as well as within-group redundancy, which provides insurance against species losses (Memmott *et al.* 2004).

An approach that combines observations of natural disassembly of communities in response to disturbance with targeted experiments (eg Zavaleta and Hulvey 2004) and/or simulations (eg Ostfeld and LoGiudice 2003; Larsen *et al.* 2005) will help to identify the key environmental factors affecting service provision over space and time. This information is essential for devising management plans.

■ Characterizing ecosystem services through a functional inventory

Conservation biologists recognized long ago that knowledge of species distributions provides the richest source of information for planning and managing protected area networks to conserve biodiversity (Margules and Pressey 2000). Similarly, understanding which populations, species, functional groups, guilds, food webs, or habitat types collectively produce ecosystem services (the "ecosystem service providers", or ESPs), is essential when planning for sustainable management of ecosystem services.

Two complementary methodologies exist. The "functional inventory" identifies the key ESPs in a given landscape and measures their functional contribution. The appropriate ecological level for defining an ESP is service-dependent: for example, at the genetic level for maintaining disease resistance of crops (Zhu *et al.* 2000), the population and/or food-web level for biological control of crop pests (Cardinale *et al.* 2003), and the habitat level for water-flow regulation by vegetation (Guo *et al.* 2000). Researchers can then estimate the total function provided by a given community or ecosystem under different management scenarios. For example, Balvanera *et al.* (2005) estimated the annual rate of carbon sequestration in tropical forests that were conserved, regrown following conversion to pasture, or selectively logged for high value timber, based on biomass accumulation rates of individual tree species. The functional inventory permits identification of key species for management (Power *et al.* 1996); correlation of functional traits with other traits, including proneness to extinction (Larsen *et al.* 2005); assessment of the level of redundancy in the system (Memmott *et al.* 2004); analysis of interaction effects that affect function (Cardinale *et al.* 2003); and finally, prediction of the functional effects of alternative management or disturbance scenarios (Balvanera *et al.* 2005). To date, inventories of this nature have been conducted for only a few functions, including biogenic mixing of ocean sediments (Solan *et al.* 2004); water flow regulation by forest habitats (Guo *et al.* 2000); crop pollination (eg Kremen *et al.* 2002); carbon sequestration (Balvanera *et al.* 2005); disease dilution (Ostfeld *et al.* in press); and others (for examples, see Kremen 2005).

Measuring "functional attribute diversity" is a complementary approach. Here, a guild or community that provides a given service is characterized by defining the "ecological distance" that separates each ESP within it (Walker *et al.* 1999, Petchey and Gaston 2002). These ecological distances may be based on morphological, ecological, or behavioral attributes of species that are likely to result in functional differences (eg tongue length for pollinators, root depth for plants). This method is useful when it is not practical to measure the functional contribution of different ESPs for a given service. An advantage of this approach is that one can subdivide the community into groups of functionally similar (qualitatively redundant) ESPs and thus predict functional resilience with species loss (Walker *et al.* 1999) or identify guilds exhibiting functional dissimilarity (ie complementarity). A disadvantage is that the relationship between aggregate function and the contributions of each ESP is less clear. In contrast, the functional inventory method identifies how much function each ESP provides, which allows a quantitative assessment of redundancy. Using both approaches would provide the most complete (qualitative plus quantitative) and useful set of information to predict functional response to changing community composition (Kremen 2005).

■ How are we affecting our ecosystem services?

Two approaches exist for assessing how environmental factors that affect the magnitude and variability of ecosystem services vary across the landscape. Researchers could focus on the abundance of an important ESP, identified

through the functional inventory, or concentrate on the function as a whole, irrespective of fluctuations in individual ESPs. The choice of approach would be informed by the results of the functional inventory. If individual ESPs are highly uneven in their functional contributions (eg dominated by a single species; Solan *et al.* 2004), an ESP-centered approach would be most useful. In contrast, if there is little quantitative or qualitative differentiation among ESPs in their functional contributions, then a function-centered approach may be best. Finally, if interactions among ESPs are thought to greatly alter function, then a function-centered approach might be more practical, although both should perhaps be used (Kremen 2005).

■ Spatial and temporal scales

Understanding the spatial and temporal scales at which ecosystem services operate will be essential for developing landscape-level conservation and land management plans. How much of a watershed's area must be maintained as forest to provide clean water for downstream communities? How should patches of natural habitat be distributed within an agricultural landscape to provide pollination and pest control services for crops, and how variable is service provision between seasons and/or years? Conversely, up to what distances might adjacent land uses affect the capacity of forest and soil ecosystems to purify water, or of natural habitat to provide pest control and pollination services? For example, Houlahan and Findlay (2004) found that land uses up to several kilometers from wetlands affect water quality, but land-use planners typically rely on narrow forest buffers of < 30 m to purify water entering rivers, streams, and wetlands. The answers to these questions about flows from ecosystem services will determine how set-asides should be distributed, and areas zoned for different land uses, in order to protect and manage the service. Because environmental effects on services may be uncorrelated across scales, studies of services should ideally be conducted at multiple, nested spatial and temporal scales (Millennium Ecosystem Assessment 2003).

■ Bringing ecosystem services into markets, environmental policies, and land-use planning

Ecological information is needed in order to design both policies and markets properly. For example, legislation under the Clean Water Act requires that wetlands destroyed by development be created elsewhere. Developers can offset wetland destruction by purchasing credits in mitigation banks consisting of restored wetlands (Bean *et al.* 1999). It is notoriously difficult, however, to replicate the functional qualities of natural wetlands through restoration (Zedler and Callaway 1999). Variation in size, shape, location, connectivity, and species composition may also substantially alter the ability of the mitigated property to replace the functions formerly supplied by the destroyed one. Thus, a unit area in

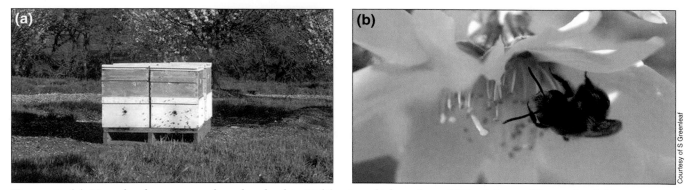

Figure 3. (a) *Honeybee boxes in an almond orchard in California, which produces 80% of the world's supply of this crop at an annual value of $1 billion. Each year, over a million colonies of honeybees are brought to California in February to pollinate almond, which cannot produce its fruit without the aide of an insect vector. Recent shortages of bee colonies have led famers to import honeybees all the way from Australia.* (b) *A wild, solitary bee* (Andrena cerasifolii), *pollinating almond in California, on a farm near wild habitat. Few wild bees are found on farms far from wild habitat* (C Kremen unpublished).

one mitigation bank may have a different ecological value than that in another, and ecological information should be used to govern allowed trades and influence market signals accordingly (Kremen 2005).

The use of local ecological data leads to valuations of marginal changes in services that can influence land-use decisions. For example, Guo *et al.* (2000) used ecological data to determine the relative importance of different forested habitats for water regulation in a Chinese watershed. They valued each unit of each habitat type by determining how it influenced units of water-flow regulation and hence electrical power generation at a hydroelectric plant. They then used this information to determine appropriate monetary compensation levels for landowners for not harvesting timber, based on the change in value of electrical power produced when a unit of a given habitat type was conserved rather than logged. Local-scale valuations of alternative land uses that include ecosystem services often show that the marginal benefits of conserving wild nature exceed those of land conversion and could be useful in determining best land-use practices (Kremen *et al.* 2000; Balmford *et al.* 2002; Turner *et al.* 2003). See Turner *et al.* (2003) for a review of various pitfalls in estimating economic values of ecosystem services.

Relatively few policies exist that provide incentives to protect ecosystem services. In the US, the Farm Bill now provides substantial funds for environmental conservation programs on farms and rangelands, including cost-sharing or direct payments for stewardship of soil, water, air, and wildlife habitat (www.usda.gov/farmbill/). Similar programs exist in the European Union and Australia. The Kyoto Protocol of the United Nations Framework Convention on Climate Change creates a mechanism for paying for the ecosystem service of carbon sequestration in agricultural and forest ecosystems. Even in the absence of such policies, markets for environmental services are emerging (reviewed in Landell-Mills and Porras 2002), using a variety of innovative mechanisms (Daily and Ellison 2002). Nonetheless, both policies and markets for ecosystem services are still in their infancy and much

work remains to be done to make these policies effective in promoting ecosystem services, including taking a systems approach that incorporates tradeoffs between services, developing monitoring and accounting techniques, creating appropriate incentive structures, developing better land management techniques, reducing transaction costs, and finding mechanisms to encourage cooperation between private and public land managers across landscapes (Landell-Mills and Porras 2002). Each of these components would benefit greatly from a deeper understanding of the underlying ecological processes controlling provision of ecosystem services (Figure 2).

■ Case studies

We present two case studies to illustrate how this approach of documenting the relationship between biodiversity change and ecosystem function in real landscapes across space and time can contribute to policies and plans for managing ecosystem services.

Pollination services for crops in Northern California

Many farmers obtain pollination services for their crops by renting colonies of honeybees (*Apis mellifera*), whose domiciles are readily transported between farm fields. In the US, the number of managed honeybee colonies declined by 1% per year, on average, over the past 50 years (Delaplane and Mayer 2000). Large die-offs in 2004 caused by parasitic mites (up to 50% in some areas; E Mussen pers comm) have led to pollinator shortages around the country. Similar reductions in availability of this key pollinator are occurring elsewhere in the world and it is clear that our heavy reliance on this single species is a risky strategy. Many other bee species, both solitary and social, also visit and pollinate crops (Figure 3), although relatively little is known about their importance. Could wild bee populations help to reduce this reliance on honeybees, and under what circumstances?

We have quantified the contributions of wild bees in

providing pollination services to watermelon, tomato, and sunflower crops in Northern California by measuring their pollination efficiencies (pollen deposited or seeds set per visit) and visitation rates (Kremen *et al.* 2002). Different but overlapping guilds of pollinators service each crop, and species contribute differentially within and between crops (eg Figure 4a). We found that wild bee communities alone (without the addition of managed honeybees) can provide partial or complete pollination services (Kremen *et al.* 2002) or enhance the services provided by honeybees through behavioral interactions (Greenleaf 2005). However, these services are rapidly eroded (Figure 4b) in response to agricultural intensification, which leads to a two-fold decline in mean richness and abundance of wild bee pollinators (Kremen *et al.* 2002). Extinction order is important; the most efficient pollinators are also the most sensitive to agricultural intensification (Larsen *et al.* 2005). In addition, density compensation does not appear to take place (Greenleaf 2005; Larsen *et al.* 2005). The proportion of wild habitat (chaparral and oak-woodland) within several kilometers of a farm is the environmental variable most strongly associated with the magnitude and stability of services, and the diversity, abundance, and productivity of foraging and nesting bees (Kremen *et al.* 2004; Greenleaf 2005; Kim *et al.* in press; Figure 5).

These findings have important economic implications. Farmers who do not have wild bees occurring naturally on their farms rent honeybees from beekeepers at considerable cost (Kremen *et al.* 2002; Figure 5). Farmers who have wild bees are partially or fully protected from sudden or gradual scarcities of honeybee colonies, whereas farmers that cannot obtain pollination services from either managed or wild pollinators may need to switch to production of crops that do not require pollination services (Southwick and Southwick Jr 1992). When pollinator shortages occur, consumers can therefore expect to pay much more for the animal-pollinated food products that constitute 15–30% of our diet (Southwick and Southwick Jr 1992).

We can use these findings, particularly the relationship between wild bee pollination services and natural habitat, to establish targets for conservation and restoration (Kremen *et al.* 2004). We have developed restoration and farm management protocols based on availability of key floral resources in natural and farmed areas of the landscape (Vaughan *et al.* 2004). We are creating spatially explicit models based on floral resource availability, bees' resource needs, and bee foraging scales, to develop alternative scenarios for managing the agro-natural landscape for pollination function. For example, could we improve pollination services equally well through landscape-scale restoration of native habitat patches off-farm, or by local-scale habitat enhancements compatible with farm management practices on-farm? Finally, we are providing this ecological information to landowners and land managers

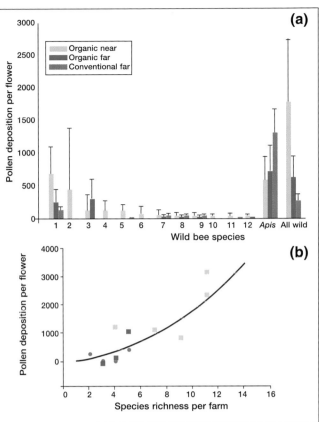

Figure 4. *Pollination services by wild bee communities to watermelon in Northern California. (a) Pollination contributions (mean pollen deposited in the lifetime of a flower, with standard error) from different species on three different farm types; farms were either conventional (using pesticides), organic (no pesticides), and far from or near to natural habitat. Each number on the x axis refers to a different species or genus of bee, ranked in order of their contributions on organic–near farms; the contribution of the honeybee (Apis) and the summed contributions of all wild bees are also shown. A flower must receive about 1000 grains of pollen to set a marketable fruit. The most important contributors either decline in abundance, and thus contribution (eg number 1), or are lost with increasing agricultural intensification (numbers 2–6). Only organic near farms could meet all the pollination needs of watermelon from wild bee pollination alone (see Total) (adapted from Kremen et al. 2002). (b) A power function with exponent >1 is the best fit to the relationship between pollination function and species richness on different farm sites, suggesting that pollination services erode rapidly as species are lost from the system (adapted from Larsen et al. 2005).*

through workshops, manuals, and demonstration sites on farms.

Lyme disease risk in the northeastern US

A similar framework has been applied to assess the role of vertebrate diversity in protecting humans from exposure to the most common vector-borne disease in the US, Lyme disease (LD). The causative agent of LD, the spirochete bacterium *Borrelia burgdorferi*, is transmitted

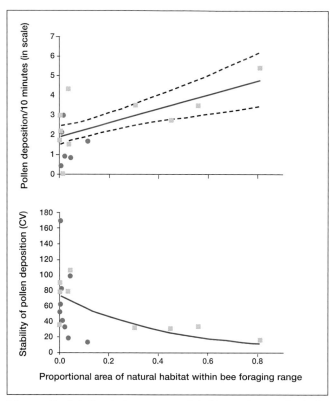

Figure 5. (a) Proximity to natural habitat enhances both the magnitude and stability of pollination services provided by wild bees to crops on organic (green squares) and conventional (orange circles) farms (Adapted from Kremen et al. 2004).

between hosts (including humans) by blood-feeding ticks (*Ixodes scapularis* in eastern and central North America). Ticks must acquire an infection during their initial (larval) blood meal in order to transmit the bacteria during the later (nymphal) meal. These ticks feed from dozens of different species of vertebrates, but the host species differ dramatically in their probability of infecting a feeding tick (Ostfeld 1997; Ostfeld and Keesing 2000).

We have quantified three host attributes that are essential in estimating species-specific roles affecting risk of human exposure to LD: (1) how many ticks an average individual of each species hosts in a given season; (2) how many host individuals occur per species per unit area; and (3) the probability that a tick feeding from a member of each host species will become infected. Together, these attributes tell us how many ticks are supported by each host species and what proportion of those ticks will become infected. Different species of mammal and bird have radically different roles influencing LD risk; white-footed mice (*Peromyscus leucopus*) infect enormous numbers of ticks, whereas most other hosts serve a protective role by acting as hosts for, but not infecting, many ticks (Figure 6a; LoGiudice et al. 2003).

Knowledge of species-specific roles in influencing exposure risk allows us to predict how risk will change as host community diversity declines. Computer simulations in which we removed host species in different sequences revealed how important the order of species loss is in influencing the ability of vertebrate communities to reduce disease risk to humans. Removal of species in entirely random order caused disease risk to decrease with decreasing diversity. However, the species most competent in pathogen transmission, the white-footed mouse, is highly resilient to habitat destruction and fragmentation, and even increases in abundance as habitat is fragmented and other vertebrate predators or competitors are lost (Nupp and Swihart 1996; Krohne and Hoch 1999). All simulations that incorporated the realistic scenario that mice are among the last species to be lost concluded that LD risk decreases strongly with increasing host diversity – in other words, high diversity communities perform a useful service by diluting the disease risk to humans (LoGiudice et al. 2003; Ostfeld et al. In press). Furthermore, imposition of different "rules" by which vertebrate communities disassemble under habitat destruction caused markedly different rates and patterns of increase in disease risk (Figure 6b). For example, using trophic level to determine the extinction sequence (from high to low trophic level) resulted in an initial decline in LD risk with species loss, followed by a marked increase as the final few species disappeared. Applying a sequence of species loss derived from empirical studies in fragmented landscapes of the midwestern US resulted in a pattern quite similar to the assumption that mice are always present (Figure 6b). Empirical studies confirm that LD risk, as measured by both proportion of ticks infected and numbers of infected ticks, is significantly higher in the smallest fragments that lacked diverse vertebrate communities (less than 2 ha in size; Allen et al. 2003). Wooded fragments of this size are typical of high-end suburbia, where it is common for people to be infected simply by spending time in their backyards. The social and economic implications of infection include diminished quality of life, school days missed, lost wages from illness, and medical insurance and treatment costs. This argues for planning landscapes to maintain larger forests with greater disease dilution capacity.

■ Conclusions

Managing for ecosystem services can have enormous scope, both for human welfare and conservation of biodiversity. For example, many major cities manage nearby forested watersheds for services (Heal 2000), and it is estimated that 13% of the terrestrial land surface could be managed for urban water use alone (Reid 2001). Now that the Kyoto Protocol has been ratified, it could potentially finance the reforestation of 3.4 million hectares per year for carbon sequestration in developing countries (Niles et al. 2002).

To manage ecosystem services in the future, we need to develop a better understanding of their underlying ecology, and use it to: (1) develop better market signals for ecosystem services, (2) create better economic strategies and environmental policies for their conservation and sustainable use, (3) understand tradeoffs between policies and practices that promote different services, and (4) develop management and conservation plans for services

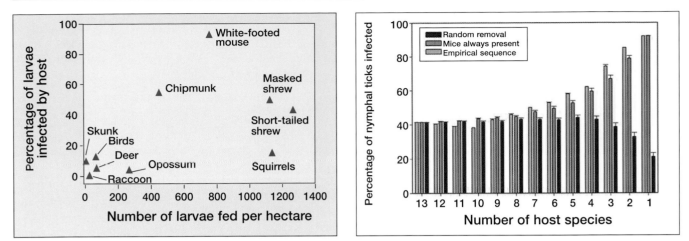

Figure 6. (a) Position of 13 species or species-groups representing two dimensions of species-specific effects on risk of human exposure to Lyme disease. Percentage of larvae infected by each host species (ie its reservoir competence) represents the probability that a feeding (uninfected) larval tick will acquire infection with the bacterial agent of Lyme disease (Borrelia burgdorferi). Number of larvae fed per hectare represents the product of the average larval burden per individual member of each species and the estimated population density of that species (Modified from Ostfeld et al. in press.). (b) Simulations showing the consequences of three different extinction scenarios in vertebrate communities for the risk of exposure to Lyme disease, as measured by infection prevalence in nymphal ticks. In all cases, initial host communities included all 13 species or species groups. In the "random removal" scenario, species were selected for removal in random sequence. In the "mice always present" scenario, mice never went extinct (see text), and all other species were selected for extinction in random sequence. For the "empirical sequence" scenario, the order of species loss approximated that observed in fragments of decreasing size in the midwestern US (see references in LoGiudice et al. 2003). Error bars represent standard errors from 100 simulations for each extinction scenario.

at the whole-system level (Figure 2).

Conducting the necessary research to develop a sufficient understanding of the ecology of ecosystem services is feasible, but it may require an investment akin to that devoted to agriculture, medicine, space exploration, or defense. Ecologists will need to mount a massive awareness campaign, aimed at the public and policy makers, to convince society of the importance of ecosystem services and to demand the resources necessary to study them (Robertson and Swinton 2005). Conducting this ecological research not in isolation, but as an integrated component of teams comprising a diversity of both scientific disciplines and resource users (Biggs *et al.* 2004, Maass and Balvanera 2005) would provide a mechanism for broad dissemination of knowledge and set the stage for adaptive management (Sayer and Campbell 2004). The agenda we propose is a tall order – but nothing less than the future of humans, and that of many other creatures, is at stake.

■ References

Allan BF, Keesing F, and Ostfeld RS. 2003. Effects of habitat fragmentation on Lyme disease risk. *Conserv Biol* **17**: 267–72.

Balmford A, Bruner A, Cooper P, *et al.* 2002. Ecology – economic reasons for conserving wild nature. *Science* **297**: 950–53.

Balmford A, Green RE, and Jenkins M. 2003. Measuring the changing state of nature. *Trends Ecol Evol* **18**: 326–30.

Balvanera P, Daily GC, Ehrlich PR, *et al.* 2001. Conserving biodiversity and ecosystem services: conflict or reinforcement? *Science* **291**: 2047.

Balvanera P, Kremen C, and Martinez-Ramos M. 2005. Applying community structure analysis to ecosystem function: examples from pollination and carbon storage. *Ecol Appl* **15**: 360–75.

Bean M, Bonnie R, and Wilcove DS. 1999. Mitigation banking as an endangered species conservation tool. New York, NY: Environmental Defense Fund. A report by Environmental Defense Fund and Sustainable Conservation.

Biggs RE, Bohensky PV, Desanker C, *et al.* 2004. Nature supporting people: the South African Millennium Ecosystem Assessment. Pretoria, South Africa: Council for Scientific and Industrial Research.

Cardinale BJ, Harvey CT, Gross K, and Ives AR. 2003. Biodiversity and biocontrol: emergent impacts of a multi-enemy assemblage on pest suppression and crop yield in an agroecosystem. *Ecol Lett* **6**: 857–65.

Daily G and Ellison K. 2002. The economy of nature. Washington, DC: Island Press.

Daily GC. 1997. Nature's services: societal dependence on natural ecosystems. Washington, DC: Island Press.

Daily GC, Soderqvist T, Aniyar S, *et al.* 2000. Ecology: the value of nature and the nature of value. *Science* **289**: 395–96.

Delaplane KS and Mayer DF. 2000. Crop pollination by bees. New York, NY: CABI Publishing.

Diaz S, Symstad AJ, Chapin FSI, *et al.* 2003. Functional diversity revealed by removal experiments. *Trends Ecol Evol* **18**: 140–46.

Folke C, Holling CS, and Perrings C. 1996. Biological diversity, ecosystems, and the human scale. *Ecol Appl* **6**: 1018–24.

Greenleaf SAS. 2005. Local-scale and foraging-scale affect bee community abundances, species richness, and pollination services in Northern California. Princeton, NJ: Princeton University Press.

Guo ZW, Xiao XM, and Li DM. 2000. An assessment of ecosystem services: water flow regulation and hydroelectric power production. *Ecol Appl* **10**: 925–36.

Heal G. 2000. Nature and the marketplace: capturing the value of ecosystem services. Covelo, CA: Island Press.

Houlahan J and Findlay CS. 2004. Estimating the "critical" distance at which adjacent land-use degrades wetland water and sediment quality. *Landscape Ecol* **19**: 677–90.

Jonsson M and Malmqvist B. 2003. Mechanisms behind positive diversity effects on ecosystem functioning: testing the facilitation and interference hypotheses. *Oecologia* **134**: 554–59.

Kim J, Williams N, and Kremen C. Effects of cultivation and proximity to natural habitat on ground-nesting native bees in California sunflower fields. *J Kansas Entomol Soc*. In press.

Kremen C. 2005. Managing ecosystem services: what do we need to know about their ecology? *Ecol Lett* **8**: 468–79.

Kremen C, Niles J, Dalton OMG, *et al*. 2000. Economic incentives for rain forest conservation across scales. *Science* **288**: 1828–32.

Kremen C, Raymond I, and Lance K. 1998. An interdisciplinary tool for monitoring conservation impacts in Madagascar. *Conserv Biol* **12**: 549–63.

Kremen C, Williams NM, Bugg RL, *et al*. 2004. The area requirements of an ecosystem service: crop pollination by native bee communities in California. *Ecol Lett* **7**: 1109–19.

Kremen C, Williams NM, and Thorp RW. 2002. Crop pollination from native bees at risk from agricultural intensification. *Proc Natl Acad Sci USA* **99**: 16812–16.

Krohne DT and Hoch GA. 1999. Demography of *Peromyscus leucopus* populations on habitat patches: the role of dispersal. *Can J Zoolog* **77**: 1247–53.

Kruess A and Tscharntke T. 1994. Habitat fragmentation, species loss, and biological control. *Science* **264**: 1581–84.

Landell-Mills N and Porras T. 2002. Silver bullet or fools' gold?: a global review of markets for forest environmental services and their impact on the poor. London, UK: International Institute for Environment and Development.

Larsen TH, Williams N, and Kremen C. 2005. Extinction order and altered community structure rapidly disrupt ecosystem functioning. *Ecol Lett* **8**: 538–47.

Limburg KE and Folke C. 1999. The ecology of ecosystem services: introduction to the special issue. *Ecol Econ* **29**: 179–82.

LoGiudice K, Ostfeld RS, Schmidt KA, and Keesing F. 2003. The ecology of infectious disease: effects of host diversity and community composition on Lyme disease risk. *Proc Natl Acad Sci USA* **100**: 567–71.

Loreau M, Naeem S, Inchausti P, *et al*. 2001. Biodiversity and ecosystem functioning: current knowledge and future challenges. *Science* **294**: 804–08.

Maass J, Balvanera PCA, Daily G, *et al*. 2005. Ecosystem services of tropical dry forests: insights from long-term ecological and social research on the Pacific Coast of Mexico. *Ecol Soc* **10**: 17.

Margules CR and Pressey RL. 2000. Systematic conservation planning. *Nature* **405**: 243–53.

Memmott J, Waser NM, and Price MV. 2004. Tolerance of pollination networks to species extinctions. *P Roy Soc Lon B Biol Sci* **271**: 2605–11.

Millennium Ecosystem Assessment. 2003. Ecosystems and human well-being: a framework for assessment. Washington DC: Island Press.

Niles JO, Brown S, Pretty J, *et al*. 2002. Potential carbon mitigation and income in developing countries from changes in use and management of agricultural and forest lands. *Philos T Roy Soc A* **360**: 1621–39.

Nupp TE and Swihart RK. 1996. Effect of forest patch area on population attributes of white-footed mice (*Peromyscus leucopus*). *Can J Zoolog* **74**: 467–72.

Ostfeld RS. 1997. The ecology of Lyme disease risk. *Am Sci* **85**: 338–46.

Ostfeld RS and Keesing F. 2000. The function of biodiversity in the ecology of vector-borne zoonotic diseases. *Can J Zoolog* **78**: 2061–78.

Ostfeld RS, Keesing F, and LoGiudice K. Community ecology meets epidemiology: the case of Lyme disease. In: Collinge SK and Ray C (Eds). Disease ecology: community structure and pathogen dynamics. Oxford, UK: Oxford University Press. In press.

Ostfeld RS and LoGiudice K. 2003. Community disassembly, biodiversity loss, and the erosion of an ecosystem service. *Ecology* **84**: 1421–27.

Palmer ME, Bernhardt E, Chornesky S *et al*. 2004. Ecology for a crowded planet. *Science* **304**: 1251–52.

Petchey OL and Gaston KJ. 2002. Extinction and the loss of functional diversity. *P Roy Soc Lond B Bio* **269**: 1721–27.

Power ME, Tilman D, Estes JA, *et al*. 1996. Challenges in the quest for keystones. *BioScience* **46**: 609–20.

Reid WV. 2001. Capturing the value of ecosystem services to protect biodiversity. In: Hollowell VC (Ed). Managing human-dominated ecosystems. St Louis, MO: Missouri Botanical Garden Press.

Robertson GP and Swinton SM. 2005. Reconciling agricultural productivity and environmental integrity: a grand challenge for agriculture. *Front Ecol Environ* **3**: 38–46.

Sayer J and Campbell B. 2004. The science of sustainable development: local livelihoods and the global environment. Cambridge, UK: Cambridge University Press.

Schindler DW. 1990. Experimental perturbations of whole lakes as tests of hypotheses concerning ecosystem structure and function. *Oikos* **57**: 25–41.

Schwartz MW, Brigham CA, Hoeksema JD, *et al*. 2000. Linking biodiversity to ecosystem function: implications for conservation ecology. *Oecologia* **122**: 297–305.

Solan M, Cardinale BJ, Downing AL, *et al*. 2004. Extinction and ecosystem function in the marine benthos. *Science* **306**: 1177–80.

Southwick EE and Southwick JRL. 1992. Estimating the economic value of honey bees (*Hymenoptera: Apidae*) as agricultural pollinators in the United States. *J Econ Entomol* **85**: 621–33.

Symstad AJ, Chapin FS, Wall DH, *et al*. 2003. Long-term and large-scale perspectives on the relationship between biodiversity and ecosystem functioning. *BioScience* **53**: 89–98.

Tilman D, Lehman CL, and Bristow CE. 1998. Diversity–stability relationships: Statistical inevitability or ecological consequence? *Am Nat* **151**: 277–82.

Turner RK, Paavola J, Cooper P, *et al*. 2003. Valuing nature: lessons learned and future research directions. *Ecol Econ* **46**: 493–510.

Vaughan M, Shepard M, Kremen C, and Black SH. 2004. Farming for bees: guidelines for providing native bee habitat on farms. Portland, OR: The Xerces Society.

Vitousek PM, Mooney HA, Lubchenco J, and Melillo JM. 1997. Human domination of Earth's ecosystems. *Science* **277**: 494–99.

Walker B, Kinzig A, and Langridge J. 1999. Plant attribute diversity, resilience, and ecosystem function: the nature and significance of dominant and minor species. *Ecosystems* **2**: 95–113.

Zavaleta ES and Hulvey KB. 2004. Realistic species losses disproportionately reduce grassland resistance to biological invaders. *Science* **306**: 1175–77.

Zedler JB and Callaway JC. 1999. Tracking wetland restoration: do mitigation sites follow desired trajectories? *Restor Ecol* **7**: 69–73.

Zhu Y, Chen H, Fan J, Wang Y, *et al*. 2000. Genetic diversity and disease control in rice. *Nature* **406**: 718–22.

Lyme disease: a case about ecosystem services

Courtney Richmond[1], Diane Ebert-May[2], and Janet Hodder[3]

One way to help students develop critical thinking skills is to focus on problems or cases where they are challenged to deal with real data and experiences (Bransford *et al.* 2004). Both problem-based learning and case studies allow students to develop the intellectual capacity to deal with complex issues, build confidence and willingness to approach topics from multiple perspectives, and encourage communication with scientists and peers from other disciplines. Students often compartmentalize content and process knowledge by discipline, whereas an interdisciplinary approach allows them to draw from multiple resources in the life sciences, mathematics, social sciences, and other disciplines. The literature is rich with examples and methods for using case studies (see References) and the majority of authors agree that if a case study is to be useful pedagogically, it must serve a specific function for the course and students. Such focus provides students with a more efficient means of achieving specific learning goals as compared to the traditional lecture approach (Herreid 1994, 1998).

Kremen and Ostfeld's paper on ecosystem services (pp 540–48) contains two case studies that provide examples of how ecological data are not often collected or interpreted in isolation. We use the Lyme disease case study to demonstrate how real data can be used to teach complex topics, while enabling students to discover how a number of disciplines can inform ecological issues. This activity is designed for an ecology course but could also be used as part of an introductory biology course.

■ Student goals

- Identify the issues and interdisciplinary components of a case study.
- Analyze data to develop a management strategy about a case study.
- Find information from scientific sources that increases knowledge about the case.
- Interrelate the ecological concepts of ecosystem services, biodiversity, functional diversity, community disassembly, and landscape ecology.
- Work productively and collaboratively in a team.

■ Instructor goals

- Design instruction using an interdisciplinary case study.
- Expose students to complex ecological concepts.

[1]Rowan University, [2]Michigan State University, [3]University of Oregon.

■ Instructional design

Problem posing: analyzing a case

Begin with a mini-lecture that includes background information on Lyme disease: for example, a brief description of the disease, how it is spread by ticks, a general description of tick life cycles, and a primer on the many possible hosts that ticks feed on, including a brief explanation about differential rates of transmission of the Lyme disease spirochete between different hosts and ticks (resources in References). In groups of two to four, students are asked, "How would you manage the problem of Lyme disease to reduce the prevalence of infected ticks?" Students are given four pieces of data to develop their management strategy (Panel 1) and to support it with evidence.

A subset of groups reports out (one minute per group) their proposed management strategy to the class. The instructor lists the different strategies on poster-size post-its; those groups who do not report identify which of the strategies most closely approximates their own. One individual from each group (ie the recorder) adds a check mark (or small post-it) to the appropriate poster. This formative assessment enables the instructor to determine students' initial level of understanding about the case and allows groups to evaluate their ideas in relation to their peers.

Next, students read the Lyme disease case study in Kremen and Ostfeld, and are told that they may include other information in the paper to revise the details of their management plan. As a tool to guide their thinking, each group generates a "Know/Need to Know" table (http://serc.carleton.edu/introgeo/icbl/strategy4.html), finds the additional information they "need to know" from scientific resources, cites the resources under the appropriate "need", and submits both the table and citations with their revised management plan. In addition, if the instructor has access to a classroom management system such as Blackboard, Angel, or WebCT, each group could post one unique (not already posted) citation on the course website as part of the homework.

Assessing student learning

Each group's revised management strategy should reflect students' comprehension of the case study and ability to use information to support recommendations to address the problem. The rubric in Panel 2 shows the criteria of an exemplary response that is provided to students before they begin the case study. "Adequate" and "Needs Improvement" categories are scaled down in terms of

---

Panel 1. Information provided to students for Lyme disease case study

- Graph of the number of tick larvae fed per hectare and the percentage of larvae fed per host species (Kremen and Ostfeld, p 546, Figure 6a)
- Graph of the relationship between forest fragment size and tick infection rates (Allan *et al.* 2003, Figure 1)
- Graph of the relationship between species richness and tick infection rates (Schmidt and Ostfeld 2001, Figure 2)
- The order in which species disappear in a system as it "disassembles" (LoGiudice *et al.* 2003, Figure 1)

First to disappear	Tree squirrels and *Sorex* shrews
	Short-tailed shrews, four species of ground-nesting birds
	Raccoons, opossums, and skunks
	Chipmunks and white-tailed deer
Last to disappear	White-footed mice

---

content, accuracy, and possible points from the "Exemplary" level response. Additional questions on exams should provide further insight to student thinking. For example:

- Why are intact, unfragmented ecosystems associated with a lower prevalence of Lyme disease?
- Use the first case study in Kremen and Ostfeld ("Pollination services for crops in Northern California", p 544) to answer the question of how and why the proportion of natural (wild) habitat surrounding a farm affects pollination services.

■ Final note

The literature on case studies is extensive, and this article represents only the tip of the iceberg in their use by students as a means to practice the analysis of information to comprehend and address interdisciplinary problems. The instructor could include many other goals and

---

Panel 2. Rubric for assessment of the management plan

Criteria for an "Exemplary" level response are provided. "Adequate" and "Needs Improvement" levels of responses are scaled down based on inclusion of content, accuracy, and possible points. Actual scoring depends on the relative weight of the assignment in the context of the course evaluation. A reference to rubrics for cooperative groups is provided.

Comprehension and analysis

- Identifies all of the issues and interdisciplinary components of the case (from the "Know" list)
- Accurately interprets data provided and uses it to support the management strategy
- Demonstrates ability to identify additional information they would "Need to Know" to build a better management strategy
- Selects appropriate citations that answer all of the "Need to Know" questions in the table
- Uses proper grammar and appropriate style in the management plan
- Group functioned as a productive team; each individual contributed (Nagel *et al.* 2005)

---

resources, thereby expanding the case over a series of classes. For example, this Lyme disease case study interconnects the ecological literature on biodiversity and ecosystem services with conservation issues, private property rights, economic concerns for developers or others likely to be negatively impacted by certain management options, and the environmental ethics that arise when human and environmental interests are at odds. Assessment data are collected at multiple points during the case study, to provide both students and the instructor with ongoing feedback about learning.

■ Acknowledgements

We thank the National Science Foundation for their long-term support of the FIRST project, Faculty Institutes for Reforming Science Teaching (DUE 0088847). All Pathways papers are peer reviewed.

■ References

Allan BE, Keesing F, and Ostfeld RS. 2003. Effect of forest fragmentation on Lyme disease risk. *Conserv Biol* **17**: 267–72.

Bransford J, Vye N, and Bateman H. 2004. Creating high-quality learning environments: guidelines from research on how people learn. In: Graham PA and Stacey NG (Eds). The knowledge economy and postsecondary education: report of a workshop. Washington, DC: National Academy Press.

Herreid CF. 1994. Case studies in science: a novel method of science education. *J Coll Sci Teach* **23**: 221–29.

Herreid CF. 1998. What makes a good case study? *J Coll Sci Teach* **27**: 163–65.

LoGiudice K, Ostfeld RS, Schmidt KA, and Keesing F. 2003. The ecology of infectious disease: effects of host diversity and community composition on Lyme disease risk. *P Natl Acad Sci* **100**: 567–71.

Nagel LM, Ebert-May D, Weber EP, and Hodder J. 2005. Learning through peer assessment. *Front Ecol Environ* **3**: 390–91.

Schmidt KA and Ostfeld RS. 2001. Biodiversity and the dilution effect in disease ecology. *Ecology* **82**: 609–19.

Online case study resources

The Starting Point project. http://serc.carleton.edu/introgeo/icbl/what.html.

National Center for Case Study Teaching in Science. http://ublib.buffalo.edu/libraries/projects/cases/case.html

Additional sources about Lyme disease

Centers for Disease Control and Prevention on Lyme Disease. http://www.cdc.gov/ncidod/dvbid/lyme/.

ESA Electronic Data Archive. http://www.esapubs.org/archive/. Washington, DC: Ecological Society of America. Archive No E084-035-A1.

Ostfeld RS and Keesing F. 2000. Biodiversity and disease risk: the case of Lyme disease. *Conserv Biol* **14**: 722–28.

Ostfeld RS and LoGiudice K. 2003. Community disassembly, biodiversity loss, and the erosion of an ecosystem service. *Ecology* **84**: 1421–27.

Ostfeld RS. Institute of Ecosystem Studies web site on Lyme disease. www.ecostudies.org/IES_lyme_disease.html. Viewed 24 October 2005.

Students: Reading Science

Overview

How often have you assigned reading for students to complete before class, and they arrive unprepared or unable to demonstrate their comprehension of the material? One learning outcome for students in the sciences is ensuring that they can both read and comprehend current literature. Too often, students in introductory biology courses are not presented opportunities to read beyond the textbook, and when they do have the chance, they view it as a solitary experience without discussion with others. In this chapter, we draw upon the power of a cooperative learning strategy—called a "jigsaw"—that promotes a learner-centered classroom in which students can practice higher-level thinking. Each member of a group becomes an expert about a particular paper or section of a paper assigned for homework and shares that expertise with their group in class the next day.

Implementation of a jigsaw may be simple or logistically complex, depending on the student learning goals and relative importance of the assignment. Here, two different applications of a jigsaw are described as cooperative learning strategies for dealing with large amounts of complex material, facilitating students' interpretation of scientific literature, and moving students toward analysis and synthesis using models. The quality of the learning community evolving in the classroom will influence the productivity of the cooperative groups in all situations. The more practice that groups have in doing and thinking about science, the more confidence and autonomy they will demonstrate. These outcomes are measurable via student surveys (Baldwin et al. 1999) and actual performance assessments.

Human-induced long-term changes in the lakes of the Jianghan Plain, Central Yangtze

Jingyun Fang, Sheng Rao, and Shuqing Zhao

The Jianghan Plain, located in the Central Yangtze area of China, is famous for its freshwater lakes, but these have undergone dramatic changes in area and number as a result of increasing human activity. We analyze the changes in lakes with an area ≥1 km² from the 1950s to 1998, using historical land-cover information and remote sensing data. The changes showed two distinct periods: the 1950s–1978 and 1978–1998. During the former period, the number of lakes fell from 414 to 250 (–39.6%) and total area decreased from 3885.4 km² to 1839.1 km² (–52.7%). During the latter period, the number of lakes rose, from 250 to 258 (+3.2%), while the area covered increased from 1839.1 km² to 2144.4 km² (+16.6%). The rapid fall in numbers of lakes from the 1950s to 1978 was largely attributed to extensive impoldering (land reclamation through draining techniques), resulting in substantial negative ecological consequences, such as increased flooding and a decline in biodiversity. In contrast, the increase in lake numbers and area from 1978 to 1998 was mainly due to the implementation of government policy prohibiting impoldering along the Yangtze River, and the return of inundated arable lands for aquaculture by local people.

Front Ecol Environ 2005; 3(4): 186–192

Freshwater lakes store renewable freshwater for human use and provide habitats for aquatic fauna and flora (Johnson *et al.* 2001). Despite their value, freshwater lakes have been greatly modified and degraded by human activities (Beeton 2002; Bronmark and Hansson 2002). How freshwater lakes change as a result of human activities, and the ecological consequences of those changes, has received increasing attention (Richter *et al.* 1997; Wilcove *et al.* 1998), but there have been surprisingly few studies conducted at the decadal time scale in heavily populated regions.

Central Yangtze (China) is an ideal place to study human-induced changes in freshwater lakes and their ecological consequences. As the human population grew, impoldering, a type of land conversion that encroaches on lakes and their associated wetlands for agricultural purposes, through the construction of dikes for agricultural purposes, became a major human activity in the region. This land reclamation practice was accelerated from the early 1950s to the late 1970s (Shi 1989), resulting in substantial negative consequences including increased flooding, decreased lake and wetland area, and a decline in biodiversity (Zhao *et al.* 2005).

The Jianghan Plain was the site of a historically famous swamp, *Yun-meng Ze* (cloud-dream swamp), which experienced extensive impoldering before the end of the 1970s, resulting in rapid loss of lake area. In the early 1950s, there were 1332 lakes greater than approximately 0.07 km² in size

(roughly equal to 100 *mu*, the Chinese unit of area) and 322 lakes greater than about 3.5 km² (Hydroelectric Bureau of Hubei Province 1991). However, there are now fewer than 300 lakes covering an area of more than 1 km². Although some studies have investigated shrinkage of lakes in some parts of the Jianghan Plain (Li and Zhang 1997), no integrated analysis on the changes in size and number of lakes, and the possible causes, has been conducted for the Plain as a whole on a decadal scale.

In this study, we used five decades of historical land-cover information and remote sensing data to (1) estimate changes in the size and number of the lakes in the Jianghan Plain from the 1950s to 1998, and (2) explore the causes of these changes and their ecological consequences.

■ Study site and methods

Site description

The Jianghan Plain is located in the northern part of the Central Yangtze River drainage basin, Hubei Province, China, and ranges from 28° 08' to 30° 08' N in latitude and from 111°12' to 114°47' E in longitude, with an altitude of <40 m in most parts (Figure 1). It is the largest plain in south China, encompassing a total area of 55 456 km² and 25 counties/cities. Geologically, it stems from the lower Yangtze and Hunan-Hubei-Guizhou platform and the old Jianghan basin of the late Paleozoic, and was formed in the past several hundred years by depositions from the Yangtze River and Han River (Liu 1994). The climate is subtropical, with an annual precipitation of 1000–1500 mm, and a mean annual temperature of 16.5°C (Cai and Du 2000). The zonal vegetation formerly consisted mainly of ever-

Department of Ecology, College of Environmental Sciences and Key Laboratory for Earth Surface Processes of the Ministry of Education, Peking University, Beijing, China, 100871 (jyfang@urban.pku.edu.cn)

green broadleaf forests and deciduous and evergreen broadleaf mixed forests, but almost all of these natural forests were logged. Currently, only small fragments of the zonal vegetation remain in hilly areas and the dominant natural vegetation in the plain consists of meadow and marsh communities. The zonal soil types include yellow-brown soil and red soil, but have been replaced with cropland and paddy soils in most areas (Liu 1994).

The Jianghan Plain contains a large number of lakes, most of which are dammed and fluvial lakes. Prior to impoldering, these lakes played an important role in flood mitigation, as well as providing water for drinking, irrigation, and aquaculture. Because this area supports a large and continuously growing human population, however, many lakes have been reclaimed for agricultural and aquaculture use. Consequently, the regional environment has been greatly altered over the past 50 years.

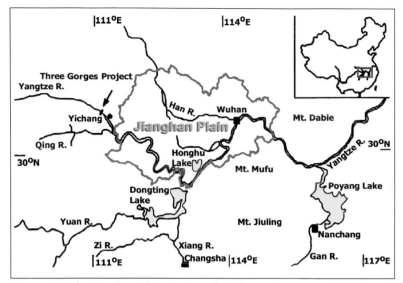

Figure 1. *The Jianghan Plain is situated in the northern part of the Central Yangtze River basin, Hubei Province, China.*

Data and data processing

In this study, we focused on Jianghan Plain lakes greater than 1 km^2 in size, since smaller lakes could not be effectively quantified using remote sensing imagery. The numbers and surface area measurements of these lakes from the 1950s to 1998 were acquired from historical land-cover information and remote-sensing data. The data used in this study spanned approximately 50 years, divided into three periods: the 1950s, 1978, and 1998. The land-cover data for the 1950s were obtained from 17 land-cover maps with topography information (scale 1:200 000, spanning from 1955 to 1959, with a mean of year 1957), which was surveyed from November-February by the China Army General Consultation. Land-cover information from the 1970s onwards was acquired from cloud-free Landsat remote-sensing images: Landsat Multispectral Scanner (MSS) data for 1978 and Landsat Thematic Mapper (TM) data for 1998. Both Landsat MSS and TM data were obtained from China's Satellite Ground Station and the Center of Remote Sensing, the Institute of Petroleum Survey and Design, China (further details available from the corresponding author).

Because the time of year (eg dry or rainy season) significantly affects topographies and remote sensing imagery, every effort was made to collect data on lake surface area during specific periods. As a result, most of the images used in this study were from the dry season (October–December), and a few from September; historical land-cover maps with topography information were also from the dry season (November–February). Therefore, the different data sources used were consistent within specific seasons.

Each of the 17 historical maps from the 1950s was scanned into digital images at 600 dots per inch, giving a ground resolution of approximately 10 m. The land-cover

maps showing topography for the 1950s contained 40–55 land-cover types with clear boundaries. Because we focused on the changes in surface area of the original lakes, the final classification consisted of only two categories, water and non-water. We reclassified these 40–55 land-cover types into water and non-water types, first through visual interpretation, then by tracing the boundary of each water body using GIS software (Founder drawing 5.5). Vector maps of the land-cover maps were transferred to ArcView GIS software, and resampled to a resolution of 90 m x 90 m, making them comparable with those obtained by remote sensing. The image processing software ERDAS 8.4 was then used to classify the land-cover types, in order to acquire information about the Jianghan Plain lakes. To provide consistency of band spectrums for different sensors of MSS and TM, the Landsat data were interpreted using similar band combinations with RGB (MSS bands 6, 7, 5, and TM bands 4, 5, 3). All images were geo-referenced according to 1:50 000 topographical maps, and the TM images (30 m x 30 m) were degraded and resampled to a resolution of 90 m x 90 m.

The quality of the classified products is critical to the analyses of the lake changes over time. We used the method of Jensen (1996) to assess the accuracy of the classified imagery products, based on field surveys and existing lake and reservoir distribution maps of Hubei Province. The resulting classification accuracy of water bodies for 1978 and 1998 was 82% and 86%, respectively, suggesting that the classified imagery products were of high quality. Land cover information for the 1950s was obtained directly from the land-cover maps and our classification consisted of only water and non-water categories; classified products for the 1950s were therefore very precise.

The classified water-body maps (Figure 2) were exported to the ArcView GIS software. We eliminated areas occupied by rivers, and retained only information on the lakes by referencing existing lakes, water body shape, and the lake and reservoir distribution map of Hubei Province. The

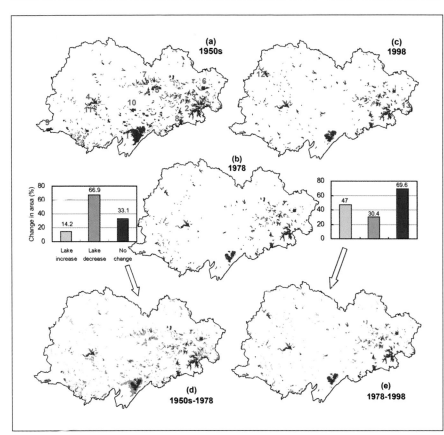

Figure 2. *Distribution of lakes in the Jianghan Plain for three periods, (a) the 1950s, (b) 1978, and (c) 1998, and overlaps of (d) the 1950s–1978, and (e) 1978–1998. The overlaps illustrate spatial distribution of lake-size decreases, increases, and areas where no change has occurred between the two periods. Insets indicate change in area (%) for the 1950s–1978 and 1978–1998. During the 1950s–1978, there was a net loss of 52.7% (inset of Figure 2d), while between 1978 and 1998, the lake area showed a net increase of 16.6% (inset of Figure 2e). The figures show major lakes that correspond to the number in Table 2: 1, Honghu Lake; 2, Liangzihu Lake; 3, Yaerhu Lake; 4, Changhu Lake; 5, Diaochahu Lake; 6, Zhangduhu Lake; 7, Laoguanhu Lake; 8, Futouhu Lake; 9, Wei River Reservoir; 10, Paihu Lake; 11, Guhu Lake; 12, Zhang River Reservoir; and 13, Huamahu Lake.*

area and perimeter of each lake were calculated for the 1950s, 1978, and 1998. The lakes were grouped into eight area size classes: 1–5, 5–10, 10–25, 25–50, 50–100, 100–200, 200–500, and 500–1000 km². We then calculated corresponding total surface area of lakes and number of lakes for each of the area size classes, including 13 major lakes that were larger than 50 km² in area (see Figures 2a and 2c).

■ Results

Figure 2 shows the distribution of lakes in the Jianghan Plain for the 1950s, 1978, and 1998, and changes in area (%) for two periods, from the 1950s to 1978 and from 1978–1998 (see Figure 2d, e insets). The changes were grouped into three categories: lake size increase, decrease, and no change for these two periods. These results were obtained by overlapping the distribution of lakes between the 1950s and 1978 and between 1978 and 1998. Both size

and number of lakes decreased rapidly from the 1950s to 1978 (Figures 2a, 2b, and 2d), but did not show any apparent change between 1978 and 1998 (Figures 2b, 2c, and 2e), implying an inconsistent pattern for these two periods. During the first period, the total surface area of the lakes decreased by 52.7% from 3885.4 km² in the 1950s to 1839.1 km² in 1978 (Table 1 and inset of Figure 2d). This decrease in lake size also occurred in most of the lake size classes for this period. For example, the total area of the lakes in the size classes 1–5 km², 25–50 km², and 500–1000 km² decreased by 38.2%, 36.7%, and 100%, respectively (Table 1). Only in the size class 200–500 km² did lake area increase, by 53.8%, due to degradation of Honghu Lake (the largest lake in the Plain) from 678.9 km² (size class 500–1000 km²) in the 1950s to 223 km² (size class 200–500 km²) in 1978 (Tables 1 and 2). During this period, the number of lakes decreased by 39.6%, from 414 to 250. The number of lakes within each size class also declined sharply. For example, the number of lakes of 1–5 km² declined from 297 in the 1950s to 188 in 1978. Lakes of 50–100 km² declined from six in the 1950s to one in 1978 (Table 1). The largest lake, Honghu, switched size class from 500–1000 km² in the 1950s to 200–500 km² in 1978, resulting in an increase in the number of lakes in the size class 200–500 km² from one in the 1950s to two in 1978 (Table 1).

In contrast to the changes seen between the 1950s and 1978, both the area and number of lakes tended to increase between 1978 and 1998. The total surface area of the lakes increased by 16.6%, from 1839.1 km² in 1978 to 2144.4 km² in 1998 (Figure 2e and inset). The only exception was shown by lakes in the size class 1–5 km², which decreased slightly in size, by 1.2%. The sizes of lakes in all other size classes increased. The total area of the lakes increased by 18.4% (5–10 km²), 11.8% (10–25 km²), 10.4% (25–50 km²), 173.1% (50–100 km²), 18.9% (100–200 km²), and 13.3% (200–500 km²), respectively (Table 1). The total number of lakes increased slightly, from 250 in 1978 to 258 in 1998 (3.2%), but this change differed from that seen in the lake size classes. For example, the number of lakes in the size class 1–5 km² continued to decline from 188 in 1978 to 182 in 1998, while those of 5–10 km² increased from 29 in 1978 to 36 in 1998, and those of 10–25 km² from 23 to 28 (Table 1). The number of lakes in the size classes 25–50 km²,

Table 1. Changes in the area and number of lakes and changing percentages for different size classes in the Jianghan Plain, Central Yangtze

Area classes (km²)	Lake area (km²)			Change in area (%)		Number of lakes			Change in number (%)	
	1950s	1978	1998	1950s-1978	1978-1998	1950s	1978	1998	1950s-1978	1978-1998
1–5	626.3	387.2	382.5	-38.2	-1.2	297	188	182	-36.7	-3.2
5–10	367.4	207.5	245.6	-43.5	18.4	50	29	36	-42.0	24.1
10–25	727.3	360.3	402.9	-50.5	11.8	47	23	28	-51.1	21.7
25–50	335.1	212.0	234.1	-36.7	10.4	9	6	6	-33.3	0.0
50–100	439.7	69.7	190.5	-84.1	173.3	6	1	3	-83.3	200.0
100–200	392.4	112.9	134.2	-71.2	18.9	3	1	1	-66.7	0.0
200–500	318.3	489.5	554.7	53.8	13.3	1	2	2	100.0	0.0
500–1000	678.9	0	0	-100.0	NA	1	0	0	-100.0	NA
Total	3885.4	1839.1	2144.4	-52.7	16.6	414	250	258	-39.6	**3.2**

100–200 km², and 200–500 km² remained constant during this period.

The changes in each lake greater than 50 km² in size were investigated further (Figure 2a and 2c; Table 2). Between the 1950s and 1978, each of these lakes decreased in size, or was separated into several smaller lakes (termed a sublake), but then expanded slightly or showed no significant variation between 1978 and 1998. For example, Honghu Lake decreased from 679.8 km² in the 1950s to 223 km² in 1978, but then increased to 290.3 km² by 1998. Changhu Lake decreased from 125.9 km² in the 1950s to 112.9 km² in 1978, but increased to 134.2 km² by 1998. The second largest lake, Liangzihu, as well as Futou Lake and Wei River Reservoir, declined from the 1950s to 1978, then showed no significant change between 1978 and 1998. Yaerhu Lake, Diaochahu Lake, Zhangduhu Lake, and Laoguanhu Lake were divided into a number of sublakes. Interestingly, Paihu Lake and Guhu Lake shrank considerably between the 1950s and 1978, but several sublakes reappeared in 1998. The Zhang River Reservoir was established between the 1950s and 1978, and its size increased from 36.6 km² in 1978 to 67.4 km² in 1998. Three separate sublakes became linked during the 1950s to form Huamahu Lake, which covered an area of 53.2 km² by 1998.

By overlaying the lake distribution maps from each of the study periods (1950s–1978 and 1978–1998), the spatial distributions and data on the three lake change categories (decrease, increase, and no change) were obtained (Figures 2d and 2e). Only 33.1% of lakes could be categorized as "no change" between the 1950s and 1978, suggesting that 66.9% of lakes disappeared during this period. The net decrease in lake surface area was calculated as the difference between the decrease in water surface area (66.9%) and the surface area covered by the newly established reservoir (14.2%). The net loss of lake surface area between the 1950s and 1978 was therefore 52.7% (Figure

Table 2. Size of lakes larger than 50 km² for three periods: 1950s, 1978, and 1998 in the Jianghan Plain, Central Yangtze

No.	Lake name	Location Centroid latitude	Centroid longitude	Lake size (km²) and notes 1950s	1978	1998
1	Honghu Lake	28°35'	113°	678.9	223.0	290.3
2	Liangzihu Lake	28°58'	114°02'	318.3	266.4	264.3
3	Yaerhu Lake	29°08'	114°08'	164.8	Separated into five sublakes: 25.1, 9.8, 6.6, 5.0, and 1.0 km²	Separated into five sublakes: 23.3, 14.2, 8.0, 6.2, and 1.2 km²
4	Changhu Lake	29°07'	112°16'	125.9	112.9	134.2
5	Diaochahu Lake	29°21'	113°20'	101.7	4.5, 3.6	2.9, 1.6, 1.3
6	Zhangduhu Lake	29°21'	114°12'	95.4	40.4, 4.5, 3.0, 2.7	42.3, 5.3, 2.9, 1.5
7	Laoguanhu Lake	29°27'	113°06'	89.5	8.5, 2.1, 1.8	9.6, 1.9
8	Futouhu Lake	28°47'	113°47'	83.3	69.7	69.9
9	Wei River Reservoir	28°43'	111°28'	61.6	32.5	31.4
10	Paihu Lake	28°59'	112°55'	56.3	10.8	11.5, 6.7, 2.3, 1.2
11	Guhu Lake	29°02'	112°13'	53.6	2.1	2.9, 2.0, 1.7, 1.2, 1.0
12	Zhang River Reservoir	29°39'	111°53'	No	36.6	67.4
13	Huamahu Lake	29°04'	114°31'	17.1, 9.1, 3.1	8.2, 5.3, 2.1	53.2

Figure 3. *A number of lakes and associated wetlands have been reclaimed for agricultural and aquacultural use in the Jianghan Plain: (a) rice field; (b) radish field; (c) cotton field; and (d) mussel cultivation for the production of pearls.*

2d inset). The net increase in lake size between 1978 and 1998 was 16.6% (difference between 47% and 30.4%), with 69.6% of the lake area remaining unchanged (Figure 2e inset).

■ Discussion

The rapid decrease in size and number of lakes in the Jianghan Plain resulted largely from accelerated impoldering practices in the Central Yangtze between the early 1950s and the late 1970s. Three unprecedented periods of impoldering occurred in the Jianghan Plain between 1957 and 1976 (Huang 2001). As a result, the amount of arable land increased by 2704 km^2 (Committee for Agricultural Division of Hubei Province 1995). This represents 1.3 times the total area lost from lakes ≥1 km^2 between the 1950s and 1978. In other words, 76% of the arable land gained during this period was due to reclamation of land from lakes ≥1 km^2 in size; the remaining 24% probably resulted from the reclamation of land from lakes of less than 1 km^2 in size.

This accelerated impoldering activity was caused primarily by the increasing demands on ecosystem services imposed by the rising human population. The population in the Jianghan Plain was estimated as 1127.8×10^4 in 1953, increasing to 2021.5×10^4 in 1982, 2119.5×10^4 in 1991, and 2352.4×10^4 by 1998 (Sun 1994; Hubei

Statistical Year Book 1992, 1999). A rapid rate of increase, 29.8×10^4/year, occurred between 1953 and 1982, coinciding with the period of lake disappearance. This period of reclamation from lakes to arable land was necessary to satisfy the increasing need for crop production and aquaculture (Figures 3 and 4). This human-induced long-term shift was also seen in Dongting Lake, a large lake in the Central Yangtze (Zhao *et al.* 2005).

Natural processes, such as interannual variability in climate and lake sediment, may also influence changes in lake size. Variations in precipitation are strongly associated with water body area (Yin and Li 2001). We therefore used 50-year time series records of annual mean precipitation from 1951 to 2000 from all 10 climatic stations over the Jianghan Plain to examine the effects of the interannual variations in precipitation on changes in lake size (Figure 5). No significant trends were identified over the 50 years of the study period, with the exception of a much greater rainfall for the years 1954 (1802 mm) and 1991 (1761.2 mm). The 50-year average annual precipitation was 1115.6 mm, and annual precipitation for the years 1957, 1978, and 1998 was 1129.9 mm, 1032.1 mm, and 1171.6 mm, respectively. This suggests that the interannual variability in precipitation may not be a significant factor in lake size change in this study area.

In addition, the natural accumulation of silt from the Yangtze River may also be a contributing factor in the

Figure 4. *An increasing human population has led to an overuse of water surface in lakes of the Jianghan Plain: (a) fish aquaculture with retiary boxes; (b) collecting aquatic plants for fish food; (c) cultivation of water bamboo (Zizania caduciflora), a persistent perennial root plant; and (d) lotus cultivation.*

shrinkage of lakes in the Jianghan Plain; however, this was much less important than the effects of reclamation practices, because the Yangtze River has been blocked off from this area since the early 1950s (Hydroelectric Bureau of Hunan Province 1989). For this reason, the sedimentation rate from lakes is very low. For example, the sediment deposition rate of Honghu Lake was 0.72–1.9 mm per year for a number of decades (Pu et al. 1994).

We therefore believe that increased impoldering has been a major driver in the decrease in number and area of lakes in the Jianghan Plain between the 1950s and 1978, while the slight increase in lake numbers and area between 1978 and 1998 can be attributed to changes in government policy restricting impoldering and requiring local people to return arable lands to the lakes.

The rapid decline in the size and number of lakes in Jianghan Plain appears to have significantly restricted hydrological and ecological services, such as flood retention and provision of support for biodiversity. The frequency of floods in the Plain increased considerably; the average interval between unusual floods in Hubei Province had been as long as 10 years in the 1950s, but the interval declined to 3.3 years during the 1970s, and to only 2.5 years during the 1990s (Yin and Li 2001). Biodiversity decreased at an alarming rate. For example, the number of fish species in the Plain decreased from 101 in the early 1950s to 82 in 1982, and the number of vascular plants and indigenous fishes in the largest lake (Honghu Lake) decreased from 92 and 74 species in the 1960s to 68 and 54 species, respectively, in the 1980s (Liu and Cao 1998).

These impacts, and an awareness of the importance of

wetlands, motivated the Chinese Government to prohibit impoldering along the Central Yangtze since the late 1990s (Wang 1998). Meanwhile, local people are willing to return inundated arable lands to the lake, or even to convert these lands to lakes/ponds for aquaculture (including lotus root cultivation and fish production), responding to changing market demands and thereby improving their financial income. For example, the area used for fish cultivation increased from 58.9 km^2 in 1990 to 100 km^2 in 1999 in Honghu City, an increase of 69.8% (Statistical Bureau of Hubei Province 1991, 2000). Consequently, the total area and number of lakes in the Jianghan Plain increased between 1978 and 1998. A study of land conversion in the Honghu Lake area between 1987 and 1998 showed similar results to our own, with the area covered by water nearly doubling, from 457.5 km^2 in 1987 to 854.1 km^2 in 1998 (Zhao et al. 2003).

In conclusion, changes in surface area and numbers of lakes in the Jianghan Plain over a 50-year period, quantified by historical land-cover maps and remote sensing imagery, show two distinct periods: the 1950s–1978 and 1978–1998. During the earlier period, the total surface area and number of lakes decreased rapidly, resulting in significant negative ecological consequences; during the latter period, the trend reversed and lake number and area increased slightly. Such changes are generally consistent with those from a field survey of the middle and large lakes and reservoirs in Hubei Province, conducted by the Committee for Agricultural Division of Hubei Province (1995). They reported that the size/number of lakes ≥0.07 km^2 in the Province decreased from 8528 km^2/1332 in 1949 to 2373 km^2/310 in 1977, then increased to 2983 km²/843 (including sublakes separated from major lakes) in 1988, respectively.

However, the restored or newly established lakes and aquaculture ponds may not function in the same way as the original, natural lakes, because these are human-dominated systems. For instance, six species of aquatic plants disappeared from Changhu Lake between 1981 and 2001 (Peng *et al.* 2003), although lake size increased during this period, suggesting that natural habitats cannot simply be replaced by human-made ecosystems. Further studies are needed in this area.

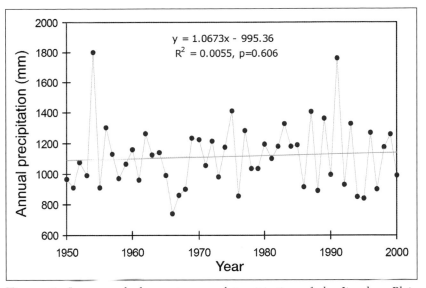

Figure 5. *Interannual change in annual precipitation of the Jianghan Plain between 1951 and 2000. The precipitation data are from an average of 10 climatic stations situated across the Plain. No significant trend in precipitation can be seen over the 50 year period.*

■ Acknowledgment

We are grateful to Y Zhang and LG Cao for partly digitalizing historical topographic maps, and GC Lei for discussions on the project. This study was funded by the State Key Basic Research and Development Plan (#G2000046801), WWF-Beijing Office (CN0079), and National Natural Science Foundation of China (# 40024101).

■ References

Beeton AM. 2002. Large freshwater lakes: present state, trends, and future. *Environ Conserv* **29**: 21–38.

Bronmark C and Hansson LA. 2002. Environmental issues in lakes and ponds: current state and perspectives. *Environ Conserv* **29**: 290–307.

Cai SM and Du Y. 2000. The characteristics of the lake resources and its development and protection on the Jianghan lakes region. *J Nat Sci Central China Norm Univ* **34**. 476–81.

Committee for Agricultural Division of Hubei Province. 1995. Study on large and middle lakes and reservoirs of Hubei Province. Wuhan, PR China: Chinese Scientific and Technology University Press.

Huang JL. 2001. Historical thought on land exploitation in recent 500 years in Jianghan Plain. *J Nat Sci Central China Norm Univ* **35**: 485–88.

Hydroelectric Bureau of Hubei Province. 1991. Atlas of the changes of lakes in Hubei Province between 1950–1988. Wuhan, PR China: Hydroelectric Bureau of Hubei Province Publication.

Hydroelectric Bureau of Hunan Province. 1989. Compilation of basic data on Dongting Lake area, Hunan Province – the fourth fascicule. Changsha, PR China: Hydroelectric Bureau of Hunan Province Publication.

Jensen JR. 1996. Introductory digital image processing: a remote sensing perspective. New York, NY: Prentice Hall.

Johnson N, Revenga C, and Echeverria J. 2001. Managing water for people and nature. *Science* **292**: 1071–72.

Li RD and Zhang XY. 1997. A study on the recent changes of lake area in the Four-lake area of Hubei province using remote sensed images. *Remote Sens Technol Appl* **12**: 26–31.

Liu HY and Cao YY. 1998. Study on the development of Jianghan Plain wetland and its effects on environment. *Geogr Terr Res* **14**: 16–20.

Liu WD. 1994. Land types and comprehensive physical regionalization in the Jianghan Plain. *Acta Geogr Sin* **49**: 73–83.

Peng YH, Jian YX, Ni LY, *et al.* 2003. Aquatic plant diversity and its changes in Changhu Lake of Hubei Province in China. *Acta Bot Yunnanica* **25**: 173–80.

Pu PM, Cai SM, and Zhu HH. 1994. Three Gorges Project and the environment of lakes and wetlands in Central Yangtze. Beijing, PR China: Science Press.

Richter BD, Braun DP, Mendelson MA, and Master LL. 1997. Threats to imperiled freshwater fauna. *Conserv Biol* **11**: 1081–93.

Shi CY. 1989. A general outline of Chinese Lakes. Beijing, PR China: Science Press.

Statistical Bureau of Hubei Province. 1991. Hubei Agricultural Statistical Year Book. Beijing, PR China: Chinese Statistical Press.

Statistical Bureau of Hubei Province. 1992. Hubei Agricultural Statistical Year Book. Beijing, PR China: Chinese Statistical Press.

Statistical Bureau of Hubei Province. 1999. Hubei Statistical Year Book. Beijing, PR China: Chinese Statistical Press.

Statistical Bureau of Hubei Province. 2000. Hubei Statistical Year Book. Beijing, PR China: Chinese Statistical Press.

Sun JX. 1994. The population of china towards the 21st century – HuBei fascicule. Beijing, PR China: Chinese Statistical Press.

Wang, K Y. 1998. The management and exploitation of Dongting Lake. Changsha, PR China: Hunan People Publishing House.

Wilcove DS, Rothstein D, Dubow J, *et al.* 1998. Quantifying threats to imperiled species in the United States. *Bioscience* **48**: 607–15.

Yin HF and Li CG. 2001. Human impact on floods and flood disasters on the Yangtze River. *Geomorphology* **41**: 105–09.

Zhao SQ, Fang JY, Miao SL, *et al.* 2005. The 7-decade degradation of a large freshwater lake in Central Yangtze River, China. *Environ Sci Technol* **39**: 431–36.

Zhao SQ, Fang JY, Ji W, and Tang ZY. 2003. Lake restoration from impoldering: impact of land conversion on riparian landscape in Honghu Lake area, Central Yangtze. *Agric Ecosyst Environ* **95**: 111–18.

Collaborative learning – a jigsaw

Christopher Finelli[1], Diane Ebert-May[2], and Janet Hodder[3]

Reading and understanding primary research literature is a challenge for students as they can be intimidated by scientific jargon and the unfamiliar style of scientific prose (Epstein 1972; White 2001). It is, however, an important skill that should be developed well before they graduate. Students' abilities to accomplish this are often underestimated, especially in the case of nonscience majors who are capable of reading the biological literature and of approaching it critically (Gillen et al. 2004). The paper by Fang et al. (pp 186–192) provides an example of how to bring primary literature into both large and small classes, using a cooperative learning strategy known as a "jigsaw".

Although over 600 experimental and 100 correlational studies indicate that cooperative learning promotes higher achievement (Springer et al. 1999; Johnson et al. 1998), faculty are often wary about implementation in large classes, where logistics are a challenge and poor attendance can hinder group work. In practice, cooperative learning techniques encourage class attendance and participation (Ebert-May et al. 1997). For cooperative learning to be most effective, faculty need to understand the techniques and students need directions and practice of the skills necessary for effective group work (Maloof 2005). The jigsaw strategy for cooperative learning may be most effective by mid to late semester (see NISE 2005), especially in large classes.

We model two ways to implement a jigsaw; the first is based on the components of the research paper and the second is derived from concepts presented in the paper. Practice using this technique will advance students' abilities to read research and understand the concepts of the paper better than when the paper is explained by the instructor, or when students are asked to read a paper individually for class discussion.

■ Student goals

- Gain understanding of the content of a primary research article
- Demonstrate expertise in reading and interpreting scientific literature
- Build high-quality interactions with their peers
- Transfer the knowledge and skills about science as a process to other research papers

■ Instructor goals

- Use jigsaw as a strategy for cooperative learning
- Facilitate students' understanding of complex material in scientific literature

[1]Louisiana Universities Marine Consortium, [2]Michigan State University, [3]University of Oregon

Implementing jigsaws

Students must be comfortable and effective with group work to use jigsaws in large classes. At the beginning of the semester, students form permanent groups composed of four or five students. Everyone reads the entire paper as homework, but each student in a group becomes an "expert" on part of the paper. During the next class session, all the experts for each section of the paper meet, share their knowledge, and clarify their understanding. After 15 minutes, groups reform and discuss the paper. All members of the group learn from each other and put together different parts of the paper. For variations on this approach refer to the National Institute for Science Education (NISE) website. The jigsaw can be logistically challenging, but it enables faculty to decrease the "functional" size of a large class to small groups of students.

Choosing the right paper

Choice of primary research to read in class is critical. Papers should reflect central themes within the discipline and be easily understood by the students. For example, Fang et al. is an original research paper with conceptually simple methods (quantifying wetland loss by comparing maps). Fang et al. touch on central issues in ecology, such as biodiversity and ecosystem services, and this paper may be best suited for an advanced environmental science course. However, the jigsaw technique can be applied to any research paper.

Jigsaw 1. Using components of the paper

The first jigsaw focuses on dissection of the paper into component parts: abstract and introduction, methods, results and discussion. The leading questions in Panel 1 serve to further guide experts in each group.

Jigsaw 2. Using content themes

An alternative jigsaw technique is to dissect a paper using content that relates to the learning goals of a course. Each student takes a topic, and an understanding of the paper is gained through discussion of the following:

- Wetland conversion (impoldering): Why? How? Benefits or negative impacts?
- Ecosystem goods and services: What are they? Why are they important?
- Biodiversity: What is it? How is it measured? Why is it important?

Assessment of jigsaws

Assessment of a jigsaw in a large class becomes manageable by assessing some components as group work (which measurably reduces the volume of grading) and other components as individual work. Panel 2 is a rubric that explains

Panel 1. Guiding questions for expert groups

- *Abstract and Introduction:* What broad disciplinary topic does the paper address? Why was the research conducted? What is the authors' primary hypothesis? Are there any terms you do not understand?

- *Methods:* When and where was the research conducted? What techniques are used to gather data? How were the data analyzed? Do any methods require further explanation?

- *Results:* What are the primary findings or trends? Are the conclusions supported by the data? Were any findings not expected by the authors? What were effective ways of presenting the results, and what ways were less effective?

- *Discussion:* Was the primary hypothesis supported? Were there any unexplained results? Do authors suggest future research? What alternative conclusions are explored?

For a similar approach, see: http://helios.hampshire.edu/~apmNS/design/RESOURCES/HOW_READ.html

the ideal expert understanding students should gain from Jigsaw 1 and can be used in a variety of ways. It could be given to groups as a way to self-check their understanding of the paper. Or the expert on the section in each group could write a summary of the section, based on the guiding questions in Panel 1; the rubric is then used to assess these summaries. Responses are evaluated in terms of the specific student objectives and the degree to which students achieved understanding in comparison to the ideal response. A similar rubric can be constructed for Jigsaw 2. Other assessments could include asking students to design the next possible research questions and methods

Panel 2. Rubric for ideal understanding of Fang et al.

Abstract and Introduction: Expert groups should identify the primary hypothesis that wetland loss resulted from impoldering, connect biodiversity and ecosystem services as important topics in ecology, and define impoldering as a technique of wetland conversion.

Methods: Expert groups should explain that Fang et al. analyzed the changes in number and coverage of lakes > 1 km², identify the location of the study as Jianghan Plain, southeastern China, and the temporal span as 1950s–1998, and identify the use of remote sensing and historical maps. Advanced student experts should note that the authors resampled their data to standardize spatial resolution, and also standardized the season from which images were chosen.

Results: Expert groups should identify the substantial reduction in the number and coverage of lakes from the 1950s to 1978 and a reversal of this trend between 1978 and 1998. They should explain the presence of anomalous results, such as the increase in the number and area of lakes in the 200–500 km² class between 1950s and 1978 and the decrease in number and area of small lakes (1–5 km²) from 1978 to 1998. Students should convey this to their peers using the figures and tables.

Discussion: Expert groups should convey the primary conclusion that lake loss in the 1950s and 1960s resulted from extensive draining of lakes to increase agricultural production, and should explain that the increase in the number and area of lakes from 1978 to 1998 resulted from a change in government policy. They should note that the alternative hypothesis that changes in wetlands resulted from climatic shifts during the same time period is rejected. Finally, students should note that biodiversity and ecological services have not returned to their past levels.

for one of the topic areas. Or, as we have suggested in previous Pathways articles, students can develop models (box models, concept maps) that illustrate the interconnections of concepts in the paper.

Assessment of knowledge transfer and group dynamics

The principles of cognitive science and learning theory indicate that information learned in one context will transfer to a different context if we teach in ways that encourage transfer (Halpern 2004). Students' ability to transfer knowledge and skills from this exercise can be assessed in numerous ways by assigning another paper or sections of a paper. The questions in Panel 1 can be used to assess students' understanding of any research paper through quizzes or short writing assignments.

Finally, assessment of group dynamics provides important feedback to students and instructors. Individuals within groups comment on quantity (percent contribution) and quality (written comments) of each other's contributions. The instructor collects these by group and provides general feedback to the entire class about trends, or specific feedback to less functional groups.

■ Acknowledgements

We thank the National Science Foundation for their long-term support of the FIRST project, Faculty Institutes for Reforming Science Teaching (DUE 0088847). All Pathways papers are peer reviewed.

■ References

Ebert-May D, Brewer CA, and Allred S. 1997. Innovation in large lectures – teaching for active learning. *BioScience* **47**: 601–07.

Epstein HT. 1972. An experiment in education. *Nature* **235**: 203–05.

Gillen CM, Vaughan J, and Lye BR. 2004. An online tutorial for helping nonscience majors read primary research literature in biology. *Adv Physiol Educ* **28**: 95–99.

Halpern DF. 2004. Using the principles of cognitive science and learning theories to enhance learning and teaching. www.pkal.org/template2.cfm?c_id=993. Viewed 12 April 2005.

Johnson DT, Johnson RT, and Smith KL. 1998. Active learning: cooperation in the college classroom. Edina, MA: Interaction Book Company.

Maloof J. 2005. Using the jigsaw method of cooperative learning to teach from primary sources. www.doit.gmu.edu/inventio/main.asp?pID=spring04&sID=maloof&tID=1. Viewed 22 March 2005.

NISE (National Institute for Science Education). 2005. Doing CL. Jigsaw. www.wcer.wisc.edu/archive/cl1/CL/doingcl/jigsaw.htm. Viewed 7 April 2005.

Springer L, Stanne ME, and Donovan S. 1999. Effects of small-group learning on undergraduates in science, mathematics, engineering, and technology: a meta-analysis. *Rev Educ Res* **69**: 21–51.

White HB III. 2001. A PBL course that uses research articles as problems. In: Duch B, Groh SE, and Allen D (Eds). The power of problem-based learning. Sterling, VA: Stylus Publishing.

Loss of foundation species: consequences for the structure and dynamics of forested ecosystems

Aaron M Ellison[1]*, Michael S Bank[1], Barton D Clinton[2], Elizabeth A Colburn[1], Katherine Elliott[2], Chelcy R Ford[2], David R Foster[1], Brian D Kloeppel[3], Jennifer D Knoepp[2], Gary M Lovett[4], Jacqueline Mohan[1], David A Orwig[1], Nicholas L Rodenhouse[5], William V Sobczak[6], Kristina A Stinson[1], Jeffrey K Stone[7], Christopher M Swan[8], Jill Thompson[9], Betsy Von Holle[1], and Jackson R Webster[10]

In many forested ecosystems, the architecture and functional ecology of certain tree species define forest structure and their species-specific traits control ecosystem dynamics. Such foundation tree species are declining throughout the world due to introductions and outbreaks of pests and pathogens, selective removal of individual taxa, and over-harvesting. Through a series of case studies, we show that the loss of foundation tree species changes the local environment on which a variety of other species depend; how this disrupts fundamental ecosystem processes, including rates of decomposition, nutrient fluxes, carbon sequestration, and energy flow; and dramatically alters the dynamics of associated aquatic ecosystems. Forests in which dynamics are controlled by one or a few foundation species appear to be dominated by a small number of strong interactions and may be highly susceptible to alternating between stable states following even small perturbations. The ongoing decline of many foundation species provides a set of important, albeit unfortunate, opportunities to develop the research tools, models, and metrics needed to identify foundation species, anticipate the cascade of immediate, short- and long-term changes in ecosystem structure and function that will follow from their loss, and provide options for remedial conservation and management.

Front Ecol Environ 2005; 3(9): 479–486

We are living in an era of unprecedented and rapid ecological change (Reid *et al.* 2005). Through habitat conversion, over-consumption of resources, and worldwide introductions of pests and pathogens, humans are causing species extinctions at a record rate: the sixth extinction crisis in the billion-year history of eukaryotic life on Earth (Eldridge 1998). The loss of a common or abundant foundation species (sensu Dayton 1972; see Panel 1), which by virtue of its structural or functional attributes creates and defines an entire ecological community or ecosystem, can have dramatic effects on our perception of the landscape and broad consequences for associated biota, ecosystem function, and stability. Foundation species differ from keystone predators (Paine 1966) in that the former usually occupy low trophic levels whereas the latter are usually top predators. They are also distinct from core species (Hanski 1982) in that foundation species are not only locally abundant and regionally common but also create locally stable conditions required by many other species. They also serve to stabilize fundamental ecosystem processes such as productivity and water balance.

Trees are most likely to be foundation species in forested ecosystems, as their architecture and functional and physiological characteristics define forest structure and alter microclimates, while their biomass and chemi-

In a nutshell:

- In many ecosystems, a single foundation species controls population and community dynamics and modulates ecosystem processes
- The loss of foundation species acutely and chronically impacts fluxes of energy and nutrients, hydrology, food webs, and biodiversity
- Human activities, including logging and the introduction of exotic pests and pathogens, often functionally remove foundation tree species from forests
- Foundation species that are currently being lost from North American forests include eastern hemlock, Port-Orford cedar, and oaks

[1]Harvard University, Harvard Forest, 324 North Main Street, Petersham, MA 01366 *(aellison@fas.harvard.edu); [2]USDA Forest Service Southern Research Station, Coweeta Hydrologic Lab, Otto, NC, 28763; [3]University of Georgia, Institute of Ecology, Athens, GA 30602; [4]Institute of Ecosystem Studies, Millbrook, NY 12545; [5]Wellesley College, Department of Biological Sciences, Wellesley, MA 02481; [6]College of the Holy Cross, Department of Biology, Worcester, MA 01610; [7]Oregon State University, Department of Botany and Plant Pathology, Corvallis, OR 97331; [8]University of Maryland, Baltimore County, Dept of Geography & Environmental Systems, Baltimore, MD 21250; [9]University of Puerto Rico, Institute for Tropical Ecosystem Studies, San Juan, PR 00931; [10]Virginia Polytechnic Institute and State University, Department of Biology, Blacksburg, VA 24061

Figure 1. *(a) An old-growth eastern hemlock* (Tsuga canadensis) *stand, (b and inset) a stand declining following 10 years of infestation by the introduced hemlock woolly adelgid* (Adelges tsugae), *and (c) dense regeneration of black birch* (Betula lenta) *saplings on a site formerly dominated by eastern hemlock in southern Connecticut. Nearly all hemlock trees in this 150-hectare forest in southern Connecticut were killed in the mid-1990s by hemlock woolly adelgid.*

cal makeup contribute substantially to ecosystem processes. Foundation tree species are declining throughout the world due to a number of factors, including introductions and outbreaks of nonindigenous pests and pathogens, irruptions of native pests, over-harvesting and high-intensity forestry, and deliberate removal of individual species from forests. We use three examples from North America to illustrate consequences for both terrestrial and aquatic habitats of the loss of foundation tree species: the ongoing decline of eastern hemlock (*Tsuga*

canadensis) resulting from an introduced insect and pre-emptive salvage logging; the local extirpation of white-bark pine (*Pinus albicaulis*) caused by interactions among a nonnative pathogen, a native insect, and human alteration of fire regimes; and the functional removal of American chestnut (*Castanea dentata*) by an introduced pathogen. Our examples focus on trees in systems we know best, but they are broadly representative of a wide range of foundation species and illustrative of their role in forests throughout the world (Panel 2).

■ The rise and fall of eastern hemlock

Majestic hemlock groves (Figure 1) evoke reverence, affection, and poetry (Frost 1923). Eastern hemlock (*Tsuga canadensis*), one of the most long-lived, shade-tolerant trees in North America, dominates about 1×10^6 ha of forest from the southern Appalachians to southern Canada and west to the central Lake states (McWilliams and Schmidt 2000). In the north, hemlock typically occurs in nearly pure stands with species-poor understories. In the south, hemlock grows in mixed stands in narrow riparian strips and moist coves, often with dense understories of rhododendron (*Rhododendron maximum*). In hemlock-dominated stands, the combination of deep shade and acidic, slowly decomposing litter results in a cool, damp microclimate, slow rates of nitrogen cycling, and nutrient-poor soils (Jenkins *et al.* 1999). Canopies of evergreen hemlocks have a higher leaf area index and lower transpiration rates per unit leaf area than canopies of co-occurring deciduous trees (Catovsky *et al.* 2002). Although hemlocks have much greater whole-tree respiration rates in the spring and fall, when deciduous trees are leafless, during the summer hemlocks transpire about 50% of the total water released by deciduous trees (J Hadley unpublished). These characteristics of hemlock, along with its high snow-interception rates, mediate soil

---

Panel 1. The many definitions of foundation species

Following nomenclatural priority, we adopt Dayton's (1972) terminology and general definition of a foundation species: *a single species that defines much of the structure of a community by creating locally stable conditions for other species, and by modulating and stabilizing fundamental ecosystem processes.*

Subsequent authors, working in different habitats and apparently unaware of historical antecedents, have suggested terms with some or all of the attributes of foundation species, including:

Core species (Hanski 1982) are locally abundant and regionally common; associated **satellite species** are sparse and rare. An associated metapopulation model (the **core–satellite hypothesis**) explains relationships between a species' local abundance and its regional distribution.

Dominant species (Grime 1984) competitively exclude subordinate species by garnering a disproportionate share of resources and contributing most to productivity.

Keystone predators (Paine 1966) preferentially consume dominant competitors and enhance local biodiversity by preventing exclusion of weaker competitors. Holling's (1992) **extended keystone hypothesis** posits that all terrestrial ecosystems are controlled and organized by a small set of **keystone species**.

Structural species (Huston 1994) create physical structures of environments, produce variability in physical conditions, provide resources, and create habitat for **interstitial species**.

Ecosystem engineers (Jones *et al.* 1994) cause physical state changes in biotic or abiotic materials and modulate availability of resources to other species. Class 5 **autogenic ecosystem engineers** are directly analogous to Dayton's foundation species.

moisture levels, stabilize stream base-flows, and decrease diel variation in stream temperatures. As a result, streams flowing through hemlock forests support unique assemblages of salamanders, fish, and freshwater invertebrates that are intolerant of seasonal drying (Snyder *et al.* 2002). Hemlock stands also shelter deer and other wildlife.

Populations of eastern hemlock have declined precipitously three times since the Pleistocene glaciation: approximately 5500 years ago, coincident with regional climate change and an outbreak of an insect similar to the extant eastern hemlock looper (*Lambdina fiscellaria*; Bhiry and Filion 1996); about 200 years ago, following forest conversion to agriculture, increases in fire, and extensive logging for timber and tannin (McMartin 1992); and from the mid-1980s to the present, due to an introduced insect, the hemlock woolly adelgid (*Adelges tsugae*; Figure 1). This rapidly spreading insect kills trees of all sizes and age-classes within 4–15 years of infestation (Orwig *et al.* 2002). Hemlock has no apparent resistance to the adelgid; it rarely recovers from attack (Orwig *et al.*

2002), and there are currently no effective biological or chemical controls of the adelgid in forested ecosystems. The insect's impact is further exacerbated by pre-emptive salvage logging, in which hemlock, which has modest economic value, is cut in anticipation of future infestation (Orwig *et al.* 2002).

Hemlock could functionally disappear from eastern forests in the next several decades. This species generally does not re-establish following adelgid-induced mortality (Figure 1), but is replaced throughout its range by hardwood species, including birch (*Betula* spp), oaks (*Quercus* spp) and maples (*Acer* spp) (Orwig *et al.* 2002). In the southeastern United States, hemlock is replaced by yellow poplar (*Liriodendron tulipifera*; J Vose *et al.* unpublished) when *Rhododendron* is absent. Decline of hemlock may lead to the local loss of its uniquely associated ants (Ellison *et al.* 2005) and birds (Tingley *et al.* 2002), cause regional homogenization of floral and faunal assemblages (Ellison *et al.* 2005), change soil ecosystem processes (Jenkins *et al.* 1999; Figure 2), and alter hydrological

---

Panel 2. Additional examples of foundation species from forests around the world

Bald cypress (*Taxodium distichum*) dominates deepwater swamps of southeastern North America (Sharitz and Mitsch 1993). Its presence and density affect the water table and flow of sediment and nutrients, and control structure and composition of associated plant and animal communities (Sharitz and Mitsch 1993). Intensive logging and removal of bald cypress dramatically alter hydrology and nutrient cycling, reduce primary productivity, and increase sedimentation (Sun *et al.* 2001).

Douglas fir (*Pseudotsuga menziesii*) dominates young and old-growth forests at low and mid-elevations west of the Cascade Range and at higher elevations in the interior of the Pacific Northwest of North America. Live trees, snags, and fallen logs provide unique habitats for wildlife, including endangered and rare species such as the spotted owl (*Strix occidentalis*). The evergreen foliage controls light levels, microclimate, and gas exchange from the forest floor to the canopy (Parker *et al.* 2004). Logging alters C and N cycling, wildlife abundance, and plant successional dynamics (Halpern *et al.* 2005). Unlike the other foundation species discussed in this paper, Douglas fir is not currently threatened, as it is strongly favored by current forest management practices. However, many old-growth stands in the Pacific Northwest have been lost to logging over the past decades. High-intensity fires resulting from long-term fire suppression practices, introduced pests or changes in the ecological dynamics of native pests, or changes in forest management that pose mortality risks to old-growth Douglas fir stands could have important ecological impacts in the future.

Fraser fir (*Abies fraseri*) is a locally abundant endemic species that occurs in six discrete, high-altitude areas in the southern Appalachians (Hollingsworth and Hain 1991). There, Fraser fir defines high-elevation spruce-fir communities, with tightly associated animal and plant species. Fraser fir has been declining since the balsam woolly adelgid (*Adelges piceae*) was introduced in the 1930s (Hollingsworth and Hain 1991). Its loss increases the susceptibility of its co-dominant, red spruce (*Picea rubens*), to windthrow, and both species are suffering additional effects of climate warming and air pollution (Hamburg and Cogbill 1988).

Jarrah is a unique Australian forest type comprised mainly of ***Eucalyptus marginata*.** This species experiences mass collapse and sudden death following waterlogging, which increases infection of jarrah roots by zoospores of *Phytophthora cinnamomi* (Davison and Tay 1987), a soil-born pathogenic fungus introduced into Western Australia in 1921 that affects ~2000 of the 9000 extant plant species there (Wills 1992). Following invasion by *P cinnamomi*, richness of woody perennial species in the jarrah understory declines significantly, whereas richness of monocots, herbaceous perennials, annuals, and geophytes are largely unaffected (Wills and Keighery 1994).

Port-Orford cedar (*Chamaecyparis lawsoniana*) is endemic to southwestern Oregon and northern California, grows on ultramafic and non-ultramafic soils, in riparian and upland sites, and occurs in the most diverse plant associations in the region. On ultramafic soils, Port-Orford cedar is often the only riparian tree species. It is a foundation species for both terrestrial and aquatic habitats: it recycles calcium to surface soils, provides shade, and stabilizes soil and stream banks (Hansen *et al.* 2000). Its highly rot-resistant wood provides habitat heterogeneity and alters hydrology. The non-native, water-dispersed, and generally lethal root pathogen *Phytophthora lateralis* has spread into virtually all natural forest stands from nursery plants infected in the early 1920s (Hansen *et al.* 2000).

Mangroves (*Rhizophora* spp) form dense, often monospecific stands in estuarine and coastal forests throughout the tropics; these forests have some of the highest reported net primary productivity of any ecosystem on the planet (Ellison and Farnsworth 2001). Removal of mangroves leads to rapid build-up of acid sulfides in the soil, increased shoreline erosion and sedimentation onto offshore coral reefs, and collapse of intertidal food webs and inshore fisheries (Ellison and Farnsworth 2001). More than 2% of mangrove forests are lost annually, as forests are cut for fuel, coastal development, and wood fiber used to produce rayon.

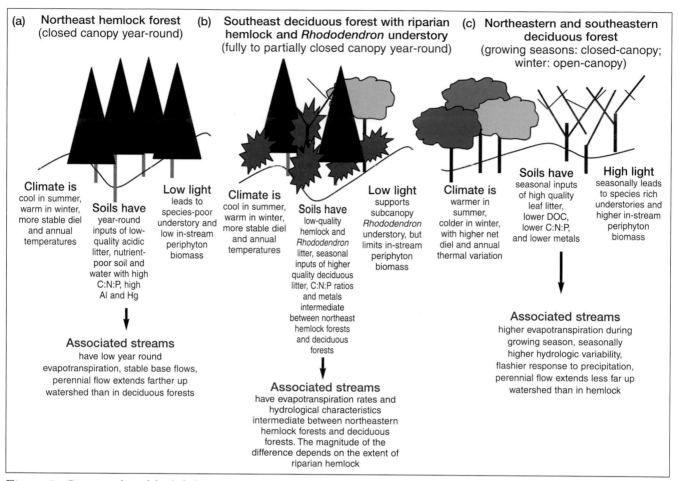

(a) Northeast hemlock forest
(closed canopy year-round)

Climate is cool in summer, warm in winter, more stable diel and annual temperatures

Soils have year-round inputs of low-quality acidic litter, nutrient-poor soil and water with high C:N:P, high Al and Hg

Low light leads to species-poor understory and low in-stream periphyton biomass

Associated streams have low year round evapotranspiration, stable base flows, perennial flow extends farther up watershed than in deciduous forests

(b) Southeast deciduous forest with riparian hemlock and *Rhododendron* understory
(fully to partially closed canopy year-round)

Climate is cool in summer, warm in winter, more stable diel and annual temperatures

Soils have low-quality hemlock and *Rhododendron* litter, seasonal inputs of higher quality deciduous litter, C:N:P ratios and metals intermediate between northeast hemlock forests and deciduous forests

Low light supports subcanopy *Rhododendron* understory, but limits in-stream periphyton biomass

Associated streams have evapotranspiration rates and hydrological characteristics intermediate between northeastern hemlock forests and deciduous forests. The magnitude of the difference depends on the extent of riparian hemlock

(c) Northeastern and southeastern deciduous forest
(growing seasons: closed-canopy; winter: open-canopy)

Climate is warmer in summer, colder in winter, with higher net diel and annual thermal variation

Soils have seasonal inputs of high quality leaf litter, lower DOC, lower C:N:P, and lower metals

High light seasonally leads to species rich understories and higher in-stream periphyton biomass

Associated streams higher evapotranspiration during growing season, seasonally higher hydrologic variability, flashier response to precipitation, perennial flow extends less far up watershed than in hemlock

Figure 2. *Conceptual model of shifts in terrestrial and aquatic ecosystem processes following loss of eastern hemlock from (a) northern and (b) southern forests, and (c) conversion to hardwood-dominated stands.*

regimes (Figure 2).

The effects of adelgid-induced hemlock mortality on stream ecosystems will be extensive. For example, hemlock streams support significantly more taxa of aquatic invertebrates than paired mixed-hardwood stands, and nearly 10% of the taxa are strongly associated with the presence of hemlock (Snyder *et al.* 2002). Hemlock death may result in a rapid pulse of large amounts of wood that decays more slowly than coarse woody debris from hardwoods. Large hemlock logs in streams retain sediment and organic matter and create novel habitat types. In general, large hemlock logs are abundant in streams draining forests where hemlock is an important riparian species. Although logs from adelgid-killed hemlocks may persist in streams for decades to centuries, eventually the loss of hemlock will reduce in-stream wood, leading to a decline in sediment retention and productivity.

Logging of hemlock initiates more rapid and greater ecosystem changes than the adelgid because of the abrupt vegetation and environmental changes, removal of wood, soil scarification, and the presence of extensive slash left by logging operations (Kizlinski *et al.* 2002). Nitrogen availability and nitrification rates are significantly higher in cut forests than in adelgid-damaged ones, increasing the threat of nutrient losses and changing food availabil-

ity in nearby aquatic systems (Kizlinski *et al.* 2002; C Swan unpublished).

■ The shifting mosaic of whitebark pine

Whitebark pine forms extensive contiguous stands in high elevation forests of the Rocky Mountains of Wyoming, Montana, Idaho, and Alberta, and smaller disjunct populations in eastern and southwestern Oregon, California, and Nevada. This dominant late-successional species (Figure 3) grows as dense krummholz (stunted trees growing at or just below treeline at higher elevations forming a very low, cushiony mat) at its upper elevational limit, whereas at lower elevations and less extreme sites, it grows in association with other conifers and its dominance is maintained by periodic fire (Arno 2001). Whitebark pine has occupied its current range for approximately 8000 years. In western North America, extensive forests of whitebark pine, spruce (*Picea* spp) and poplar (*Populus* spp) developed after glacial retreat. As warming continued from 8000–4000 years ago, whitebark pine became restricted to high elevation sites (MacDonald *et al.* 1989).

Whitebark pine cover at upper elevations retards snowmelt and modulates runoff and stream flows (Farnes

Figure 3. *High-elevation stands of whitebark pine* (Pinus albicaulis). *This species is transformed from* (a) *healthy stands to* (b) *dead stands through the interaction of fire suppression, the introduced pathogen* Cronartium ribicola *that causes white pine blister rust (inset), and the native bark beetle* Dendroctonus ponderosae.

1990). At lower elevations, post-fire mid-successional whitebark pine stands provide shade and cool soil, facilitating establishment of diverse plant communities and associated cryptogams, invertebrates, and microbes, while its seeds serve as a major seasonal food source for many species of mammals and birds (Mattson *et al.* 2001).

Throughout its range, whitebark pine is declining due to the combined effects of an introduced pathogen, *Cronartium ribicola*, a native bark beetle, *Dendroctonus ponderosae,* and fire-suppression policies (Kendall and Keane 2001). The pathogen *C ribicola*, which causes white pine blister rust, was introduced from Eurasia into western North America in 1910 on imported white pine (*Pinus strobus*) seedlings planted near Vancouver, British Columbia (MacDonald and Hoff 2001). After its introduction, *C ribicola* spread in a series of episodic pulses throughout western North America and by the late 1930s was established throughout the west, where it devastated pine stands (MacDonald and Hoff 2001). Fire exclusion allowed further replacement of whitebark pine by more shade-tolerant species and at lower elevations promoted the growth of dense stands of lodgepole pine (*Pinus contorta*). In turn, lodgepole pine supports high populations of *D ponderosae* beetles that disperse into adjacent whitebark pine stands when beetle populations irrupt. In a positive feedback loop, drought- and disease-stressed whitebark pines are further susceptible to beetle attack.

Loss of whitebark pine alters watershed hydrology immediately as flashiness of streams increases, and changes the dynamics of wildlife populations and succession over longer time scales. Cone crops of whitebark pine have declined due to interactions between white pine blister rust, fire exclusion, and bark beetles. Carrying capacities of species dependent on whitebark pine seeds have also declined with the cone supply of this irreplaceable species (Mattson *et al.* 2001).

■ The shrub that was a tree: American chestnut

American chestnut was once a foundation species in eastern North American forests (Figure 4). Chestnut and oak were co-dominants in the southern Appalachians for nearly 4000 years and reached the northeast from 2500–1500 years ago (Paillet 2002). Chestnut provided

important resources for wildlife and humans, and locally exerted a strong influence on ecosystem structure and function (Paillet 2002). Chestnut blight, caused by the canker pathogen *Cryphonectria parasitica*, was introduced from Asia in the late 19th century. The blight was first noted in New York in 1904, spread rapidly (~37 km yr^{-1}) across the range of chestnut, and within 50 years had converted this stately tree to a rarely flowering understory shrub across approximately 3.6 million ha (Anagnostakis 1987).

Chestnut has a rapid growth rate and sprouting ability, wood with an extremely high tannin content, and leaves with a relatively low C:N ratio. Therefore, fundamental forest ecosystem processes, including decomposition, nutrient cycling, and productivity, probably changed substantially following chestnut's replacement by other species. Decomposition of chestnut wood is much slower than other co-occurring hardwoods and its high tannin concentrations could restrict the mobilization of nutrients in soils. Additionally, chestnut's fast growth rate (Jacobs and Severeid 2004) might have resulted in rapid sequestration of carbon and nutrients.

Chestnut dominated a wide range of environments and its decline is thought to have altered both terrestrial and aquatic processes. There is evidence to suggest that the abundance of chestnut along riparian corridors of the southern Appalachians was due to production of allelochemicals that prevented establishment of what we now consider "typical" riparian shrub and tree species, including eastern hemlock and rhododendron (Vandermast *et al.* 2002). Ironically, therefore, the loss of one foundation species – American chestnut – may have facilitated the establishment of another – eastern hemlock – which in turn is now threatened.

In most forested headwater streams, autumn leaf inputs serve as the predominant energy base for aquatic ecosystems. Where chestnut was replaced by oak, relatively rapidly decaying chestnut leaves with high nutritional quality for aquatic macroinvertebrates were replaced by more slowly decaying oak leaves with lower nutritional quality (Smock and MacGregor 1988). As a consequence, leaf-processing and consumption rates would have declined, decreasing growth rates and adult body mass in macroinvertebrate shredder communities. Many

Figure 4. American chestnut. (a) Chestnut timber, Great Smoky Mountains of western North Carolina (circa 1910), a foundation species that was transformed in the mid-20th century to an understory shrub (b; small shrub in center) by the introduced pathogen Cryphonectria parasitica, *which causes chestnut blight* (c; chestnut in the Blue Ridge Plateau killed by the blight, circa 1946).

stream macroinvertebrates have life cycles closely synchronized to the dynamics of detrital decay, and this change in detrital quality undoubtedly affected the macroinvertebrate assemblage, although there are no data to support this supposition. Furthermore, slowly decomposing chestnut wood persists for decades in stream channels, altering channel structure and providing habitat for fish and invertebrates. For example, in an Appalachian headwater stream sampled in the late 1990s, Wallace *et al.* (2001) found that 24% of the large (> 10 cm diameter) woody debris still consisted of American chestnut that had died over 50 years earlier.

■ Functional loss versus total loss

As foundation species decline, their control of ecosystem structure and processes may wane long before the species itself disappears completely. For example, as hemlock stands decline, tree death opens the canopy, drastically altering the understory microclimate and causing the loss of unique habitat. Similarly, shrubby chestnut contributes little to leaf area, wood production, or nuts, so that while it is still present in many forests, the American chestnut tree is functionally extinct.

The potential effects on ecosystem function and community composition caused by the loss of foundation species can be either exacerbated or ameliorated by patterns of decline in time and space. For example, logging and diseases such as chestnut blight or white pine blister rust have resulted in rapid loss of foundation species over broad areas. This contrasts with the slow death of individuals over decades or partial loss of a species through removal or death of only one age or size class, as in beech bark disease (Griffin *et al.* 2003). Similarly, whether the spatial pattern of individual deaths occurs in mosaic fashion or as an advancing wave influences the timing and magnitude of loss of a foundation species (Holdenreider *et al.* 2004), and perhaps the ultimate outcome. Forest fragmentation often occurs in mosaic patterns across the

landscape (eg Halpern *et al.* 2005), whereas epidemiological models of plant pathogens or species invasions indicate that changes in forest structure occur in wave-like patterns (Johnson *et al.* 2004). Such studies suggest that where complex spatial and temporal patterns of species loss occur, the effects at any particular location are unlikely to be a linear function of area altered or changes in species' dominance. Indeed, threshold responses, including transitions to new types of ecosystems, should be expected where key dependent variables, such as mast production, herbivore or detritivore abundance, or adult survival, result from a complex web of indirect relationships (eg Ebenman and Jonsson in press).

■ Responding to the loss of foundation species

Because foundation tree species tend to be common, abundant, and large, our responses to their loss often come late and are conducted at inappropriate scales. For example, the ongoing attempt to recreate the American chestnut by backcrossing the few remaining fertile individuals with resistant species from Europe and Asia holds out the promise of specimen trees in suburban lawns but is unlikely to reforest four million hectares with hybrid chestnuts. Similarly, chemical control of the hemlock woolly adelgid requires injecting trees annually and can only target isolated single trees or small groves. Biological control of the adelgid using non-native, generalist, predaceous beetles is being explored with uneven regard for the long history of unexpected impacts that can accompany the importation of exotic insects (eg Howarth 1991; Boettner *et al.* 2000). Although several million beetles are released every year, there have been no systematic attempts to determine whether self-sustaining populations have become established or how effective they are at actually controlling the adelgid in the field. Overall, we would be much more likely to conserve foundation species and the systems they create if we set aside very large reserves of intact forests and adopted techniques that preserve ecosystem integrity in managed forest stands (Foster *et al.* 2005).

■ Conclusions

There is no sign that the currently increasing rates of resource extraction, climate change, or global movement of pests and pathogens will slow any time soon. Foundation species have disappeared before and they will continue to disappear. Despite nearly half a century of research on foundation species (Panel 1), our understanding of the consequences of their loss is based on a small number of case studies, as we usually identify foundation species only after they have declined dramatically. Our examples illustrate how foundation tree species can control both terrestrial forest processes and the dynamics of aquatic systems within their watersheds. However, detailed information on the importance of foundation species for key ecosystem processes are scarce. Likewise, the impact on water quality from the loss of foundation species could be substantial and merits further study.

Long-term monitoring can reveal how losses of foundation species alter rates and trajectories of succession, leading in some cases to novel forest types (such as black birch forests in New England) with unexpected dynamics. However, monitoring is not enough. Ecologists have long appreciated the complex nature of interactions among species, and we encourage direct, experimental approaches that use current losses of foundation species as an opportunity to determine how the removal of a single species can have immediate and profound effects on other species and ecosystem processes.

The dynamics of communities and ecosystems shaped by foundation species are dominated by a small number of strong interactions (Figure 2). Such systems are relatively fragile and susceptible to switching between alternative stable states following even small perturbations (Dudgeon and Petraitis 2005). At the same time as many forested systems are losing their foundation species, they are simultaneously and synergistically threatened by climate change, atmospheric deposition, drought, and invasion of exotic species, all of which may increase their overall fragility. Temperate-zone forests, such as those we have highlighted here, have few tree species relative to the species-rich tropical forests that garner much attention from ecologists and conservation biologists. When there are only one or two foundation species in a forest, there is little functional redundancy in many important respects, and their loss is likely to lead to rapid, possibly irreversible, shifts in biological diversity and system-wide changes in structure and function (Ebenman and Jonsson in press). Regrettably, the lack of detailed knowledge of the natural history of most species in most forests, and the abandonment of courses and curricula in natural history (Dayton 2003), will leave us unaware of the collapse of the intricate webs of interactions and processes that are lost when foundation species disappear.

These species provide fundamental structure to a system, and thus are by definition irreplaceable. For example, with-out hemlock, hemlock forests cease to exist, and no other native conifer possesses the same suite of structural and functional characteristics that simultaneously define its position in the system and control system-wide dynamics and processes. Many recognized foundation tree species (Panel 2) that have been identified are conifers, but it remains an open question whether conifers are disproportionately represented among foundation species. We need new research tools, models, and metrics that will allow us to identify foundation species a priori and to anticipate the cascade of immediate, short- and long-term changes in ecosystem structure and function that follow their loss. Community viability analysis (Ebenman and Jonsson in press) may provide some of these tools, but its utility awaits empirical evaluation. Ongoing declines of many foundation species (Panel 2) provide timely, though unfortunate, opportunities to develop such tools and models.

■ Acknowledgements

We thank A Barker-Plotkin, P Dayton, E Farnsworth, S Jefts, J Jones, J Malloway, B Mathewson, R McDonald, T Spies, and F Swanson for useful discussion and constructive comments on the manuscript. This work was supported by the Harvard Forest, NSF grants DEB 00–80592, DEB 02–18001, DEB 02–18039, DEB 02–36154, and DEB 02–36897, and the US Forest Service, and is a cross-site contribution of the Andrews, Baltimore, Coweeta, Harvard Forest, Hubbard Brook, and Luquillo Long-Term Ecological Research Programs.

■ References

Anagnostakis SA. 1987. Chestnut blight: the classical problem of an introduced pathogen. *Mycologia* **79**: 23–37.

Arno SF. 2001. Community types and natural disturbance processes. In: Tomback DF, Arno SF, and Keane RE (Eds). Whitebark pine communities, ecology and restoration. Washington, DC: Island Press.

Bhiry N and Filion L. 1996. Mid-holocene hemlock decline in eastern North America linked with phytophagus insect activity. *Quaternary Res* **45**: 312–20.

Boettner GH, Elkinton JS, and Boettner CJ. 2000. Effects of a biological control introduction on three nontarget native species of Saturniid moths. *Conserv Biol* **14**: 1789–1806.

Catovsky S, Holbrook NM, and Bazzaz FA. 2002. Coupling whole-tree transpiration and canopy photosynthesis in coniferous and broad-leaved tree species. *Can J For Res* **32**: 295–309.

Davison EM and Tay FCS. 1987. The effect of waterlogging on infection of *Eucalyptus marginata* seedlings by *Phytophthora cinnamomi*. *New Phytol* **105**: 585–94.

Dayton PK. 1972. Toward an understanding of community resilience and the potential effects of enrichments to the benthos at McMurdo Sound, Antarctica. In: Parker BC (Ed). Proceedings of the colloquium on conservation problems in Antarctica. Lawrence, KS: Allen Press.

Dayton PK. 2003. The importance of the natural sciences to conservation. *Am Nat* **162**: 1–13.

Dudgeon S and Petraitis PS. 2005. First year demography of the foundation species, *Ascophyllum nodosum*, and its community implications. *Oikos* **109**: 405–15.

Ebenman B and Jonsson T. Using community viability analysis to identify fragile systems and keystone species. *Trends Ecol Evol* doi:10.1016/j.tree.2005.06.011. In press.

Eldrige N. 1998. Life in the balance: humanity and the biodiversity crisis. Princeton, NJ: Princeton University Press.

Ellison AM and Farnsworth EJ. 2001. Mangrove communities. In: Bertness MD, Gaines SD, and Hay ME (Eds). Marine community ecology. Sunderland, MA: Sinauer Associates.

Ellison AM, Chen J, Díaz D, *et al.* 2005. Changes in ant community structure and composition associated with hemlock decline in New England. In: Onken B and Reardon R (Eds). Proceedings of the 3rd symposium on hemlock woolly adelgid in the eastern United States. Morgantown, WV: USDA Forest Service.

Farnes PE. 1990. SNOTEL and snow course data describing the hydrology of whitebark pine ecosystems. In: Schmidt WC and McDonald KJ (Eds). Proceedings of a symposium on whitebark pine ecosystems: ecology and management of a high mountain resource. Ogden, UT: USDA Forest Service Intermountain Research Station.

Foster DR, Kittredge D, Donahue B, *et al.* 2005. Wildlands and woodlands: a vision for the forests of Massachusetts. Petersham, MA: Harvard Forest.

Frost R 1923. Dust of snow. In: New Hampshire: a poem with notes and grace notes. New York, NY: Henry Holt and Co.

Griffin JM, Lovett GM, Arthur MA, *et al.* 2003. The distribution and severity of beech bark disease in the Catskill Mountains, NY. *Can J For Res* **33**: 1754–60.

Grime JP. 1984. Dominant and subordinate components of plant communities: implications for succession, stability and diversity. In: Gray AJ and Crawley MJ (Eds). Colonization, succession and stability. Oxford, UK: Blackwell.

Halpern CB, McKenzie D, Evans SA, *et al.* 2005. Initial responses for forest understories to varying levels and patterns of green-tree retention. *Ecol Appl* **15**: 175–95.

Hamburg SP and Cogbill CV. 1988. Historical decline of red spruce populations and climatic warming. *Nature* **331**: 428–31.

Hansen EM, Goheen DJ, Jules ES, *et al.* 2000. Managing Port-Orford cedar and the introduced pathogen *Phytophthora lateralis*. *Plant Dis* **84**: 4–10.

Hanski I. 1982. Dynamics of regional distribution: the core and satellite species hypothesis. *Oikos* **38**: 210–21.

Holdenrieder O, Pautasso M, Weisberg PJ, *et al.* 2004. Tree diseases and landscape processes: the challenge of landscape pathology. *Trends Ecol Evol* **19**: 446–52.

Holling CS. 1992. Cross-scale morphology, geometry, and dynamics of ecosystems. *Ecol Monogr* **62**: 447–502.

Hollingsworth RG and Hain FP. 1991. Balsam woolly adelgid (Homoptera, Adelgidae) and spruce-fir decline in the southern Appalachians: assessing pest relevance in a damaged ecosystem. *Florida Entomol* **74**: 179–87.

Howarth FG. 1991. Environmental impacts of classical biological control. *Ann Rev Entomol* **36**: 485–509.

Huston MA. 1994. Biological diversity: the coexistence of species on changing landscapes. Cambridge, UK: Cambridge University Press.

Jacobs DF and Severeid LR. 2004. Dominance of interplanted American chestnut (*Castanea dentata*) in southwestern Wisconsin, USA. *Forest Ecol Manag* **191**: 111–20.

Jenkins, J, Aber JD, and Canham CD. 1999. Hemlock woolly adelgid impacts on community structure and N cycling rates in eastern hemlock forests. *Can J For Res* **29**: 630–45.

Johnson DM, Bjørnstad ON, and Liebhold AM. 2004. Landscape geometry and travelling waves in the larch budmoth. *Ecol Lett* **7**: 967–74.

Jones CG, Lawton JH, and Shachak M. 1994. Organisms as ecosystem engineers. *Oikos* **69**: 373–86.

Kendall KC and Keane RE. 2001. Whitebark pine decline: infection, mortality, and population trends. In: Tomback DF, Arno SF, and Keane RE (Eds). Whitebark pine communities, ecology and restoration. Washington, DC: Island Press.

Kizlinski ML, Orwig DA, Cobb RC, *et al.* 2002. Direct and indirect ecosystem consequences of an invasive pest on forests dominated by eastern hemlock. *J Biogeogr* **29**: 1489–503.

MacDonald GI and Hoff RJ. 2001. Blister rust: an introduced plague. In: Tomback DF, Arno SF, and Keane RE (Eds). Whitebark pine communities, ecology and restoration. Washington, DC: Island Press.

MacDonald GM, Cwynar LC, and Whitlock C. 1989. Late quaternary dynamics of pines: northern North America. In: Richardson DM (Ed). Ecology and biogeography of *Pinus*. New York, NY: Cambridge University Press.

Mattson DJ, Kendall KC, and Reinhart DP. 2001. Whitebark pine, grizzly bears, and red squirrels. In: Tomback DF, Arno SF, and Keane RE (Eds). Whitebark pine communities, ecology and restoration. Washington, DC: Island Press.

McMartin B. 1992. Hides, hemlocks, and Adirondack history. Utica, NY: North Country Books.

McWilliams WH and Schmidt TL. 2000. Composition, structure, and sustainability of hemlock ecosystems in eastern North America. In: McManus KA, Shields KS, and Souto DR (Eds). Proceedings: symposium on sustainable management of hemlock ecosystems in eastern North America, June 22–24, 1999. Durham, NH: USDA Forest Service.

Orwig DA, Foster DR, and Mausel DL. 2002. Landscape patterns of hemlock decline in New England due to the introduced hemlock woolly adelgid. *J Biogeogr* **29**: 1475–87.

Paillet F. 2002. Chestnut: history and ecology of a transformed species. *J Biogeogr* **29**: 1517–30.

Paine RT. 1966. Food web complexity and species diversity. *Am Nat* **100**: 65–75.

Parker GG, Harmon MA, and Lefsky JQ. 2004. Three-dimensional structure of an old-growth *Pseudotsuga tsuga* canopy and its implications for radiation balance, microclimate, and gas exchange. *Ecosystems* **7**: 440–53.

Reid WV, Mooney HA, Cropper A, *et al.* 2005. Millennium ecosystem assessment synthesis report. Washington, DC: Millennium Assessment and World Resources Institute.

Sharitz R and Mitsch WJ. 1993. Southern floodplain forests. In: Echternacht AC (Ed). Biodiversity of the southeastern United States: lowland terrestrial communities. New York, NY: John Wiley and Sons.

Smock LA and MacGregor CM. 1988. Impact of the American chestnut blight on aquatic shredding macroinvertebrates. *J N Am Benthol Soc* **7**: 212–21.

Snyder CD, Young JA, Smith D, *et al.* 2002. Influence of eastern hemlock (*Tsuga canadensis*) forests on aquatic invertebrate assemblages in headwater streams. *Can J Fish Aquat Sci* **59**: 262–75.

Sun G, McNulty SG, Shepard JP, *et al.* 2001. Effects of timber management on the hydrology of wetland forests in the southern United States. *Forest Ecol Manag* **143**: 227–36.

Tingley MW, Orwig DA, Field R, *et al.* 2002. Avian response to removal of a forest dominant: consequences of hemlock woolly adelgid infestations. *J Biogeogr* **29**: 1505–16.

Vandermast DB, Van Lear DH, and Clinton BD. 2002. American chestnut as an allelopath in the southern Appalachians. *Forest Ecol Manag* **165**: 173–81.

Wallace JB, Webster JR, Eggert SL, *et al.* 2001. Large woody debris in a headwater stream: long-term legacies of forest disturbance. *Int Rev Hydrobiol* **86**: 501–13.

Wills RT. 1992. The ecological impact of *Phytophthora cinnamomi* in the Stirling Range National Park, Western Australia. *Aust J Ecol* **17**: 145–59.

Wills RT and Keighery GJ. 1994. Ecological impact of plant disease on plant communities. *J Roy Soc W Aust* **77**: 127–31.

Problem solving: a foundation for modeling

J Hodder[1], G Middendorf[2], and D Ebert-May[3]

Reading and discussing primary literature is central to communicating science. Students need practice in reading the literature for purposes beyond gaining information. Literature can be used to both increase knowledge and comprehension and to engage students in higher-level thinking (Bloom 1956; Levine 2001; Gillen *et al.* 2004; Finelli *et al.* 2005). Because science is also about making predictions and testing models, using information gained from reading to construct models allows students to develop problem-solving skills (Starfield *et al.* 1994). Ellison *et al.* (pp 479–486) provide information on how the removal of foundation species has affected the structure and function of a wide range of forest communities. In this article, we show how the Ellison *et al.* paper can be used to help students make connections between their prior knowledge and new information. Students explain the causes and effects of forest decline and the ecological processes involved by developing an explicit model that interconnects the data presented in the paper. They confer with their peers to explain and refine their models and then use the knowledge represented in their models to make predictions about novel situations. In this way, students actively develop their understanding of science and practice their ability to solve problems.

■ Student goals

- Demonstrate expertise in reading and interpreting scientific literature to solve problems.
- Analyze and apply information to design models that explain changes in ecosystem processes.
- Transfer understanding of ecosystem processes in forests to other ecosystems.

■ Instructor goals

- Use a jigsaw assignment as an effective way to analyze literature.
- Use group and individual instructional strategies to enable students to actively construct understanding of foundation species effects on ecosystem function by building descriptive models.
- Assess understanding of ecosystem functions by giving students novel examples to apply their understanding and test predictions.

■ Instructional design

Prepare for building models

Engage students by showing them the photographs in

[1]*University of Oregon*, [2]*Howard University*, [3]*Michigan State University*

Figures 1, 2, and 4 in Ellison *et al.* Students then describe the changes they see in hemlock, whitebark pine, and American chestnut forests and predict why these changes occurred (think individually, then share with their neighbor, ie "think–pair–share"; http://tiee.ecoed.net/teach/tutorials/neighbor.html). Select several pairs to report to the class; both individuals from the pair should be prepared to speak. Follow with a discussion of how scientists often synthesize and condense data into descriptive models that integrate processes. Show and discuss the components of several examples of such models, including ones derived from the examples in Panel 2 of Ellison *et al.*

Active homework

For homework, students form three-person groups. Each group member is responsible for constructing a model about how the removal of the foundation species affected ecosystem function of one of the three forest examples in the paper. Students are instructed to include information on the ecological processes and the biotic and abiotic factors that influenced the change from the historical situation to present-day conditions (eg Panel 1 for the hemlock forest). Students bring two copies of their models to class, one to hand in (for a grade or check) and the other to use when they explain the model to their group.

In class

Students share the details of their models within their groups and look for commonalities and differences in the causes and effects of foundational tree removal. Based on this, they create a summary table (formative assessment), listing the causal factors that influenced declines of foundation species for each of the three ecosystems (Panel 2). Groups then present their findings (post-it posters are a useful tool) along with an instructor-led discussion on the varieties of pathways and effects leading to ecosystem change.

An assessment of whether students fully understand the material is to ask them to apply their knowledge of ecosystem processes to a different system. For example, the instructor could present data from Jackson *et al.* (2001), showing how removal of predators as a result of overfishing has fundamentally altered the functioning of the world's coastal ecosystems in a similar manner to that seen in the removal of foundation species. Another example involves work in the Sonoran desert (McGregor *et al.* 1962; Pierson and Turner 1998) that reveals the keystone role of saguaro populations. Based on instructor-supplied material or their own literature searches, students predict

Panel 1. Example of model showing changes in ecosystem processes in an eastern hemlock forest

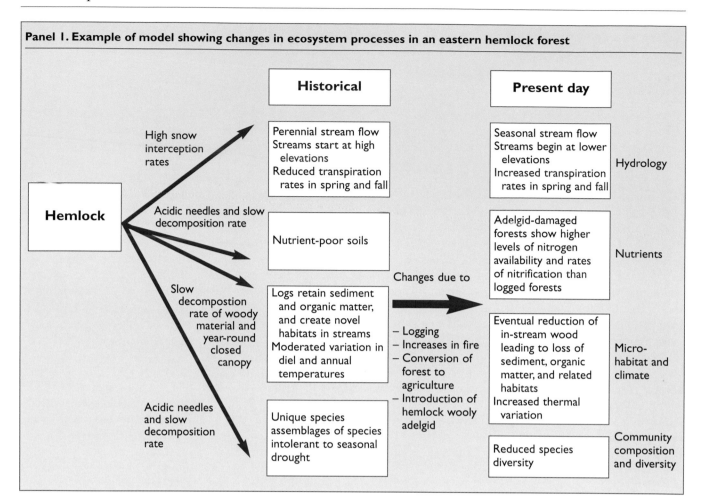

the consequences of predator loss in ocean systems, or of a foundation species in the desert, and then construct a descriptive model that describes the resulting ecosystem changes. This assessment may be done by individuals or groups. Ideally, results will show if students can make connections about the factors influencing the changes in ecosystem structure from their work on the Ellison *et al.* paper.

■ Final note

Students have been building conceptual models in their minds for as long as they can remember. However, what they have not done often, if ever, is build explicit models so both they and their peers can understand and use them. Modeling provides a venue for students to critically read and process information about ecological problems from the literature. It also allows instructors to assess students' thinking.

■ Acknowledgements

We thank the National Science Foundation for their long-term support of the FIRST project, Faculty Institutes for Reforming Science Teaching (DUE 0088847). All Pathways papers are peer reviewed.

■ References

Bloom BS. 1956. Taxonomy of educational objectives, handbook I: the cognitive domain. New York, NY: David McKay Co Inc.

Finelli C, Ebert-May D, and Hodder J. 2005. Collaborative learning – a jigsaw. *Front Ecol Environ* **4**: 220–21.

Gillen CM, Vaughn J, and Lye BR. 2004. An online tutorial for helping nonscience majors read primary research literature in biology. *Adv Phys Edu* **28**: 95–99.

Jackson JBC, Kirby MX, Berger WH, *et al.* 2001. Historical overfishing and the recent collapse of coastal ecosystems. *Science* **293**: 629–37.

Levine E. 2001. Reading your way to scientific literacy. *J Coll Sci Teach* **31**: 122–25.

McGregor SE, Alcorn SM, and Olin G. 1962. Pollination and pollinating agents of the saguaro. *Ecology* **43**: 259–67.

Pierson EA and Turner RM. 1998. An 85-year study of saguaro (*Carnegiea gigantea*) demography. *Ecology* **79**: 2676–93.

Starfield AM, Smith KA, and Blelock AL. 1994. How to model it: problem solving for the computer age. Edina, MN: Burgess International Group Inc.

Panel 2. Causal factors influencing decline of foundation species

Causal factors	Hemlock	Whitebark pine	Chestnut
Native pest or pathogen		Yes	
Introduced pest or pathogen	Yes	Yes	Yes
Increased rates of fire	Yes		
Reduced rates of fire (suppression)		Yes	
Logging	Yes		
Conversion of forest to agriculture	Yes		

Chapter 5

Faculty and Students: Assessing Multiple Ways

Overview

"How am I going to find time to grade more stuff?" is, by far, the most frequent response from faculty when we discuss assessment in all its various forms. Time is a genuine issue. The assessments in these papers provide different kinds and quality of data about student learning and suggest that the investment in time may be worth the return. Scoring rubrics are an essential part of assessment. Rubrics provide students with expectations and a guide for how they are assessed, and save time with grading (Handelsman et al. 2007).

In a nutshell, assessment is data collection with the purpose of answering questions about students' understanding, skills, and attitudes, and is central to scientific teaching. Just as in science, data informs conclusions and drives the next questions—in teaching, assessments provide feedback to students and help instructors determine the degree to which students have achieved the intended outcomes. Assessments can drive the next steps of instruction. Because learning is a complex process, we are challenged to create assessments that genuinely measure the learning goals we want our students to achieve. While it is easier and more efficient to assess students' knowledge and comprehension, it is more difficult and time-consuming to assess students' problem solving and critical thinking skills. In scientific teaching we want students to construct understanding by asking questions, designing experiments, working with data, identifying patterns, making models and predictions, and testing the models in new experiments (Etkina et al. 2005).

One goal of the units in this chapter is to improve students' abilities to learn science by solving problems. The instructor's goals are to assess what students have learned both during (formative) and at the conclusion of (summative) the activity. Designing appropriate assessments is the challenge, because multiple-choice questions, although easy to grade, provide incomplete evidence of students' accomplishments. On the other hand, extended-response questions, which have the potential to reveal more about student thinking, are time-consuming to grade. These articles offer ideas for multiple forms of both formative and summative assessments that when combined provide more reliable and valid insight into students' understanding about the science they are learning. For example, we ask students to represent a concept or process in multiple ways, such as in analogies, models, pictures, applications, and extended responses. We also illustrate several in-class problems designed as group activities to teach students, in part, how to make models, such as concept maps, flow charts, or box diagrams.

How will you find time to grade these assessments? Scoring rubrics are tools that provide specific criteria by which the assessments (e.g., exam questions, homework, papers, projects) are evaluated. Point values are associated with these criteria. In most rubrics the criteria are grouped into categories so the instructor and the student can discriminate among the categories by level of performance. Rubrics are necessary for grading because they provide an objective, external standard against which student performance is compared. We give students rubrics *before* they undertake an assignment or answer test questions, and consequently, if followed, students know what "we want" on assignments and have a roadmap for performing well. Rubrics are analogous to guidelines for writing grant proposals or preparing a paper for submission to a journal—none of us would proceed without one. Hence, students need rubrics in hand to meet their expected outcomes for performance based on the learning goals. Rubrics make grading easier, fairer, and less contentious, and students' performance improves. Ultimately, rubrics save time!

Novel weapons: invasive success and the evolution of increased competitive ability

Ragan M Callaway and Wendy M Ridenour

When introduced to new habitats by humans, some plant species become much more dominant. This is primarily attributed to escape from specialist consumers. Release from these specialist enemies is also thought by some to lead to the evolution of increased competitive ability, driven by a decrease in the plant's resource allocation to consumer defense and an increase in allocation to size or fecundity. Here, we discuss a new theory for invasive success – the "novel weapons hypothesis". We propose that some invaders transform because they possess novel biochemical weapons that function as unusually powerful allelopathic agents, or as mediators of new plant–soil microbial interactions. Root exudates that are relatively ineffective against their natural neighbors because of adaptation, may be highly inhibitory to newly encountered plants in invaded communities. In other words, the novel weapons of some plant invaders provide them with an advantage that may arise from differences in the regional coevolutionary trajectories of plant communities. Furthermore, the selective advantage of possessing a novel weapon may result in rapid evolution of that weapon – for example, the production of greater quantities of allelopathic or antimicrobial root exudates. Direct selection of competitive traits provides an alternative to the "grow versus defend" trade-offs that underpin the theory of the evolution of increased competitive ability.

Front Ecol Environ 2004; 2(8): 436–443

In the 13th century, eastern and central Europe experienced one of the most surprising invasions in human history. The Mongols, once restricted to a small portion of central Asia, swept into Russia, Hungary, Poland, and Germany and consistently defeated much larger European armies. It was only the death of the Mongol leader, Ogedai Khan, in 1242, and the ensuing internal politics, that prevented Europe from becoming a collection of vassal states. The reasons for the success of the Mongol invasion were complex. Although it was in large part due to brilliant strategy and discipline, these strengths were derived from the possession of a novel weapon, the recurve bow carried by most Mongolian soldiers (Figure 1). The recurve bow

---

In a nutshell:
- The success of some exotic invasive plant species may be due to the possession of "novel weapons", biochemicals that native species have never encountered
- The novel weapons hypothesis raises the possibility of coevolution among plants in different regions of the Earth, and that mixing species from different regions increases the chances of disrupting the ecological processes that lead to species coexistence and greater community diversity
- Novel weapons suggest an alternative mechanism for the evolution of increased competitive ability in invasive plants. If invaders possess allelochemical weapons that provide greater competitive advantages in their new habitats than in their original ranges, then selection may act directly on those traits. We call this the "allelopathic advantage against resident species" hypothesis or "AARS"

Division of Biological Sciences, The University of Montana, Missoula, MT 59812 (ray.callaway@mso.umt.edu)

fired arrows faster, farther, and with greater force than anything the Europeans had ever experienced. Such novel weapons have played a role in many human invasions, but novel biological weapons have only recently been considered as possible drivers of invasions by non-human exotic species. Here, we explore the possibility that novel weapons, biochemical in nature, play a part in the exotic plant invasions that are currently sweeping the world.

One of the mysteries in ecology is how exotic plants occurring at low densities in their native ranges attain extremely high densities in their introduced ranges (Figure 2). Although only a small fraction of introduced species have enjoyed such dramatic changes in fortune, these have had extensive economic impacts and suggest the existence of very powerful, yet poorly understood, ecological processes. A number of explanations for this invasion success have been proposed (Mack et al. 2000), but consumer-based hypotheses predominate – the "natural enemies hypothesis" (Williams 1954; Elton 1958; Crawley 1987, 1997; Mack et al. 2000; Maron and Vilà 2001; Levine et al. 2002) and a recent expansion of the natural enemies hypothesis, "the evolution of increased competitive ability" (EICA; Blossey and Nötzold 1995; Müller-Schärer et al. 2004).

The natural enemies hypothesis attributes exotic plant success to the fact that upon introduction many exotics are liberated from their specialist herbivores and pathogens. Exotics are thought to gain a substantial advantage because their populations are no longer directly suppressed by specialist consumers and pathogens, and because they obtain a competitive advan-

---

tage over natives that may suffer disproportionately from attacks by these native enemies.

The EICA hypothesis argues that exotics long liberated from their native specialist enemies should lose costly traits that helped them resist those enemies. By evolving to allocate less resources to traits that conferred resistance to their specialist enemies, which are absent in the introduced range, exotics can use more resources for traits that provide greater competitive advantage, such as size or fecundity. Although the EICA hypothesis refers only to competitive ability, it was explicitly developed in the context of the "grow or defend" paradigm of allocation trade-offs (Herms and Matson 1992) and therefore reference to EICA implicitly attributes increased competitive ability to such trade-offs. The novel weapons hypothesis, described in detail below, addresses both invasive success and the evolution of increased competitive ability.

Convincing evidence exists for the natural enemies hypothesis as an explanation of some successful exotic invasions (Wolfe 2002; Mitchell and Power 2003; Reinhart *et al.* 2003; Siemann and Rogers 2003; Callaway *et al.* 2004; DeWalt *et al.* 2004; Jakobs *et al.* 2004), but there are reasons to be hesitant about accepting enemy release as the only reason for invasive success. First, there is evidence that the effects of natural enemies are weak on some invaders (Callaway *et al.* 1999; Ridenour and Callaway 2003; Lesica and Hanna 2004; Maron and Vilá 2001). Also, consumer effects can be similar in native and introduced ranges, (Beckstead and Parker 2003; Maron and Vilá 2001; Reinhart and Callaway in press), and in some habitats natives and exotics appear to receive similar amounts of damage (Agrawal and Kotanen 2003). Second, the literature on consumer–plant interactions in natural systems suggests that the relative impact of consumers is often minimal (Crawley 1989). Finally, little is known about the comparative effects of herbivores or pathogens on invasive plants in their native ranges versus their invaded ranges (see DeWalt *et al.* 2004 for an exception), and virtually nothing is known about the relative effects of consumers on the population ecology of invaders in native versus invaded ranges.

There is evidence for EICA (Daehler and Strong 1997; Willis and Blossey 1999; Siemann and Rogers 2001; 2003a,b; Leger and Rice 2003) and against it (Willis *et al.* 2000; Vilá *et al.* 2003; van Kleunen and Schmid 2003; Bossdorf *et al.* 2004; Maron *et al.* 2004). Although some invaders have been shown to be either larger or more fecund than similar species back in their native ranges, these studies have not shown that size confers greater competitive ability. Furthermore, no studies have explicitly linked greater size to the reallo-

Figure 1. A Mongol warrior wielding the recurve bow.

cation of resources or energy from defense against specialist herbivores to competitive ability.

■ Biochemical novel weapons

The role of consumer interactions in plant invasions must be crucial, but interactions between plants as determinants of invasive success have been overlooked. The novel weapons hypothesis that we propose holds that some exotics transform from native weaklings to invasive bullies by exuding biochemicals that are highly inhibitory (allelopathic) to plants or soil microbes in invaded communities, but relatively ineffective against natural neighbors that had adapted over time (Rabotnov 1982; Mallik and Pellisier 2000). Like the "guns, germs, and steel" used by human European invaders against indigenous peoples (Diamond 1997), the possession of novel weapons by some plant invaders provides them with an advantage that arises from regional differences in coevolutionary trajectories (Thompson 1999). To be precise, the definition of novel weapons here is limited to biochemicals released from invasive plants that affect native plants or the native soil biota, and with which native plants interact. For example, invasive plants may release biochemicals that alter the soil biota in ways that disadvantage native plants.

One manifestation of different regional evolutionary trajectories may be the huge number of different biochemicals produced by plants. So far, a compositionally diverse array of over 100 000 different low-molecular-mass natural products has been identified, many of which appear to be species-specific (Bais *et al.* 2002, 2003; Flores 1999). Far more are likely to be discovered. This rich diversity is probably due to selection pressures for many

Courtesy of J Anthony

Figure 2. *An invasive monoculture of kudzu* (Pueraria montana) *in the southeastern US. As with many exotic invasive plants, kudzu causes much more damage in its invasive range than in its native range.*

different jobs, including soil nutrient acquisition, defense against herbivory, root communication, and antimicrobial protection. Alternatively, many biochemicals may be metabolic byproducts without particular functions. As described below for the examples of *Centaurea maculosa*, *Centaurea diffusa*, and *Picea-Vaccinum* communities, there is no reason to think that novel weapons must have originally evolved for the purpose of poisoning other plants. There may be good reason, however, to think that biochemicals, once evolved, can affect other plants, that other plants or microbes may evolve to tolerate the chemicals exuded by their neighbors, and that possession of novel weapons may lead to their proliferation.

The novel weapons hypothesis does have some strikes against it. First, little unambiguous evidence for it exists – what is known is presented below. Second, the allelopathic mechanisms on which the hypothesis partially rests have a murky history (Callaway 2002), and allelopathy has been dismissed, perhaps unfairly, by many in plant community theory in favor of resource-driven interactions. On the other hand, biogeographic studies of allelopathic effects of invasive plants in natural and invaded communities may provide a new line of evidence for the role of allelopathy in community theory (Baldwin 2003; Fitter 2003). Finally, the notion that plant communities consist, even to a small extent, of species adapted to each other's rhizosphere biochemistry is unsettling to people raised on Whittaker's (1951) ideas about individualistic plant communities. Nevertheless, recent evidence suggests that geographic coevolutionary trajectories (Thompson 1999) based on unique biochemistry may affect plant coexistence and the development of communities; disruption of these trajectories by invaders may therefore have profound consequences (see also Callaway and Hierro in press; Callaway *et al.* in press).

Diffuse knapweed (*Centaurea diffusa*), a relatively minor member of a diverse genus, occurs naturally across Europe and Asia. Although capable of high densities immediately after agricultural disturbance in native systems, it is rarely as abundant, widespread, and dominant in its natural geographic range as it is in the western North American communities it has invaded (RM Callaway pers obs). While working in the foothills of the Caucasus Mountains, Callaway and Aschehoug (2000) observed that many of the genera outcompeted by *C diffusa* in North America appeared to coexist in relative peace with *C diffusa* in their native range (Figure 3). It did not seem likely that *C diffusa* would possess some profound competitive advantage for resources over North American species, yet not have similar advantages over species that were similar in size and phylogeny in the Caucasus. To test this, Callaway and Aschehoug collected seeds of *C diffusa* and several coexisting grass species in the Caucasus. They then grew the Caucasian species and related North American species in competition with the Caucasian *C diffusa*. Most importantly, they included treatments in which these competing species were grown in sand mixed with a small amount of activated carbon, a compound that absorbs organic molecules and has been used in previous experiments to ameliorate the allelopathic effects of root exudates of *Centaurea maculosa* and other species (Mahall and Callaway 1992; Ridenour and Callaway 2001).

They found that *C diffusa* suppressed the growth of North American species by about 70% more than it suppressed the growth of Caucasian species. Furthermore, activated carbon sharply reduced the inhibitory effect of *C diffusa* on the North American plants, but not its effect on the Caucasian plants. The story is more complicated, however, as *C diffusa* strongly suppressed the ability of North American species to acquire phosphorus-32 (^{32}P; a radioactive isotope of phosphorus), but had no influence on the Caucasian species in this regard. The effect on the North American plants was not altered by the presence of activated carbon. The reason for this difference is not known; it is possible, however, that activated carbon interfered with the phosphorus-chelating properties of *C diffusa*'s root exudates (see below) as well as their toxic properties, and allelo-tolerant Eurasian grasses suffered from the adsorption of their neighbor's P-chelating root exudates.

Providing more mechanistic detail, Vivanco *et al.* (2004) identified a chemical in the root exudates of *C diffusa*, 8-hydroxyquinoline, which had not previously been reported as a natural product and which has strong metal-chelating properties. Although they have similar effects, 8-hydroxyquinoline is not related to (±)-catechin. They also found that experimental communities built from North American grass species were far more susceptible to invasion by *C diffusa* than communities built from Eurasian species, regardless of the biogeographical origin of the soil biota. These results correspond well with those of Callaway and Aschehoug (2000). In addition, 8-hydroxyquinoline applied to plants growing in field soils in pots suppressed the growth of North American species about 30% more than it did the growth of Caucasian species. Considered as a package, the results of Callaway and Aschehoug (2000) and Vivanco *et al.* (2004) raise the possibility that Eurasian plants have evolved tolerance to the root exudates of *C diffusa* and a particular chemical constituent of *C diffusa's* root exudates, while North American plants have not. This suggests the possibility of evolved compatibility among plants within natural communities, and that the disruption of this compatibility can destroy these communities.

Mallik and Pellissier (2000) conducted experiments comparing the effects of leaves, leaf extracts, and humus from *Vaccinium myrtillis*, a widespread understory shrub in coniferous forests of Eurasia that has strong allelopathic effects, on an exotic North American neighbor, *Picea mariana*, and on a long-term native neighbor, *Picea abies*. They found that V *myrtillus* generally had stronger biochemical effects on the exotic plant than on the native one. Their results also support the idea of a coevolutionary aspect to allelopathy (Rabotnov 1982).

Figure 3. *(a) Palouse prairie in eastern Oregon; (b) prairie south of the Caucasus in the eastern part of the Republic of Georgia. The regions share many genera which are similar in size and morphology.* Centaurea diffusa *is native to the Caucasus region and invasive in the Palouse and intermountain prairies of North America.*

Similar evidence exists for a plant in the same genus as *C diffusa*, the even nastier invader *C maculosa*. Probably introduced with alfalfa seed from Europe, it now occupies over 7 million acres of the US (http://www.fs.fed.us/database/feis/plants/forb/cenmac/all.html; Figure 4). Like *C diffusa*, *C maculosa* is not a dominant, or even common, species in Europe. In the US, *C maculosa* has been the target of an aggressive biological control effort, with 13 species of insects introduced to control the weed. So far, biocontrol has not been successful (Müller-Schärer and Schroeder 1993; Pearson and Callaway 2003), suggesting that the lack of specialist insect herbivores is a minor component of its invasive success. In fact, specialist biocontrol root herbivory may stimulate the growth and competitive ability of *C maculosa* (Callaway *et al.* 1999;

Ridenour and Callaway 2003), an odd phenomenon that may be due to the effects of herbivory on the exudation of allelochemicals into the rhizosphere (GC Thelen and RM Callaway unpublished).

By integrating ecological, physiological, biochemical signal transduction, and genomic approaches to the root exudates of *C maculosa*, Bais *et al.* (2003) were able to isolate (-)-catechin, a chemical that has phytotoxic properties and is produced by *C maculosa* roots. Although unrelated chemically to 8-hydroxyquinoline, and not as rare in natural systems, (-)-catechin has been found in only a few plant species. Further supporting the novel weapons hypothesis, the germination and growth of European grasses were more resistant to (-)-catechin than were the germination and growth of naïve North American plants of the same genus.

Using a biogeographic approach similar to that of

Courtesy of G Thelen

Figure 4. Centaurea maculosa, *an invader of many communities in North America. The roots of this species exude large amounts of (±)-catechin, an isomer with chelating, phytotoxic, and antimicrobial properties.*

Callaway and Aschehoug (2000), Prati and Bossdorf (2004) compared the allelopathic effects of *Alliaria petiolata* (garlic mustard), an aggressive invader of the understory of forests in North America, on the germination of two closely related species that co-occur with *Alliaria*, the American *Geum laciniatum* and the European *Geum urbanum*. Although no specific biochemical has been identified, they found that invasive North American populations of *A petiolata* greatly reduced the germination of naïve North American *G laciniatum* seeds, but had no effect on "experienced" European *G urbanum* seeds. Native European *A petiolata*, on the other hand, substantially reduced seed germination of North American *G laciniatum* and European *G urbanum* in similar proportions – a result that partially supports the novel weapons hypothesis.

The weak effects of root exudates of invasive species on their old neighbors and the strong effects of the same exudates on new and naïve neighbors suggest that plants can evolve tolerance to the unique rhizosphere biochemistry of co-occurring species. The scale at which evolved tolerance exists is unknown. It is unlikely that entire floras have evolved in response to particular root exudates, but it does seem that (-)-catechin and 8-hydroxyquinoline have influenced the evolution of at least some of the plant species living in the vicinity of *C maculosa* and *C diffusa*, perhaps in much the same way that herbicides exert strong selective pressures on plants. However, no coevolutionary relationships are possible with an herbicide.

Closely related species can differ in their sensitivity to the same allelochemical when they are from different continents, while distantly related plants can have similar sensitivities if they are from the same region. Thus, the historical coevolutionary trajectories discussed here are probably the result of relatively recent evolution and not from more ancient phylogenetic relationships. Such recent adaptation would suggest the possibility of future rapid evolution in plant populations that are experiencing invasion now. The evolution of exotics can be rapid (Müller-Schärer *et al.* 2004); perhaps natives can evolve tolerance to the competitive traits of invaders and ultimately coexist more evenly.

As mentioned above, there is no reason to think plants evolved to exude (-)-catechin and 8-hydroxyquinoline exclusively to gain a competitive advantage. Both chemicals are powerful chelators of nutrients such as phosphorus. Also, 8-hydroxyquinoline is an antimicrobial agent (Vivanco *et al.* 2004) and (-)-catechin is always exuded in a racemic form with an antimicrobial enantiomer (a molecule with a reversed, or mirror image), (+)-catechin (Bais *et al.* 2002). Other invasive species can have antimicrobial activity (Ehrenfeld 2003) and allelopathic chemicals released by some invasive species may alter nitrogen fixation (Wardle *et al.* 1994, 1998). Both (-)-catechin and 8-hydroxyquinoline could have evolved in response to selection pressure to improve nutrient acquisition and prevent microbial infection, and these chemicals are ineffective against native neighbors that have evolved tolerance. Perhaps it is only when these chemicals are introduced to naïve communities that their toxicity is manifest.

Many invasive species appear to have undergone a lag phase, during which they spread very slowly or not at all (Kowarik 1995). If the novel weapons hypothesis is a valid explanation for some invasions, then it would seem that species with these weapons would be highly successful from the beginning, and not undergo a lag phase. On the other hand, lag phases may occur for many other reasons, including the evolution of increased competitive ability and biological inertia in the resident community (von Holle *et al.* 2003). Lag phases might therefore occur even in exotic species that possess novel weapons.

■ **Antimicrobial novel weapons**

We have emphasized how novel biochemical interactions among plants may disrupt communities that are invaded by new species. However, plant–soil microbe interactions are also mediated by biochemical processes that are subject to the same kinds of selective forces. In other words, the effects of novel biochemical weapons on soil biota may also drive invasions. Combining plant and microbial species that have not shared evolutionary trajectories might also cause the striking changes in community composition and dominance that characterize many invasions.

Different microbial communities are associated with different plant species (Bever 1994; Grayston and Campbell 1996; Westover *et al.* 1997; Priha *et al.* 1999, 2001; Grayston *et al.* 2001; Klironomos 2002), probably due to species-specific rhizosphere biochemistry and the addition or removal of particular resources. It is reasonable to expect exotic species to also have species-specific effects on soil microbes, because they can have a strong influence on nutrient cycling (Vitousek 1990; Ehrenfeld *et al.* 2001). It is not known whether microbial changes caused by invaders are different enough from those that occur in native communities to allow invaders with little influence to transmogrify into dominant components of communities and exclude other species.

A great deal of evidence suggests that soil biota have important effects on the success of invasive plants (Klironomos 2002; Mitchell and Power 2003; Reinhart *et al.* 2003; Callaway 2004; Reinhart and Callaway in press; Wolfe and Klironomos unpublished) and that interactions between plants and their soil biota are based, in part, on biochemistry. However, despite the potential for biochemically based novel interactions between invasive plants and soil biota and our inclusion of such interactions in the novel weapons hypothesis, as yet there are no clear links between novel biochemistry, soil microbial communities, and invasive success. Invasive species such as *Alliaria petiolata* (garlic mustard) provide intriguing opportunities for such links. Like most members of its family, *Alliaria* is not mycorrhizal, and its root exudates are harmful to arbuscular mycorrhizae found in the soils where it invades in North America (Roberts and Anderson 2001). Comparative experiments on the effects of *Alliaria* on mycorrhizae in its native soils versus its effects on mycorrhizae in invaded soils could provide an empirical link between biochemical mechanisms, the importance of their novelty, and soil microbial communities.

■ Novel weapons as a mechanism for EICA

Despite the fact that the EICA hypothesis refers specifically to competitive ability, the underlying mechanism is explicitly rooted in the allocational trade-offs between investment in growth and investment in defense (Blossey and Nötzold 1995). However, there is no reason that selection for increased competitive ability should only arise from grow versus defend-type trade-offs. The mechanisms driving competitive ability, specifically the biochemical mechanisms described above, may also be the subject of selection.

Regardless of the factors that originally select for the novel chemical composition of the root exudates of invaders (eg need for nutrient chelation, defense, or antimicrobial action), possessing novel weapons is likely to have important evolutionary implications. If invaders possess traits, such as allelochemical weapons, that provide greater competitive advantages in their new habitats than in their original ranges, then selection pressure for the traits conferring competitive advantages may be much greater on the genotypes in the invaded regions than on the conspecific genotypes remaining at home. In other words, individuals that pump out a lot of effective poison might grow and reproduce more than individuals that do not. The rationale for exploring this alternative mechanism for the evolution of increased competitive ability, which we refer to as "allelopathic advantages against resident species" (AARS), is based on increasing evidence for the importance of rhizosphere biochemistry in invasions (Hierro and Callaway 2003). To be precise, we see AARS as a subset of the EICA hypothesis, but occurring as a consequence of an exotic species possessing a novel weapon. There are specific predictions of the "grow or defend" allocational trade-off hypothesis of EICA, and there are specific predictions of AARS. First, individuals from invasive populations should be better competitors where they have invaded than individuals from the source populations of the invader. However, this competitive superiority will not necessarily be related to the commonly measured greater size or fecundity because competitive superiority may not be directly related to resource uptake. The fundamental prediction of AARS is that invasive populations will be more allelopathic than source populations. Presumably this could occur as a result of selection for more toxic compounds, or selection for the production of greater amounts of an existing toxin. To our knowledge, there is no unambiguous evidence for such a biogeographical difference. For *C diffusa* and *C maculosa*, the concentrations of their allelochemicals (8-hydroxyquinoline and (±)-catechin) are about twice as high in the rhizospheres of invasive populations than in rhizospheres of native populations (Bais *et al.* 2003; Vivanco *et al.* 2004), but the effects of different microbial consumption rates or population densities have not been separated from individual exudation rates. It should be mentioned that there is no *a priori* reason to assume that directional selection will increase allelopathic output. If a very small amount of chemical is very effective at first, but not as effective later (a rapidly saturating benefit curve), and if the cost of production increases at least linearly, it is feasible that allelochemical production could decrease in the new range. Only empirical studies will tell.

■ Conclusions

Investigation of the role of species-specific rhizosphere biochemistry in plant ecology and evolution may provide insight into remarkable phenomena involving successful plant invasions. Recent research suggests conceptual parallels between the success of exotic human invasions and the success of exotic plant invasions – the possession of novel weapons.

■ Acknowledgements

We gratefully acknowledge support provided to Ragan Callaway from the National Science Foundation, the USDA, The Aldo Leopold Wilderness Institute, and the Civilian Research and Development Foundation.

■ References

Agrawal AA and Kotanen PM. 2003. Herbivores and the success of exotic plants: a phylogenetically controlled experiment. *Ecol Lett* **6**: 712–15.

Bais HP, Walker TS, Stermitz FR, *et al.* 2002. Enantiomeric-dependent phytotoxic and antimicrobial activity of (±)-catechin. A rhizosecreted racemic mixture from spotted knapweed. *Plant Physiol* **128**: 1173–79.

Bais HP, Vepachedu R, Gilroy S, *et al.* 2003. Allelopathy and exotic plants: from genes to invasion. *Science* **301**: 1377–80.

Baldwin IT. 2003. At last, evidence of weapons of mass destruction. *Science STKE* pe42.

Beckstead J and Parker IM. 2003. Invasiveness of *Ammophila arenaria*: release from soil-borne pathogens? *Ecology* **84**: 2824–31.

Bever JD. 1994. Feedback between plants and their soil communities in an old field community. *Ecology* **75**: 1965–77.

Blossey B and Nötzold R. 1995. Evolution of increased competitive ability in invasive nonindigenous plants: a hypothesis. *J Ecology* **83**: 887–89.

Bossdorf O, Prati D, Auge H, and Schmid B. 2004. Reduced competitive ability in an invasive plant. *Ecol Lett* **7**: 346–53.

Callaway RM. 2002. The detection of neighbors by plants. *Trends Ecol Evol* **17**: 104–05.

Callaway RM and Aschehoug ET. 2000. Invasive plants versus their new and old neighbors: a mechanism for exotic invasion. *Science* **290**: 521–23.

Callaway RM, DeLuca T, and Ridenour WM. 1999. Herbivores used for biological control may increase the competitive ability of the noxious weed *Centaurea maculosa*. *Ecology* **80**: 1196–201.

Callaway RM and Hierro JL. Resistance and susceptibility of plant communities to invasion: revisiting Rabotnov's ideas about community homeostasis. In: Reigosa, MJ, N Pedrol and L González (Eds.) Allelopathy: a physiological process with ecological implications. Boston, MA: Kluwer Academic Press. In press.

Callaway RM, Hierro JL, and Thorpe AS. Evolutionary trajectories in plant and soil microbial communities: plant invasions and the geographic mosaic of coevolution. In: Sax DF, Gaines SD, and Stachowicz JJ (Eds). Exotic species bane to conservation and boon to understanding: ecology, evolution and biogeography. Sunderland, MA: Sinauer. In press.

Callaway RM, Thelen GG, Rodriguez A, and Holben WE. 2004. Release from inhibitory soil biota in Europe may promote exotic plant invasion in North America. *Nature* **427**: 731–33.

Crawley MJ. 1987. What makes a community invasible? In: Gray AJ, Crawley MJ, and Edwards PJ (Eds). Colonization, succession and stability. London, UK: Blackwell Scientific.

Crawley MJ. 1989. Insect herbivores and plant population dynamics. *Annu Rev Entomol* **34**: 531–64.

Crawley MJ. 1997. Plant ecology. London, UK: Blackwell Science.

Daehler CC and Strong DR. 1997. Reduced herbivory resistance in introduced smooth cordgrass (*Spartina alterniflora*) after a century of herbivore-free growth. *Oecologia* **110**: 99–108.

DeWalt SJ, Denslow JS, and Ickes K. 2004. Natural-enemy release facilitates habitat expansion of the invasive tropical shrub *Clidemia hirta*. *Ecology* **85**: 471–83.

Diamond J. 1997. Guns, germs, and steel: the fates of human societies. New York, NY: Random House.

Elton CS. 1958. The ecology of invasions. London, UK: Methuen.

Ehrenfeld JG. 2003. Effects of exotic plant invasions on soil nutrient cycling processes. *Ecosystems* **6**: 503–23.

Ehrenfeld JG, Kourtev P, and Huang W. 2001. Changes in soil functions following invasions of exotic understory plants in deciduous forests. *Ecol Appl* **11**: 1287–300.

Fitter A. 2003. Making allelopathy respectable. *Science* **301**: 1337–38.

Flores HE. 1999. "Radical" biochemistry: the biology of root-specific metabolism. *Trends Plant Sci* **4**: 220–26

Grayston SJ and Campbell CD. 1996. Functional biodiversity of microbial communities in the rhizosphere of hybrid larch (*Larix eurolepis*) and Sitka spruce (*Picea sitchensis*). *Tree Physiol* **16**: 1031–38.

Grayston SJ, Griffith GS, Mawdsley JL, Campbell CD, and Bardgett RD. 2001. Accounting for variability in soil microbial communities of temperate upland grassland ecosystems. *Soil Biol Biochem* **33**: 533–51.

Herms DA and Mattson WJ. 1992. The dilemma of plants: to grow or defend. *Q Rev Biol* **67**: 283–335.

Hierro JL and Callaway RM. 2003. Allelopathy and exotic plant invasion. *Plant Soil* **256**: 25–39.

Jakobs G, Weber E, and Edwards PJ. 2004. Introduced plants of the invasive *Solidago gigantea* (Asteraceae) are larger and grow denser than conspecifics in the native range. *Divers Distrib* **10**: 11–19.

Klironomos J. 2002. Feedback with soil biota contributes to plant rarity and invasiveness in communities. *Nature* **417**: 67–70.

Kowarik I. 1995. Time lags in biological invasions with regard to the success and failure of alien species. In: Py ek P, Prach K, Rejmánek M, and Wade M (Eds). Plant invasions – general aspects and special problems. Amsterdam, Netherlands: SPB Academic Publishing.

Leger EA and Rice KJ. 2003. Invasive California poppies (*Eschscholzia californica* Cham.) grow larger than native individuals under reduced competition. *Ecol Lett* **6**: 257–64.

Lesica P and Hanna D. 2004. Indirect effects of biological control on plant diversity vary across sites in Montana grasslands. *Conserv Biol* **18**: 444–54.

Levine JM, Vilá M, D'Antonio CM, *et al.* 2002. Mechanisms underlying the impacts of exotic plant invasions. *P Roy Soc Lond B Bio* **270**: 775–81.

Mack RN, Simberloff D, Lonsdale WM, *et al.* 2000. Biotic invasions: causes, epidemiology, global consequences and control. *Ecol Appl* **10**: 689–710.

Mahall BE and Callaway RM. 1992. Root communication mechanisms and intracommunity distributions of two Mojave Desert shrubs. *Ecology* **73**: 2145–51.

Mallik AU and Pellissier F. 2000. Effects of *Vaccinium myrtillus* on spruce regeneration: testing the notion of coevolutionary significance of allelopathy. *J Chem Ecol* **26**: 2197–209.

Maron JL and Vilà M. 2001. Do herbivores affect plant invasion? Evidence for the natural enemies and biotic resistance hypotheses. *Oikos* **95**: 363–73.

Maron JL, Vilá M, Bommarco R, *et al.* 2004. Rapid evolution of an invasive plant. *Ecol Mono* **74**: 261–80.

Mitchell CG and Power AG. 2003. Release of invasive plants from fungal and viral pathogens. *Nature* **421**: 625–27.

Muir AD and Majak W. 1983. Allelopathic potential of diffuse knapweed (*Centaurea diffusa*) extracts. *Can J Plant Sci* **63**: 989–96.

Müller-Schärer H and Schroeder D. 1993. The biological control of *Centaurea* spp. in North America: do insects solve the problem? *Pestic Sci* **37**: 343–53.

Müller-Schärer H, Schaffner U, and Steinger T. 2004. Evolution in invasive plants: implications for biological control. *Trends Ecol Evol* **19**: 417–22.

Pearson DE and Callaway RM. 2003. Indirect effects of host-specific biocontrol agents. *Trends Ecol Evol* **18**: 456–61.

Prati D and Bossdorf O. 2004. Allelopathic inhibition of germination by *Alliaria petiolata* (Brassicaceae). *Am J Bot* **91**: 285–88.

Priha O, Grayston SJ, Pennanen T, and Smolander A. 1999. Microbial activities related to C and N cycling, and microbial community structure in the rhizospheres of *Pinus sylvestris*, *Picea abies* and *Betula pendula* seedlings in an organic and mineral soil. *FEMS Microbiol Ecol* **30**: 187–99.

Priha O, Grayston SJ, Hiukka R, *et al.* 2001. Microbial community structure in soils under *Pinus sylvestris*, *Picea abies* and *Betula pendula*. *Biol Fert Soils* **33**: 17–24.

Rabotnov TA. 1982. Importance of the evolutionary approach to the study of allelopathy. *Ékologia* No 3: **May–June**: 5–8.

Ridenour WL and Callaway RM. 2001. The relative importance of allelopathy in interference: the effects of an invasive weed on a native bunchgrass. *Oecologia* **126**: 444–50.

Ridenour WL and Callaway RM. 2003. Root herbivores, pathogenic fungi, and competition between *Centaurea maculosa* and *Festuca idahoensis*. *Plant Ecol* **169**: 161–70.

Reinhart KO and Callaway RM. Soil biota facilitate exotic *Acer* invasions in Europe and North America. *Ecol Appl*. In press.

Reinhart KO, Packer A, Van der Putten WH, and Clay K. 2003. Plant–soil biota interactions and spatial distribution of black cherry in its native and invasive ranges. *Ecol Lett* **6**: 1046–50.

Roberts KJ and Anderson RC. 2001. Effect of garlic mustard [*Alliaria petiolata* (Beib. Cavara and Grande)] extracts on plants and arbuscular mycorrhizal (AM) fungi. *Am Midl Nat* **146**: 146–52.

Siemann E and Rogers WE. 2001. Genetic differences in growth of an invasive tree species. *Ecol Lett* **4**: 514–18.

Siemann E and Rogers WE. 2003. Increased competitive ability of an invasive tree limited by an invasive beetle. *Ecol Appl* **13**: 1503–07.

Thompson JN. 1999. Specific hypotheses on the geographic mosaic of coevolution. *Am Nat* **153**: 1–14.

Van Kleunen M and Schmid B. 2003. No evidence for evolutionary increased competitive ability (EICA) in the invasive plant *Solidago canadensis*. *Ecology* **84**: 2824–31.

Vilà M, Gomez A, and Maron JL. 2003. Are alien plants more competitive than their native conspecifics? A test using *Hypericum perforatum*. *Oecologia* **137**: 211–15.

Vitousek PM. 1990. Biological invasions and ecosystem processes: towards an integration of population biology and ecosystem studies. *Oikos* **57**: 7–13.

Vivanco JM, Bais HP, Stermitz FR, *et al.* 2004. Biogeographical variation in community response to root allelochemistry: novel weapons and exotic invasion. *Ecol Lett* **7**: 285–92.

Von Holle D, Delacourt HR, and Simberloff D. 2003. The importance of biological inertia in plant community resistance to invasion. *J Veg Sci* **14**: 425–32.

Wardle DA, Nicholson KS, Ahmed M, and Rahman A. 1994. Interference effects of the invasive plant *Carduus nutans* L against the nitrogen fixation ability of *Trifolium repens* L *Plant Soil* **163**: 287–97.

Wardle DA, Nilsson M-C, Gallet C, and Zackrisson O. 1998. An ecosystem-level perspective of allelopathy. *Biol Rev* **73**: 301–19.

Westover KM, Kennedy AC, and Kelley SE. 1997. Patterns of rhizosphere microbial community structure associated with co-occurring plant species. *J Ecol* **85**: 863–73.

Whittaker RH. 1951. A criticism of the plant association and climatic climax concepts. *Northwest Sci* **25**: 17–31.

Williams JR. 1954. The biological control of weeds. In: Report of the Sixth Commonwealth Entomological Congress. London, UK.

Willis AJ and Blossey B. 1999. Benign climates don't explain the increased plant size of non-indigenous plants: a cross-continental transplant experiment. *Biocontrol Sci Techn* **9**: 567–77.

Willis AJ, Memmott J, and Forrester RI. 2000. Is there evidence for the post-invasion evolution of increased size among invasive plant species? *Ecol Lett* **3**: 275–83.

Wolfe LM. 2002. Why alien invaders succeed: support for the escape-from-enemy hypothesis. *Am Nat* **160**: 705–11.

New series: invitation to authors

This paper is the first in a new occasional series under the heading "Concepts and Questions". These essay-style articles will provide authors with the opportunity to outline innovative theories not yet accepted by the scientific community, to discuss old ideas that deserve to be revisited in the light of new information, or to provide interesting commentaries on a hot topic in ecology, environmental science, or a related specialty.

Criteria: *The topic and level of writing must be accessible and interesting, even to those unfamiliar with the subject. Length: about 2500–3000 words; abstract: up to 150 words; references: 25–30. All essays will be subject to peer review before they are accepted for publication, with emphasis placed on the clarity and logic of the arguments.*

Please contact the Editor-in-Chief, Dr Sue Silver (suesilver@esa.org) for further information.

Novel assessments: detecting success in student learning

Kathy S Williams[1], Diane Ebert-May[2], Doug Luckie[2], Janet Hodder[3], Suzanne Koptur[4]

How can we gather evidence that shows that all students understand the concepts and processes of science? This question is central to the idea of "scientific teaching" (Handelsman *et al.* 2004). As scientists, we learn to question anecdotal data and to challenge our peers to use multiple procedures to collect reproducible results. A similar approach is possible when assessing students' knowledge about a topic. This article illustrates how multiple methods can be used to assess student understanding of the "novel weapons hypothesis" presented in the Callaway and Ridenour review of theories regarding invasive plant species (see pp 436–443). The paper introduces students to concepts of natural selection, fitness, competition, and invasion of exotic species. The assessments we describe here engage students in diverse ways to demonstrate their understanding.

Multiple and varied assessments give students feedback about their progress, help instructors to determine their next instructional steps, and communicate to students what they need to know and do, and motivate them to continue challenging themselves to learn (Pellegrino *et al.* 2001). Learning through assessment offers students ways of building their understanding by using models, theories, and "cause and effect" explanations that support successful knowledge transfer (Mayer *et al.* 1996). The use of multiple representations, such as definitions, analogies, visual models, and examples, helps students to understand and remember scientific concepts, while allowing them and the instructor to assess their understanding. The "novel weapons" paper provides students with opportunities to build a deeper understanding of basic biological concepts and develop problem-solving skills, as they explore theories and hypotheses about plant invasions.

■ Student learning goals

Students will:
- Describe factors that cause differential growth or reproduction in plants
- Predict ways in which plants affect one another
- Propose and explain traits that would convey competitive advantages to invading species
- Design an experiment to test two hypotheses about control of plant growth

■ Faculty teaching goals

Instructors will:
- Use multiple forms of assessment (eg probing knowledge, paired questions, concept maps, and solving an experimental problem) to help recognize how well students understand scientific concepts
- Provide students with guidance and practice in using different forms of assessment, such as concept maps (Pellegrino *et al.* 2001)

■ Instructional design

Students read the Calloway and Ridenour paper as homework, focusing on the learning goals noted above. This instructional design alternates assessments used inside or outside the class with short lectures or discussions. Just as research results direct scientists to their next experiments, student responses obtained in these assessments inform subsequent discussion or lecture segments.

Assessment 1. A knowledge probe shows students' understanding about the cause of variation in plants. Use an illustration or photo of a small plant and a large plant. Inform students that these plants are growing in the same habitat, in the same population, and are the same age. Ask students to write for 5 minutes, explaining at least three factors that might cause the difference in sizes between the plants. Student groups then discuss responses and selected groups report their ideas. Information gathered from this initial knowledge probe is used to direct subsequent instruction.

Assessment 2. Paired questions query students' understanding about origins of variation. A multiple choice question about the process of evolution is followed by a written response asking for *a rationale* for the answer to the multiple choice. This will allow instructors to identify knowledge gaps. For example:

Part A. According to the process of natural selection, how did exotic plants most likely come to produce novel toxic biochemicals that improved their competitive ability when they invaded a new habitat?
- (a) Invading exotic plants needed to change in order to survive, so beneficial new traits developed.
- (b) Variations in exotic plant chemicals occurred by chance, and exotics producing chemicals that reduced the success of competing natives produced more offspring.
- (c) Mutations occurred in the invading exotics so they could adapt and succeed in the new environment.
- (d) Differences between the exotic and native environ-

[1]*San Diego State University*; [2]*Michigan State University*; [3]*University of Oregon*; [4]*Florida International University*

ments caused production of different chemicals by exotic and native plants.

Part B. Give one reason each for rejecting the three responses you did not choose.

Ask students to show their answer to the multiple choice question by raising their hand, voting with a numbered note card, or using a personal response system. Then, after short discussions, individuals or groups of students should explain the problems with the erroneous responses, and use comments to clarify the correct concepts.

Assessment 3. Concept mapping asks students to link ideas about evolution and interactions among plants. Concept maps (Panel 1) are illustrations of relationships among concepts organized hierarchically (Novak 1998). Tools such as concept maps, flow charts, and Venn diagrams reveal student understanding about associations and organization of many concepts, elements not easily assessed by multiple choice questions, or even extended responses. Knowledge diagramming tools like concept maps enable students to organize and retrieve ideas, then construct new knowledge and link it to their prior knowledge. The ability to connect seemingly disparate terms and ideas is one of the skills that distinguishes expert from novice problem solvers (Novak 1998). A meta-analysis of 19 studies revealed that concept mapping had positive effects on student achievement and attitudes toward science (Horton *et al.* 1993), although constructing concept maps requires practice throughout a course. Key concepts from Callaway and Ridenour include: competitive advantage, natural selection, fitness, growth, survival, reproduction, exotic species, native species, limiting resources, and novel phytochemical weapons. The instructor then reviews the maps, identifies incorrect links, and learns what students consider relevant, accurate relationships and the hierarchical organization of concepts. Students can add new concepts to their maps throughout a course, making new connections.

Assessment 4. An experimental problem allows students to show their understanding of experimental design and the complexity of interactions and selection pressures. Students are asked to design experiments to test hypotheses from the paper about the control of plant growth. This could be written homework (individual) or a written in-class problem (group activity) with assessment by the instructor and/or peers. For example:

Part A. Design greenhouse experiments to test two hypotheses from the reading:

H1: Chemical exudates of an exotic species, such as knapweed, reduce performance (or fitness) of native species.

H2: Exotic species out-compete native species in acquiring essential nutrients, such as nitrogen and phosphorous.

Part B. Assume that your results provide support for Hypothesis 1, showing that by exuding novel phytochemicals that inhibit native plant growth, exotic plants out-

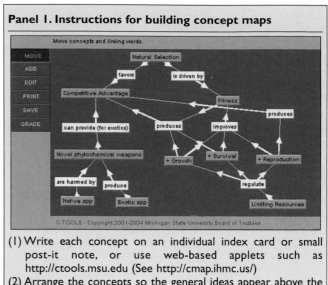

Panel 1. Instructions for building concept maps

(1) Write each concept on an individual index card or small post-it note, or use web-based applets such as http://ctools.msu.edu (See http://cmap.ihmc.us/)
(2) Arrange the concepts so the general ideas appear above the sub-ideas
(3) Add linking lines and then add linking verbs that explain the relationships between the concepts

compete natives. Now imagine you repeat the experiment in a field plot and find that natives grow and/or reproduce as well as or better than exotics! Propose three possible reasons, related to factors affecting fitness, for your field results.

■ Final note

Callaway and Ridenour review concepts proposed to explain relationships among native and invading species that have long challenged scientists, and also present an engaging storyline that will capture and hold the interest of undergraduates. Multiple assessments inform instructors *and students* about their progress towards understanding. With these data, instructors can direct their subsequent instruction.

■ Acknowledgements

We thank the National Science Foundation for their long-term support of the FIRST project, Faculty Institutes for Reforming Science Teaching (DUE 0088847), C-TOOLS Creating Visual Tools to See Student Learning (DUE 0206924), and Ray Callaway.

■ References

Handelsman J, Ebert-May D, Beichner R, *et al.* 2004. Policy forum: scientific teaching. *Science* **304**: 521–22.

Horton B, McConney AA, Gallo M, *et al.* 1993. An investigation of the effectiveness of concept mapping as an instructional tool. *Science Education* **77**: 95–11.

Mayer RE, Bove W, Bryman A, *et al.* 1996. When less is more: meaningful learning from visual and verbal summaries of science textbook lessons. *J Educ Psychol* **88**: 64–73.

Novak J. 1998. Learning, creating, and using knowledge: concept maps as facilitative tools in schools and corporations. Mahwah, NJ: Lawrence Erlbaum Associates.

Pellegrino J, Chudowsky N, Glaser R (Eds). 2001. Knowing what students know. Washington, DC: National Academy Press.

Effects of deposited wood on biocomplexity of river corridors

Angela Gurnell[1], Klement Tockner[2], Peter Edwards[3], and Geoffrey Petts[4]

Under natural conditions, most rivers are bordered by riparian woodland. Many studies have highlighted the ecological importance of these wooded zones, but the impact of riparian woodland dynamics on the complexity of the active tract (the area of bare sediment adjacent to the river) has been overlooked. This paper highlights the impact of downed trees and sprouting driftwood on the development of islands and associated ponds within the active tract of large rivers and the effects of these features on the abundance and diversity of plants and animals, and points to the benefits of riparian woodland for channel restoration.

Front Ecol Environ 2005; 3(7): 377–382

Many natural rivers are relatively wide and shallow, with an extensive tract of bare sediments during the low flow season – the active tract. Many (called braided rivers) have more than one mobile channel, bounded by bars of bare sediment, while others (island-braided rivers) are also characterized by vegetated islands. Most are lined by riparian woodlands. Along these natural rivers, floods erode, transport, and deposit not only sediment but also trees. Deposited trees, and islands that evolve from them, sustain a suite of aquatic and terrestrial habitats that would otherwise not be present on river bar surfaces. Previous research from a wide range of bioclimatic regions has focused on forested headwater catchments and on the important role of dead wood – trees eroded from hillslopes and terraces – in the ecology of streams and rivers (Maser and Sedell 1994; Gregory et al. 2003). The roles of wood

In a nutshell:

- Deposited driftwood capable of regrowth dramatically accelerates the process of island formation along large floodplain rivers
- Deposited trees, pioneer islands, and fully developed islands are associated with a suite of adjacent and closely linked habitat types across a range of spatial scales on otherwise relatively homogenous river bar surfaces
- The suite of linked habitats supports high biodiversity and the simple index of shoreline length has been positively correlated with both abundance and diversity of animals
- These wood-cored features depend on a supply of wood capable of regrowth, space for habitat turnover, and dynamic river processes
- In river restoration, a relaxation in the intensity of river margin management could provide the space to regenerate riparian woodlands and create a sustainable supply of large wood to yield important enhancements in the biocomplexity of large-river systems

[1]Department of Geography, King's College London, London WC2R 2LS, UK; [2]Department of Limnology, EAWAG, 8600 Dübendorf, Switzerland; [3]Geobotanical Institute, ETH, Zürich, 8044, Switzerland; [4]School of Geography, Earth and Environmental Sciences, University of Birmingham, Birmingham B15 2TT, UK (g.e.petts@bham.ac.uk)

within large floodplain rivers have received relatively little attention. Some notable medium to large systems where the interplay between driftwood, riparian trees, and physical processes has been the focus of a great deal of research include the Queets (eg Abbe and Montgomery 1996, 2003; Naiman et al. 2000), Willamette (eg Sedell and Frogatt 1984; Dykaar and Wigington 2000) and Drôme (eg Piégay et al. 1999) rivers. We have shown that the role of wood is particularly marked when the deposited trees are able to sprout and anchor themselves to bar surfaces through the growth of adventitious roots (Gurnell et al. 2001); such trees are predominantly "soft-wood" riparian species and in the northern temperate zone are dominated by one family, the Salicaceae (poplars and willows; Karrenberg et al. 2002). Hitherto, the benefits derived from this "living wood" have been largely overlooked. Here we synthesize our findings from research on the Tagliamento River in Italy, one of the few remaining large floodplain-river systems in Europe where trees and large living-wood pieces still interact freely with river processes, forming island-braided reaches of channel (Figure 1). This paper examines the processes that lead to the formation of island-braided rivers and shows how the dynamics of these islands influence biocomplexity – the variety and arrangement of terrestrial and aquatic habitats, and the diversity and distribution of species they support – and comments on their future management and restoration.

■ Wood as a driver of island development

There has been extensive research on the roles of downed trees in river channels of forested headwater catchments, where dead wood induces hydraulic, morphologic, and textural complexity (Gregory et al. 2003). In larger floodplain rivers logjams can also form stable structures that influence local water depths and flow velocities and provide long-term protection for mature forest patches within the river corridor. From observations on the Queets River

Figure 1. *An island-braided section of the Tagliamento River, Italy. Pioneer islands surround the established island, with newly deposited trees draped across the bar adjacent to the main channel (foreground). The inset shows trees deposited across an expanse of bare gravel by a recent flood.*

and nutrients from the decomposing plant material. From our observations on the Tagliamento River, we have demonstrated an additional mechanism for island growth, where regrowth from living driftwood dramatically accelerates the process of island formation. This mechanism appears to be important for sustaining islands within river corridors characterized by rapid channel migration and frequent disturbance by floods (Gurnell *et al.* 2001; Gurnell and Petts 2002). Along the Tagliamento, rates of tree growth from living wood (Figure 2) can be four times faster than growth from seeds and small vegetative propagules and islands of more than 200 m in length can form in less than 20 years (Francis *et al.* in press). The availability of riparian tree species capable of regenerating in this way is obviously a key component of this system, but appropriate local conditions are also required, especially adequate moisture levels. On the Tagliamento, dynamic braided reaches lacking islands have a similar supply of wood but occur where regrowth from driftwood is severely limited by locally arid conditions caused by deeper alluvial groundwater levels and rapid drainage from surface waters.

(Washington, USA), Abbe and Montgomery (1996, 2003) developed a model of island formation downstream from an initial deposited tree or wood jam at the head of a mid-channel bar and eventual integration of the island into the floodplain. This island development model was driven by the accumulation of dead wood and the growth of vegetation from propagules deposited in the protected lee of the wood. In such locations, the wood supports vegetation growth by acting as a "resource node" (Pettit and Naiman 2005), where fine sediments accumulate, retaining moisture

■ Wood as a driver of physical complexity

Trees transported by floods become snagged on river bars, typically with their root bole oriented upstream. The hydraulic impact of an individual tree creates a set of closely linked topographic habitats (Figure 3a) on what would otherwise be a relatively homogeneous and smooth surface of bare sediments. Deep hollows are often scoured at the upstream flow divergence around the root bole of the tree; scouring exposes lag deposits of coarse sediment. Plumes of sand are deposited in the sheltered area bordering, and in the lee of, the tree's stem and canopy. Large wood pieces and large sediment particles become trapped, forming jams against the upstream face of the root bole, and reinforcing the hydraulic impact of the tree.

The build-up of wood and coarse sediment around the root bole, the adjacent scour hole, and sand plume may develop over a sequence of inundations. Given suitable tree species and environmental conditions, some wood pieces and the core deposited tree may sprout, developing root networks that reinforce the accumulating sediments and a canopy that

Figure 2. *Early regrowth of poplar (*Populus nigra*) from a tree deposited by floodwaters along the Tagliamento in the second growing season, showing over 2m of growth.*

further enhances the hydraulic impact of the tree (Figure 3b). As a result, the area of hydraulically induced scour, sedimentation, and growing vegetation may enlarge to form a patch of vegetation or "pioneer island" (Edwards *et al.* 1999; Figure 4). Such pioneer islands may subsequently continue to grow and coalesce to form larger, more mature islands (Figure 3c; Gurnell *et al.* 2001).

Individual deposited trees, pioneer islands, and more mature islands all support the same suite of linked habitats, but the relative size of these habitats increases with the size of the vegetated area. For example, deposited trees and pioneer islands (length typically < 30 m) are often associated with small shallow scour holes supporting ephemeral ponds (Figure 5). Established islands (length typically > 100 m) are often associated with large, deep scour holes extending below the alluvial water table and sustaining ponds for prolonged periods (see Figure 6). These ponds provide an important addition to the range of habitats within the active tract. They are different from those associated with remnant cutoff channels, contributing thermal heterogeneity by damping diel (ie within a 24-hour cycle) fluctuations. Along the middle of the Tagliamento, scour pools associated with wood accumulations at the head of islands have a lower average daily temperature (18 °C) and lower diel variation (5 °C) than ponds located on open gravel (20.5 °C and 9.5 °C, respectively; Karaus *et al.* 2005). Because scour and deposition of sediment during bar-inundation can cause rapid creation, infilling, and lateral displacement of the low-lying ponds around the margins of aggrading islands, the turnover of ponds is an order of magnitude more rapid than islands (Van der Nat *et al.* 2003).

Whereas individual trees and islands have an important local effect on flow resistance and bar surface form, clusters of deposited trees can have an important aggregate effect across entire bars. We hypothesize that as the density of snagged trees and pioneer islands increases across a bar surface, their aggregate effect on flow resistance can change a bar surface from a fine sediment source to a fine sediment sink during flood events (Figure 7). In the former case, a low density of trees and pioneer islands allows fine sediment particles to be flushed from the bar surface and washed downstream by floodwaters, leaving a coarse gravel pavement (Figure 7a). In the latter case, closely spaced trees and pioneer islands filter fine sediments from the water and create backwaters that enhance the rate of sedimentation. The deposition of fine sediments and vegetation propagules around vegetated patches can lead to rapid extension of the vegetated surface (Figure 7c). We

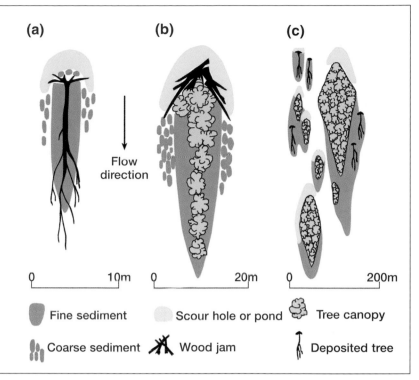

Figure 3. *Island development from living wood. (a) A deposited tree inducing the development of a suite of linked habitats; (b) a tree sprouting and inducing scour, deposition of fine sediment, and trapping of wood pieces to form a pioneer island; (c) an island complex with deposited trees, pioneer islands, and established islands distributed across an extensive gravel surface.*

also suggest that an intermediate density of trees and pioneer islands could maximize habitat diversity by causing the scouring of fine sediments along high-velocity flow pathways between sedimentation zones of closely spaced patches of wood, trees, and pioneer islands (Figure 7b).

■ Wood and biocomplexity

It is well established that wood jams in streams provide: flow and habitat heterogeneity; refugia for fish and invertebrates; sites of biofilm production that serve as food for grazing organisms; high organic matter retention; nursery habitat for fish; and perches for birds and other animals. Within large dynamic rivers, such as the Tagliamento, the suite of habitats created around individual deposited trees and islands form complex patches of high biodiversity within a relatively barren landscape of exposed sediment (Figure 6). Seed germination and sprouting wood produce a diverse vegetation cover on the building, fine-sediment surfaces. In addition, the root bole of deposited trees often contains soil, established plants, and a seed bank. This increases plant species diversity and greatly accelerates and influences the initial trajectory of succession, not least because some species may be "alien" to the particular location along the river continuum (Tockner *et al.* 2003).

As deposited trees evolve into pioneer islands, the number of plant species increases with vegetated area. On the Tagliamento, Kollmann *et al.* (1999) surveyed 89 recently

Figure 4. *A pioneer island developing from a single buried willow, showing the features described in Figure 3b with wood debris accumulating around the root bole, gravel scour around the growing debris jam, and fine sediment deposition downstream.*

deposited trees (< 1 year since deposition) and 22 pioneer islands (2–5 years) and showed that, on average, 17.3 (sd = 1.1) plant species were associated with the former and 26.2 (sd = 2.1) species with the latter. They also showed that the association between the number of plant species and habitat area was sustained across the developmental sequence of island types (deposited tree → pioneer island→ building island → established island).

On the Tagliamento, ponds associated with islands pro-

duce large amounts of algal biomass that may drive metabolism and provide habitat for a high proportion of juvenile fish. However, it is the physical proximity of the different habitats (scour holes, accumulations of sediment of different caliber, wood jams, vegetated patches; eg Figures 4, 5, and 6) that is of particular importance. For example, islands provide a source of organic matter for adjacent ponds and are a habitat from which the pond can be recolonized. Ponds are a food source for island fauna and algae can be an important food source for grazers, while the range of linked habitats are important for amphibians. Snags and islands provide stable habitat for invertebrates and are often areas of high secondary production, which may be important as drift. The islands are characterized by a high proportion of rare species of some taxa, such as ground beetles (Carabidae) that have high dispersal capacity, but the highest abundance is found along shorelines (up to 150 individuals m^{-2} on the Tagliamento), where prey organisms (ie emerging insects and aquatic drift) are concentrated. Moreover a study of amphibians within one reach of the Tagliamento found that amphibian richness within a given habitat type decreased with distance from islands (Tockner *et al.* in press). At a large scale, one simple index that appears to be helpful in demonstrating the impact of islands and channel complexity is shoreline length. This index has been positively correlated with both the abundance and diversity of animals. Table 1 provides comparative data for two adjacent reaches of the Tagliamento River (a bar-braided and adjacent island-braided reach; the latter is shown in Figure 1) and provides indices of their overall physical complexity, richness, and diversity of animal species.

It is also important to realize that any particular bar will not sustain the same position along the spectrum described in Figure 7 indefinitely. In particular, a bar surface that has been the subject of heavy accumulation of fine sediment and vegetation growth can be reset to a lower cover of vegetation and fine sediment during large, erosive floods. In natural settings, rivers have space to move, so that at the landscape scale different zones of the river corridor can support different densities of snagged trees, vegetated patches, and islands. The spatial distribution of both individual features and zones of features of different age, profile, and density, are highly dynamic. Dynamic zones, similar to those depicted in Figure 7, can be present

Figure 5. *A well-established pioneer island with a large wood debris jam trapped against its upstream face and an adjacent scour hole that contains an ephemeral pond. The scour hole is bordered by fine sediment deposited by receding floodwaters and also by wind that has redistributed sand from the surrounding bar surface.*

within and between reaches and are subject to major contrasts in habitat turnover rates that promote substantial variations in biodiversity. For example, along the middle Tagliamento, aquatic habitat change caused by individual floods was observed to be 35% in the island-braided compared to 56% in the bar-braided reach (described in Table 1), showing that woody vegetation slowed turnover in these habitats, whereas habitat composition remained relatively stable (Arscott *et al.* 2002).

■ Conclusions and management implications

Our observations on the Tagliamento River highlight the important role played by the transport and deposition of downed riparian trees, particularly species that can sprout, in enhancing biocomplexity within valley corridors along large, multi-thread

Figure 6. *A deep pond at the head of an island on the Tagliamento River, showing a massive wood jam. The islands form a complex patch within an extensive expanse of bare gravel (view looking downstream).*

gravel-bed rivers. Deposited trees create biocomplexity from the scale of the individual tree to the entire river corridor. Islands and their associated ponds are a dominant habitat couplet within the otherwise bare expanses of gravel (see Figure 6); the range of mesohabitats associated with this primary couplet (eg log piles, sand drapes, algal mats, and patches in different stages of succession) contribute to the high physical complexity of island-dominated reaches. The large size, braided pattern, relatively unmanaged riparian woodland, and large wood load of the Tagliamento River may be unique within Europe, and we have proposed that the future conservation of the Tagliamento should provide a benchmark for the European Water Framework Directive (Tockner *et al.* 2003). However, we also believe that our observations are applicable to other multi-thread and meandering systems and are germane to restoring reaches of larger rivers. Indeed, along large sand-bed rivers, wood deposition may be the only mechanism for creating habitat diversity (Erskine and Webb 2003).

We contend that island-braided rivers, although rare today, would have been a common style of gravel-bed river before the introduction of river engineering and flow regulation for water supply, flood control, hydroelectric power production, and navigation. Historical records support this contention for Europe (Gurnell and Petts 2002; Tockner *et al.* 2003) and North America (Maser and Sedell 1984), and research on impacts of dams has illus-

trated how island-braided rivers have changed to single-thread ones over the historical period (eg on the Peace River, British Columbia and Alberta, Canada; Church 1995). However, the loss of island-braided reaches is not only related to increased intensity of river management over the past 200 years; it is also likely to have been part of a longer, slower change in large river dynamics, whereby island complexes disappear from sections

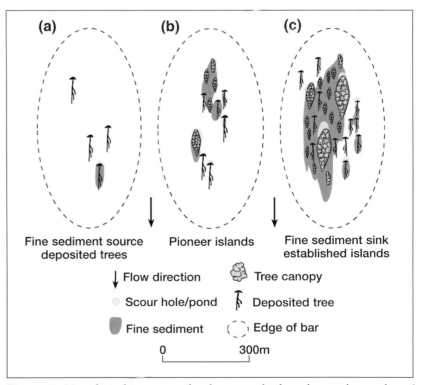

Figure 7. *Hypothetical impact on the character of a large bar as the number of snagged trees and pioneer islands increases, and in the functioning of the bar surface from (a) a fine sediment source to (c) a fine sediment sink during flood events.*

Table 1. Biocomplexity of the active zone of an island-braided compared to a bar-braided reach, Tagliamento River, Italy.

Approximate reach dimensions	Bar-braided	Island-braided
Channel slope (m m^{-1})	0.0035	0.0029
Reach length (km)	1.4	1.8
Width of active zone (m)	1000	800
Physical characteristics		
Large wood (t ha^{-1})	15–73	102–158
Channels (half-life expectancy; months)	4.1	7.7
Aquatic habitat diversity (H')	1.6	2.0
Average number of ponds	7	22
Average shoreline length (km km^{-1})	13.7	20.9
Animal species richness and diversity		
Amphibian species: γ-diversity	5	7
Carabid beetle species: γ-diversity	34	47
Benthic invertebrates: α-diversity	30	27
Benthic invertebrates: β-diversity	10.5	21
Benthic invertebrates: γ-diversity	50	53

Diversity indices: α-diversity - the number of species in each habitat; β-diversity - the turnover of species between habitats; γ-diversity - the total species pool.

starved of wood. Wood-cored islands of the type described in this paper are dynamic structures that can only exist where there is space for habitat turnover and a supply of downed trees of species capable of regrowth, as well as suitable environmental conditions for regrowth. In river restoration, a relaxation in the intensity of river margin management could provide the space to regenerate riparian woodland and create a sustainable supply of large wood to yield important enhancements in the biocomplexity of any large-river system. Island development through the incorporation of trees and wood, would have a major impact in enhancing habitat and biodiversity at both local and reach scales, especially where the tree species concerned are capable of sprouting from driftwood.

■ Acknowledgements

We thank JV Ward and J Kollmann for stimulating discussions and for their long-term collaboration in research on the Tagliamento River. Many students have participated in this research; we would also particularly like to acknowledge the work of D Arscott, R Francis, S Karrenberg, C Rust, and D van der Nat. This article was written while KT was on sabbatical at the Institute of Ecosystem Studies (Millbrook, NY, USA). The ideas presented were developed during research supported by grants from ETH-Forschungskommission (0-20572-98) and the UK NERC (GR9/03249, NER/B/S/2000/00298, NER/D/S/2000/01263, NER/T/S/2001/00930).

■ References

Abbe TB and Montgomery DR. 1996. Large woody debris jams, channel hydraulics and habitat formation in large rivers. *Regul River* **12**: 201–21.

Abbe TB and Montgomery DR. 2003. Pattern and process of wood debris accumulation in the Queets river basin, Washington, USA. *Geomorphology* **51**: 81–107.

Arscott DB, Tockner K, and Ward JV. 2002. Geomorphic dynamics along a braided-river corridor in the Alps (Fiume Tagliamento, NE Italy). *Ecosystems* **5**: 802–14.

Church M. 1995. Geomorphic response to river flow regulation: case studies and time scales. *Regul River* **11**: 3–22.

Dykaar BB and Wigington PJ. 2000. Floodplain formation and cottonwood colonisation patterns on the Willamette River, Oregon, USA. *Environ Manage* **25**: 87–104.

Edwards PJ, Kollmann J, Gurnell AM, *et al.* 1999. A conceptual model of vegetation dynamics on gravel bars of a large Alpine river. *Wetlands Ecol Manage* **7**: 141–53.

Erskine WD and Webb AA. 2003. Desnagging and resnagging: new directions in river rehabilitation in SE Australia. *River Res Appl* **19**: 233–49.

Francis RA, Gurnell AM, Petts GE, and Edwards PJ. 2006. Riparian tree establishment on gravel bars: interaction between plant growth strategy and the physical environment. International Association of Sedimentologists. Special Publication. In press.

Gregory S, Boyer K, and Gurnell AM (Eds). 2003. The ecology and management of wood in world rivers. Bethesda, MD: American Fisheries Society.

Gurnell AM, Petts GE, Hannah DM, *et al.* 2001. Riparian vegetation and island formation along the gravel-bed Fiume Tagliamento, Italy. *Earth Surf Proc Land* **26**: 31–62.

Gurnell AM and Petts GE. 2002. Island dominated landscapes of large floodplain rivers, a European perspective. *Freshwater Biol* **47**: 581–600.

Karaus U, Alder L, and Tockner K. 2005. "Concave islands": habitat heterogeneity and dynamics of parafluvial ponds in a gravel-bed river. *Wetlands* **25**: 26–37.

Karrenberg S, Edwards PJ, and Kollmann J. 2002. The life history of Salicaceae living in the active zone of floodplains. *Freshwater Biol* **47**: 733–48.

Kollmann J, Vieli M, Edwards PJ, *et al.* 1999. Interactions between vegetation development and island formation in the Alpine river Tagliamento. *Appl Veget Sci* **2**: 25–36.

Maser C and Sedell JR. 1994. From the forest to the sea. Delray Beach, FL: St Lucie Press.

Naiman RJ, Bilby RE, and Bisson PA. 2000. Riparian ecology and management in the Pacific Coastal rain forest. *BioScience* **50**: 996–1011.

Pettit NE and Naiman PJ. 2005. Flood deposited wood debris and its contribution to heterogeneity and regeneration in a semi-arid riparian landscape. *Oecologia*. In press.

Piégay H, Thevenet A, and Citterio A. 1999. Input, storage and distribution of large woody debris along a mountain river continuum, the Drôme River, France. *Catena* **35**: 19–39.

Sedell JR and Frogatt JL. 1984. Importance of streamside forests to large rivers: the isolation of the Willamette River, Oregon, USA, from its floodplain by snagging and streamside forest removal. *Verhandl Internatl Verein Theor Angew Limnol* **22**: 1828–34.

Tockner K, Ward JV, Arscott DB, *et al.* 2003. The Tagliamento River: a model ecosystem of European importance. *Aquat Sci* **65**: 239–53.

Tockner K, Klaus I, Baumgartner C, and Ward JV. 2005. Amphibian diversity and nestedness in a dynamic floodplain river (Taglimento, NE Italy). *Hydrobiologia*. In press.

Van der Nat D, Tockner K, Edwards PJ, *et al.* 2003. Habitat change in braided flood plains (Tagliamento, NE Italy). *Freshwater Biol* **48**: 1–14.

Learning through peer assessment

Linda M Nagel[1], Diane Ebert-May[2], Everett P Weber[2], Janet Hodder[3]

Ecological succession is driven by disturbance, both natural and human-induced, and change occurs at multiple scales, both temporal and spatial. Understanding the mechanisms involved in succession requires the integration of many ideas, some of which may contradict students' belief that succession is only a unidirectional and linear model. The notion of ecosystems as static, or as eventually reaching a final state of equilibrium, needs to be critically challenged by students; ecosystems are stochastic, and this dynamism is the only constant (White and Pickett 1985, Kozlowski 2002). Gurnell *et al.* (pp 377–82) present a novel succession model that provides a context for students to analyze, synthesize, and integrate basic ecological concepts across scales and between groups of organisms.

In previous Pathways articles, we described cooperative learning strategies that are based on the growing body of research showing the cognitive, motivational, affective, and social benefits of college students working in small groups (Bruffee 1999). Here we introduce formative peer assessment strategies to determine the effectiveness of cooperative learning experiences. A major concern of faculty and students about cooperative learning is accountability. In theory, teams are formed to accomplish a common goal and necessarily involve both positive interdependence, where all members must cooperate to complete the task, and individual and group accountability for the work (Smith *et al.* 2005). Peer assessment enables students to measure the effectiveness of group work, to fully understand the purpose of the instruction and assessment criteria, to monitor learning, and to improve their ability to transfer what they have learned to new situations. Formative peer assessment and feedback is more helpful in improving student learning than summative assessment that generally measures specific outcomes (Sheppard 2004).

■ Student goals

- Identify biological and physical components of a dynamic river system.
- Build a model that integrates the components of a river system, showing the response following disturbance.
- Demonstrate understanding that ecological systems are complex, and that there may be more than one correct model for any given system.
- Use peer assessment to learn from and provide substantive feedback to peers.

■ Instructor goals

- Use conceptual model building as a tool for facilitating

[1]*Michigan Technological University*, [2]*Michigan State University*, [3]*University of Oregon*

and assessing students' understanding of succession.
- Facilitate students' understanding of and ability to practice peer assessment.

■ Preceding class

Succession is often included as a topic within a unit on ecosystems. Introduce the concepts of disturbance and succession by engaging students with a series of time-lapse sequenced pictures of succession, including classic linear sequences (eg old field succession) and a set showing disturbance (eg Yellowstone fire or a local example). By working through these examples, students are prepared to make predictions about succession from the Gurnell paper. Models are simplified approximations that provide useful starting points for studying complex natural processes.

Homework

Using information from the Gurnell paper, identify the biological and physical components of this river system. Create a visual model (eg a box model with arrows) that illustrates how the habitats and organisms change in a particular sequence over time. Include in the model the disturbance that is driving this system. As you construct the model, think about what is happening and why. Each individual brings to class one copy of her/his model (use carbonless paper, powerpoint, or CTOOLS [www.ctools.msu.edu]) for each group member.

■ Next class meeting

Peer assessment of models

During class, students use the rubric in Panel 1 to provide constructive comments about each other's models. Then together, they use their models to derive and draw the most complete and explicit model of the river system. The teams use their revised model to develop a response to the following questions and turn in one answer set per group, to be scored as a group assignment. Figure 1 is an example of a model showing how floods can influence habitats, organisms, and processes across scales and groups.

Assessment (group)

1. How does the biomass in the model change over time? Why?
2. Which species appear and disappear over time? What species traits are unique to the (a) wood jam stage and (b) established island stage?
3. Predict the diversity of species in both the wood jam and established island stages. Describe possible interactions among species.
4. Using your group's model, predict what will happen to the established island stage when there is another

---

Panel 1: Rubric for assessing disturbance models

Event   – accurately identified (1 point)
Habitats   – created by disturbance (1 point)
Organisms – impacted by disturbance event (or resulting
              from creation of habitat) (1 point)
Processes – logical progression of response to events –
              includes early (wood jam), mid (pioneer), and late
              (established islands) stages (3 points)

---

small flood and another large flood. Limit the response to three sentences for each scenario.

5. In general, what components of succession are stochastic, and what components are static?

After the groups turn in their work, the instructor selects two or three different models to display and discuss. If the classroom is not equipped with a document camera, the instructor can select two or three groups to draw their model on a transparency while the groups are working. By comparing models, the students should infer that there are multiple rather than single pathways for succession within a system.

Peer assessment of cooperative work skills

Since this activity will take an entire class meeting, it is critical that students spend time productively. Peer assessment (Panel 2) provides feedback to the instructor about the effectiveness of groups in this activity (Liu *et al.* 2002), and about students' ability to apply complex concepts related to succession. It can also be used as a regular learning and assessment tool during a course.

Students receive the assessment criteria before they begin the activity. Each group member evaluates all other team members' contribution by applying a point distribution system for both quantity and quality. The quantity scale should add up to 100% (eg, 25% equal share in a 4-person group) for the teamwork assessment (criteria 1) and quality for each individual contribution (criteria 1–5) is based on a point system from 4 to 0 (highest to none). Each item in Panel 2 is derived from criteria used in engineering and science for assessing collaborative work (Sheppard 2004). Other criteria can be added, depending on the goals of the cooperative groups.

Analysis

The assessments are collected, averaged, and combined with the instructor's score of the group model and ques-

Panel 2. Assessment of cooperative work skills					
Criteria		S1	S2	S3	S4
1. Teamwork, did an equal share of the work, % estimate	Quantitative				
	Qualitative				
2. Kept an open mind, considered other's ideas	Qualitative				
3. Contributed useful ideas	Qualitative				
4. Model prepared prior to class (in this case, homework)	Qualitative				
5. Communicated ideas clearly/ effectively	Qualitative				

S = Student

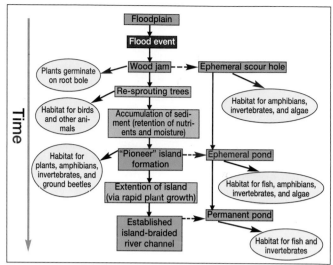

Figure 1. *Model showing how floods influence the components of a river.*

tions. As with any assignment, the weighting of each component of this activity is determined a priori and is linked to the goals of the course.

■ Final note

Collaborative work enables students to deepen their understanding of ecological succession by developing and applying a model of a river system. The two types of peer assessment modeled are intended to drive both cognitive and behavioral attributes of learning, as students challenge each other about what they think they know. A comparison between the groups' models and associated written assessments provides evidence about students' ability to use models to understand concepts.

■ Acknowledgements

We thank the National Science Foundation for their long-term support of the FIRST project, Faculty Institutes for Reforming Science Teaching (DUE 0088847). All Pathways papers are peer reviewed.

■ References

Bruffee KA. 1999. Collaborative learning: higher education, interdependence, and the authority of knowledge (2nd edn). Baltimore, MD: The Johns Hopkins University Press.

Kozlowski TT. 2002. Physiological-ecological impacts of flooding on riparian forest ecosystems. *Wetlands* **22(3)**: 550–561.

Liu J, Thorndike Pysarchik D, and Taylor WW. 2002. Peer review in the classroom. *BioScience* **52**: 824–29.

Sheppard L. 2004. Peer assessment of student collaborative processes in undergraduate engineering education. Final Report to the National Science Foundation, Award Number 0206820, NSF Program 7431 CCLI-ASA, Sheri Sheppard, *et al.* Stanford Center for Innovations in Learning.

Smith K, Sheppard S, Johnson D, and Johnson R. 2005. Pedagogies of engagement: classroom-based practices. *J Eng Educ.* **Jan**: 87–101.

White PS and Pickett STA. 1985. The ecology of natural disturbance and patch dynamics. Orlando, FL: Academic Press, Inc.

Can crop transgenes be kept on a leash?

Michelle Marvier[1] and Rene C Van Acker[2]

Debates about the benefits and risks of genetically modified (GM) crops need to acknowledge two realities: (1) the movement of transgenes beyond their intended destinations is a virtual certainty; and (2) it is unlikely that transgenes can be retracted once they have escaped. Transgenes escape via the movement of pollen and seeds, and this movement is facilitated by the growing number of incidents involving human error. Re-examination of our risk management policies and our assumptions about containment is essential as genes coding for pharmaceutical and industrial proteins are being inserted into the second generation of GM food crops. Even the best designed risk management can be foiled by human error, a reality that is underestimated by most GM crop-risk analyses. Thus, our evaluation of risk should assume that whatever transgene is being examined has a good chance of escaping.

Front Ecol Environ 2005; 3(2): 99–106

Genetically modified organisms (GMOs) are now a part of everyday life in the US, with ingredients from GM crops present in the majority of our processed foods (Hopkin 2001). GM crops are also a major feature of our landscape. In 2003, GM crops were grown on 42.8 million hectares within the US alone, an area larger than the entire state of California (James 2003). Genetic engineering promises society everything from crops with improved agronomic and nutritional qualities to frivolities, such as colored lawns and fluorescing pet fish (Figure 1). The possibilities seem to be limited only by our imaginations (Dunwell 1999). Thus far, however, commercially available GMOs have been almost exclusively limited to crops of major economic importance (eg corn, soybean, cotton, and canola), and the commercially introduced traits have been primarily agronomic (eg insect or herbicide resistance; Figure 2).

Different degrees of confinement are warranted for different types of GM crops, depending primarily on the nature of the genetically altered traits and the breeding system of the crops and related species. For those GM varieties that have been deregulated by the US Department of Agriculture (ie approved for widespread commercial production), confinement is typically not expected. However, there are special cases in which there has been an intent to locally segregate or contain transgenes even for deregulated varieties. For example, some commercially approved GM crops are restricted from being grown in particular states where there are concerns regarding hybridization with weedy relatives; thus, GM cotton can be grown in all states except Florida and Hawaii (EPA 2000). In another well known case, it was assumed that potential risk could be avoided by requiring that seeds remain segregated according to their allowed use; for example, StarLink corn was intended as animal feed but not as human food. The accumulated experiences regarding containment of crops with altered agronomic properties – both before and after their deregulation – provide clear lessons about our ability to contain transgenes.

A second body of evidence regarding containment comes from the last 4 or 5 years of experience with crops that are engineered to cheaply and efficiently produce pharmaceutical and industrial proteins (Giddings et al. 2000; see Table 1 for examples of pharmaceutical proteins currently in development). For these varieties there are no realistic expectations of deregulated production – their cultivation will, in all likelihood, forever be limited to "confined" field trials. Examples of the confinement measures for the cultivation of these crops include geographic isolation, scouting for and destroying escaped plants that sprout in subsequent seasons (volunteer plants), and the dedication of equipment for use only on the regulated crop. Inexpensive production of drugs, vaccines, and enzymes would provide benefits to society, but these crops may also represent new risks and they certainly pose new challenges to our ability to contain transgenes while growing plants outdoors.

The issue of containing transgenes has become a flashpoint in the current debate about biotechnology. If trans-

In a nutshell:

- The movement of transgenes beyond their intended destinations is a virtual certainty
- It is unlikely that transgenes can be retracted once they have escaped
- Human error can foil even the best designed strategies for risk management
- Evaluation of risk should assume that transgenes have a good chance of escaping
- The second generation of GM plants includes traits which could put humans, as well as ecosystems, at risk following transgene escape

[1]Biology Department and Environmental Studies Institute, Santa Clara University, CA (mmarvier@scu.edu); [2]Department of Plant Science, University of Manitoba, Winnipeg, MB, Canada.

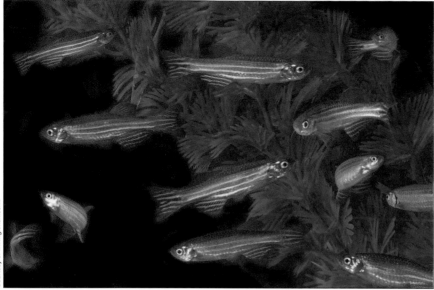

Courtesy of www.glofish.com.

Figure 1. *These transgenic GloFish illustrate one end of the spectrum for novelty and frivolity of GM organisms that are currently on the market.*

genes can be contained, then regulations can be much more permissive about which traits are allowed in crop plants; on the other hand, if transgenes will inevitably escape and spread widely, despite our best intentions (or predictions) of containment, then we need to be much more cautious about what traits are allowed – not only for widespread commercial release, but also in plants that would be grown in small, presumably contained, plots.

Twenty years of accumulated experience with biotechnology provides us with a wealth of examples and evidence that bear on the question of transgene containment. In this review we provide information to support and emphasize two critical points: (1) the movement of transgenes beyond their intended destinations is a virtual certainty; and (2) it is unlikely that transgenes can be retracted once they have escaped. These points support the need for caution in considerations of the release of GM crops.

■ Genes move a lot, and often to unintended places

The movement of transgenes follows many different routes. The most obvious one is via pollen, which can be carried long distances by either wind or pollinators (eg Rieger *et al.* 2002; Chilcutt and Tabashnik 2004). Genes can also escape after a crop has been harvested and plowed under because volunteer and feral crop populations can appear in subsequent years and act as potential sources for the reintroduction of transgenes (Gulden *et al.* 2003). Genes also travel great distances when, knowingly or unknowingly, humans transport crop seeds over huge distances, including between continents.

One of the best documented examples of far-ranging gene spread involves canola (*Brassica napus* L). Canola has been genetically engineered to tolerate glyphosate herbicide (Roundup Ready canola) and, separately, to tolerate glufosinate herbicide (Liberty Link canola). With the unconfined commercial release of GM canola in Canada, transgene movement from canola crop to canola crop was predicted (CFIA 1995), but the speed and extent of movement surprised everyone. By 1998, after only two seasons of commercial cultivation of GM herbicide-tolerant canola types in western Canada, volunteer canola plants carrying GM resistance traits were found in many fields where farmers were not intentionally growing these GM varieties (Hall *et al.* 2000). More importantly, even though the original GM canola possessed either glyphosate tolerance or glufosinate tolerance, individual plants of volunteer canola appeared that possessed both forms of resistance.

Hybridization with other species can be an important additional route for transgene escape. Most crops hybridize with non-crop species in at least some part of their global ranges (Ellstrand *et al.* 1999). Some, such as canola, readily hybridize with related weed species, and we should expect many such hybrids to be created every year. Based on pollen dispersal data, distributions of canola fields, and distributions of weedy mustard populations, Wilkinson *et al.* (2003) estimate that tens of thousands of canola–weed hybrids are produced each year in the UK alone (Figure 3).

Hybridization and gene flow are often controlled by age-old agronomic practices for maintaining seed purity. The most common isolation technique depends on geographic isolation combined with buffers and windbreaks grown around field trials of GM crops (USDA 2003a). Unfortunately, isolation can be broken because pollen flow can cross barriers and surprisingly large distances (Rieger *et al.* 2003; Friesen *et al.* 2003). For example, Reiger *et al.* (2003) studied the movement of canola pollen and detected pollen-mediated gene flow nearly 3 km from a source field. In addition, Watrud *et al.* (2004) found that gene flow from GM creeping bentgrass occurred over 21 km from the source.

Because classical isolation techniques do not provide complete containment, genetic engineers have argued that they can devise technological solutions to the problem of gene movement. The three most familiar and feasible technical solutions are (1) transformation of chloroplasts rather than nuclear DNA (Daniell *et al.* 1998), because chloroplasts are primarily maternally inherited in most species; (2) the controversial "terminator technology" in which plants are genetically engineered to produce sterile seeds (controversial because this interferes with farmers' ability to save seed), and (3) cytoplasmic male sterility, which involves mitochondrial genes that prevent production of functional pollen. The National Research Council (NRC 2004) recently reviewed these and other bioconfinement tools and concluded that no method is likely to be completely effective. The NRC suggested that rather than relying on bioconfinement, we should put care into selecting host species for certain traits. All GM crops do not warrant the same level of concern. Even among the pharmaceutical crops, there may be certain pharmaceutical proteins that are completely benign to humans and the environment. However, it might be appropriate to restrict plants producing the more high-risk proteins to contained facilities or to disallow their production in food plants entirely (NRC 2004). Clearly, many transgenic proteins will fall in between these two extremes, and the degree of confinement required should depend upon the level of risk to human and environmental health, as well as the risk to public confidence.

■ Human error and transgene movement

Recent experiences with GM crops suggest that containment will inevitably fail, frequently as a result of human error. Examples include accidental commingling of GM with non-GM seeds or food products, accidental release of unapproved transgenes into commercial seed, and the failure of industry and growers to follow USDA protocols for field trials. Yet risk assessment applied to GM crops has tended to overlook the importance and apparent ubiquity of human error and its consequences for transgene escape. A brief summary of a few recent mishaps highlights important issues that should be considered in future risk assessments.

Several major biotech firms were recently fined for violations of safety protocols during field trials of GM crops not yet approved for commercial production. In December 2002, Dow AgroSciences was fined for not establishing proper barriers and windbreaks around a GM cornfield (Gillis 2002a). In that same month, Pioneer Hi-Bred (a subsidiary of DuPont) was fined for growing GM corn in a field that was too near to another corn field, potentially allowing cross-pollination (Gillis 2002a). Pioneer was fined again in March 2003 for failing to report detected contamination among the neighboring corn fields within the allotted time (Gillis 2003a). Similarly, in October 2003, Monsanto was fined for violations that occurred in 2001 field trials of GM corn and cotton (Gillis 2003b).

A disturbing example of human error involved corn genetically modified to produce a vaccine that prevents diarrhea in pigs. In November 2002, the USDA discovered that ProdiGene had failed to comply with federal regulations in two field trials, conducted in Nebraska and Iowa (Gillis 2002b, 2003c). In both locations, ProdiGene failed to destroy volunteer corn plants in the subsequent

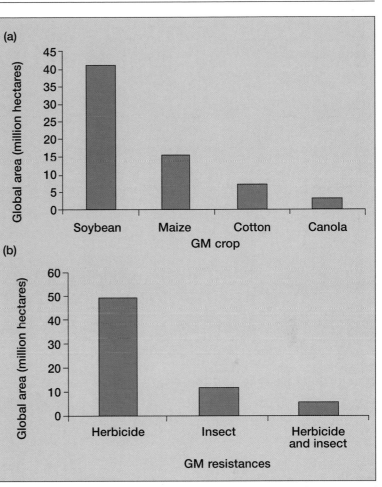

Figure 2. *Global area planted with crops genetically modified for improved agronomic properties in 2003. Areas are shown (a) by crop and (b) by trait. Total worldwide area planted with GM crops in 2003 was 67.7 million hectares. Data are from James (2003).*

growing season. In Nebraska, the volunteer corn had been shredded and mixed among soybeans at a grain elevator, necessitating the destruction of 500 000 bushels of soybeans. In Iowa, 155 acres of corn surrounding a test site had to be destroyed because of possible contamination, via pollen, from volunteer plants. ProdiGene was fined $250 000 – one of the largest fines ever levied by the US against a biotech company for a violation of containment regulations.

A particularly puzzling mishap involved transgenes that seem to have escaped industry control and entered the commercial market prior to federal approval (Pollack 2002). In a letter to the USDA (November 9, 2001), Monsanto admitted that small quantities of a non-approved type of GM herbicide-tolerant canola, called GT200, could be present within commercial canola sold in the US. Monsanto requested that the USDA grant retroactive approval of GT200. Although it had never been sold in North America and was not found in commercial canola in the US, GT200 was detected in Canadian canola. Monsanto could not explain how the transgene came to be present in Canadian canola. Aventis CropScience was similarly concerned that some

Table 1. Examples of pharmaceutical crops currently in development

Company/institution	Protein	Crop	Examples of potential uses
Meristem Therapeutics	Lipase	Rice	Supplement digestive enzymes in cystic fibrosis patients and others
	Various monoclonal antibiodies	Tobacco	Therapeutic proteins to treat cancer and various infectious diseases
	Human serum albumin	Tobacco	Expand blood volume following severe bleeding
	Lactoferrin	Maize	Defense protein that can treat numerous infections
	Collagen	Tobacco	Wound dressings, tissue engineering and artificial skin, wrinkle and scar treatments
Prodigene	Trypsin	Maize	Protease used in insulin production, cell culture, manufacture of vaccines, and wound care
	Aprotinin	Maize	Protease inhibitor used in cell culture, protein purification, and wound care
Ventria	Lactoferrin	Rice and barley	See above
	Lysozyme	Rice	Small enzyme that attacks the protective cell walls of bacteria; can treat numerous infections
Planet Biotechnology	Antibody to *Streptococcus mutans*	Tobacco	Prevent tooth decay (*Streptococcus mutans* is the bacteria that causes tooth decay)
Chlorogen Inc	Human serum albumin	Tobacco	See above
Iowa State University	*E coli* LT-B subunit protein	Corn	Vaccine against *E coli* infection

This list is not exhaustive but is meant to illustrate the diversity of pharmaceutical proteins that are in development and the variety of crops that are being used to produce them.

of its GM canola may also have been inadvertently released prior to federal approval.

Seed purity has long been an important issue for agronomists and plant breeders. Recently, Friesen *et al.* (2003) and Downey and Beckie (2002) tested non-GM canola seedlots that were grown in western Canada and found that after only 6–7 years of commercial production of GM canola, the majority of tested seedlots contained at least trace amounts of genetically engineered herbicide-tolerance traits. In fact, 97% (32 of 33) of the seedlots tested by Friesen *et al.* (2003), and 59% (41 of 70) of the seedlots tested by Downey and Beckie (2002) had foreign transgenes present at detectable levels (above 0.01%). The contamination could have resulted from inadvertent mechanical mixing of certified seedlots during harvest or handling, or contamination (possibly from pollen-mediated gene flow) occurring in earlier generations of pedigreed seed production (ie Breeder or Foundation seed). This high level of contamination in pedigreed seed is noteworthy and disturbing because it shows that even stringent segregation systems were not sufficient to deliver pure non-GM canola seed to farmers in western Canada.

Finally, a probably harmless, yet embarrassing human error was committed by researchers at the University of California (UC). It was recently discovered that the Charles M Rick Tomato Genetics Resource Center at UC Davis had unknowingly distributed seeds of tomatoes containing an approved GM trait to researchers in 14

countries over the past 7 years (Lee and Lau 2003). At least one research project was derailed by receiving this seed. The university has been attempting to recall the approximately 30 seed samples, and has apologized to the recipients.

Although in isolation none of the above examples are terribly alarming, taken together they reveal a worrisome pattern; smart, highly trained, and conscientious people make mistakes, and those mistakes may be repeated and go unnoticed for years. Moreover, although most field trials are performed properly, the rules established to prevent the spread of transgenes from experimental GM varieties are occasionally neglected. The door for transgene escape is occasionally flung wide open. These and similar incidents should serve as a wake-up call to industry, to regulators, and to the public. Transgene movement beyond their intended destination is, for all practical purposes, a foregone conclusion. Unless regulatory oversight and enforcement are improved, containment will fail (Taylor and Tick 2003). As a result, regulatory policies that assume risk control is possible through containment should be re-examined.

■ No turning back

Unlike most of the agricultural technologies introduced in the past, the decision to introduce transgenic crops on a broad scale may be irreversible. Even persistent pesticides will eventually break down if we simply stop using them, but models from theoretical population genetics suggest that transgenes can persist in the environment for very long time periods. Transgenes that have a selective advantage (eg resistance traits for a herbicide that is used frequently) can easily persist in a gene pool for many generations (Van Acker *et al.* 2003). Even selectively neutral or slightly detrimental genes can persist for long periods, especially if gene flow is ongoing (Ellstrand *et al.* 1999). Although there have been no field experiments that directly assess whether we can remove or recall transgenes once they have escaped into natural gene pools, two lines of evidence suggest that it would be

Figure 3. *A field of canola* (Brassica napus L) *in bloom.*

extremely difficult to perform a recall once a transgenic organism becomes widespread. First, although the presence of transgenes will not necessarily make a plant more invasive or harmful, the many failed attempts to eradicate non-native species should alert us to the potential difficulty of eradicating living organisms in general, once they are released or have escaped into the environment. Efforts to eradicate non-native species are often prohibitively expensive and typically involve spraying large quantities of highly toxic compounds that also affect non-target species, including humans (Myers *et al.* 2000). The US, for example, spends about $45 million each year to control a single non-native plant, purple loosestrife (*Lythrum salicaria*; Pimentel *et al.* 2000). Despite these efforts, purple loosestrife continues to spread rapidly and is now present in 48 states (Pimentel *et al.* 2000).

Second, we need only look to the well known story of StarLink corn to see just how hard it can be to recall a transgene once it has become widespread. Engineered to express insecticidal cry9 protein, StarLink corn was approved for animal feed but not human consumption. It did not, however, remain segregated – in 2000, cry9 was discovered in a wide variety of processed foods. Despite a massive recall of food products and extraordinary efforts to recover StarLink seed, the cry9 transgenes still persisted at detectable levels in US corn supplies 3 years later (USDA 2003b). The lingering presence of StarLink demonstrates that once a transgene makes its way into the general food supply, it may take many years and enormous effort to get rid of it (Figure 4). In contrast to

StarLink corn, it is expected that transgenes coding for pharmaceutical and industrial proteins will never become widespread in the first place. However, the StarLink experience shows that should there ever be a massive containment failure, by which an undesirable transgene somehow manages to gain a strong foothold in the seed supply, it may not be possible to subsequently eradicate that gene.

Even with minimal uncertainty regarding the human and environmental safety of GM traits, it would generally be prudent to maintain some non-GM seed lineages for cases where we want to establish cropping systems that are free of GM traits. Unfortunately, recent tests performed on traditional seed varieties of corn, soybeans, and canola in the US, and of canola in Canada, have found pervasive transgenic contamination (Friesen *et al.* 2003; Mellon and Rissler 2004). Although the levels of contamination were generally low (typically less than 1%

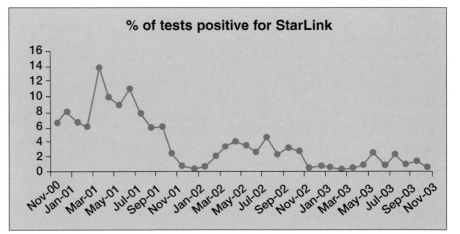

Figure 4. *Persistence of StarLink transgenes in US corn. Because the tests for StarLink are performed on a voluntary basis and not on a statistical sampling of the total US corn crop, the values may not accurately reflect the overall levels of contamination. What is important to note, however, is the lingering presence of StarLink in the samples, despite extensive efforts to recall the transgene. Data from USDA (2003b).*

Figure 5. With increased soil cultivation (tillage) comes increased risk of erosion – a trend that can be slowed and possibly reversed by the adoption of no-till practices.

of individual seeds contain transgenes, although levels of contamination were occasionally much higher), the findings have some unsettling implications for the future. Contamination such as that uncovered by a Union of Concerned Scientists study (Mellon and Rissler 2004) shows just how hard it may be to obtain GM-free seeds in the future.

Does transgene escape matter?

It is not certain whether escape of transgenes, in and of itself, constitutes risk, but escape does enhance the possibility of risk. A particularly well-documented demonstration of possible environmental consequences comes from Snow et al. (2003). Commercial sunflowers readily hybridize with weedy sunflowers. Snow and colleagues showed that if a transgene coding for an insecticidal compound moves into weedy sunflowers, the weeds experienced reduced herbivory and produced more seeds. Thus, a problem weed could be made even worse by transgene escape.

Concerning human health, GM foods that are currently on the market do not appear to have caused any great harm, but a recent review by Pryme and Lembcke (2003) highlights a striking lack of published, independent studies examining effects of GM food and feed on mammals. In contrast to commercialized varieties, there could be serious health consequences if transgenes coding for certain pharmaceutical and industrial proteins were to escape into crops being grown for food or feed – this potential for harm is precisely why the USDA requires strict confinement measures during the cultivation, processing, and transport of these varieties.

Movement of deregulated transgenes into non-GM crop fields can also have important effects on broad agricultural practices. The clearest example of this concerns reduced tillage farming. In reduced tillage cropping systems, non-selective glyphosate herbicide (Roundup) is used instead of tillage to control weeds prior to crop seeding. Reduced tillage provides substantial and measurable economic benefits to farms, in addition to broader environmental benefits (Lafond *et al.* 1992; McRae *et al.* 2000; Derksen *et al.* 2002; Agriculture and Agri-Food Canada 2003; Figure 5). Although the adoption of reduced tillage practices was well underway before GM glyphosate-resistant crops (eg Roundup Ready canola and soy) were first introduced in Canada, the adoption of Roundup Ready crops has facilitated further adoption of reduced tillage practices. Unfortunately, the widespread movement of transgenes conferring glyphosate resistance now threatens the viability of reduced tillage practices. The ubiquitous appearance of Roundup-tolerant volunteer canola in western Canada (Friesen *et al.* 2003) makes glyphosate a selective herbicide; reduced tillage farmers (even those not growing Roundup Ready canola) must now add a second herbicide to the pre-seeding glyphosate treatment. This adds cost and reduces the economic feasibility of reduced tillage cropping. It also adds herbicide load on the environment (Van Acker *et al.* 2003).

Finally, transgene escape has important implications for those farmers and organizations that are hoping to avoid or minimize the occurrence of GM traits on their land or in their crops and thus, for food processors and consumers who wish to keep certain traits out of food products. If a farmer wants to be certified as organic, or a food provider wants to reassure the public that some food is GM-free, there must be frequent testing and discarding of contaminated seed or grain lots. All this will cost money and create additional costs for entire production systems; currently, where the service is available, genetic purity testing for individual seedlots costs approximately $500.

GM crops on the horizon

Although widespread planting of transgenic crops such as herbicide-resistant canola may have environmental consequences, it is typically thought that human health is not at risk. This may change if pharmaceutical and industrial crop production becomes widespread. In 2002, the USDA approved 20 permits for field trials (130 acres on 34 sites) involving plants engineered to produce pharmaceutical proteins (USDA 2003a; see also USDA 2005). A great deal of attention is paid to developing and enforcing confinement protocols for the production of pharmaceutical crops. However, the history of mistakes with previous GM plants suggests that similar mistakes could occur with pharmaceutical crops, where the consequences of lost containment may be more dire. The National Research Council (2004) states that an "organism that is typically grown to produce a common and widespread food product probably would be a poor choice as a precursor for an industrial compound, unless that organism were to be grown under stringent conditions of confinement. Alternative non-food host organisms should be sought for genes that code for transgenic products that need to be kept out of the food supply." However, of the over 200 field trials conducted to date for GM crops producing pharmaceutical or industrial products, over 75% involved corn – a wind-pollinated and out-crossing food crop (UCS 2003). Moreover, even *Nature Biotechnology*, a journal that most would label as pro-biotechnology, challenged the wisdom of using corn for pharmaceutical production. The editorial board of *Nature Biotechnology* (2004) wrote: "It seems that an industry in which the PhD is the intellectual norm is either incapable of learning a simple lesson from the past or cannot bring itself to act appropriately, despite what it has learned previously". Pharmaceutical crops make the issue of containment and human error a matter of public health as well as an environmental concern.

Conclusions

GM crops are here to stay, and they may produce numerous societal benefits, including inexpensive production of drugs and more nutritious foods. Advocates of biotechnology often point to the precision of the technology and our mastery of DNA as reassuring. Perhaps it is, but we will never be able to master and fully eliminate human error. The inevitability of mistakes, and therefore of transgene escape, must be factored into our policies, regulations, and risk assessments for GM plants. There is therefore a pressing need for the development of models that simulate the entire lifecycle of those transgenic crops that do require confinement – from the time when seeds leave a company's custody until they are planted in a field, harvested, processed, and successfully shipped to a processing facility. These models should include detailed information about all possible routes for transgene escape, including biological processes such as long-distance pollen dispersal, seed movement by animals, and viability of seeds following consumption by animals. Just as importantly, these models must include routes of transgene escape that result from human error, such as a failure to perform appropriate scouting for volunteers, inadvertent mixing of GM and non-GM products, inadequate cleaning of equipment, and violations of procedures for chain of custody. There are many possible points at which containment could be breached, and data are needed to estimate probabilities at each of these points. These models, if properly parameterized, should help regulators to identify where to build in redundancies to improve confinement, and many of these redundancies will need to be aimed at human error. However, we must keep in mind that even the best designed risk management with redundancy and enforcement can still be foiled by human error. We should not have confidence in our ability to keep GM

plants on a tight leash. Rather, total containment can never be assured or assumed, and our evaluation of risk should be predicated on the idea that transgenes always have some chance of escaping. Re-examination of our risk management policies and of our assumptions about containment is essential as we move into the second generation of GM crops, some of which will have the potential for serious adverse effects.

Acknowledgements

M Marvier was supported by a grant from the Biotechnology Risk Assessment Research program of the National Center for Environmental Research of the US EPA.

References

Agriculture and Agri-Food Canada. 2003. Greenhouse gas mitigation program for Canadian agriculture. www.agr.gc.ca/progser/ghgm_e.phtml. Viewed 30 January 2004.

Canadian Food Inspection Agency. 1995. Decision Document DD95-02: Determination of environmental safety of Monsanto Canada Inc's Roundup® herbicide-tolerant *Brassica napus* canola line GT73. Ottawa, Canada: Canadian Food Inspection Agency. http://www.inspection.gc.ca/english/plaveg/bio/dd/dd9502e.shtml Viewed 30 January 2004.

Chilcutt CF and Tabashnik BE. 2004. Contamination of refuges by *Bacillus thuringiensis* toxin genes from transgenic maize. *P Nat Acad Sci USA* **101**: 7526–29.

Daniell H, Datta R, Varma S, *et al.* 1998. Containment of herbicide resistance through genetic engineering of the chloroplast genome. *Nat Biotechnol* **16**: 345–48.

Derksen DA, Anderson RL, Blackshaw RE, and Maxwell B. 2002. Weed dynamics and management strategies for cropping systems in the northern great plains. *Agron J* **94**: 174–85.

Downey RK and Beckie H. 2002. Isolation effectiveness in canola pedigreed seed production. Internal research report. Saskatoon, Canada: Agriculture and Agri-Food Canada, Saskatoon Research Centre.

Dunwell JM. 1999. Transgenic crops: the next generation, or an example of 2020 vision. *Ann Bot – London* **84**: 269–77.

Ellstrand NC, Prentice HC, and Hancock JF. 1999. Gene flow and introgression from the domesticated plants into their wild relatives. *Annu Rev Ecol Syst* **30**: 539–63.

Friesen LF, Nelson AG, and Van Acker RC. 2003. Evidence of contamination of pedigreed canola (*Brassica napus*) seedlots in western Canada with genetically engineered herbicide resistance traits. *Agron J* **95**: 1342–47.

Giddings G, Gordon A, Brooks D, and Carter A. 2000. Transgenic plants as factories for biopharmaceuticals. *Nat Biotechnol* **18**: 1151–55.

Gillis J. 2002a. EPA fines biotechs for corn violations. *The Washington Post*. December 13; E: 03.

Gillis J. 2002b. Soybeans mixed with altered corn; suspect crop stopped from getting into food. *The Washington Post*. November 13; E: 01.

Gillis J. 2003a. Firm fined for spread of altered corn genes; Government wasn't told soon enough. *The Washington Post*. April 24; E: 04.

Gillis J. 2003b. Monsanto fined for crop tests; modified corn, cotton improperly handled. *The Washington Post*. October 18; E: 01.

Gillis J. 2003c. US will subsidize cleanup of altered corn. *The Washington Post*. March 26; E: 01.

Gulden RH, Shirtliffe SJ, and Thomas AG. 2003. Harvest losses of canola (*Brassica napus*) cause large seedbank inputs. *Weed Sci* **51**: 83–86.

Hall L, Topinka K, Huffman J, *et al*. 2000. Pollen flow between herbicide-resistant *Brassica napus* is the cause of multiple-resistant *B napus* volunteers. *Weed Sci* **48**: 688–94.

Hopkin K. 2001. The risks on the table. *Sci Am* **April**: 60–61.

James C. 2003. ISAAA Briefs No. 30-2003 – Global status of commercialized transgenic crops: 2003. International Service for the Acquisition of Agri-biotech Applications. www.isaaa.org. Viewed 25 October 2004.

Lafond GP, Loeppky H, and Derksen DA. 1992. The effects of tillage systems and crop rotations on soil water conservation, seedling establishment and crop yield. *Can J Plant Sci* **72**: 103–115.

Lee M. and Lau E. 2003. 2003. Biotech seeds shipped in error. *Sacramento Bee*. December 19; A:1.

McRae T, Smith CAS, and Gregorich LJ (Eds.). 2000. Environmental sustainability of Canadian agriculture: report of the agri-environment indicator project. Ottawa, Canada: Agriculture and Agri-Food Canada.

Mellon M and Rissler J. 2004. Gone to seed: transgenic contaminants in the traditional seed supply. Cambrige, MA: Union of Concerned Scientists. www.ucsusa.org/food_and_environment/biotechnology/page.cfm?pageID=1315. Viewed 30 January 2005.

Myers JH, Simberloff D, Kuris AM, and Carey JR. 2000. Eradication revisited: dealing with exotic species. *Trends Ecol Evol* **15**: 316–20.

NRC (National Research Council). 2004. Biological confinement of genetically engineered crops. Washington, DC: The National Academies Press.

Nature Biotechnology. 2004. Drugs in crops – the unpalatable truth. *Nat Biotechnol* **22**: 133.

Pimentel D, Lach L, Zuniga R, and Morrison D. 2000. Environmental and economic costs of nonindigenous species in the US. *BioScience* **50**: 53–65.

Pollack A. 2002. Unapproved canola seed may be on farms, makers say. *New York Times*. April 16; C: 4.

Pryme IF and Lembcke R. 2003. In vivo studies on possible health consequences of genetically modified food and feed – with particular regard to ingredients consisting of genetically modified plant materials. *Nutr Health* **17**: 1–8.

Rieger MA, Lamond M, Preston C, *et al*. 2002. Pollen-mediated movement of herbicide resistance between commercial canola fields. *Science* **296**: 2386–88.

Snow AA, Pilson D, Riesberg LH, *et al*. 2003. A Bt transgene reduces herbivory and enhances fecundity in wild sunflower. *Ecol Appl* **13**: 279–86.

Taylor MR and Tick JS. 2003. Post-market oversight of biotech foods: is the system prepared? Washington, DC: Pew Initiative on Food and Biotechnology. http://pewagbiotech.org/research/postmarket. Viewed 30 January 2005.

UCS (Union of Concerned Scientists). 2003. Food and environment: pharm and industrial crops. The next wave of agricultural biotechnology. www.ucsusa.org/pharm/pharm_open.html. Viewed 30 January 2005.

USDA 2003a. Field testing of plants engineered to produce pharmaceutical and industrial compounds. *Federal Register* **68**: 11337–40.

USDA 2003b. StarLink test results. US Department of Agriculture, Grain Inspection, Packers and Stockyards Administration.

USDA 2005. Release Permits for Pharmaceuticals, Industrials, Value Added Proteins for Human Consumption, or for Phytoremediation Granted or Pending by APHIS as of January 3, 2005. www.aphis.usda.gov/brs/ph_permits.html. Viewed 30 January 2005.

EPA (US Environmental Protection Agency). 2000. Biopesticides registration action document: preliminary risks and benefits section. *Bacillus thuringiensis* plant-pesticides. www.epa.gov/scipoly/sap/2000/october/brad3_enviroassessment.pdf. Viewed 30 January 2005.

Van Acker RC, Brûlé-Babel AL, and Friesen LF. 2003. An environmental risk assessment of Roundup Ready wheat: risks for direct seeding systems in western Canada. Winnipeg, Canada: Canadian Wheat Board. www.cwb.ca/en/topics/biotechnology/report/index.jsp. Viewed 30 January 2004.

Watrud LS, Lee EH, Fairbrother A, *et al*. 2004. Evidence for landscape-level, pollen-mediated gene flow from genetically modified creeping bentgrass with CP4 EPSPS as a marker. *P Natl Acad Sci USA* **101**: 14533–38.

Wilkinson MJ, Elliott LJ, Allainguillaume J, *et al*. 2003. Hybridization between *Brassica napus* and *B rapa* on a national scale in the United Kingdom. *Science* **302**: 457–59.

Unleashing problem solvers: from assessment to designing research

Diane Ebert-May[1], Janet Hodder[2], Everett Weber[1], and Douglas Luckie[1]

"Can transgenes be kept on a leash?" ask Marvier and Van Acker in the preceding review article (pp 99–106). "No", they answer, "the movement of transgenes beyond their intended destination is a virtual certainty", and furthermore "it is unlikely that transgenes can be retracted once they have escaped". Would these bold statements engage students, revealing the realities and complexities of genetically modified (GM) crops? How can we use the critical analyses presented by these authors to guide our undergraduates towards developing their own analytical skills?

Students' abilities to analyze controversial subjects are often limited by their lack of understanding of basic science fundamental to the issue. In this case, their approach to the debate about GM crops may be driven by common misconceptions about, for example, gene expression, traits, or even the difference between an allele and a mutation. Students may not know that genes flow between non-GM crops, a normal, commonly occurring process. Hence, a common belief is that traditional methods of crop breeding are completely safe, while all transgenic crops are potentially dangerous (Beringer 2000; CSU 2004). Ideally, we want students to understand the body of knowledge surrounding a subject so they can transfer and apply their knowledge to solve novel, complex problems. In this two-step approach to scientific teaching, we use Marvier and Van Acker's paper as the context for assessing students' comprehension and problem-solving abilities. We then provide instructors with a framework for thinking about what these assessments mean and how they could form the basis of a researchable question.

■ Student goals

- Demonstrate understanding of biological principles relevant to genetic modification of crops.
- Explain the pathways and processes of gene flow from GM crops to other plants.

■ Instructor goals

- Probe student understanding of concepts fundamental to GM technology and, based on the student responses, design instruction that addresses student needs.
- Use data from student assessments to pose a significant question about their learning that can be investigated empirically.

[1]Michigan State University, [2]University of Oregon

First step: students move from comprehension to problem solving

The following questions are designed to check students' knowledge and comprehension of biological principles after they read the paper. Questions are derived directly from the content in Marvier and Van Acker and are generally known concepts that are difficult for students to understand.

Knowledge and comprehension questions

Students could support each response with an example to demonstrate deeper understanding.

- What is a gene? A transgene?
- What is a trait? (eg ultimate source [DNA], expression [protein], transfer from generation to generation [reproduction/meiosis])
- How does an allele differ from a mutation? A transgene?
- How can the genotype of an organism influence the phenotype?
- What does hybridization mean? (eg crop/weed, GMO crop/non-GMO crop hybridization)
- What is gene flow? Dispersal?
- How does sexual reproduction occur in plants?
- Do transgenes and mutations have selective advantage?

While comprehension of the facts above is important for thinking and problem solving, students also need opportunities to work on problems that allow them to build connections between concepts that help them gain long-term understanding (Anderson and Krathwohl 2001). Rather than suggest a specific instructional design, we recommend having students work in groups to address some of the comprehension issues revealed by their responses to the questions above. Box models and concept maps provide visual data about students' higher-level thinking (Novak 2003). The following assessment requires understanding of a number of concepts and promotes discussion within groups.

Application and analysis problem

Students examine the different types of genetically modified crops described in Marvier and Van Acker. They select one of the crops and fill in the box model below. In each box, they put the name of the organism at the top and the cellular component of the organism that is involved in transgene transfer at the bottom. They use arrows to connect the movement of the transgene from the organism in the laboratory to organisms in the field. The number of boxes depends on the number of transfers. Next to each arrow, students explain the

Panel 1. Assessment using canola as the crop

Students begin with a blank template. This sample box model was drawn using web-based C-TOOLS (http://ctools.msu.edu/); post-it notes or a box model template on paper also work.

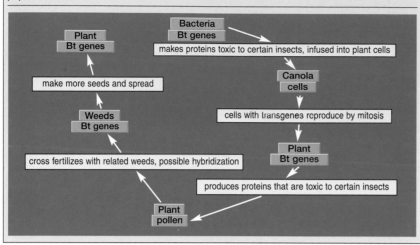

processes that enabled the movement of the transgene and the expression of the trait. Students can also indicate possible places in the pathway where transgenes could escape and explain why this might happen (Panel 1).

Second step: instructors move from assessment to designing research on learning

What did students' responses to the concept questions and problem tell the instructor about their understanding? For

Panel 2. Guidelines for planning research in education

* What did the assessment data suggest about student understanding?

* Why didn't students understand critical concepts? This can lead to a researchable question worth pursuing.

* What has been done already about students' understanding of these concepts and does the research you have proposed have the potential to contribute to the knowledge base?

* How and why will you select the methods? Consider design research methods as a way to refine teaching practices (Collins *et al.* 2004; Suter and Frechtling 2000). Design research is used by engineers, computer scientists, and now educators.

* What kinds of data will you collect, direct (eg tests, reports, performance, observations, interviews) and/or self-report (eg surveys)?

* How will you analyze the data? Both descriptive and univariate statistics are useful tools. Also, extended response answers from students can be coded and counted, then statistics used, as shown in Ebert-May *et al.* (2003).

* How could the results influence instruction? Would you modify the instructional design, the assessment, the students' role, your role?

* Where should the study be reported? A summary of possible journals appears on the FIRST II website (www.first2.org).

example, did students understand the relationship between gene modification, movement, and expression, or the connection of genotype to phenotype? If not, what can an instructor do? One pathway is to investigate students' difficulties in understanding as a research problem, using the guidelines in Panel 2.

■ Final note

This article is intentionally less prescriptive than our previous Pathways to Scientific Teaching papers. Our observations and those of others indicate that many faculty are implementing new teaching strategies in their courses, yet few are asking questions and systematically gathering data that have the potential to contribute to our understanding of how students learn (Shavelson and Towne 2003; D'Avanzo 2003). Ultimately, this type of research will contribute to the continuing improvement of undergraduate science instruction and catalyze further exploration into learning.

■ Acknowledgements

Our thanks to D Sibley for box models and the National Science Foundation for their long-term support of the FIRST project, Faculty Institutes for Reforming Science Teaching (DUE 0088847), C-TOOLS Creating Visual Tools to See Student Learning (DUE 0206924), and M Marvier. All Pathways articles are peer reviewed.

■ References

Anderson LW and Krathwohl DR (Eds). 2001. A taxonomy for learning, teaching and assessing. New York, NY: Addison Wesley Longman, Inc.

Beringer J. 2000. Releasing genetically modified organisms: will any harm outweigh any advantage? *J Appl Ecol* **37**: 207–14.

Collins A, Joseph D, and Bielaczyc K. 2004. Design research: theoretical and methodological issues. *J Learn Sci* **13**: 15–42.

CSU (Colorado State University). 2004. Transgenic crops: an introduction and resource guide. www.colostate.edu/programs/life sciences/Transgenic Crops. Viewed January 30, 2005.

D'Avanzo C. 2003. Application of research on learning to college teaching: ecological examples. *Bioscience* **53**: 1121–28.

Ebert-May D, Batzli J, and Lim H. 2003. Disciplinary research strategies for assessment of learning. *Bioscience* **53**: 1221–28.

Novak J. 2003. The promise of new ideas and new technology for improving teaching and learning. *Cell Biol Educ* **2**: 122–32.

Shavelson RJ and Towne L. 2002. Scientific research in education. Washington, DC: National Academy Press.

Suter L and Frechtling J. 2000. Guiding principles for mathematics and science education research methods: report of a workshop. NSF Report 00-113. Washington, DC: National Science Foundation.

Chapter 6

Students: Preparing Homework for Class

Overview

What happens when we design an active-learning activity for class, and the students arrive unprepared to participate? In a learner-centered classroom, it is essential that students prepare prior to class so that they can contribute to individual or group-based activities during class. The goal of active homework on a regular basis is for students to become engaged in the homework and increasingly reflective about their learning. In this chapter we include examples of active homework in which students are required to do more than just read material. These preclass activities engage students in relevant work that prepares them to deepen their understanding of concepts in class and provides the instructor insight into their thinking.

Grading any homework is overwhelming in terms of time; however, the judicious use of rubrics helps streamline the process and increase the quality of student responses. Active homework is intended to give students practice and motivate them for class the next day. Recent research indicated that assigning points for just doing the homework does not improve performance (Freeman et al. 2007). Therefore, the rubrics and scoring schemes we use for grading homework provide students straightforward feedback about the level of their performance. The process of assigning grades using rubrics is efficient and the criteria transparent to the students before they begin the task.

Losing pieces of the puzzle: threats to marine, estuarine, and diadromous species

Carrie V Kappel

The number of marine species at risk of extinction is rising. Understanding the threats that contribute to extinction risk in the seas is thus critical to conservation. When major threats to marine, estuarine, and diadromous species on the US Endangered Species Act and IUCN Red lists were ranked according to the number of species they affect, strong consensus in the ranking of threats across species and between institutions emerged. Overexploitation is the most frequent threat to vulnerable marine species, with approximately half of threatened species caught as bycatch in fisheries. Habitat degradation, the primary threat to terrestrial species, ranks second in impact on marine species. Loss of listed marine species would probably affect ecosystem function and delivery of ecosystem services because many of these species are strong interactors, including ecosystem engineers, taxa that provide important nutrient links between terrestrial and marine ecosystems, and a disproportionate number of high trophic-level predators.

Front Ecol Environ 2005; 3(5): 275–282

Human history has noted the disappearance of five seabirds, three marine mammals, and four gastropods from the world's oceans. According to a recent review of marine extinctions, another 18 species may have gone extinct globally, although their taxonomic status is uncertain, while 103 species have been lost from substantial portions of their ranges (Dulvy *et al.* 2003).

Despite evidence of marine extinctions, fewer marine than terrestrial species have been flagged as vulnerable under the US Endangered Species Act (ESA), the World Conservation Union (IUCN) Red List, or the Convention on International Trade in Endangered Species of Wild Fauna and Flora (CITES). However, the number of marine species on these lists has grown recently and is expected to continue to rise with mounting threats and increased attention to the status of marine populations and ecosystems (International Institute for Sustainable Development 2002; Baillie *et al.* 2004; Armsworth *et al.* in press a; Figure 1).

In part, the increase in listings represents growing recog-

In a nutshell:
- Most marine species face multiple threats
- Overexploitation is the most pervasive of these threats, affecting commercial and non-commercial species alike
- Bycatch is comparable in impact to targeted harvest and threatens approximately half of the listed marine species
- Habitat degradation, the second greatest threat, is particularly problematic for coastal species affected by land-based impacts
- By assessing the relative impacts of different threats and building understanding of species' ecological roles, we can develop conservation priorities

Hopkins Marine Station, Stanford University, 100 Oceanview Boulevard, Pacific Grove, CA 93950 (ckappel@stanford.edu)

nition that marine species may be as vulnerable to extinction risk as terrestrial species, despite commonly held perceptions to the contrary (Roberts and Hawkins 1999; Dulvy *et al.* 2003; Hutchings and Reynolds 2004). In 1996, IUCN sparked a debate in the scientific literature by listing several commercially important species, including southern bluefin tuna, Atlantic cod, and North Sea haddock. Although some scientists and managers objected to the "one size fits all" decline threshold (IUCN Criterion A) that triggered the listing of these species (eg Matsuda *et al.* 1997), others have argued that there is no convincing evidence that marine species are less vulnerable to extinction than terrestrial species, and that high fecundity, naturally variable populations, and large dispersal potential do not necessarily confer resistance to overexploitation (Hutchings 2001; Dulvy *et al.* 2003; Hutchings and Reynolds 2004).

Many recent papers have pointed to overfishing as a major cause of declines in marine populations (Pauly *et al.* 1998; Musick *et al.* 2000; Jackson *et al.* 2001; Myers and Worm 2003). Dulvy *et al.* (2003) found that 55% of known local to global marine extinctions were attributable to exploitation. However, to date no one has looked in a quantitative way at threats to the full list of vulnerable marine species. On land, the most common threat to vulnerable species is habitat loss, rather than overexploitation (Wilcove *et al.* 1998). This difference may represent, at least in part, a temporal lag in exploitation of the seas. We have long since abandoned the harvest of substantial numbers of wild land animals or plants for human consumption, and instead have turned to domesticated biomass and industrial agriculture, which is a primary contributor to terrestrial habitat degradation (Wilcove *et al.* 1998). However, each year, over 80 x 10⁶ tons of wild biomass are harvested from the oceans (FAO

Figure 1. *Humpback whale* (Megaptera novaeangliae) *breaching in Monterey Bay, CA. Humpbacks are listed as endangered under the ESA and vulnerable by the IUCN.*

Fisheries Department 2004); thus, overexploitation has the potential to be a major threat to both target and non-target species through direct harvest, bycatch, depletion of prey, habitat alteration, or other indirect effects. To design and implement effective biodiversity conservation approaches for the oceans, we must understand the relative impacts of the full spectrum of risks facing marine species, from overexploitation to habitat loss to climate change.

Major threats to marine biodiversity in general and to vulnerable species in particular have been qualitatively reviewed elsewhere (National Research Council 1995; Pew Oceans Commission 2003; US Commission on Ocean Policy 2004; Armsworth *et al.* in press a). Table 1 briefly summarizes the threat categories evaluated here. The primary objective of this paper is to provide a synopsis of the current status of threats to vulnerable species by using two separate datasets, comprised of nearly 300 species, to evaluate the relative importance of these threats, and to rank by how many at-risk species they impact. ("Species at risk" refers to marine, estuarine, or diadromous species listed as vulnerable, endangered, or critically endangered on the IUCN Red List and/or endangered, threatened, candidate, or species of concern under the ESA.) Marine and estuarine threats are compared to terrestrial and freshwater stressors, and the potential impact that the loss of strongly interactive species or groups of species would have on ecosystem function and delivery of ecosystem goods and services is also discussed. Finally, suggestions are offered for how we should proceed with research, conservation, and management efforts to better understand and minimize extinction risk in the world's oceans.

■ Ranking the threats

As of May 1, 2004, 168 marine, estuarine, or diadromous species from US and foreign waters were listed or being considered for listing under the ESA (Figure 2). Under the Act, subspecies and distinct population segments (DPSs) can be treated as "species" in the listing process;

"species" is thus used here to refer to any taxa listed under the ESA. Results for species defined in this manner are detailed here; however, threat rankings were also reanalyzed using biological species and subspecies rather than DPSs, in an attempt to determine whether or not species with multiple DPSs (eg salmonids) caused bias in the results.

Threats to these taxa were tallied using Federal Register rulings, status reviews, and recovery plans published by the listing agencies of the National Oceanic and Atmospheric Administration (NOAA) Fisheries and US Fish and Wildlife Service (FWS). Threats were categorized as "known" (historical or ongoing) or "potential" (uncertain or future), as indicated by the listing agency (Table 1). Major and minor threats were not separated, as this information was not consistently provided. Multiple threats were recorded for most species. Single threats that could be counted in multiple categories were tallied in both. For example, habitat degradation due to destructive fishing gear was classified as both habitat loss and overexploitation.

An additional 225 species, subspecies, or stocks (55 in common with the ESA list) for which information on threats was available were compiled from the IUCN Red List (IUCN 2004a; Figure 2). This information came from assessments of taxonomic groups conducted by specialists who categorize major threats according to a common hierarchy (IUCN 2004b). Red List threats were placed into the Table 1 categories to make the two datasets comparable. For marine birds, additional information on threats and on potential correlates of vulnerability (eg ground nesting) was obtained from Birdlife International, the organization that assessed marine birds for the IUCN Red List (BirdLife International 2004). The full list of species and threats is available in Web Table 1.

These datasets have important limitations: both ESA and IUCN listings are based on expert opinion, and the biologists who prepare listing notices and status reviews may or may not use quantitative or experimental data to evaluate threats. In fact, such data are often unavailable. ESA listing notices, for instance, frequently lack important data, including information about impacts of invasive species, habitat degradation, and pollutants (Easter-Pilcher 1996). The level of detail varies considerably among taxa and with date of listing. Recent listings have resulted in more detailed documentation of status, causes of decline, and threats to recovery of petitioned species than earlier listings. Threats cited in listing documentation are partly a reflection of the scientific understanding of the time, so recently recognized impacts such as climate change are underrepresented. In addition, although the datasets cover a wide taxonomic range, they are weighted towards certain groups of species, largely because studies and management of marine

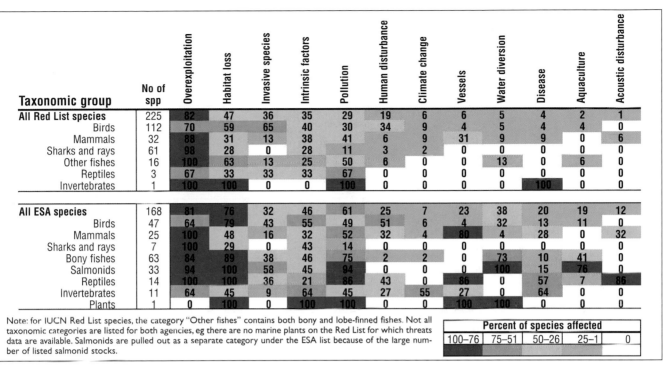

Taxonomic group	No of spp	Overexploitation	Habitat loss	Invasive species	Intrinsic factors	Pollution	Human disturbance	Climate change	Vessels	Water diversion	Disease	Aquaculture	Acoustic disturbance
All Red List species	225	82	47	36	35	29	19	6	6	5	4	2	1
Birds	112	70	59	65	40	30	34	9	4	5	4	4	0
Mammals	32	88	31	13	38	41	6	9	31	9	9	0	6
Sharks and rays	61	98	28	0	28	11	3	2	0	0	0	0	0
Other fishes	16	100	63	13	25	50	6	0	0	13	0	6	0
Reptiles	3	67	33	33	33	67	0	0	0	0	0	0	0
Invertebrates	1	100	100	0	0	100	0	0	0	0	100	0	0
All ESA species	168	81	76	32	46	61	25	7	23	38	20	19	12
Birds	47	64	79	43	55	49	51	6	4	32	13	11	0
Mammals	25	100	48	16	32	52	32	4	80	4	28	0	32
Sharks and rays	7	100	29	0	43	14	0	0	0	0	0	0	0
Bony fishes	63	84	89	38	46	75	2	2	0	73	10	41	0
Salmonids	33	94	100	58	45	94	0	0	0	100	15	76	0
Reptiles	14	100	100	36	21	86	43	0	86	0	57	7	86
Invertebrates	11	64	45	9	64	45	27	55	27	0	64	0	0
Plants	1	0	100	0	100	100	0	0	100	100	0	0	0

Note: for IUCN Red List species, the category "Other fishes" contains both bony and lobe-finned fishes. Not all taxonomic categories are listed for both agencies, eg there are no marine plants on the Red List for which threats data are available. Salmonids are pulled out as a separate category under the ESA list because of the large number of listed salmonid stocks.

Percent of species affected				
100–76	75–51	50–26	25–1	0

Figure 2. *Impacts of threats on different taxonomic groups. The proportions of species affected by different threats were compared between the ESA and IUCN lists and within individual taxonomic groups for each list. Cells in the table are color-coded to reflect the relative magnitude of each threat to the given group.*

ecosystems are similarly imbalanced; commercially important taxa are overrepresented, for instance, as are large-bodied vertebrates. Invertebrates and marine plants and algae, on the other hand, are drastically underrepresented. Despite such limitations, these datasets represent the most comprehensive and taxonomically broad assessment of the current threats to marine species and combine available data and expert opinion from a variety of sources and fields.

■ The seascape of risks

The most common threat to marine and diadromous species on both lists is overexploitation (Figures 2 and 3a). Overharvest impacts 82% of Red List and 81% of ESA species at risk, through direct harvest, incidental catch and bycatch, and indirect effects, such as trophic cascades, competition for prey, and habitat destruction due to destructive fishing gear. The relative importance of these is shown in Figure 3b: 65% of ESA species are affected by targeted harvest, 42% by incidental catch or bycatch, and 8% by indirect effects, while for IUCN species the proportions are 58%, 48%, and 17%, respectively. Habitat loss ranks second in importance on the IUCN list, affecting 47% of imperiled species, followed by invasive species, which impact 36% (Figure 3a). For ESA species, habitat degradation also ranks second (76%) and pollution third (61%). On both lists the top three threats are pervasive: overexploitation, habitat loss, and/or invasive species affect every Red List species, either singly or in combination. Similarly, 98% of ESA species are affected by overexploitation, habitat loss, and pollution, or some com-

bination of these. Results were similar whether the unit considered was a population or a biological species/subspecies (C Kappel, unpublished). Red List threat rankings were unaltered, and percentages affected differed by ≤ 1% for every threat. Considering species rather than populations had a slightly greater effect on results for ESA species. Ranks of the top four threats were unaltered, but water diversion and aquaculture both went down in rank (from fifth to a tie for sixth and from tenth to eleventh place, respectively), while human disturbance went up from seventh to fifth. Percentages affected by each threat differed, on average, by 4.4%.

Overharvest, bycatch, and the indirect effects of fishing

Tallies of threats to ESA and Red List species lead to the same conclusion: overexploitation is the most common threat to listed species. Both of these lists are biased towards commercial species; in fact, about half the listed taxa have been, or currently are, commercially exploited. At the same time, however, the vast majority of species were affected, demonstrating that impacts of exploitation go beyond target species, an assertion supported by the large proportions of species affected by bycatch and/or incidental catch (Figure 3b). The majority of the world's fisheries affect multiple species, and even sustainable levels of exploitation of a primary target species can lead to non-sustainable impacts on less valuable, non-target species taken incidentally (eg skates and rays in the Irish Sea; Dulvy *et al.* 2003).

Table 1. Threats categories used in analysis

Threat	Description	Examples of species affected
Overexploitation	Targeted harvest via fishing, hunting, or collecting; bycatch or incidental catch; and indirect effects including trophic cascades, competition for prey, and habitat degradation due to destructive fishing gear	• Sturgeons (Collins *et al.* 2000) • White abalone (Hobday and Tegner 2000) • Loggerhead and leatherback turtles (Lewison *et al.* 2004) • Vaquita (Rojas-Bracho and Taylor 1999; D'Agrosa *et al.* 2000)
Habitat destruction	Degradation or loss of habitat due to various causes	• Salmonids (Slaney *et al.* 1996) • Abbott's booby (Reville *et al.* 1990)
Climate change	Direct and indirect effects of anthropogenic global climate change (eg changes in prey availability, altered water temperature, salinity, and pH, increased storm frequency, etc)	• Seabirds (Croxall *et al.* 2002) • Corals (Hoegh-Guldberg 1999; Knowlton 2001) • Marine mammals (Langtimm and Beck 2003; Tynan and DeMaster 1997)
Pollution	Contamination, terrestrial runoff, and eutrophication, sedimentation, thermal pollution, and marine debris	• Marine mammals (MMC 1999) • Florida manatee (Beck and Barros 1991)
Vessel interaction	Boat collisions and acoustic and visual disturbance due to vessel traffic	• Northern right whale (Clapham *et al.* 1999, Nowacek et al. 2004a) • Florida manatee (Nowacek *et al.* 2004b)
Disease	Native and non-native pathogens	• Black abalone (Friedman *et al.* 1997) • Acroporid corals (Gladfelter 1982; McClanahan and Muthiga 1998) • Sea turtles (Aguirre *et al.* 1998)
Water diversion	Diversion of water and flow modification in rivers, streams, coastal wetlands, bays, and estuaries, for hydropower and irrigation, navigation, and coastal development (could be considered a particular type of habitat destruction)	• Salmonids (Slaney *et al.* 1996) • Tidewater goby (Lafferty *et al.* 1996)
Invasive species	Direct and indirect effects of non-native invaders, such as competition, predation, spread of disease, and habitat modification	• Sea turtles (Allen *et al.* 2001) • Seabirds (Moors and Atkinson 1984)
Aquaculture & hatcheries	Direct and indirect effects of aquaculture and hatcheries operations on wild populations, including competition for food, predation by escaped or released individuals, spread of disease, habitat destruction, genetic pollution, water quality degradation	• Snake River spring chinook salmon (Levin *et al.* 2001) • Pacific salmonids (Volpe *et al.* 2000)
Increased human presence	Disturbance from increased human activity, especially to marine animals that come to shore to nest, breed, or rest	• Hawaiian monk seal (Gerrodette and Gilmartin 1990)
Acoustic disturbance	Disturbance from underwater explosions, sonar, or other acoustic sources	• Marine mammals (NRC 2003)
Natural threats and Intrinsic factors	Intrinsic factors such as limited dispersal or range size, slow growth rate, or poor recruitment, and natural threats such as predation, storms, or flooding	• Skates and rays (Dulvy *et al.* 2002)

Habitat loss on land and in the seas

Habitat degradation, the leading driver of terrestrial endangerment, is the second most pervasive threat to marine species at risk. In fact, it may be that habitat loss is the number two threat to aquatic species, specifically because it is the primary threat on land. This is suggested by the prevalence of species for which habitat degradation was counted as a substantial threat and that spend some part of their lives associated with terrestrial, freshwater, or estuarine habitats. Over 85% of the ESA species that utilize these ecosystems in addition to marine habi-

tats – and all of the diadromous species – are impacted by habitat degradation, most likely because their life cycles expose them to the effects of terrestrial land conversion. In addition, all but one of the fully marine species affected live in coastal (nearshore or continental shelf) habitats, where activities on land and near the shore may contribute to habitat loss. Degradation of oceanic and deepwater habitats, though less commonly cited, may be increasing in frequency as a threat to marine species, particularly as advances in navigation technology allow exploitation of formerly inaccessible areas.

The persistent and pervasive problem of pollution

Pollution affects large numbers of ESA species. However, strong causal links between pollution and population level effects in marine species have generally been difficult to demonstrate (Nisbet 1994; Marine Mammal Commission 1999). Clear evidence comes from catastrophic and chronic oil spills (eg Peterson *et al.* 2003; Wiese and Robertson 2004) and selected organochlorine impacts (eg links between DDT, DDE, and PCBs, and bird declines; Nisbet 1994). Evidence for a link between persistent organic pollutants and decreased health and reproductive success in turtles and marine mammals is emerging (Marine Mammal Commission 1999; Keller *et al.* 2004). The large numbers of species thought to be vulnerable to pollution is in keeping with the ubiquity of the problem. Even remote ecosystems are plagued by pollutants: for example, over 111 metric tons of derelict fishing gear and other debris were removed from the uninhabited Northwest Hawaiian Islands in 2003 (NOAA Fisheries 2003b). The Arctic Ocean is now a net source for contaminants such as the pesticide lindane (HCH), deposited from the atmosphere in the 1940s–1980s (MacDonald *et al.* 2000). The widespread distribution and long-term persistence of these pollutants, combined with the small population sizes of many species at risk, could translate to population-level impacts.

Invasive species impacts and the IUCN Red List

A major difference between ESA and IUCN threat rankings is the greater importance of invasive species impacts to IUCN Red List taxa. This difference is probably driven by several factors. First, half the Red List species assessed for the purposes of this review are birds. Of these, 65% are affected by invasive species (Figure 2). By contrast, birds make up less than 30% of marine and coastal ESA species, and invasive species were highlighted as a cause of decline or a threat to recovery in only 43% of these taxa. Breeding traits of many marine birds may explain their vulnerability to invasive species. Eighty-two percent of Red List marine birds are ground nesting, and three-quarters are adapted to breeding on oceanic islands, which often lack native predators, leaving them vulnerable to introductions of rats, cats, and other predators of eggs, nestlings, and adults.

Why wasn't climate change ranked higher?

Surprisingly, climate change was not frequently listed as a threat, despite recent modeling which suggests that as many as 15–37% of terrestrial species may go extinct due to global warming by 2050 (Thomas *et al.* 2004). One would expect that factors such as climate change that have only recently gained attention would be underrepresented in earlier listings. In keeping with this, pollution, climate change, invasive species, and disease, in particular, have been cited more frequently in recent ESA listings. It is likely that reporting of these threats will

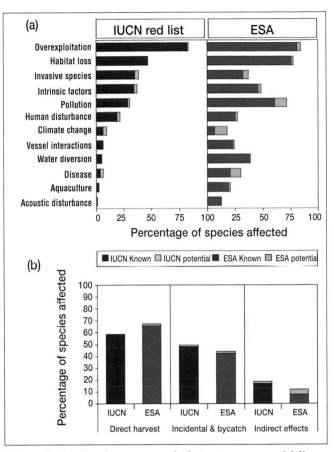

Figure 3. *Results of assessment of relative importance of different threats to marine species at risk. (a) Comparison of proportions of IUCN (n=225) and ESA (n=168) species affected by each threat. (b) Breakdown of the top threat, overexploitation, into the percentages of species affected by direct, targeted harvest versus incidental catch and bycatch, or indirect effects such as habitat degradation, competition for prey, or trophic cascades.*

increase in the future, as indicated by the proportions of species for which these were listed as a "potential" threat: pollution 11%, climate 13%, disease 10%, and invasive species 5%.

The science of threats assessment

Simple lists of threats cannot predict population or ecosystem effects of combining multiple stressors. A key challenge for ecologists is to develop statistical, modeling, and experimental techniques to build our capacity to predict how threats combine and interact to affect vulnerable species. For biodiversity conservation planning, we require spatially explicit data, preferably collected over the long term, so that spatiotemporal trends in threats can be evaluated. These data should derive from assessments of multiple species and ecosystems and should be evaluated within the context of species and ecosystem vulnerability to particular threats.

Threats assessment aimed at endangered species recovery requires quantitative data and experimental evidence to reveal causes of declines and roadblocks to recovery. For example, Peery *et al.* (2004) used a multi-pronged approach to test multiple competing hypotheses about causes of marbled murrelet declines in California. Like elasticity analyses of population matrix models, which highlight the life stages of vulnerable species that exert the greatest effect on population growth rates, mechanistic tests of the relative importance of different threats can direct us towards effective recovery strategies (Caswell 2000; Peery *et al.* 2004).

■ Functional roles of vulnerable species

It is sometimes assumed that loss of threatened species would not lead to ecosystem-level changes because these species were probably rare to begin with and therefore unlikely to have played important roles in ecosystem function. However, examination of the currently listed marine and estuarine species indicates that the world might indeed feel the loss of these species, many of which are top predators, ecosystem engineers, and key links between marine and terrestrial ecosystems. Soulé *et al.* (2003, 2005) term these species "strongly interactive" and provide guidelines for assessing the types and degree of interaction that include promotion of species diversity, provision or modification of habitat, and alteration of nutrient dynamics, among other factors. As the authors point out, the ESA contains language that provides a rationale for attending to species interactions: "The purposes of this Act [the ESA] are to provide a means whereby the ecosystems upon which threatened and endangered species depend may be conserved" (section 16 USC § 1531 [b]). They recommend that the goal for recovery of strongly interactive species should be "ecological effectiveness", with a particular desired ecosystem state as the management endpoint (Soulé *et al.* 2005).

The average trophic level of the taxa reviewed here is 3.7, indicating that most of these species are secondary or tertiary predators (Web Table 2). Species within top trophic levels have been shown to be more susceptible to extinction than lower level species (Pauly *et al.* 1998; Duffy 2003; Petchey *et al.* 2004), and tend to be more heavily exploited and more vulnerable to bioaccumulation of pollutants and temperature shifts as well (Pauly *et al.* 1998; Myers and Worm 2003; Petchey *et al.* 2004). Top-down effects of predators have been shown to be critical in structuring some marine ecosystems (eg Menge 2000). For example, rebounding populations of over-hunted sea otters, a keystone predator in Pacific kelp forest ecosystems, reversed large-scale declines in kelp cover by eating urchins which had been overgrazing the kelp (Estes and Duggins 1995). We know little about the exact ecological roles of most listed species, and the impacts of their loss would doubtless be varied and context-dependent. Nonetheless, strongly interactive top predators should be priority targets for recovery efforts.

Species at lower trophic levels may also provide key ecosystem functions. Caribbean acroporid corals, (*Acropora palmata*, *A cervicornis*, and *A prolifera*), which are currently candidates for listing under the ESA and are at present listed under CITES, were once the ecological dominants on shallow-water reefs in Florida and the Caribbean (Goreau 1959; NOAA Fisheries 2003a; Figure 4). These corals, which represent the only staghorn and tall tabular corals in this region, provided important biogenic habitat for many species of fish and invertebrates (Bellwood *et al.* 2004). Live coral cover and habitat complexity provided by these species is positively correlated with abundance and diversity of fishes (Gladfelter and Gladfelter 1978). The elkhorn (*A palmata*) and staghorn (*A cervicornis*) zones have virtually been eliminated from the Caribbean through disease, hurricanes, bleaching, and algal overgrowth (NOAA Fisheries 2003a). The number of obligate species that depend on these corals is unknown, as is the extent of diversity loss that would result from extinction of Caribbean acroporids.

Many vulnerable marine species use terrestrial, freshwater, and estuarine habitats at points in their life histories, and thus have the potential to serve as important conduits for nutrient flux between marine and terrestrial systems. Guano production by seabirds, for example, can greatly affect community structure on or around seabird colonies (eg Bosman and Hockey 1986; Anderson and Polis 1999). Similarly, the return of spawning salmon to Pacific Northwest streams represents a tremendous annual input of marine nutrients to freshwater and riparian ecosystems and has cascading effects (Gende *et al.* 2002; Schindler *et al.* 2003). Loss of either seabirds or salmonids, two groups that are nearly universally threatened, could have ecosystem-level ramifications.

Figure 4. Acropora palmata, *commonly known as elkhorn coral, in the Bahamas. A palmata, which once formed dense stands, has declined precipitously throughout the Caribbean and is now listed as a candidate species under the ESA, along with* Acropora cervicornis *and* Acropora prolifera.

The consequences of marine extinctions will remain a black box until more is known about the natural histories, interactions, and ecological roles of marine species. Nonetheless, the roles played by top predators, ecosystem engineers, and species that link marine and terrestrial systems may be essential to marine ecosystem function. Unfortunately, for some species, we may not learn what pieces of the puzzle they represent until it is too late.

Figure 5. *Seabird–fisheries interactions off the coast of Argentina. Some current fishing practices lead to high seabird mortality.*

■ Conservation implications

The results of this analysis are clear: marine species face a gauntlet of threats, chief among which are overexploitation, habitat degradation, pollution, and invasive species. Bycatch, in particular, is a major risk to nearly half the species examined. In one sense, these results are hopeful; the leading cause of endangerment, overharvest, is also the most controllable. Furthermore, unlike pollution, which may persist long past the point where its production has stopped, or habitat degradation, where recovery to pristine levels is unlikely, the threat of overharvest is removed (though alterations to habitats and food webs may persist) once halted. Then, of course, the hard business of recovery must begin.

Unfortunately, despite the potential for control, we have a poor track record of managing overexploitation (Hutchings and Reynolds 2004). Fisheries around the world have undergone serial depletion and collapses of species from ever-lower trophic levels as we "fish down marine food webs" (Pauly *et al.* 1998). The recent shift towards ecosystem-based management in fisheries holds promise for slowing and potentially reversing this trend, but we currently lack both the data and the governance structures needed to successfully account for environmental forcing, habitat dynamics, and species interactions in fisheries management (Pew Oceans Commission 2003; Pikitch *et al.* 2004; US Commission on Ocean Policy 2004). Conservation of vulnerable marine species presents a similar challenge, as data on life-history traits, habitat requirements, and interactions with other species and with the environment are nearly always lacking. However, this analysis suggests that a high priority first line of action would be to reduce non-target catch in the world's fisheries through bycatch quotas and mandatory observer programs, changes to fishing gear and practices, and international agreements to halt destructive fishing practices (Hall *et al.* 2000; Melvin and Parrish 2001). Programs that provide incentives to fishermen to devise innovative bycatch reduction methods (for example changing the depth at which hooks are set or using thawed bait that sinks rather than floating, to avoid seabird mortality), show promise (Figure 5). No-take marine reserves, which could be used to reduce impacts on sensitive species by providing spatial refugia from overharvest and other threats have, so far, seldom been applied to marine endangered species conservation (Armsworth *et al.* in press b).

In addition, we must address the fundamental problem of overcapitalization in the world's fisheries and establish governance structures that provide incentives for fishermen (eg via property rights) to promote conservation and sustainable fishing of portfolios of species (Edwards *et al.* 2004; Hilborn *et al.* 2004). Finally, it is critical to recognize that impacts of fishing do not act in isolation, even in populations for which overexploitation is the primary threat. Habitat degradation, pollution, and invasive species interact with disease, climate change, and other stressors to exacerbate existing problems in many populations. An effective conservation program for the oceans must address the threats on all fronts.

Species-by-species conservation is difficult, expensive, and inefficient. It is likely to be even more so in marine systems, where the implementation and monitoring of restoration and conservation measures are logistically challenging. What is needed is a broader approach to biodiversity conservation – one aimed at preventing species from collapsing to the point where extinction is imminent – and a means to prioritize how limited funds should be spent. A threats-based approach, wherein we focus first on alleviating the most serious threats to the strongly interactive species that play key ecosystem roles is recommended. A clear understanding of the nature of the threats, and of their separate and joint effects on multiple species, habitats, and ecological interactions, is vital if we are to develop effective conservation strategies to prevent the loss of a significant portion of marine biodiversity.

■ Acknowledgements

I am indebted to P Armsworth and F Micheli for involving me in the collaboration that first piqued my interest in marine species at risk. This manuscript was greatly improved by the helpful comments of K Heiman, R Martone, F Micheli, and C Palmer. It is dedicated to Will, for his unwavering confidence in my ability to study creatures underwater.

■ References

Anderson WB and Polis GA. 1999. Nutrient fluxes from water to land: seabirds affect plant nutrient status on Gulf of California islands. *Oecologia* **118**: 324–32.

Armsworth PR, Kappel CV, Micheli F, and Bjorkstedt EP. Endangered marine species. In: Scott JM, Goble DD, Davis F, and Heal G (Eds). The Endangered Species Act at 30: renewing the conservation promise. Washington, DC: Island Press. In press.

Armsworth PR, Kappel CV, Micheli F, and Bjorkstedt EP. Working seascapes. In: Scott JM, Goble DD, Davis F, and Heal G (Eds). The Endangered Species Act at 30: conserving biodiversity in human-dominated landscapes. Washington, DC: Island Press. In press.

Baillie JEM, Hilton-Taylor C, and Stuart SN (Eds). 2004. 2004 IUCN Red List of threatened species. A global species assessment. Gland, Switzerland and Cambridge, UK: IUCN.

Bellwood DR, Hughes TP, Folke C, and Nystrom M. 2004. Confronting the coral reef crisis. *Nature* **429**: 827–33.

BirdLife International. 2004. World bird database. www.birdlife.net/datazone/index.html. Viewed 1 December 2004.

Bosman AL and Hockey PAR. 1986. Seabird guano as a determinant of rocky intertidal community structure. *Mar Ecol-Prog Ser* **32**: 247–57.

Caswell H. 2000. Prospective and retrospective perturbation analyses: their roles in conservation biology. *Ecology* **81**: 619–27.

Duffy JE. 2003. Biodiversity loss, trophic skew and ecosystem functioning. *Ecol Lett* **6**: 680–87.

Dulvy NK, Sadovy Y, and Reynolds JD. 2003. Extinction vulnerability in marine populations. *Fish and Fisheries* **4**: 25–64.

Easter-Pilcher A. 1996. Implementing the Endangered Species Act. Assessing the listing of species as endangered or threatened. *BioScience* **46**: 355–63.

Edwards SF, Link JS, and Rountree BP. 2004. Portfolio management of wild fish stocks. *Ecol Econ* **49**: 317–29.

Estes JA and Duggins DO. 1995. Sea otters and kelp forests in Alaska: generality and variation in a community ecological paradigm. *Ecol Monogr* **65**: 75–100.

FAO Fisheries Department. 2004. The state of world fisheries and aquaculture (SOFIA) 2004. Rome, Italy: FAO.

Gende SM, Edwards RT, Willson MF, and Wipfli MS. 2002. Pacific salmon in aquatic and terrestrial ecosystems. *BioScience* **52**: 917–28.

Gladfelter WB and Gladfelter EH. 1978. Fish community structure as a function of habitat structure on West Indian patch reefs. *Rev Biol Trop* **26**: 65–84.

Goreau TF. 1959. The ecology of Jamaican coral reefs.1. Species composition and zonation. *Ecology* **40**: 67–90.

Hall MA, Alverson DL, and Metuzals KI. 2000. By-catch: problems and solutions. *Mar Pollut Bull* **41**: 204–19.

Hilborn R, Punt AE, and Orensanz J. 2004. Beyond band-aids in fisheries management: fixing world fisheries. *Bull Mar Sci* **74**: 493–507.

Hutchings JA. 2001. Conservation biology of marine fishes: perceptions and caveats regarding assignment of extinction risk. *Can J Fish Aquat Sci* **58**: 108–21.

Hutchings JA and Reynolds JD. 2004. Marine fish population collapses: consequences for recovery and extinction risk. *BioScience* **54**: 297–309.

International Institute for Sustainable Development. 2002. Summary of the twelfth conference of the parties to the Convention in International Trade in Endangered Species of wild fauna and flora: 3-15 November 2002. http://www.iisd.ca/cites/COP12/.

IUCN. 2004a. 2004 IUCN Red List of threatened species. www.Redlist.org. Viewed 1 December 2004.

IUCN. 2004b. Threats authority file (version 2.1). www.redlist.org/info/major_threats.html. Viewed 1 December 2004.

Jackson JBC, Kirby MX, Berger WH, *et al.* 2001. Historical overfishing and the recent collapse of coastal ecosystems. *Science* **293**: 629–38.

Keller JM, Kucklick JR, Stamper MA, *et al.* 2004. Associations between organochlorine contaminant concentrations and clinical health parameters in loggerhead sea turtles from North Carolina, USA. *Environ Health Perspect* **112**: 1074–79.

MacDonald RW, Barrie LA, Bidleman TF, *et al.* 2000. Contaminants in the Canadian Arctic: 5 years of progress in understanding sources, occurrence and pathways. *Sci Total Environ* **254**: 93–234.

Marine Mammal Commission. 1999. Marine mammals and persistent ocean contaminants: proceedings of the Marine Mammal Commission workshop, Keystone, Colorado, October 12-15, 1998. Keystone, CO: Marine Mammal Commission.

Matsuda H, Yahara T, and Uozumi Y. 1997. Is tuna critically endangered? Extinction risk of a large and overexploited population. *Ecol Res* **12**: 345–56.

Melvin EF and Parrish JK (Eds). 2001. Seabird bycatch: trends, roadblocks, and solutions. Fairbanks, AK: University of Alaska Sea Grant, AK-SG-01-01.

Menge BA. 2000. Top-down and bottom-up community regulation in marine rocky intertidal habitats. *J Exp Mar Biol Ecol* **250**: 257–89.

Musick JA, Harbin MM, Berkeley SA, *et al.* 2000. Marine, estuarine, and diadromous fish stocks at risk of extinction in North America (exclusive of Pacific salmonids). *Fisheries* **25**: 6–30.

Myers RA and Worm B. 2003. Rapid worldwide depletion of predatory fish communities. *Nature* **423**: 280–83.

National Research Council. 1995. Understanding marine biodiversity: a research agenda for the nation. Washington, DC: National Academy Press.

Nisbet ICT. 1994. Effects of pollution on marine birds. In: Nettleship DN, Burger J, and Gochfeld M (Eds). Seabirds on islands: threats, case studies and action plans. Cambridge, UK: BirdLife International. p 8–25.

NOAA Fisheries. 2003a. Candidate corals: *Acropora palmata* (elkhorn coral) and *Acropora cervicornis* (staghorn coral). www.nmfs.noaa.gov/habitat/ecosystem/AcorporaWorkshop.htm. Viewed 1 December 2004.

NOAA Fisheries. 2003b. Marine debris removal. www.pifsc.noaa.gov/crd/marine_debris.html. Viewed 1 December 2004.

Pauly D, Christensen V, Dalsgaard J, *et al.* 1998. Fishing down marine food webs. *Science* **279**: 860–63.

Peery MZ, Beissinger SR, Newman SH, *et al.* 2004. Applying the declining population paradigm: diagnosing causes of poor reproduction in the marbled murrelet. *Conserv Biol* **18**: 1088–98.

Petchey OL, Downing AL, Mittelbach GG, *et al.* 2004. Species loss and the structure and functioning of multitrophic aquatic systems. *Oikos* **104**: 467–78.

Peterson CH, Rice SD, Short JW, *et al.* 2003. Long-term ecosystem response to the Exxon Valdez oil spill. *Science* **302**: 2082–86.

Pew Oceans Commission. 2003. America's living oceans: charting a course for sea change. Arlington, VA: Pew Oceans Commission.

Pikitch EK, Santora C, Babcock EA, *et al.* 2004. Ecosystem-based fishery management. *Science* **305**: 346–47.

Roberts CM and Hawkins JP. 1999. Extinction risk in the sea. *Trends Ecol Evol* **14**: 241–46.

Schindler DE, Scheuerell MD, Moore JW, *et al.* 2003. Pacific salmon and the ecology of coastal ecosystems. *Front Ecol Environ* **1**: 31–37.

Soulé ME, Estes JA, Berger J, and Del Rio CM. 2003. Ecological effectiveness: conservation goals for interactive species. *Conserv Biol* **17**: 1238–50.

Soulé ME, Estes JA, Miller B, and Honnold DL. 2005. Strongly interacting species. Conservation policy, management, and ethics. *BioScience* **55**: 168–76.

Thomas CD, Cameron A, Green RE, *et al.* 2004. Extinction risk from climate change. *Nature* **427**: 145–48.

US Commission on Ocean Policy. 2004. An ocean blueprint for the 21st century: final report of the US Commission on Ocean Policy – pre-publication copy. Washington, DC: US Commission on Ocean Policy.

Wiese FK and Robertson GJ. 2004. Assessing seabird mortality from chronic oil discharges at sea. *J Wildl Manage* **68**: 627–38.

Wilcove DS, Rothstein D, Dubow J, *et al.* 1998. Quantifying threats to imperiled species in the United States. *BioScience* **48**: 607–15.

Active homework – preparation for active classes

Diane Ebert-May[1], Debra L Linton[2], Janet Hodder[3], Tammy Long[1]

Instructors faced with teaching large introductory science courses and dealing with the diverse backgrounds in knowledge, skills, and motivation of 100–500 students have genuine concerns about engaging all students in learning, something more easily achieved in small courses. Low attendance in large lectures, often down to 30–40% by the end of the term, indicates disengagement and lack of involvement by students (Cooper and Robinson 2000). While lectures, as a rule, have limited educational value because people learn by doing rather than by watching and listening (Felder 1997; Powell 2003), the majority of college faculty teach classes in a traditional lecture mode.

Some faculty are still skeptical about pedagogy that advocates using inquiry, active, and collaborative learning instructional strategies to facilitate students' learning, especially in large courses. Their pervasive concern about *covering* content overrides finding additional time for in-class activities that allow students to *uncover* the meaning of concepts. Finding time for grading additional student work is another formidable challenge for faculty. A well-designed active learning exercise effectively replaces a lecture on the same topic, with student understanding and retention potentially exceeding learning gained from a traditional lecture format (Gardiner 1994; Mazur 1997; Handelsman 2004). However, the success of this approach depends on students coming to class prepared to participate in the activity. In this article we focus on active homework – a strategy intended to better prepare students for active learning in class. Regular active homework assignments can help students become more involved in learning, without the overburden of impossible grading loads for faculty.

Research with K-12 students shows a positive effect of homework on student achievement, an effect that increases as students get older (Cooper *et al.* 1998). Information about the effects of homework on learning by college students is unknown because research is lacking. The concept of homework in introductory college physics, chemistry, and mathematics is primarily problem solving (Bonham *et al.* 2003). In contrast, homework in introductory biology generally focuses on readings from a textbook or papers associated with lecture topics (NRC 1997). Students may read and highlight the pages assigned for the class, but do not apply or analyze the information they read to solve problems that help further their understanding. We use the Kappel article (pp 275–282) to model ways to engage students in active homework to advance learning both inside and outside the classroom.

[1]*Michigan State University,* [2]*Cuyahoga Community College,* [3]*University of Oregon*

■ Student goals

- Increase the efficiency and effectiveness of students' time on homework to prepare for active learning during class.
- Understand the biological concepts underpinning major ecological problems in marine environments.
- Build connections between ecological problems and choices they can make in their own lives.

■ Instructor goals

- Guide students with active homework that prepares them for class.
- Motivate students to become proficient self-learners.
- Use the outcomes of the homework to build on specific content and concepts in subsequent classes.

■ Instructional design: from home to class....

Kappel's article provides an overview of threats to marine environments, pointing out that overharvest, habitat loss, and invasive species have major effects on marine communities. The following activities are examples designed to enable students to gain an understanding of the biological concepts that result from these threats. The homework concentrates on changes in community structure as a result of overharvest or introduced species, and the role of strongly interacting species on ecosystems.

Homework directions

After reading the Kappel article, students
- Print out kelp forest Food Web A from the course website (original at http://research.amnh.org/biodiversity/crisis/images/otter1.gif).
- Use a highlighter to identify the links in the food web representing the relationships among sea otters, urchins, and kelp.
- Draw a diagram (model) that explains why kelp forests disappear when sea otters are removed.
- Use the food web to predict the effect of decreases in sea otter populations on herbivorous fish, abalones, sea stars, and large crabs. Explain the predictions in writing.

Students bring their homework to class, with questions 2, 3, and 4 on separate pieces of paper. Now the instructor has choices – if the homework is graded, the instructor can ask students to turn in either question 3 or 4 after using them in class, thereby reducing the numbers of papers to grade. Students know a priori that all homework is treated this way and, in some cases, will not be graded at all. If the homework is not graded, the concepts from the homework will be assessed in subsequent exams.

Active learning in class

Engage students by asking them to compare their diagrams of kelp forest disappearance to Food Web B, projected to the class, from the web page http://research.amnh.org/biodiversity/crisis/images/otter2.gif. The instructor then selects several groups to explain their predictions from question 4 to the class and records them on the overhead. The instructor then gives a brief synopsis of the role of strongly interacting species and covers the current sea otter declines in Alaska (Estes *et al.* 1998; Maldini *et al.* 2004).

Assessment

At the end of this mini-lecture, students use the homework and class discussion to demonstrate their ability to apply their understanding to a new scenario. Using Food Web A they add killer whales, seals and sea lions (information from the instructor's lecture) and predict changes in the food web. Again, selected groups report out to sample the classes' understanding, although written responses from all students or groups provide more complete data.

Additional examples on how the loss of marine species can affect marine environments are provided in Table 1 in the Kappel paper (p 277). Homework could be developed for the loss of species because of introduced species; for example, introduced foxes on Alaskan islands have altered nutrient input from nesting birds and this, in turn, has influenced vegetation communities (Croll *et al.* 2005). Another case involves the multiple threats that are causing the decline of Caribbean acroporid corals.

The next example is an approach for students to actively explore their own impact on the marine environment by examining the harvest methods and environmental effects associated with the seafood they consume. This activity could serve as a prelude to a class on ecosystem-level impacts of overharvesting, including the effects of overfishing and bycatch, or to introduce topics about marine conservation such as marine reserves and bycatch reduction efforts.

Individual impact

In class, students make a table that lists the five most common seafood items in their diet. They indicate the method by which they think the seafood is harvested and any impacts on the environment or other species that might result from this practice. For homework students are directed to the Monterey Bay Aquarium Seafood Watch at www.mbayaq.org/cr/seafoodwatch.asp to look up information on their seafood items and confirm or expand the responses on their table. Students decide which of their seafood selections raises

the most serious concerns about environmental effects and which the least. In class, groups of students discuss the homework and choose a "best and worst pick" (available to them locally) from their selections. The instructor polls group results for the most common best and worst choices and records them. Reporters from groups are asked to explain the choices and dissenting views are encouraged. The homework prepares students to further learn about effects of harvest on coastal and open ocean communities.

■ Final note

The concept of actively engaging students in homework to prepare for class is seldom considered in large courses. Instructors may use quizzes or online questions to hold students accountable for reading, but pay less attention to designing active homework that flows directly into active learning during class. This instructional strategy takes little time relative to the pay-off for both students and instructors. Assessment data based on instructors' specific learning goals will show the degree to which this approach to scientific teaching results in increased student engagement, accountability, and ability to understand the connections of complex ecological models.

■ References

Bonham S, Deardorff D, and Beichner R. 2003. Comparison of student performance using web and paper-based homework in college-level physics. *J Res Sci Teach* **40**: 1050–71.

Cooper JL and Robinson P. 2000. The argument for making large classes seem small. San Francisco: Jossey-Bass.

Cooper H, Lindsay JJ, Nye B, and Greathouse S. 1998. Relationships among attitudes about homework, amount of homework assigned and completed, and student achievement. *J Educ Psychol* **90**: 70–83.

Croll DA, Mason JL, Estes JA, *et al.* 2005 Introduced predators transform subarctic island from grassland to tundra. *Science* **307**: 1959–61.

Estes JA, Tinker MT, Williams TM, and Doak DF. 1998. Killer whale predation on sea otters linking oceanic and near shore ecosystems. *Science* **282**: 473–76.

Felder R. 1997. Beating the numbers game: effective teaching in large classes. American Society for Engineering Education, Milwaukee, WI. http://www.ncsu.edu/effective_teaching/Papers/Largeclasses.htm. Viewed 8 May 2005.

Gardiner L. 1994. Redesigning higher education: producing dramatic gains in student learning. Washington, DC: George Washington University. ASHE-ERIC Higher Education Report No 7.

Handelsman J, Ebert-May D, Beichner R, *et al.* 2004. Scientific teaching. *Science* **304**: 521–22.

Maldini D, Calkins D, Atkinson S, and Meehan R. 2004. Alaska sea otter research workshop: addressing the decline of the southwestern Alaska sea otter population. Fairbanks, AL: Alaska Sea Grant. Publication AK-SG-0403.

Mazur E. 1997. Peer instruction: a users manual. Upper Saddle River, NJ: Prentice Hall.

NRC (National Research Council). 1997. Science teaching reconsidered. Washington, DC: National Academy Press.

Powell K. 2003. Spare me the lecture. *Nature* **25**: 234–36.

The ecological–societal underpinnings of Everglades restoration

Fred H Sklar[1], Michael J Chimney[1], Susan Newman[1], Paul McCormick[2], Dale Gawlik[3], ShiLi Miao[1], Christopher McVoy[1], Winifred Said[1], Jana Newman[1], Carlos Coronado[1], Gaea Crozier[1], Michael Korvela[1], and Ken Rutchey[1]

The biotic integrity of the Florida Everglades, a wetland of immense international importance, is threatened as a result of decades of human manipulation for drainage and development. Past management of the system only exacerbated the problems associated with nutrient enrichment and disruption of regional hydrology. The Comprehensive Everglades Restoration Plan (CERP) now being implemented by Federal and State governments is an attempt to strike a balance between the needs of the environment with the complex management of water and the seemingly unbridled economic growth of southern Florida. CERP is expected to reverse negative environmental trends by "getting the water right", but successful Everglades restoration will require both geochemical and hydrologic intervention on a massive scale. This will produce ecological trade-offs and will require new and innovative scientific measures to (1) reduce total phosphorus concentrations within the remaining marsh to 10 µg/L or lower; (2) quantify and link ecological benefits to the restoration of depths, hydroperiods, and flow velocities; and (3) compensate for ecological, economic, and hydrologic uncertainties in the CERP through adaptive management.

Front Ecol Environ 2005; 3(3): 161–169

Understanding the ecology of the Everglades at all landscape scales, from the ubiquitous mats of calcareous periphyton to the Florida panther, is a tall order, even for an $8.3 billion restoration program (see www.evergladesplan.org). Although most of this money will be used for land acquisition and re-engineering south Florida's vast water management system, $10 million will be spent annually for ecological monitoring and assessment. Everglades restoration is intertwined with both science and public policy (Davis and Ogden 1994). Providing flood control and water supply to urban and agricultural areas competes with the water needs of the environment. As such, the fate of the Everglades is a dramatic case study of a global issue: freshwater allocation. Decision makers from around the world are watching south Florida, to see how wetland restoration will be balanced against economic development and societal demands.

Efforts to drain the Everglades first began on a small scale in the 1880s and culminated almost 70 years later with Congressional authorization to build today's complex system of canals and water-control structures (Light and Dineen 1994). Understanding the impact of these events is crucial to understanding Everglades restoration. The drainage projects of the early 20th century uncovered the fertile "black gold" soil for farming by diverting the Everglades' headwaters – Lake Okeechobee – to the Atlantic and Gulf of Mexico, and later by channelizing the Everglades themselves. These initiatives precipitated a 100-year legacy of development and environmental degradation in south Florida.

The economic growth of south Florida is easy to see on a satellite image (Figure 1). Four thousand square kilometers of former marsh have been developed into highly productive farmland and a portion of the cities and towns that are home to more than 6 million people. The environmental damage to the remaining Everglades is not as apparent, but is just as widespread. Between 1880 and 1940, water tables declined by as much as 2.7 m (McVoy

In a nutshell:
- Since 50% of the historic Everglades is gone and cannot be restored, the ecological underpinnings of Everglades restoration will instead establish conservation criteria intended to reverse current negative environmental trends by "getting the water right"
- Restoration plans account for the lack of a coordinated regional effort to regulate future development in southern Florida
- A critical precursor to restoration will be the construction of more than 24 000 ha of treatment wetlands, whose outflow of total phosphorus concentrations will need to approach 10 µg/L
- Restoration will require numerous socioeconomic (eg recreational fishing) and ecological (eg removal of canals) trade-offs
- Flexibility in the design and implementation of Everglades restoration, needed to balance uncertainties and optimize trade-offs, will depend upon the ability of State and Federal agencies to develop an adaptive management approach

[1]*Everglades Division, South Florida Water Management District, West Palm Beach, FL 33416-4680 (fsklar@sfwmd.gov)*; [2]*US Geological Survey, Leetown Science Center, Kearneysville, WV 25430*; [3]*Department of Biological Sciences, Florida Atlantic University, Boca Raton, FL 33431-0991*

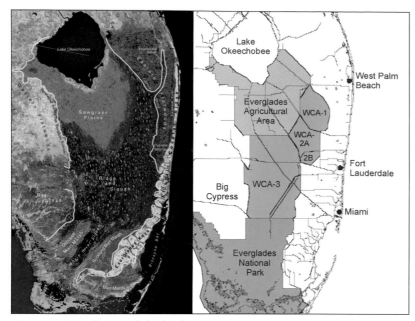

Figure 1. (a) The Everglades landscape as it is thought to have appeared prior to development compared with (b) today's highly managed, compartmentalized system.

et al. in press). As a result of drainage, the region's rich organic soils began to subside, due to physical compaction, microbial oxidation, and periodic burning. Over the decades, more than 2 m of soil has been lost in what is now designated the Everglades Agricultural Area (Figure 2), and topographic changes actually reversed the direction of

Figure 2. Drainage was especially effective in the Everglades Agricultural Area, where exposure has oxidized much of the original peat soil. The top of the concrete post shown was at ground level when it was driven down to the underlying limestone caprock in the 1920s.

water flow (Davis 1943). Low water tables within the Everglades allowed saltwater intrusion into coastal aquifers and contaminated urban wellfields (Allison 1943).

The problems associated with both flood control and over-drainage prompted Congress to create the Central & South Florida Project in 1948; this authorized the US Army Corps of Engineers (USACOE) to impound the northern Everglades, creating the Water Conservation Areas (WCAs; Figure 1). However, these measures only slowed the rate of environmental damage. The WCAs divided what was a shallow, free-flowing wetland into a series of ponded compartments that operated more as storage reservoirs. These hydrologic changes led to the loss of hundreds of tree islands (Sklar and van der Valk 2002) and altered the characteristic ridge and slough landscape patterning (Science Coordinating Team 2003). In addition, high phosphorus (P) loads in runoff from developed areas have damaged portions of the historically nutrient-poor Everglades (McCormick et al. 2002). The goals of Everglades restoration are to restore the region's hydrology and reduce nutrient enrichment to the greatest extent practicable.

■ Plants behaving badly

The encroachment of native cattail (*Typha* spp) into sawgrass (*Cladium* spp) marsh and slough (*Nymphaea, Nuphar, Utricularia,* and *Eleocharis* spp) communities was triggered by alterations in hydrology and nutrient enrichment, and is one of the most visible signs of an Everglades in decline. For example, dense coverage of cattail in WCA–2A increased from 422 ha in 1991 to more than 1643 ha by 1995, an increase of some 350% (Rutchey and Vilchek 1999; Figure 3). Cattail expansion has reduced prey availability for wading birds (Crozier and Gawlik 2002) and altered periphyton (attached algae) productivity, which in cascade fashion contributes to decreased dissolved oxygen (DO) concentrations (McCormick and Laing 2003) and altered food webs. This invasive species is difficult to control since it stores large amounts of P (Miao and Sklar 1998) and is well adapted to present-day water depths and nutrient regimes (Newman et al. 1996).

The feedback mechanisms between soil P and cattail growth forecast the fate of the Everglades without restoration. At the far northern end of the Everglades, soil P concentrations are substantially elevated near points where urban and agriculture runoff enters the marsh (Newman et al. 1997). Surficial soil P has increased threefold since the 1970s along a nutrient gradient downstream of the WCA–2A inflow structures. In 1998, over 73% of WCA–2A had soil P concentrations >500 mg/kg, as compared to only 48% in 1990 (Figure 3).

The loss of tree islands is another symptom of environmental degradation in the area. These "biodiversity hotspots" are small (1–10 ha) topographic highs within the ridge and slough landscape, and are ecologically important because they provide critical habitat for many plants and animals (Sklar and van der Valk 2002). From 1940 to 1995, WCA–3 experienced a 45% loss in the abundance and a 61% decline in total acreage of tree islands due to frequent peat fires and high water levels. Prolonged submergence of wetland forests inhibits plant growth and regeneration for even the most water-tolerant species (McKelvin *et al.* 1998). A tree island model for WCA–2A suggests that 30 cm of water and 120 days per year of continuous flooding is sufficient to cause physiological stress and eventual replacement of the forest structure by marsh vegetation (Wu *et al* 2002).

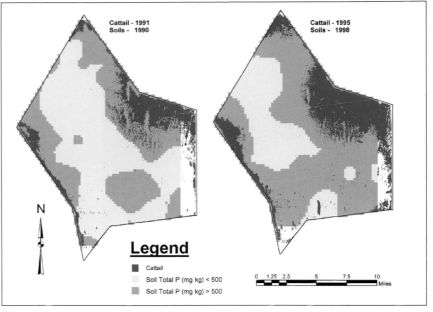

Figure 3. *Temporal and spatial changes in soil total phosphorus content and cattail coverage in WCA–2A in the northern Everglades.*

■ Animals beset with flood and drought

Geographic shifts in nesting patterns and a 90% decline in abundance of wading birds were two early signs of an ecosystem in decline (Ogden 1994). On one hand, reduced flow to Everglades National Park (ENP) led to the reduction of nesting areas for many wading birds during dry years. Conversely, deep water in the WCAs greatly affected species such as ibises, which require a continuous dry down (approximately 0.5 cm/day) during breeding to concentrate prey in depressions (eg sloughs and alligator holes; Gawlik 2002). When water levels increase due to water management or rain, prey disperse, forcing wading birds to abandon their nests (Frederick and Collopy 1989).

Historically, important invertebrate prey, such as the apple snail (*Pomacea paludosa*), were able to survive short periods (5–6 weeks) of desiccation (Darby *et al.* 2002) or, like crayfish (*Procambarus* sp), were able to burrow deep into the soil to find water. However, current Everglades water levels are too low and hydroperiods too short to adequately support these populations (Kitchens *et al.* 1994; Acosta and Perry 2001). Everglades restoration is expected to increase ground-water levels and create more refugia for these species during the dry season.

The dynamic between small fishes and the American alligator (*Alligator mississippiensis*) is another important ecological factor for Everglades restoration. Alligators dig holes that often serve as fish habitat during the dry season. Alligators do so because they need deep, open water for courtship and mating; successful mating and nest building leads to more holes and consequently more fish refugia. However, current compartmentalization of the Everglades can result in abrupt water-depth changes, which can either flood alligator nests or render them vulnerable to predation (Mazzotti and Brandt 1994). To restore successful alligator

nesting while creating refugia for fish, it will be necessary to buffer rapid hydrologic changes and mimic the range of pre-drainage water depths.

The 420 animal species native to the Everglades are, to varying degrees, adapted to the pre-drainage hydrology of the region. However, restoring Everglades hydrology may not necessarily meet the long-term requirements of every extant animal. A particular water regime that is beneficial to one species is not always ideal for others. For example, the Cape Sable seaside sparrow (*Ammodramus maritimus mirabilis*), a federally endangered species displaced by hydrologic changes in ENP, requires a water depth of around 10 cm to begin breeding because its nests, which are placed at the base of vegetation, are flooded or lost to predators if water depth is too high or too low, respectively (Nott *et al.* 1998). To accommodate the sparrow's breeding cycle, inflow to ENP is reduced early in the dry season, allowing water levels to recede. However, reducing flow through the Park creates ponding stress on tree islands in upstream portions of the Everglades. To deal with this dilemma, and potentially create "trade-offs" (see below), the restoration planners have focused on the water needs of a subset of indicator species, which include lower trophic-level prey organisms such as small (<8 cm) fishes, crayfish, and apple snails, and higher trophic-level predators such as wood storks (*Mycteria americana*), white ibis (*Eudocimus albus*), and alligators (MAP 2004).

■ First, clean the water!

Atmospheric deposition was the primary source of nutrient inputs to the pre-drainage Everglades. The best available science suggests that surface-water P concentrations across most of the Everglades typically ranged from 4 to 10 µg/L and loading rates averaged less than 0.1 g P/m^2 /year

Figure 4. *(a) Floating mats of white periphyton disappear within an experimental mesocosm that is periodically dosed with phosphorus. (b) Sets of four 100-m long flumes evaluate chronic, low P dosing in Everglades National Park (see Gaiser et al. in press).*

(McCormick *et al.* 2001). In contrast, total phosphorus (TP) concentrations in drainage canals conveying urban and agricultural runoff to the Everglades have ranged from 100–1000 μg/L over the past three decades.

For restoration of the Everglades to succeed, it will be necessary to reduce nutrient loads, particularly P, entering the landscape from agricultural and urban areas. But how much P is too much? The answer was found along the nutrient gradient in WCA–2A. In addition to the cattail invasion described earlier, an important ecosystem change in nutrient enriched areas was the loss of the once abundant calcareous periphyton mats and an increase in algae, indicative of eutrophication (McCormick and O'Dell 1996). This shift in species resulted in a 6- to 30-fold decrease in areal periphyton productivity in enriched areas. Subsequent reduced DO levels (McCormick and Laing 2003) lead to increased abundance of organisms tolerant of low-oxygen conditions, such as oligochaete worms (Rader and Richardson 1994).

Because other aspects of wetland biogeochemistry and hydrology also vary in the Everglades, the assertion that excess P was the primary cause of ecological changes was tested using enclosed fertilizer plots (eg Craft *et al.* 1995), mesocosms (Figure 4), and flumes (Pan *et al.* 2000; Childers *et al.* 2002). Despite differences in methodology, biotic responses were consistent among experiments and corresponded with many of the ecological changes documented along nutrient gradients. For example, adding P to mesocosms resulted in the loss of the calcareous periphyton mat within several weeks to months, caused a shift from a periphyton-based to a detritus-based system, and increased nitrogen mineralization (Newman *et al.* 2001).

Based on an evaluation of these data, the Florida Department of Environmental Protection (FDEP) determined that key biological changes occurred in the Everglades when water column TP exceeded a mean of 9.8 to 14.7 μg/L (Figure 5). In December 2001, FDEP recommended a TP concentration threshold of 10 μg/L to protect the ecological integrity of the entire system (FDEP 2000).

The question now is: how do

Table 1. Hydrological conditions in the Everglades: then and now*

	NSM v4.5 (Pre-drainage for the remnant Everglades)	SFWMM v3.5 (Current drainage for the remnant Everglades)
Average depth (cm)		
Annual	22.6	30.2
Dry season (Nov – May)	19.5	27.5
Wet season (Jun – Oct)	26.5	33.9
Average hydroperiod (days)		
Annual	309	295
Dry season (Nov – May)	172	160
Wet season (Jun – Oct)	138	134
Droughts in Everglades National Park		
# of Events	11	20
Average duration (Weeks)	5	7
Discharge to the Gulf of Mexico (m³ x 10⁶)		
Annual	1932	871
Dry season (Nov – May)	930	323
Wet season (Jun – Oct)	1002	549

NSM = Natural Systems Model; SFWMM = South Florida Water Management Model. Driven by 1965–1995 rainfall patterns, these two models are used to understand how water is currently distributed in the Everglades and how it would have been distributed if all roads, canals, control structures and people were removed from the remnant Everglades.

*The hydrologic goals of Everglades restoration are largely based upon the NSM. The amount of hydrologic change is based upon a comparison of the NSM and SFWMM. The smaller footprint of the remnant Everglades compared to the historic footprint creates a bias towards lower NSM depths when water depths may have been historically greater (McVoy *et al.* in press).

we reduce TP concentrations to a mere 10 µg/L? The answer depends on the adequacy of three approaches: (1) on-farm, best management practices (BMPs); (2) six or more large treatment wetlands, known as Stormwater Treatment Areas (STAs) (Chimney and Goforth 2001; Figure 6); and (3) Advanced Treatment Technologies (ATT), to enhance STA performance. The BMPs, initially expected to reduce the TP load from farms by 25%, have far exceeded their goal. Annual TP loads in agricultural runoff decreased by an average of 54% from 1996 to 2000, compared to a 10-year baseline period (1979–1988). The STAs, designed to achieve an interim outflow TP concentration of 50 µg/L (Walker 1995), have also largely exceeded expectations. With the exception of one STA, mean outflow TP concentrations have ranged from 17 to 47 µg/L.

Three types of ATTs have been investigated: chemical (treatment with aluminum or iron salts), biological (wetlands dominated periphyton or submerged aquatic vegetation [SAV]), and hybrid (combination of chemical and biological approaches) technologies. While chemical treatment achieved outflow TP concentrations at or below 10 µg/L, concerns about high capital and operating costs, disposal of residuals, and the potential impact of the effluent on the Everglades remain unresolved. Because of this uncertainty, chemical treatment was not considered a viable option; instead, research efforts are now focused on optimizing the "green" technologies. One scenario would reconfigure the STAs into treatment trains of sequential cells dominated by emergent macrophytes → SAV → periphyton. As currently envisioned, the STAs will encompass more than 24 000 ha when completed, making them the largest complex of constructed wetlands in the world.

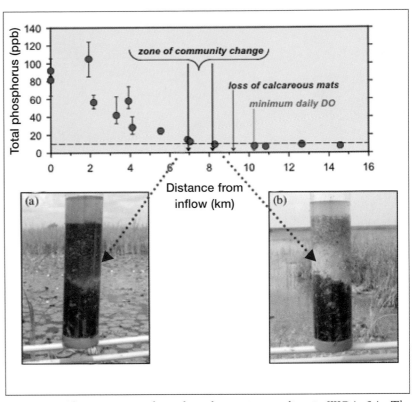

Figure 5. *Change point analysis along the nutrient gradient in WCA–2A. The graph illustrates the decrease in water column total phosphorus concentration with increasing distance from the inflow structures. A sediment core taken from a nutrient enriched area (a) has a dark, highly organic surficial layer, while a core from an unimpacted area (b) shows a characteristic calcareous sediment.*

■ Every restoration plan needs a model (or two)

While researchers have gathered an extensive body of historical information on pre-drainage Everglades hydrology, the synthesis of this material is in progress and the role of flow velocities and direction needs further study (CROGEE 2003). As a result, restoration planning has relied heavily upon a mathematical model, the Natural Systems Model (NSM), to estimate pre-drainage and pre-impoundment water depths, hydroperiods, and, to a lesser extent, flow vectors based on 1965–1995 rainfall patterns. The NSM may be the most important landscape model ever developed for environmental restoration, and yet it cannot be calibrated or "confirmed". Instead, it relies on the calibration of another model, the South Florida Water Management Model (SFWMM), which is similar to the NSM, except that it includes present-day infrastructure (eg canals, levees, etc) and is driven by current (1965–1995) rainfall patterns, soil elevations, and operational rules for flood protection and water supply.

The hydrologic goals of Everglades restoration were derived from a comparison of NSM and SFWMM output (Figure 7). Differences in water depth, hydroperiods and discharge rates (Table 1) were used to help set initial restoration targets. However, the current NSM water depths appear too low and flow directions seem illogical to some (McVoy *et al.* in press). The intent is to return the hydrology of the present-day Everglades to "NSM-like" conditions. However, due to the high uncertainty of NSM, these goals will almost certainly need to be modified through adaptive management (see "Under the underpinnings").

■ Dances with wolves: litigation and legislation

The restoration of the Everglades has been fraught with litigation, beginning with a lawsuit brought by the Federal government in 1988 alleging that the state of Florida was in violation of its own water quality standards for the Everglades. In the ensuing years, numerous other lawsuits and administrative actions were brought by a variety of interested parties (Rizzardi 2001). A settlement

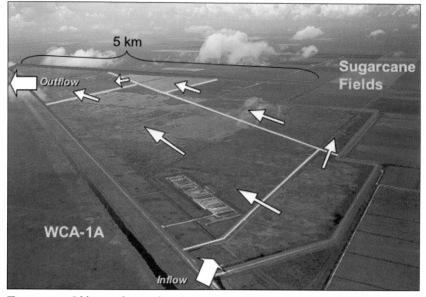

Figure 6. *Oblique photo of a Stormwater Treatment Area (STA) in south Florida. Arrows indicate direction of water flow through the wetland; yellow lines mark interior levees that divide the STA into separate treatment cells.*

that guide the implementation of CERP: (1) Programmatic Regulations will "ensure the protection of the natural system consistent with the goals and purposes of the Plan (CERP), including the establishment of interim goals to provide a means to evaluate success of the Plan"; and (2) CERP will "ensure that new scientific or technical information that is developed through the principles of adaptive management...are integrated into the plan".

The SFWMD, together with the USACOE, are obligated to "ensure that restoration does not diminish current levels of water supply or flood control". Everglades restoration is therefore a two-fold challenge: it must restore hydrologic regimes and clean water while simultaneously devision alternative means of improving regional water management for economic and societal development.

to the federal lawsuit included the purchase of large tracts of farmland for conversion into STAs. Never in the history of US wetland science has a conversion of this scale been attempted. The Florida legislature codified the settlement agreement in the 1994 Everglades Forever Act (EFA). The EFA established a taxing mechanism to fund land acquisition and STA construction, at a cost of about $800 million. The EFA also specified that by 2001, the FDEP had to establish a P threshold where, "In no case shall such phosphorus criterion allow waters in the Everglades Protection Area to be altered so as to cause an imbalance in the natural populations of aquatic flora or fauna".

In the event that a P threshold was not adopted by this deadline, a default standard of 10 µg/L would become law. The Florida legislature amended the EFA in 2003, which resulted in moderating provisions and an extension of the time required to achieve long-term water quality goals (the P-rule). Although the P-rule was challenged by both environmental and agricultural interests in 2004, the state won the challenges and therefore a criterion of 10 µg/L is in place and a procedure for assessing compliance is required to be in place by 2006.

The EFA is only half of the legal and legislative story; the Comprehensive Everglades Restoration Plan (CERP) comprises the other. The CERP, authorized by Congress as part of the Water Resources and Development Act of 2000, is a massive hydrologic restoration program for the whole of south Florida. CERP includes some 60 projects to be constructed over the next 30 years, which will extensively modify the existing water management system by removing some infrastructure while adding new components.

In anticipation of a contentious political environment and in recognition of the fact that Everglades restoration is different from most USACOE projects, the following language was incorporated into the Programmatic Regulations

■ Trade-offs and uncertainties abound

Successful Everglades restoration will ultimately be determined by reconciling society's needs and values with that of the ecosystem. Unlike the cycle of opportunistic growth -> maintenance -> release -> reorganization, as detailed in Holling's (1978) paper on natural succession, the human economic system seems to be one of opportunistic growth -> opportunistic growth -> opportunistic growth. As a result, the re-engineering of the south Florida water management system may conflict with ecological restoration and create issues of social concern that pit dollars against nature.

Despite all the attention, Everglades restoration is not a done deal. In fact, every one of its 60 or so cost-shared projects must be ecologically and economically "justified", using procedures that quantify tax-payer costs against ecological benefits. For very expensive projects, such as the construction of an elevated highway to enhance sheet-flow across the marsh, justification can be very contentious because the uncertainties associated with calculating the benefits greatly exceed the uncertainties for calculating the costs.

These uncertainties become magnified by conflicting interpretations, non-linear feedback mechanisms, slow response times, and a lack of data. As a result, "exact" solutions are not possible; instead, Everglades restoration is challenged by seven major uncertainties:
(1) What will be the structure of the surrounding watershed in 2050? This uncertainty is associated with estimates of population growth and the potential impacts of converting farmland to housing developments or mining operations to maximize economic returns. This will affect both water quantity and water quality. Trade-offs will occur, especially during floods and

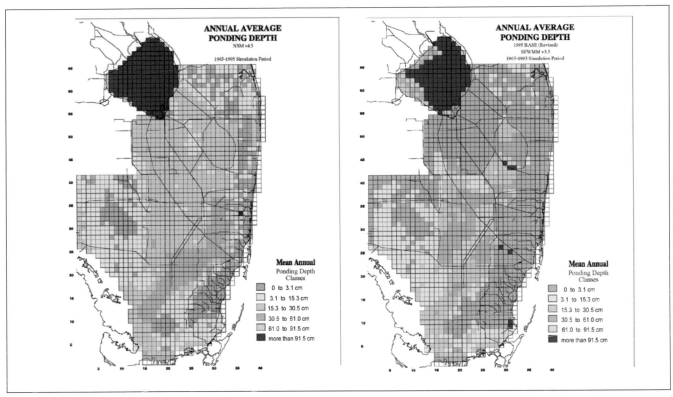

Figure 7. *The difference between (a) the historical extent and (b) the current boundaries of the Everglades is shown here in terms of surface water depths. Much of the historic Shark River Slough (shown as a dark green flow-way) is now east of the existing levee system and outside the current footprint of the Everglades. What remains is approximately 30 cm shallower than historically predicted. At the same time, model simulations indicate that the rest of the Everglades has become deeper.*

droughts when water is diverted to the estuaries or stored belowground in deep Aquifer Storage and Recovery (ASRs) wells, respectively.

(2) How dependent is restoration upon cutting-edge engineering and technology? Some 300 ASR injection wells are proposed to store freshwater and some 20 km of 20–30 m deep curtain walls are suggested as flood protection for urban and agricultural lands. Neither have been implemented at these scales. In the purest sense of restoration, all impediments to flow within the extant Everglades would be removed. However, even with these technologies, if all levees that separate one WCA from another were removed, then according to the SFWMM, water would drain too quickly in some places and not drain at all in others. Since these are very expensive technologies (eg $4 million/km of curtain wall), the trade-offs will be between the ecological benefits of removing all or some structures and the cost of providing flood protection and water supply.

(3) How and where in the Everglades do you measure compliance with a P threshold? This uncertainty is associated with sizing and operating STAs and with soil P dynamics downstream in the marsh. It follows that uncertainty associated with the P threshold in the Everglades will determine land acquistion, at a cost of millions of dollars. It is the precursor to a trade-off between "getting the water right" and "getting the

water quality right". If P concentrations delivered to the Everglades exceed the 10 µg/L threshold, then the hydrologic needs of the Everglades landscape may come at the expense of an expanding cattail habitat. Other water quality uncertainties, including the use of runoff elevated in sulfate and its potential effect on the methylation of mercury (Gilmour *et al.* 1998; Bates *et al.* 2002), pesticides, and other contaminants have only begun to be investigated.

(4) What are the freshwater volumes needed for Florida Bay? Too little freshwater inflow from the Everglades to Florida Bay can promote hypersaline events that are detrimental to seagrass beds. However, increasing inflows, if not fully treated, may also increase nutrient loading. The trade-off will be between "getting the salinity right" and "getting the water quality right".

(5) What are the ecological impacts of canals? The canals that were constructed to drain the Everglades are now sport-fishing habitats. However, the complete back-filling of canals will also eliminate deep-draft boating activity. The trade-off will consist of the economic benefits of recreational fishing versus the ecological benefits of sheet-flow.

(6) How do landscape patterns of tree islands, ridges and sloughs maintain their topographic differences? Restoring pre-drainage hydroperiods is expected to prevent peat fires, reverse the impacts of compartmentalization, and create more slough habitat.

Increasing the hydroperiod, however, may stress tree islands that have been losing elevation due to drainage. A return to pre-drainage depths and hydroperiods may cause tree island degradation in some regions.

(7) How do you quantify ecological benefits? The implementation of any USACOE project requires a trade-off between estimated costs and predicted benefits. Models to predict the ecological benefits have considerably greater uncertainty than those used to estimate engineering costs. Furthermore, although there are quantitative valuation techniques for ecosystem services (eg Costanza *et al.* 1993; Howarth and Farber 2002; Kant 2003), they are not easily developed or interpreted, and thus have not yet gained acceptance by government or social institutions.

■ Under the underpinnings

Ecosystem science has clearly documented the environmental impacts associated with the Central & South Florida Project, including over-drainage and excessive nutrient loading. Now, it is a matter of careful design and implementation to correct these problems and compensate for the uncertainties, and therein lies the biggest challenge to Everglades restoration.

Flexibility in the design and execution of CERP, needed to balance modeling and ecological uncertainties, optimize trade-offs, and go beyond just conservation, will depend upon an adaptive management approach (Holling 1978; Walters *et al.* 1992). Adaptive management allows for the utilization of new knowledge as it becomes available and is essential to the success of this long-term project. However, the mechanism for translating new information into new project designs and implementation schedules has yet to be devised. Limitations include the expense of modifying new construction and the long lag times associated with measuring and quantifying ecological benefits. Adaptive management may also be costly and alter benefits to particular stakeholders. Yet these changes will probably be necessary and are in fact the justification for using an adaptive management framework.

Successful adaptive management will require both public and interagency trust. Stakeholders must believe that they will not be short-changed in this process. Unfortunately, due to a long history of accommodation to special interest groups (Douglas 1947; Johnson 1974), there are concerns that social change and shifts in political power may undermine a long-term restoration program that is designed and implemented incrementally. Therefore, the adaptive management approach must contain criteria to reassure stakeholders that the goals of Everglades restoration cannot be compromised. Trust is essential, and will improve as long as the scientific basis for restoration continues to reduce uncertainty. Scientists are currently developing interim goals and a strong monitoring and assessment plan for the Everglades. These efforts will supply the data needed to reduce the ecological and economic risks associated with adaptive restoration, and hopefully provide the framework for the successful restoration of this national treasure.

■ Acknowledgements

We wish to thank the South Florida Water Management District for supporting Everglades research. A special thanks to K Tarboton, R van Zee, D Powell, J Ogden, and D Rudnick for their insightful reviews and dedication.

■ References

Acosta CA and Perry SA. 2001. Impact of hydropattern disturbance on crayfish population dynamics in the seasonal wetlands of Everglades National Park, USA. *Aquat Conserv* **11**: 45–57.

Allison RV. 1943. The need of the Everglades for a specific plan of development based on the physical and chemical characteristics of its soils and a rational handling of its natural water supply. *Soil Sci Soc Fla Proc* **5-A**: 126–31.

Bates AL, Orem WH, Harvey JW, and Spiker EC. 2002. Tracing sources of sulfur in the Florida Everglades. *J Environ Qual* **31**: 287–99.

Childers DL, Jones RD, Trexler JC, *et al.* 2002. Quantifying the effects of low-level phosphorus additions on unenriched Everglades wetlands with in situ flumes and phosphorus dosing. In: Porter JW and Porter KG (Eds). The Everglades, Florida Bay, and coral reefs of the Florida Keys: an ecosystem sourcebook. Boca Raton, FL: CRC Press.

Chimney MJ and Goforth G. 2001. Environmental impacts to the Everglades ecosystem: a historical perspective and restoration strategies. *Water Sci Tech* **44**: 93–100.

Costanza R, Wainger L, Folke C, and Maler KG. 1993. Modeling complex ecological economic systems. *Bioscience* **43**: 545–55.

Craft CB, Vymazal J, and Richardson CJ. 1995. Response of Everglades plant communities to nitrogen and phosphorus additions. *Wetlands* **15**: 258–71.

CROGEE (Committee on Restoration of the Greater Everglades Ecosystem). 2003. Adaptive monitoring and assessment for the Comprehensive Restoration Plan. Water Science and Technology Board, National Research Council. Washington, DC: The National Academies Press. www.nap.edu/catalog/10663.html. Viewed 3/1/05

Crozier GE and Gawlik DE. 2002. Avian response to nutrient enrichment in an oligotrophic wetland, the Florida Everglades. *Condor* **104**: 631–42.

Darby PC, Bennetts RE, Miller SJ, and Percival HF. 2002. Movements of Florida apple snails in relation to water levels and drying events. *Wetlands* **22**: 489–98.

Davis JH. 1943. The natural features of southern Florida. *Geol Bull* **25**. Tallahassee, FL Florida Geological Survey.

Davis SM and Ogden JC (Eds). 1994. Everglades: the ecosystem and its restoration. Delray Beach, FL: St Lucie Press.

Douglas MS. 1947. The Everglades: river of grass, America's unique natural treasure. Marietta, GA: Mockingbird Books.

FDEP. 2000. Everglades phosphorus criterion technical support document. www.dep. state.fl.us/water/wqssp/everglades/pctsd. htm. Viewed 3/1/05

Frederick PC and Collopy MW. 1989. Nesting success of five species of wading birds (Ciconiiformes) in relation to water conditions in the Florida Everglades. *Auk* **106**: 625–34.

Gaiser EE, Trexler J, Richards J, *et al.* Cascading ecological effects of low-level phosphorus enrichment in the Florida Everglades. *J Environ Qual.* In press.

Gawlik DE. 2002. The effects of prey availability on the numerical response of wading birds. *Ecol Monogr* **72**: 329–46.

Gilmour CC, Ridel GS, Ederington MC, *et al*. 1998. Methylmercury concentrations and production rates across a trophic gradient in the northern Everglades. *Biogeochemistry* **40**: 327–45.

Holling CS. 1978. Adaptive environmental assessment and management. London, UK: John Wiley & Sons.

Howarth RB and Farber S. 2002. Accounting for the value of ecosystem services. *Ecol Econ* **41**: 421–29.

Johnson L. 1974. Beyond the fourth generation. Gainesville, FL: University of Florida Presses.

Kant S. 2003. Choices of ecosystem capital without discounting and prices. *Environ Monit Assess* **86**: 105–27.

Kitchens WM, Bennetts RE, and DeAngelis DL. 1994. Linkages between the Snail Kite population and wetland dynamics in a highly fragmented south Florida hydroscape. In: Porter JW and Porter KG (Eds). The Everglades, Florida Bay, and coral reefs of the Florida Keys: an ecosystem sourcebook. Boca Raton, FL: CRC Press.

Light SS and Dineen JW. 1994. Water control in the Everglades: a historical perspective. In: Davis SM and Ogden JC (Eds). Everglades: the ecosystem and its restoration. Delray Beach, FL: St Lucie Press.

MAP (Monitoring and Assessment Plan). 2004. Comprehensive Everglades Restoration Plan (CERP) Monitoring and Assessment Plan: Part 1. Monitoring and supporting research. Restoration, Coordination and Verification (RECOVER). West Palm Beach, FL: South Florida Water Management District. http://www.evergladesplan.org/pm/ recover/recover _map_2004.cfm. Viewed 3/1/05

Mazzotti FJ and Brandt LA. 1994. Ecology of the American Alligator in a seasonally fluctuating environment. In: Davis SM and Odgen JC (Eds). Everglades: the ecosystem and its restoration. Delray Beach, FL: St Lucie Press.

McCormick PV, O'Dell MB, Shuford III RBE, *et al*. 2001. Periphyton responses to experimental phosphorus enrichment in a subtropical wetland. *Aquat Bot* **71**: 119–39.

McCormick PV, Newman S, Miao SL, *et al*. 2002. Effects of anthropogenic phosphorus inputs on the Everglades. In: Porter JW and Porter KG (Eds). The Everglades, Florida Bay and coral reefs of the Florida Keys: an ecosystem sourcebook. Boca Raton, FL: CRC Press.

McCormick PV and Laing JA. 2003. Effects of increased phosphorus loading on dissolved oxygen in a subtropical wetland, the Florida Everglades. *Wet Ecol Manage* **11**: 199–216

McCormick PV and O'Dell MB. 1996. Quantifying periphyton responses to phosphorus in the Florida Everglades: a synoptic–experimental approach. *J N Am Benthol Soc* **15**: 450–68.

McKelvin MR, Hook DD, and Rozelle AA. 1998. Adaptation of plants to flooding and soil waterlogging. In: Messina MG and Conner WH (Eds). Southern forested wetlands. Boca Raton, FL: Lewis Publishers.

McVoy CW, Park WA, Obeysekera J, and VanArman J. Predrainage landscapes and hydrology of the Everglades. Gainesville, FL: University of Florida Press. In press.

Miao SL and Sklar FH. 1998. Biomass and nutrient allocation of sawgrass and cattail along an environmental gradient in Florida Everglades. *Wet Ecosys Manage* **5**: 245–64.

Newman S, Grace JB and Koebel JW. 1996. Effects of nutrients and hydroperiod on *Typha*, *Cladium*, and *Eleocharis*: implications for Everglades restoration. *Ecol. Applications* **6**: 774-783.

Newman S, Kumpf H, Laing JA, and Kennedy WC. 2001. Decomposition responses to phosphorus enrichment in an Everglades (USA) slough. *Biogeochemistry* **54**: 229-250.

Newman S, Reddy KR, DeBusk WF, *et al*. 1997. Spatial distribution of soil nutrients in a northern Everglades marsh: Water Conservation Area 1. *Soil Sci Soc Am J* **61**: 1275–83.

Nott MP, Bass Jr OL, Fleming DM, *et al*. 1998. Water levels, rapid vegetation changes, and the endangered Cape Sable seaside-sparrow. *Anim Conserv* **1**: 23–32.

Ogden JC. 1994. A comparison of wading bird nesting colony dynamics (1931–1946 and 1974–1989) as an indication of ecosystem conditions in the southern Everglades. In: Davis SM and Ogden JC (Eds). Everglades: the ecosystem and its restoration. Delray Beach, FL: St Lucie Press.

Pan Y, Stevenson RJ, Vaithiyanathan P, *et al*. 2000. Changes in algal assemblages along observed and experimental phosphorus gradients in a subtropical wetland, USA. *Freshwater Biol* **44**: 339–53.

Rader RB and Richardson CJ. 1994. Response of macroinvertebrates and small fish to nutrient enrichment in the northern Everglades. *Wetlands* **14**: 134–46.

Rizzardi KW. 2001. Alligators and litigators: a recent history of Everglades regulation and litigation. *Fl Bar J* **75**: 18–26. www.flabar.org. Viewed 3/1/05

Rutchey K and Vilchek L. 1999. Air photointerpretation and satellite imagery analysis techniques for mapping cattail coverage in a northern Everglades impoundment. *Photogramm Eng Rem S* **65**: 185–91.

Science Coordinating Team. 2003. The role of flow in the Everglades ridge and slough landscape. Report to the South Florida Ecosystem Restoration Task Force Working Group. www.sfrestore.org/sct/docs/SCT%20Flow%20Paper%20-%20Final.pdf. Viewed 3/1/05

Sklar FH and van der Valk A (Eds). 2002. Tree islands of the Everglades. Dordrecht, Germany: Kluwer Academic.

Walker WW. 1995. Design basis for Everglades stormwater treatment areas. *Wat Res Bull* **31**: 671–85.

Walters C, Gunderson L, and Holling CS. 1992. Experimental policies for water management in the Everglades. *Ecol Appl* **2**: 189–202.

Wu Y, Rutchey K, Guan W, Vilchek L, and Sklar FH 2002. Spatial simulations of tree islands for Everglades restoration. In: Sklar FH and van der Valk A (Eds). Tree islands of the Everglades. Dordrecht, Germany: Kluwer Academic.

Unraveling complexity: building an understanding of Everglades restoration

Janet Hodder[1], Diane Ebert-May[2], and Kathy S Williams[3]

Understanding the complexity of ecosystems at all scales, macro to micro, is challenging for students (and scientists!) to unravel. Sklar and colleagues present the engaging problem of the restoration of the Florida Everglades (pp 161–169), including history, biology, hydrology, modeling, and regulatory morasses. Students need to learn how to derive and interconnect biological concepts from the literature as well as from textbooks. To do so they must connect new information with prior knowledge to make sense of the ideas and concepts presented. In this article, we model a way to guide and assess students' understanding of the biological principles featured in Sklar et al. before they come to class. Instructors use this formative assessment to modify classroom instruction, and to assess students' understanding of those principles at the end of class.

■ Student goals

- Read a complex article, derive and interconnect the biological concepts to construct understanding.
- Build models that predict how abiotic and biotic factors interact in complex systems.

■ Instructor goals

- Implement Just-in-Time Teaching (JiTT) instructional strategies.
- Analyze and use formative data from students' responses to their reading before class to guide instruction in class.
- Develop summative assessments that quantify and elucidate students' understanding of complex ecological problems and demonstrate their ability to synthesize information.

■ Before class

With the increased availability of classroom management software, such as Blackboard (www.blackboard.com), Web CT (www.webct.com), and Lon-Capa (www.lon-capa.org), faculty are using pre-class assessments designed to motivate students to read materials as well as to check their understanding. Many discussions among instructors using these systems focus mainly on how to prevent students from merely getting the correct answer from their peers. Here we introduce JiTT as a method for using pre-class assessments to help students connect new information to their prior knowledge, thereby deepening their under-

standing (Novak et al. 1999; Marrs and Novak 2004). Faculty can assess their students' competencies and modify class content accordingly.

In the JiTT model, students respond electronically to web-based assignments due shortly before class (a day or a few hours), and the instructor reads the student submissions to adjust the lesson to respond to students' replies. A goal of JiTT, or any active learning inside or outside class, is to engage students, promote more and high quality student–student interactions, faculty–student interactions, and students' study time. The example we present using JiTT and the Sklar et al. paper is not intended to stand alone in a course. Both students and faculty need to practice this type of instructional innovation to maximize its benefits. The data that faculty collect with JiTT can be used to measure improvements in students' understanding.

Before class, Sklar et al. is assigned as reading material. Warm-up questions in Panel 1 appear online and are designed to address students' prior knowledge about the ecological concepts fundamental to restoration of the Everglades and determine their understanding of the reading.

■ During class

Student responses from the warm-up assignment contribute to the content of the class and serve as an engagement tool. A mini-lecture based on the responses (10–15 minutes) can be used to clarify new biological jargon, begin to address

---

Panel 1. Warm-up questions

- Describe the differences in the appearance of the Everglades landscape today, compared with what it must have been like in the 1880s.
- The Comprehensive Everglades Restoration Plan wants to reverse the negative environmental trends by "getting the water right". Based on your understanding of the situation, what is "wrong" with the water now?

Instructors may provide additional web sources or references that allow students to explore material that supports the warm-up questions and provides information about new jargon and concepts. For this example, the website presented in Sklar et al. provides a good starting place (www.evergladesplan.org).

Students send their responses to the questions electronically to the instructor, who sees what students know about the topic and understand from the reading. Instructors use the rubric below to sort out the trends in responses.

- Unclear or unrelated information
- Accurate but incomplete response
- Accurate response but shows no interconnections of concepts
- Accurate response and demonstrates interconnections of concepts

---

[1]University of Oregon, [2]Michigan State University, [3]San Diego State University

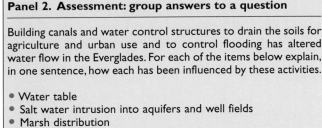

Panel 2. Assessment: group answers to a question

Building canals and water control structures to drain the soils for agriculture and urban use and to control flooding has altered water flow in the Everglades. For each of the items below explain, in one sentence, how each has been influenced by these activities.

- Water table
- Salt water intrusion into aquifers and well fields
- Marsh distribution
- Soil
- Water flowing to the Gulf of Mexico
- Phosphorus loads

Panel 3. Assessment: synthesis of biological concepts in a model (eg concept map)

How does your item influence:

- Tree islands?
- Cattails?
- Calcareous periphyton?
- Species of algae associated with eutrophication?
- Sea grass beds in the Gulf of Mexico?
- Alligator populations?

What are the biological consequences of this influence?

alternate conceptions students may have about the content, introduce new content, and help students build connections between the concepts and their own experiences. This type of teaching does not mean that faculty cannot plan the class meeting in advance. Student responses to these kinds of pre-class assessments are in many instances predictable and can be planned. Importantly, students see the warm-up as contributing to the direction of the class, thereby increasing their sense of ownership and community in the course. Once the instructor addresses alternative conceptions and clarification of ideas evident from the responses, groups of students prepare answers to the question in Panel 2.

Groups share answers, which are recorded and are used for the assessment in Panel 3. Individuals or groups are then assigned one of the items from Panel 2 to make a model such as a concept map (Williams *et al.* 2004) that explains how the item interacts with the biological factors from Panel 3.

The model in Panel 4 shows the interactions that occur as a result of increased phosphorus loads. This model provides students with a visual tool for sorting out and connecting the components of this ecosystem (drawn with www.ctools.msu.edu). Evaluation of this synthesis problem is based on the accuracy and logic of the connections and

hierarchy of the map. Level of performance can be based on the rubric for the warm-up questions.

■ Final note

This article models scientific teaching because the process of helping students unravel the complexity of an ecological issue is as important as gaining an understanding of the issue itself. Many researchable questions may arise during this process, as considered in Ebert-May *et al.* (2005). By engaging students before class, using their prior knowledge or that gained from answering the warm-up questions as a basis for some of the class content, and then having them construct models to assess their understanding, instructors can guide students to develop a more complete understanding of a topic. The limited class time instructors have with students can then be used to help students understand more difficult and complex ecological processes and concepts.

■ Acknowledgements

We thank S Koptur and H Swain for their insights and critical evaluation of this article, and the National Science Foundation for their long-term support of the FIRST project, Faculty Institutes for Reforming Science Teaching (DUE 0088847). All Pathways articles are peer reviewed.

■ References

Ebert-May D, Hodder J, and Weber E *et al.* 2005. Unleashing problem solvers: from assessment to designing research. *Front Ecol Environ* **3**: 101–02.

Marrs KA and Novak G. 2004. Just-in-Time Teaching in biology: creating an active learner classroom using the Internet. *Cell Biol Edu* **3**: 49–61. www.cellbioed.org/articles/vol3no1/article.cfm?articleI D=95. Viewed 1 March 2005.

Novak G, Gavrin A, Christian W, and Patterson E. 1999. Just-In-Time Teaching: blending active learning with web technology. Prentice Hall Series in Educational Innovation. www.jitt.org. Viewed 1 March 2005.

Williams KS, Ebert-May D, Luckie D, *et al.* 2004. Ecological controversy: analysis to synthesis. *Front Ecol Environ* **2**: 546–47.

Panel 4. Impact of phosphorus on the Everglades

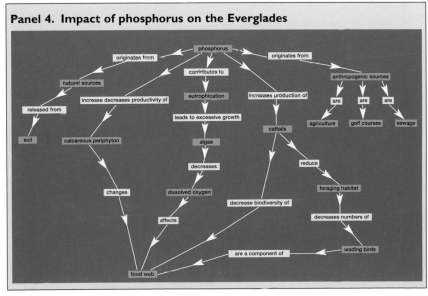

How many endangered species are there in the United States?

David S Wilcove[1] and Lawrence L Master[2]

Only about 15% of the known species in the United States have been studied in sufficient detail to determine whether or not they are imperiled. Any estimate of the total number of imperiled species in this country must therefore rely on extrapolations from this small number of comparatively well-studied species to a much larger number of poorly studied ones. We review the best available data on the status of plants, animals, and fungi in the US and conclude that the actual number of known species threatened with extinction is at least ten times greater than the number protected under the Endangered Species Act (ESA). The key to developing a more accurate picture of the extent of species endangerment is to obtain more data on the following groups (in decreasing order of priority): (1) invertebrate animals; (2) fungi; and (3) marine organisms. However, given the slow pace at which species are being protected under the ESA, and the rapid rate at which natural areas are being destroyed, a more urgent task is to develop and refine approaches to conservation that complement species-by-species protection, most notably the use of coarse filters.

Front Ecol Environ 2005; 3(8): 414–420

How many endangered species are there in the United States? This seemingly straightforward question is, in fact, unanswerable at the present time, largely because we have no clear idea how many species – endangered or not – exist there. A recent tally found that over 200 000 species of fungi, plants, and animals have been described to date in the US (Table 1; Stein *et al.* 2000) but by all accounts, large numbers of species have yet to be discovered. For example, Peter Raven, Director of the Missouri Botanical Garden, has estimated that as many as a half million species remain to be discovered (Stein *et al.* 2000; B Stein pers comm). He based this estimate on the fact that approximately 7% of the world's known vascular plant species occur in the US. Since vascular plants are a reasonably well-studied group, this value is likely to be close to the actual percentage. By extending this percentage to other types of organisms, and by assuming a worldwide total of 10 million species, Raven reasoned that as many as 700 000 species may inhabit the US.

Raven's approach is acutely sensitive to estimates of the total number of species on earth, which have ranged over more than an order of magnitude (eg May 1988; Novotny *et al.* 2002). Yet application of even low values for global species richness leads one to conclude that hundreds of thousands of undescribed species occur in the US. Invertebrate animals, fungi, and protists undoubtedly constitute the vast majority of these unknown species, although over the past decade at least 63 new vertebrate species have been described in the US, as taxonomists gain a better understanding of the genetic relationships between populations. (This figure does not include previously described subspecies that were subsequently elevated to species status).

If we do not know how many species occur in the US, we cannot be certain how many of them are at risk of extinction. But by making some reasonable assumptions, we can nonetheless estimate the number of *described* species that may be at risk of extinction. Such an estimate is a useful indicator of the scope of potential species losses. Our efforts to come up with a number may also shed light on neglected groups of species and other important data gaps that bedevil conservation efforts in the US and elsewhere.

■ Sources of information

Table 1 provides a breakdown by major groups of the 200 000+ species described to date in the US. If we knew how many of these species were in danger of extinction, we would have the answer to our question, at least with respect to known species. Under the Endangered Species Act (ESA) of 1973, the US Fish and Wildlife Service (USFWS; Department of the Interior) and the National Marine Fisheries Service (NMFS; Department of Commerce) are charged with identifying and protecting endangered species. These agencies currently (May 2005) classify 942 species (and an additional 327 subspecies and vertebrate populations) in the 50 states and District of Columbia as threatened or endangered (http://endangered.fws.gov/wildlife.html; NatureServe 2005). However, because adding a particular plant or animal to the endangered species list is a long and often controversial process, those who have studied the US endangered species list agree that it contains only a fraction of the total number of imperiled species (Master *et al.* 2000).

[1]*Woodrow Wilson School and Department of Ecology and Evolutionary Biology, Princeton University, Princeton, NJ 08544 (dwilcove@princeton.edu)*; [2]*NatureServe, 11 Avenue de Lafayette, 5th Floor, Boston, MA 02111*

By far the most complete list of US imperiled species is maintained by the nonprofit organization NatureServe, in collaboration with member natural heritage programs in all 50 states. NatureServe assigns each species to one of seven global conservation status categories (ranks) to indicate its overall risk of extinction (Table 2). These assessments and their documentation are available on NatureServe's data portal (www.natureserve.org/explorer/) and are continuously peer reviewed and updated as new information comes to light. NatureServe status ranks correspond closely to similar assessments made by other conservation science organizations (Master *et al.* 2000). For example, species considered critically endangered, endangered, vulnerable, or near-threatened under the Red List system of the World Conservation Union (IUCN) and species considered endangered, threatened, or of special concern by the American Fisheries Society are generally classified as possibly extinct, critically imperiled, imperiled, or vulnerable (ie ranked GH, G1, G2, or G3) by NatureServe. O'Grady *et al.* (2004) found that the systems employed by NatureServe and the IUCN yield similar rankings for species and that these rankings are correlated with the species' predicted extinction risk, as determined by population viability analyses.

To date, NatureServe has assigned global conservation status ranks to approximately 30 000 species in the US, or to approximately 15% of the country's known flora and fauna. Regrettably, even among the US species that have been discovered and described by scientists, the vast majority are so poorly known that they cannot be assigned a status rank. Therefore, any estimate of the total number of imperiled species in the US must be made by extrapolating from a few well-studied organisms to a much larger number of poorly studied ones.

We focus on those taxonomic groups for which over 95% of the species known to occur in the US have been assigned global conservation status ranks by NatureServe. For the purposes of this study, we define an endangered species as any species with a global rank of GH, G1, or G2. Ours is a very conservative definition of endangerment, in the sense that it excludes species with a rank of G3, some of which are classified under the ESA as endangered or threatened (eg piping plover [*Charadrius melodus*], jaguar [*Panthera onca*], loggerhead turtle [*Caretta caretta*], and 35 plant species). We also exclude from our tally all subspecies and population segments, all species that are rare in the US but relatively common in other countries, and all species for which there is persuasive evidence that they have become extinct. Table 3 provides a summary of the numbers of species in each category.

■ Endangerment patterns

The status of nearly all US vertebrates with the exception of marine fish is known with a high degree of accuracy. The percentage of imperiled species within each vertebrate class ranges from a low of 7% (mammals) to a high of 25% (amphibians); the overall value for vertebrates, again excluding marine fish, is 13% (Table 3).

In the case of invertebrates, only 11 groups, representing 4698 species (~3% of known species of invertebrates in the US) have been evaluated in sufficient detail to meet our 95% criterion. These include: freshwater mussels; freshwater snails; crayfishes; fairy, clam, and tadpole shrimps; butterflies and skippers; Saturniidae, Sphingidae, *Papaipema*, and *Catocala* moths; grasshoppers; tiger beetles; dragonflies and damselflies; stoneflies; and mayflies. In addition we include terrestrial snails from the continental US because all known species have been assigned a status rank. The terrestrial snails of Hawaii have not been ranked by NatureServe; however, all of them are almost certain to be classified as either endangered or recently extinct, with status ranks of GX–G2. Within these invertebrate groups, the percentage of imperiled species varies greatly, from a low of 6% (butterflies and skippers) to a high of 61% (freshwater snails).

In the US, animal groups closely associated with fresh

Table 1. Number of known species in the US in three kingdoms

Fungi	Plants		Animals	
Total: >37 800	Vascular: 16 230		Vertebrates: ~4900	
	Nonvascular: 2223		Invertebrates: ~143 900	
	Total: ~18 400		Total: ~148 800	

Numbers represent described native species from all 50 states, including terrestrial, freshwater, and marine species to within the 200-mile territorial limit. Data are from Stein *et al.* (2000) and NatureServe (2005).

Table 2. NatureServe's global conservation status ranks and their definitions

Status[a]	Description
GX	**Presumed extinct** – Not located despite intensive searches and virtually no likelihood of rediscovery.
GH	**Possibly extinct** – Missing; known from only historical occurrences but still some hope of rediscovery.
G1	**Critically imperiled** – At very high risk of extinction due to extreme rarity (often five or fewer populations), very steep declines, or other factors.
G2	**Imperiled** – At high risk of extinction due to very restricted range, very few populations (often 20 or fewer), steep declines, or other factors.
G3	**Vulnerable** – At moderate risk of extinction or of significant conservation concern due to a restricted range, relatively few populations (often 80 or fewer), recent and widespread declines, or other factors.
G4	**Apparently secure** – Uncommon but not rare; some cause for long-term concern due to declines or other factors.
G5	**Secure** – Common; widespread and abundant.
GU	**Unrankable** – Currently unrankable due to lack of information or due to substantially conflicting information about status or trends.
GNR	**Unranked** – Global rank not yet assessed.

[a]Note: "G" refers to global or range-wide conservation status for a species or ecological community.

water, such as mussels, crayfish, and shrimps, have higher percentages of imperiled species than do largely terrestrial groups, a pattern first noted by Master (1990). There are, however, curious exceptions to this pattern. The percentage of imperiled dragonflies and damselflies seems low relative to other freshwater invertebrates, while the percentages of imperiled terrestrial snails and grasshoppers seem unusually high relative to butterflies and moths. We can construct post hoc explanations for these anomalies – dragonflies and damselflies are strong flyers whose distributions are rarely restricted to a single watershed, whereas many snails and grasshoppers have extremely restricted distributions – but clearly, more research is warranted.

Within the vascular plants, flowering plants (monocots and dicots), gymnosperms (conifers and allied forms), and pteridophytes (ferns and allied forms) have been reasonably well surveyed. The percentages of imperiled species vary from 10% among gymnosperms to over 18% among dicots; the overall percentage of US vascular plants at risk of extinction is close to 17%. Within the nonvascular plants, only about two-thirds of the mosses, liverworts, and hornworts have been surveyed, not enough for inclusion in this analysis, but approximately 10% (136) of these are judged to be imperiled.

■ Forgotten fungi

Although fungi constitute approximately 17% of described species in the US, their conservation has attracted little attention. Only in the Pacific Northwest, where logging of old-growth forests may threaten certain species, have substantial efforts been made to identify at-risk fungi. To estimate the number of imperiled fungi in the US, we can examine the case of truffle-like (sequestrate) macrofungi in the states of Washington and Oregon. Truffle-like fungi are not a monophyletic group, but rather a collection of similar looking but unrelated species. Given their popularity in cooking, and the fact that many species occur in old-growth forests, they are better inventoried and monitored than most other types of fungi. Approximately 365 species of sequestrate macrofungi have been found in Washington and Oregon; 65 species (18%) are classified as imperiled by the US Forest Service (D Luoma pers comm), mostly due to logging of older forests. This percentage is close to the value for vascular plants, but it may be high when compared to all US fungi. NatureServe has assigned conservation status ranks to 1200 of the estimated 3800 lichens, and 6% of these species are considered imperiled. If we assume that 6–18% of known fungi are at risk of extinction, we add 2200–6800 species to the total number of imperiled species.

■ Tallying the numbers

The figures of 339 imperiled vertebrates and 2708 imperiled vascular plants are, in all likelihood, close to the actual values. With respect to invertebrates, application of even the lowest percentage value for any of the well-studied groups (ie 6% for butterflies and skippers) to all 144 000 known invertebrate species would equate to approximately 8600 at-risk invertebrates alone. Use of a higher percentage, for example 17%, which is the average of the insect groups listed in Table 3, would equate to nearly 25 000 imperiled invertebrate species. If we assume that approximately 10% of nonvascular plants are currently at risk of extinction, we can add an additional 200+ species to the roster of endangered species. For fungi, our best estimate, based on woefully inadequate data, is 2200–6800 imperiled species. Thus, a total of somewhere between 14 000–35 000 imperiled species – roughly 7–18% of the nation's known plants, animals, and fungi – appears to be a reasonable, conservative estimate for the US. This total is more than an order of magnitude greater than the number of species currently protected under the ESA.

■ Causes of endangerment

Knowing why species become endangered is as important as knowing how many are endangered. Several studies have examined the causes of species endangerment in the US, both for species classified as globally imperiled by NatureServe (Richter *et al.* 1997; Wilcove *et al.* 1998, 2000) and for species listed as threatened or endangered by USFWS and NMFS (Lawler *et al.* 2002).

Habitat loss is the most widespread cause of species endangerment in the US, affecting approximately 85% of imperiled species. Harm caused by nonindigenous species is the second most widespread threat, affecting 49% of imperiled species, followed by pollution (24%), overexploitation (17%), and disease (3%). The numbers total more than 100% because most species face multiple threats. Indeed, habitat loss is the top-ranked threat in terms of the number of species it affects for all of the groups studied by Wilcove *et al.* 1998), which included vascular plants, mammals, birds (Figure 1), reptiles, amphibians, freshwater fish, freshwater mussels, crayfish, tiger beetles, and butterflies. For the other threat categories, the rankings vary somewhat from group to group. For example, nonindigenous species are the second most frequent threat to vascular plants, birds, and butterflies. For groups with a large proportion of aquatic species (ie amphibians, fishes, freshwater mussels, crayfishes), the second-ranked threat is pollution, including nonpoint sources such as sedimentation. Overexploitation is an especially important threat to imperiled mammals (45%; second only to habitat loss), reptiles (66%; second rank), and butterflies (30%; third rank). Disease is generally at the bottom of the list in terms of the number of species it threatens, with the notable exception of birds, where it affects 37% of imperiled species, mostly in Hawaii.

In addition to threats and trends, NatureServe's ranking criteria (Table 2) emphasize population size and other factors related to rarity as major influences on a species' vulnerability to extinction. Thus, a species that is intrinsically rare but otherwise unaffected by human activities could be classified as imperiled. Wilcove *et al.* (1998), however,

Table 3. Species groups ranked by NatureServe

US species report card – species groups tracked in NatureServe's central databases

Taxonomic group	Presumed extinct (GX)	Possibly extinct (GH)	Critically imperiled (G1)	Imperiled (G2)	Vulnerable (G3)	Apparently secure (G4)	Secure (G5)	Unrankable (GU)	Unranked (GNR)	Totals	Percent of species imperiled (%GH–G2)
Vertebrates											
Mammals	1	1	11	16	45	92	253	1	1	421	7%
Birds	20	9	26	20	40	93	575	0	0	783	7%
Reptiles, turtles, and crocodilians	0	0	9	19	35	46	184	0	2	295	9%
Amphibians	1	1	29	35	43	45	104	0	0	258	25%
Freshwater fishes	16	4	91	68	110	189	318	0	2	798	20%
Vertebrates subtotals	**38**	**15**	**166**	**158**	**273**	**465**	**1434**	**1**	**5**	**2555**	**13%**
Invertebrates											
Freshwater mussels	16	18	84	41	48	46	42	3	0	298	48%
Freshwater snails	23	58	274	84	72	33	130	3	0	677	61%
Terrestrial snails	2	6	338	218	150	101	182	0	0	997	56%
Crayfishes	1	2	59	53	61	92	74	0	0	342	33%
Freshwater shrimps	0	4	8	5	8	14	40	0	0	79	22%
Butterflies & skippers	0	0	11	27	85	107	385	3	3	621	6%
Tiger beetles	0	0	6	4	14	19	60	0	1	104	10%
Stoneflies	0	16	40	74	133	165	197	0	0	625	21%
Mayflies	4	6	36	81	73	134	227	0	0	561	22%
Grasshoppers	0	21	61	106	43	90	209	55	1	586	32%
Dragonflies & damselflies	0	4	8	27	49	107	270	0	0	465	8%
Four moth groups (Saturniidae, Catocala, Sphingidae, Papaipema)	0	4	12	9	27	158	124	6	0	340	7%
Invertebrate subtotals	**46**	**139**	**937**	**729**	**763**	**1066**	**1940**	**70**	**5**	**5695**	**32%**
Vascular plants											
Dicots	9	122	925	1265	2213	3560	4296	24	156	12590	19%
Monocots	1	8	124	155	356	896	1384	4	27	2957	10%
Gymnosperms	0	0	5	6	9	32	61	0	0	113	10%
Pteridophytes	0	3	37	36	93	159	224	1	17	570	13%
Vascular plant subtotals	**10**	**133**	**1091**	**1484**	**2671**	**4647**	**5965**	**29**	**200**	**16230**	**17%**
Totals	**94**	**287**	**2194**	**2371**	**3707**	**6178**	**9339**	**100**	**210**	**24480**	**20%**

Groups are included if at least 95% of the species in the group have been assigned a global conservation status rank. For terrestrial gastropods, only species occurring in the continental US have been ranked and are included, although the unranked (GNR) Hawaiian species, if included, would be overwhelmingly ranked GX–G2. The percent of imperiled species excludes extinct (GX) species from the calculation. Many of these species are given "range ranks" (eg G1–G3), which indicate uncertainty in their conservation status. These range ranks are averaged (eg G2) for placement in the table above.

found that only 52 of 1880 species classified as imperiled (GH, G1, or G2) by NatureServe appeared not to be threatened by human activities.

After reviewing the threats listed in the recovery plans for 181 plants and animals protected under the ESA, Lawler *et al.* (2002) concluded that most threats "…are chronic, have occurred over a long time period, and are intense where they do occur. In addition, most species face multiple major threats rather than single major threats. The recovery of species under such conditions is likely to be quite difficult."

■ Consequences of endangerment

If the road to recovery for imperiled species is likely to be long and costly, decision makers and the public may demand an explanation for why such species ought to be saved. Numerous books and articles have been written about the reasons for conserving biological diversity (eg Norton 1988; Wilson 1999, 2002). These reasons include: aesthetic and moral justifications; the importance of wild species as providers of products and services essential to human welfare (Daily 1997; Panel 1); the value of particular species as indicators of environmental health or as keystone species crucial to the functioning of ecosystems; and the scientific breakthroughs that have come from the study of wild organisms.

From among the roster of imperiled species in the US one can find examples of most of these benefits. For example, the endangered scrub mint (*Dicerandra frutescens*) contains both a natural insecticide and a powerful antifungal agent

Figure 1. *The Florida scrub-jay (*Aphelocoma coerulescens*), a globally imperiled (G2 ranked) species endemic to Florida.*

(Eisner 1994). The decline of the bald eagle (*Haliaeetus leucocephalus*) and peregrine falcon (*Falco peregrinus*), both of which ended up on the US endangered species list, alerted people to the potential health hazards associated with the widespread spraying of DDT and other persistent pesticides. The reintroduction of gray wolves (*Canis lupus*) to Yellowstone National Park has not only attracted thousands of tourists to the Park, it has also resulted in a beneficial redistribution of the Park's elk (*Cervus elaphus*), which had been congregating in riparian areas and preventing the regeneration of willow and aspen stands, an important habitat for much of the Park's wildlife (Ripple *et al.* 2001). Hawaii's endemic honeycreepers, most of which are now extinct or endangered, are – quite literally – a textbook example of adaptive radiation and a continuing source of new insights into evolution. One area where endangered species may arguably play a less substantive role is in providing major ecosystem services, simply because most endangered species have limited geographical ranges and small populations. However, it is certainly possible that some currently endangered species were important providers of ecosystem services prior to their decline and will once again become so if their populations are restored.

Finally, our ignorance of the natural history of most species, especially endangered species, should temper any rush to judgment as to which, if any, are "expendable". Species that today appear to be of little consequence or importance to humanity may, upon further study, prove to be critically important. A prime example is the Pacific yew (*Taxus brevifolia*). Once disdained by loggers as a worthless "trash tree" and destroyed, it subsequently became the

---

Panel 1. No fish, no fishery

People who are skeptical about the value of conserving species often single out particular species that have vanished and then ask, "So what?" In response, one might turn to the Great Lakes for an instructive example of a fishery that was fished to extinction. Commercial fishing in the Great Lakes began in the early 19th century and reached a peak in 1899, when 147 million pounds were harvested. Among the mainstays of that fishery were seven species in the genus *Coregonus*, variously known as ciscoes, chubs, whitefish, and bloaters.

Today, the Great Lakes still support a substantial fishery but the value of the catch is greatly diminished because of dramatic changes in species composition. Two *Coregonus* species (*C johannae*, *C reighardi*) and the Great Lakes populations of another (*C nigripinnis*) are now extinct; two others (*C zenithicus*, *C kiyi*) are in danger of extinction, having disappeared from every Great Lake except Superior, and the remaining three (*C artedi*, *C clupeaformis*, *C hoyi*) have vanished from at least one lake or are much reduced in abundance. Many fishers lost their jobs, and those who remained were forced to turn to other, less desirable species to make a living.

The decline of these *Coregonus* species can be traced largely to overfishing. Fishers began by targeting the largest species. As the bigger fish declined, they switched to nets with progressively smaller mesh sizes, targeting smaller and smaller species. In Lake Michigan, fishers at the start of the 20th century used gill nets with a mesh size of up to 4.5 inches. By 1950, the most commonly used mesh size was only 2.5 inches, and by the end of that decade it was less than 2.4 inches.

Also contributing to the demise of the *Coregonus* fishes were pollution from logging, farming, industry, and urbanization, as well as the spread of non-native fishes, most notably alewives (*Alosa pseudoharengus*) and smelt (*Osmerus mordax*). Alewives and smelt compete with ciscoes and consume their eggs. Moreover, as some of the ciscoes became increasingly rare, they hybridized with commoner species, hastening their demise. The end result was extinction or endangerment of the fish and the degradation of a once great fishery.

---

source of taxol, one of the most potent anticancer compounds ever discovered (Wilson 1999).

■ Towards a better safety net

By some estimates, fewer than half the plants, animals, and fungi native to the US have been discovered and described by scientists. Yet our analysis suggests that within the pool of described species, the number threatened with extinction is at least ten times greater than the number protected under the ESA.

The steps necessary to obtain a more complete inventory of all species in the US are beyond the scope of this study. The key to achieving a more accurate tally of endangered species among known species lies in obtaining more and better data on the following groups (in decreasing order of priority): (1) invertebrate animals, especially from among the groups listed in Table 3 because the global conservation status ranks of many of these species are known only within a range of values, reflecting uncertainty about their conservation status; (2) fungi; and (3) marine organisms, including marine fishes. We give top billing to the invertebrate animals partly because they constitute the vast majority of described species and partly because there is significant variance among invertebrate groups in the proportion of imperiled species. Gathering additional information on them is almost certain to be expensive and time-consuming (Lawton *et al.* 1998) and cannot be accomplished without sufficient numbers of adequately trained taxonomists. Scientists should also work to determine the conservation status of additional invertebrate species beyond those covered in Table 3. Doing so may provide useful insights into the conservation needs of habitats not well represented by the better-known invertebrate groups.

We lack sufficient information to rigorously estimate the cost of a national initiative to address these data gaps. However, it is worth noting that state and federal agencies currently invest approximately $22 million per year in inventory and monitoring work, not including university and National Science Foundation investments that are harder to quantify. For many years, some NatureServe member programs have been conducting county inventories, at an approximate cost of $150 000 per county (M Klein pers comm). Adding $50 000 per county to increase the coverage of at-risk invertebrates and fungi and multiplying by the number of counties (3143) in the US yields a cost of $629 million. Spreading the effort over 20 years, adding $3 million year^{-1} for additional taxonomic and identification assistance and $1 million year^{-1} for new and updated status assessments yields an annual average cost of $35 million. These figures do not, of course, include additional funds needed for conservation, education and outreach, database management, inventory and description of new (undescribed) species, description and mapping of ecological systems, and related activities necessary to ensure the continued existence of our biological diversity.

No additional data are needed to conclude that the ESA by itself will not adequately protect the US's imperiled species, now or in the foreseeable future. Over the past four presidential administrations, the mean number of species added annually to the federal endangered species list has varied from 10 (George W Bush's first term) to 65 (William J Clinton's term of office; Clark 2005). This six-fold difference translates into large differences over time in the total number of species receiving federal protection, but even the relatively high rate of additions during the Clinton Administration is insufficient to quickly erase the backlog of imperiled but unprotected species. The ESA is an essential part of national conservation efforts, but the need for additional tools to complement species-specific conservation measures is clear.

An oft-cited goal of conservation biologists has been to identify those groups that can serve as surrogates or indicators for lesser-known groups. Unfortunately, the evidence to date on the efficacy of this approach is equivocal. Most studies have found little or no congruence among hotspots of different groups, including hotspots of endangered species in the US (Prendergast *et al.* 1993; Dobson *et al.* 1997; Pimm and Lawton 1998; Chaplin *et al.* 2000; but see also Howard *et al.* 1998 and Lawler *et al.* 2003 for examples of places where there is apparent congruence of hotspots among different groups). In addition, there is mounting evidence that hotspots for terrestrial species do not correspond to hotspots for freshwater species. However, in one study, hotspots for at-risk terrestrial and freshwater species, when combined, did relatively well in capturing all species – endangered and non-endangered – in these groups at potential reserve sites (Lawler *et al.* 2003).

Another approach – using ecological communities as a kind of "coarse filter" to protect little-known species – is favored by many conservation biologists and non-governmental organizations. It also reflects the reality that species exist as part of complex ecosystems and therefore depend upon the presence of numerous other components (ie species and landscape features) for their survival. But this approach too will fail to protect many imperiled species if the distributions of rare invertebrates and fungi do not correspond to the way the ecological communities are defined (Noon *et al.* 2003). While some studies have found that coarse filters can be an effective means of protecting insect and bird diversity (Panzer and Schwartz 1998; Su *et al.* 2004), other studies have concluded that such approaches fail to capture the rarer species that are often of greatest interest to conservationists (Kintsch and Urban 2002; Noon *et al.* 2003). For this reason, many biologists have argued that the most efficient and effective approach to capturing biodiversity in a network of reserves is via a combined coarse–fine filter approach (Jenkins 1976, 1985; Noss and Cooperrider 1994; Groves *et al.* 2002). Even this combined strategy will fall short if: (1) the number of imperiled invertebrates and fungi is so great that conservation institutions cannot identify and protect them on a species-by-species basis (which seems to be the case in the US); and (2) the coarse filter does not correspond to the habitat requirements and distributions of these poorly-known species.

Although imperfect, we believe the combined coarse filter–fine filter approach holds the greatest promise for protecting endangered species in the US. The refinement and testing of the coarse filter component (ie delineating ecological communities and testing the efficiency with which those communities capture imperiled and vulnerable species in some of the better known groups of species; Table 3) is one of the most critical tasks facing conservation biologists in the US. Continuing and expanded inventories of known groups and searches for undescribed species are also undeniably important, as the efficacy of conservation depends greatly on accurate information about the "fine filter" species as well. However, given the rate at which natural areas are being degraded or destroyed in the US, conservation "shortcuts" such as an efficient coarse filter are urgently needed to prevent the loss of thousands of species.

■ Acknowledgments

We thank D Luoma for providing us with valuable information on US fungi. M Ormes, A Tomaino, G Davis, J McNees, and J Cordeiro kindly assisted with data compilations from NatureServe's databases. M Klein provided information on the costs of county inventories. We also thank W Turner for his helpful comments on an earlier version of this manuscript.

■ References

Chaplin SJ, Gerrard RA, Watson HM, et al. 2000. The geography of imperilment: targeting conservation towards critical biodiversity areas. In: Stein BA, Kutner LS, and Adams JS (Eds). Precious heritage: the status of biodiversity in the United States. New York, NY: Oxford University Press.

Clark JP. 2005. Testimony of Jamie Rappaport Clark, Executive Vice President, Defenders of Wildlife, before the Senate Environment and Public Works Subcommittee on Fisheries, Wildlife and Water Hearing on the Endangered Species Act. 19 May 2005; Washington, DC: Defenders of Wildlife.

Daily GC (Ed). 1997. Nature's services: societal dependence on natural ecosystems. Covello, CA: Island Press.

Dobson AP, Rodriguez JP, Roberts WM, and Wilcove DS. 1997. Geographic distribution of endangered species in the United States. Science 275: 750–52.

Eisner T. 1994. Chemical prospecting: a global imperative. P Am Philos Soc 138: 385–92.

Groves CR, Jensen DB, Valutis LL, et al. 2002. Planning for biodiversity conservation: putting conservation science into practice. Bioscience 52: 499–512.

Howard PC, Viskanic P, Davenport TRB, et al. 1998. Complementarity and the use of indicator groups for reserve selection in Uganda. Nature 394: 472–75.

Jenkins RE. 1976. Maintenance of natural diversity: approach and recommendations. In: Proceedings of the Forty-first North American Wildlife and Natural Resources Conference, Washington, DC.

Jenkins RE. 1985. The identification, acquisition, and preservation of land as a species conservation strategy. In: Hoage, RJ (Ed).

Animal extinctions. Washington, DC: Smithsonian Institution Press.

Kintsch JA and Urban DL. 2002. Focal species, community representation, and physical proxies as conservation strategies: a case study in the Amphibolite Mountains, North Carolina, US. Conserv Biol 16: 936–47.

Lawler JJ, Campbell SP, Guerry AD, et al. 2002. The scope and treatment of threats in endangered species recovery plans. Ecol Appl 12: 663–67.

Lawler JJ, White D, Sifneos JC, and Master LL. 2003. Rare species and the use of indicator groups for conservation planning. Conserv Biol 17: 875–82.

Lawton JH, Bignell DLE, Bolton B, et al. 1998. Biodiversity inventories, indicator taxa and effects of habitat modification in tropical forest. Nature 391: 72–76.

Master LL. 1990. The imperiled status of North American aquatic animals. Biodiversity Network News 3: 1–8.

Master LL, Stein BA, Kutner LS, and Hammerson GA. 2000. Vanishing assets: conservation status of US species. In: Stein BA, Kutner LS, and Adams JS (Eds). Precious heritage: the status of biodiversity in the United States. New York, NY: Oxford University Press.

May RM. 1988. How many species are there on earth? Science 241: 1441–49.

NatureServe. 2005. NatureServe central databases. Arlington, VA: NatureServe.

Noon BR, Murphy DR, Beissinger SR, et al. 2003. Conservation planning for US national forests: conducting comprehensive biodiversity assessments. BioScience 53: 1217–20.

Norton BG (Ed). 1988. The preservation of species: the value of biological diversity. Princeton, NJ: Princeton University Press.

Noss RF and Cooperrider A. 1994. Saving nature's legacy: protecting and restoring biodiversity. Washington, DC: Island Press.

Novotny V, Basset Y, Miller SE, et al. 2002. Low host specificity of herbivorous insects in a tropical forest. Nature 416: 841–44.

O'Grady JJ, Burgman MA, Keith DA, et al. 2004. Correlations among extinction risks assessed by different threatened species categorization systems. Conserv Biol 18: 1624–35.

Panzer R and Schwartz MW. 1998. Effectiveness of a vegetation-based approach to insect conservation. Conserv Biol 12: 693–702.

Pimm SL and Lawton JH. 1998. Planning for biodiversity. Science 279: 2068–69.

Prendergast JR, Quinn RM, Lawton JH, et al. 1993. Rare species, the coincidence of diversity hotspots and conservation strategies. Nature 365: 335–37.

Richter BD, Braun DP, Mendelson MA, and Master LL. 1997. Threats to imperiled freshwater fauna. Conserv Biol 11: 1081–93.

Ripple WJ, Larsen EJ, Renkin RA, and Smith DW. 2001. Trophic cascades among wolves, elk and aspen on Yellowstone National Park's northern range. Biol Conserv 102: 227–34.

Stein BA, Adams JS, Master LL, et al. 2000. A remarkable array: species diversity in the United States. In: Stein BA, Kutner LS, and Adams JS (Eds). Precious heritage: the status of biodiversity in the United States. New York, NY: Oxford University Press.

Su JC, Debinski JM, Jakubauskas ME, and Kindscher K. 2004. Beyond species richness: community similarity as a measure of cross-taxon congruence for coarse-filter conservation. Conserv Bio 18: 167–73.

Wilcove DS, Rothstein D, Dubow J, et al. 1998. Quantifying threats to imperiled species in the United States. BioScience 48: 607–15.

Wilson EO. 1999. The diversity of life. New York, NY: WW Norton and Co.

Wilson EO. 2002. The future of life. New York, NY: Knopf.

Here today, not gone tomorrow?

Evelyn Gaiser[1], Kristen Rosenfeld[2], Diane Ebert-May[3], Everett P Weber[3], and Amanda McConney[4]

Extinction has been a fact of life since long before humans arrived on Earth. Now that humans have contributed to the issues of scale and novel causes of endangered species, questions addressing how many species there are in the US, and which ones are at risk, are increasingly relevant. Wilcove and Master (pp 414–420) provide an estimate of the number of described species in the US that may be at risk of extinction, including neglected groups of species. The article highlights the opportunity that the NatureServe databases provide to search for rare plant and animal species by US county or watershed – in effect, in students' own backyards.

At first, it may appear that concepts about species extinction are not difficult for students to understand. However, students' misconceptions about this topic include the belief that the only important endangered species are the "charismatic megafauna", and that some populations in a community are not important, therefore their elimination has no effect (Munson 1994). Furthermore, students often assume that we know definitively how many species exist and how many are endangered.

■ Student goals

- Demonstrate skills in using web-based data.
- Calculate the proportion of major groups of endangered organisms and explain any variance among groups.
- Analyze, based on life-history strategies, why some species are endangered in a habitat and others are not.

■ Instructor goals

- Design active homework.
- Practice cooperative learning strategies in large classes.
- Use formative assessment data in class to identify student conceptions.
- Analyze summative assessment data to make decisions about instruction.

■ Instructional design

Pre-assessment at the end of previous class

Students write a minute paper about the following questions:
- What major groups of organisms are endangered in the US? What proportion of endangered species belong to each major group you identified?
- How do we know which species (or groups) are endangered?
- What are the major causes of species endangerment?

The instructor subsamples (if class is large) the responses and, at the beginning of the next class, reports trends to students.

[1]Florida International University, [2]North Carolina State University, [3]Michigan State University, [4]Archbold Biological Station

Active homework

Students read Wilcove and Master and use the NatureServe database to find out the status of all species in their home county. Record the name, group (eg mammals, birds, reptiles, amphibians, fish, invertebrates, plants, and fungi), and status of species in the GH, G1, and G2 categories. They then select a species from their county that is on the endangered list, read the comprehensive report, and print it out to bring to class. Based on the paper and website, they should write the best answers to the following questions:

1. What is the current population size of the species?
2. What is its range of distribution?
3. How does it reproduce? (How many offspring, how often, under what conditions?)
4. How does it disperse? (Is it territorial or does it have a large range? How are offspring/seeds/pollen distributed?)
5. Does it have any specific resource requirements (eg specific prey items, physicochemical needs).

■ In class

Process homework

When students arrive, there are large post-its with graphs of numbers of species versus conservation status (GH, G1, G2) for each of the eight major groups of organisms positioned around the room. In a large class use duplicate sets. Individuals write their species names on small post-its and plot them as a function of conservation status on the appropriate graphs. To avoid counting species more than once, students who have the same species should place their post-it notes on top of each other. When all the data are plotted, each student team is responsible for collecting and tabulating data from the large post-its. Ask individual students to quickly count the number of species per group of organisms. Each team then calculates the percentage of species (sum of GH, G1, G2) represented by each major group of organisms.

Ask groups of students to discuss, interpret the data on the graphs, and write one response per group (this reduces grading substantially) to the following questions:
1. Are the groups of organisms endangered in roughly the same proportion? If not, predict possible reasons why the proportions of groups vary.
2. Describe and explain any differences between the class proportions and those presented by Wilcove and Master.

Analysis

A mini-lecture addressing potential reasons for species vulnerability to extinction is intended to guide students through further analysis. The instructor calls on a sample of students to report the name of an endangered species they investigated, and fills in a table, as shown in Panel 1.

Panel I. Example: characteristics of endangered species in the Florida Everglades

Species	Pop size	Range	Reproduction	Mobility	Extinction cause	Requirements
Puma concolor coryi (Florida panther)	<50	South Florida swampland	90–96 d gestation, 2–3 offspring every 2 years, mature at 3 years	200–400 mi^2 range	Habitat and prey loss	Carnivore
Papilio aristodemus ponceanus - (Schaus' swallowtail)	<1000 (1989)	Dade and Monroe Counties, FL	Annual eggs; Lengthy pupal diapause	Does not migrate; very isolated	Habitat loss, pollutants	Larvae feed mainly on *Amyris elemifera* (highly seasonal plant)
Ammodramus maritimus mirabilis (Cape Sable sparrow)	6000 (1981)	South Florida wet grassland	3–4 eggs, 20 day parental care, nests flood-prone	Does not migrate; territorial	Habitat loss (wet grassland), poor habitat management	Invertebrates and grain
Galactia smallii (Small's milk pea)	11	Everglades pine rocklands	1–5 flowers that produce leguminous fruit	Localized populations	Fire repression, habitat loss	Rockland habitat

All data are from NatureServe.org

After some answers are recorded, the instructor provides additional data on endangered species and similar but not endangered relatives. In Panel 1 above, the instructors might compare *Galactia smallii* to *G floridana*, a widespread species that is not endangered (also found in the pine rocklands). A discussion of factors that might cause these two species to differ in their response to management can follow (eg genetic diversity, pollinator diversity, mode of reproduction and response to fire). See if students note that minimal information is available for many taxa, but is copious for the "charismatic megafauna".

■ Summative assessment

At the end of class, students write an extended response to the following questions: (1) What three general life-history attributes make a species more or less vulnerable to extinction? (2) State how each of these attributes affects extinction vulnerability and our ability to predict it.

■ Analysis of assessment

Student responses can provide the instructor with more information than merely "percent correct". By formally coding student responses, the instructor can determine misconceptions and gaps in student knowledge. An example for the assessment above is shown in Panel 2. The accuracy of the reasoning for each life-history trait described in each essay is tallied. By examining the finished data, the instructor can determine: (1) traits for which students provided correct reasoning; (2) traits students felt were important but were not sure why (trait listed without a reason); and (3) traits that students reasoned incorrectly, thereby illuminating possible misconceptions. Subsequent instruction can address vital concepts still missing from student understanding.

Panel 2. Sample concept tally sheet

Life-history attribute	Correct	Missing	Incorrect	Total
Range		/////		5
Reproduction	/			1
Mobility	///////	//	/	10
Population size	/	///	////	8
Extinction cause	///////	/		8
Resource specialization	////////	//	/	11

■ Final note

Student misconceptions uncovered in the assessment analysis probably also pertain to topics beyond threatened species, such as population dynamics, biodiversity, and functional groups. Many other ecological misconceptions are cited by Stamp and Armstrong (2005). The information gained from this analysis should be used to guide future instruction and assessment, to ensure that difficult concepts important to the discipline are achieved through active learning.

■ Acknowledgements

We thank the National Science Foundation for their long-term support of the FIRST project, Faculty Institutes for Reforming Science Teaching (DUE 0088847). All Pathways papers are peer reviewed.

■ References

Munson BH. 1994. Ecological misconceptions. *J Environ Educ* **25**: 30–34

Stamp N and Armstrong M. 2005. Overcoming ecological misconceptions. Binghamton University, State University of New York. http://ecomisconceptions.binghamton.edu/. Viewed 13 September 2005.

Chapter 7

Faculty: Moving from Assessment to Research

Overview

How do we determine if the innovations in our courses actually improve student learning? The tremendous amount of effort to develop and implement scientific teaching units in a course requires evidence in the form of assessment data that gives meaningful feedback to the instructor and students. This chapter describes a framework that can guide faculty towards research about their teaching and student learning. One trigger to move in this direction is when faculty realize that students are not learning what they expected them to learn. Identifying "what" students are not learning is often followed by the question, "Why aren't they learning that concept?" The decision to undergo systematic study of teaching practice and student learning to answer this question is important and takes time, just like the time and energy required to do scientific research.

When faculty inquire into learning, they draw on what they know and do as scientists. Once the question about learning is identified, the next step is to mine the assessment data available to determine the patterns of learning. With extended-response questions, classifying student responses for comprehension and higher-level thinking is accomplished by coding the data. These data are used to explore research questions about why students do not understand particular concepts. As in science, there is a literature base to consult, predictions to make, and a research design to determine. If the instructor is thinking about publishing the findings of the study in the literature, an application to the Institutional Review Board for human subjects is required. The intent of the papers in this chapter is to model the research process in several different contexts.

E-commerce and *Caulerpa*: unregulated dispersal of invasive species

Linda J Walters[1]*, Katherine R Brown[1], Wytze T Stam[2], and Jeanine L Olsen[2]

Professional aquarists and hobbyists are thought to be the source of invasions of the aquarium strain of the green macroalga *Caulerpa taxifolia* in the Mediterranean, southern California, and Australia. The US Department of Agriculture, Animal and Plant Health Inspection Service (USDA–APHIS) restricted interstate commerce and importation of the Mediterranean clone of *C taxifolia* prior to the California invasion and is currently deciding if it should strengthen regulation of this genus as more species of *Caulerpa* are being described as invasive. Here we document the importance of e-commerce as a mode of dispersal for many species of *Caulerpa* in the United States. We purchased *Caulerpa* from 30 internet retailers and 60 internet auction sites representing 25 states and Great Britain. Twelve different *Caulerpa* species were confirmed using DNA sequencing. Only 10.6% of sellers provided the correct genus and species names with their shipments. Thirty purchases of "live rock" provided four species of *Caulerpa*, as well as 53 additional marine species. Our results confirm the extensive e-commerce availability of this invasive genus and its high dispersal potential via postal services and hobbyists. We recommend that both eBay and the USDA maximize regulation of *Caulerpa*.

Front Ecol Environ 2006; 4(2): 75–79

Many species of the green macroalga *Caulerpa* (Chlorophyta: Ulvophyceae) are highly invasive and the economics and ecological impacts associated with these introductions are well documented (eg de Villèle and Verlaque 1995; Davis *et al.* 1997; Meinesz 1999; Williams and Grosholz 2002a). For example, monocultures of the aquarium strain of *Caulerpa taxifolia* extend hundreds of kilometers along the Mediterranean coastline (Meinesz *et al.* 2001), have clogged nine waterways in New South Wales and two more in South Australia (Schaffelke *et al.* 2002; Millar 2004; A Davis pers comm), and infested two lagoons in southern California (Jousson *et al.* 2000). In all cases, this invasive strain of *C taxifolia* grew faster, larger, and in deeper and colder waters than its native tropical counterpart (Belsher and Meinesz 1995; Williams and Grosholz 2002b). DNA studies confirmed that the aquarium strain of *C taxifolia* originated near Brisbane, Australia, and was subsequently transported via the aquarium trade (Jousson *et al.* 1998; Wiedenmann *et al.* 2001; Muesnier *et al.* 2002). In the Mediterranean and the Canary Islands, *Caulerpa racemosa* is now also recognized as invasive (Verlaque *et al.* 2003, 2004). Similarly, non-native *Caulerpa brachypus* was first recognized in southeastern Florida waters in 2001, where extensive blooms were overgrowing or displacing native flora and fauna (Jacoby *et al.* 2004).

Despite its invasive reputation, many members of the genus *Caulerpa* (especially *C racemosa*, *C prolifera*, and some of the "feather *Caulerpas*": *C taxifolia*, *C sertularioides*, and *C mexicana*) remain extremely popular with aquarium hobbyists because they are attractive in salt water tanks and are easy to clonally propagate (Smith and Walters 1999; Padilla and Williams 2004). The genus *Caulerpa* is also touted by hobbyists for its many additional virtues, most notably its ability to remove nutrients from closed aquarium systems and to act as fish food. However, as their aquaria become overgrown or situations change, hobbyists may either sell their extra stock on eBay or dispose of their unwanted algae (and animals) in nearby waters, thus setting the stage for a new invasion (Whitfield *et al.* 2002; Semmens *et al.* 2004).

"Live rock" is extremely popular with aquarists because it is inexpensive, and can potentially harbor a huge diversity of marine organisms (including *Caulerpa* spp). Many consider it to be an essential component of saltwater aquariums, as it acts as a substrate for sessile species, a refuge for fishes and mobile invertebrates, and as a biological filtration system. Live rock consists of either pieces of hard coral directly harvested from reefs or rocks allowed to cure under aquaculture conditions.

In response to a stakeholder request, the Mediterranean clone of *C taxifolia* was added to the Noxious Species List in 1999 by the US Department of Agriculture, Animal and Plant Health Inspection Service (USDA–APHIS), making interstate transport and importation illegal. Only the Mediterranean clone was included in this initial request. The term "Mediterranean clone" has been replaced by the more neutral "aquarium strain" by many scientists, and this term will be used here.

In 2001, California imposed stricter guidelines than the Federal Government in response to the two southern

[1]*Department of Biology, University of Central Florida, Orlando, FL 32816 USA* *(ljwalter@pegasus.cc.ucf.edu); [2]Department of Marine Biology, Center for Ecological and Evolutionary Studies, University of Groningen, The Netherlands*

Californian invasions by the aquarium strain of *C taxifolia*; it became illegal to sell or possess *C taxifolia* or eight other species, some of which are easily confused with *C taxifolia* (*C mexicana*, *C sertulariodes*, *C ashmeadii*, *C floridana*, *C cupressoides*), and others that are considered invasive (*C racemosa*, *C scalpelliformis*, *C verticillata*). The city of San Diego took this a step further and made it illegal to possess any species of *Caulerpa*. There has been local success in eradicating *Caulerpa* in southern California, but at a cost of over $5 million (R Woodfield pers comm). Now a more concerted approach is necessary at the national level. The Aquatic Nuisance Species (ANS) Task Force released a National Management Plan for the genus *Caulerpa* in the fall of 2005, focused on supporting *Caulerpa* research and outreach, and the USDA–APHIS is currently considering whether to enhance regulation of this genus. Although both the ANS Task Force and USDA–APHIS acknowledge the potential importance of e-commerce as a mode of dispersal for these species, until now the importance of this vector has not been directly measured.

■ Methods

Between April 2003 and April 2005, using our central Florida address, we determined the diversity and availability of *Caulerpa* species via e-commerce and local retail outlets. The study involved 22 volunteers and over 200 internet search hours; we therefore consider our findings to be representative of the online availability of the genus. Volunteers chose their search dates and each time a volunteer began a search, he/she had 48 hours to find all the sources of *Caulerpa* available via online retail and eBay auctions, using their own choice of keywords. Keywords ranged from the obvious (eg *Caulerpa*, macroalgae) to less obvious terms, such as refugia, sea grapes, or marine cactus. Online purchases were made once from each dealer with any species of *Caulerpa* in stock, and from all unique eBay auctions that we won between March 11 and November 16, 2004 and between February 1 and March 18, 2005. We purchased *Caulerpa* from 51% of the online retailers we identified (*Caulerpa* was frequently out of stock) and 44% of the auctions. In addition, we obtained *Caulerpa* spp from 25 of 47 (53%) saltwater aquarium retail shops in central Florida (all Yellow Page-listed shops in the Tampa, Orlando, and Daytona Beach areas). We compared our data to those of Zaleski and Murray (in press), who conducted a similar survey of 50 southern California retailers between November 2000 and August 2001.

To determine the likelihood of purchasing live rock with *Caulerpa* growing on it, we purchased rocks from ten online retailers, ten eBay auctions, and ten local retailers during the same periods as described above. On the internet, "live rock" was the only keyword we used and we purchased it from the first ten retailers and eBay auctions we encountered that would sell us quantities of 10 kg or less.

Many distributors only wanted to supply 100 kg or more, shipped directly from the country of origin. All of the purchased live rock was maintained in separate, recirculating aquaria for 1 month.

■ Results and discussion

From 90 internet sites (30 online commercial retailers and 60 eBay auctions), *Caulerpa* spp were shipped to central Florida from shipping addresses in Great Britain and 25 US states, 52% of which were landlocked (Figures 1 and 2). Figures 1 and 2 document extensive interstate transport of this genus, especially via eBay. We separated our purchases into online retail versus eBay auctions for two reasons. First, internet retailers should be aware of federal regulations pertaining to the organisms they sell as part of their livelihood, while this may or may not be the case with eBay vendors, many of whom are home hobbyists. Information about restrictions on shipping *Caulerpa* to California was found on only two of the 30 retail websites from which we purchased material. eBay states that sellers are responsible for knowing all federal and state regulations for all live plants, animals, or animal products they sell and that vendors stand to have their accounts suspended and forfeit all eBay fees on the cancelled listings for breaking federal regulations. Of the 60 eBay auctions we won, only three vendors included information showing that they were aware of the restrictions on interstate transport of *Caulerpa*. In addition, one eBay vendor of *C prolifera* proudly, and correctly, stated that this species was permitted in, and could be shipped to, California. We never saw the aquarium strain of *C taxifolia* specifically listed on eBay, but "feather *Caulerpa*" was frequently seen for sale. Twelve of the 30 internet retailers were located in Florida and collected macroalgae locally, on demand. We also bought from two out-of-state retailers that supply live

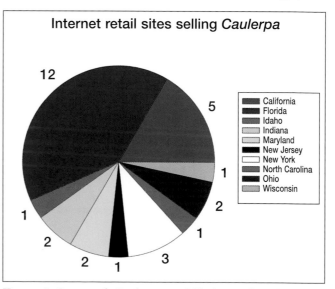

Figure 1. *States with* Caulerpa *available for purchase from commercial internet retailers. Numbers associated with pie-charts indicate the number of retailers.*

materials to educational institutions that contracted with south Florida harvesters to supply *Caulerpa* as needed. Thus, 47% of our internet retail purchases never crossed state lines. *Caulerpa* spp were purchased from seven eBay auctions listing Florida as their address (12%). This suggests much greater interstate dispersal of *Caulerpa* from eBay auctions than from internet retailers. It is also important to note that all of our purchases were delivered via the US postal service or one of many private shipping services; USDA–APHIS has no direct regulatory inspection authority over these entities.

Caulerpa costs varied greatly among sellers, with the least expensive being local retailers. The average cost for a handful of any species of the genus *Caulerpa* locally was $4.00. Not included in this average is the free *Caulerpa* that we received from 43% of the local retailers. We always purchased the smallest amount available online. Units of purchase also varied greatly among dealers, ranging from 2–3 individuals to enough to fill a quart-size plastic bag (22 x 17 cm) to "enough for a class of 35 students". The average cost for any single species of *Caulerpa* from internet retailers was $43.08, and $18.09 from eBay. In both cases, this price included packing and shipping charges, which ranged from $10 to over $35 per shipment.

From all purchased material, 13 different *Caulerpa* species were identified by us at the University of Groningen, using DNA sequencing (Figure 3). Details of all sequences and relationships for all collections, along with those of Zaleski and Murray (in press), will soon be submitted to GenBank and for publication (Stam *et al.* unpublished). Four species were available from all sources, whereas *C cupressoides* was only available via the internet (Figure 3). Of the 12 species shipped to central Florida, two species, *Caulerpa serrulata* and *C taxifolia*, have not been reported in Florida's coastal waters (Littler and Littler 2000; C Glardon pers comm).

Specimens of *C taxifolia* were purchased only once, from a southern California internet retailer (November 2004) and were listed online as "green feather *Caulerpa*". It proved to be the non-invasive type, based on DNA sequence analysis (Stam *et al.* unpublished). The one finding of *C taxifolia* suggests that this species is not being widely distributed in the US via e-commerce, hopefully as a result of awareness campaigns and USDA–APHIS regulations. The potential success of this early (pre-California invasion) USDA decision to restrict the aquarium strain of *C taxifolia* indicates that a genus-wide ban could be very effective in preventing future invasions and associated, extremely costly eradication efforts.

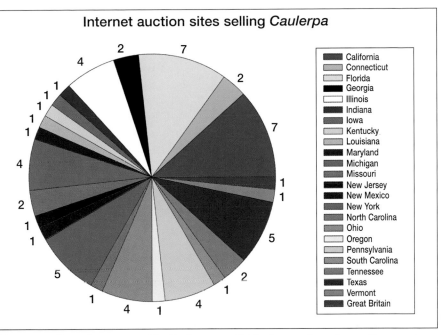

Figure 2. *States/countries with* Caulerpa *available for purchase from eBay auctions. Numbers associated with pie-charts indicate the number of auctions.*

Reported origins of live rock included Haiti, the Caribbean, Florida Keys, Marshall Islands, Pohnpei, Fiji, Tonga, Samoa and Vanuatu. Following one-month laboratory cultivation, we observed *C racemosa, C sertularioides, C mexicana,* and *C verticillata,* plus 25 other species of macroalgae, 27 species of invertebrates, and multiple species of cyanobacteria. In many cases, *Caulerpa* was not visible on the rocks until the fourth week of cultivation. Costs of live rock ranged from $20.29 per pound from internet retailers, $6.82 per pound from eBay vendors (both include shipping), to $7.23 per pound from local retailers.

From our e-commerce purchases, we learned that both retailers and eBay vendors frequently do not identify their product scientifically, by including the genus and species (14.1% included both genus and species). When all purchases were considered, sellers correctly identified *Caulerpa* at the species level only 10.6% of the time. Misidentifications at the species level occurred 3.5% of the time (all associated with "feather *Caulerpas*"), while only the name *Caulerpa* (or green *Caulerpa* or *Caulerpa* algae) was used 15.7% of the time. The genus name *Caulerpa* plus a common name descriptor (eg grape *Caulerpa*, feather *Caulerpa*) was used in 44.4% of cases, while only a common name (eg grape weed, fern algae, etc) was used 11.1% of the time. The term "green macroalgae" was used 5.1% of the time and the term "fish food" was used on one occasion. At the genus level, mistakes occurred in 9.6% of cases. This is in part because *Caulerpa* is a popular internet keyword, which encourages sellers to mislabel their stock. We found: "red grape *Caulerpa*" (actually *Botrycladia*), "red feather *Caulerpa*" (actually *Gelidiella*), "red *Gracilaria Caulerpa*" (actually *Gracilaria*), "lettuce *Caulerpa*" (actually *Ulva*), "*Caulerpa Halimeda* macroalgae" (actually *Halimeda opuntia*), and

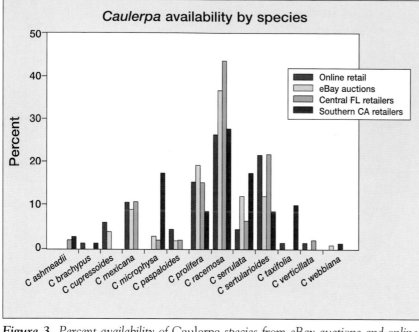

Figure 3. *Percent availability of* Caulerpa *species from eBay auctions and online, Central Florida, and Southern California retail sources.*

"*Chaetomorpha Caulerpa*" (actually *Chaetomorpha*). This high level of unreliability and variability makes both morphological identification by customs agents and internet tracking of *Caulerpa* difficult.

Finally, we discovered that *Caulerpa*, especially species of *Caulerpa* with feathery blades, was frequently pictured in entire aquarium set-ups for sale on internet auction sites. Items had to be collected in person, so we were able to acquire *C racemosa* and *C mexicana* by this means from only one auction initiated in Clermont, Florida. In total, ten states were represented in 13 auctions for complete, 30–120-gallon tank set-ups.

■ Improving the future

Internet availability of the genus *Caulerpa*, as well as numerous other algal species and invertebrates, represents a serious threat to Florida's coastlines in terms of non-native introductions from hobbyists. The $5 million spent on *Caulerpa* eradication in California would be equivalent to 142 857 purchases of loose *Caulerpa* at an average of $35 per purchase. If 1% of these hobbyists dumped *Caulerpa* into nearby waters and 1% of these releases became established, then at least $70 million (14 eradications x $5 million/response) will be required to achieve eradication. Pressuring eBay to eliminate all auctions of *Caulerpa* and enhanced federal regulation of *Caulerpa* would be considerably more cost-effective.

Commercial retail of invasive species is not limited to marine macroalgae or live rock. For example, Semmens *et al.* (2004) found 16 species of non-native, marine fishes in Florida waters; their data suggest aquarium dumping as the source for all these species. Only limited information was available online and in local retail shops to alert con-

sumers to the dangers of "aquarium dumping". Locally, only two of 47 retailers had signs asking patrons not to dump unwanted organisms. On the internet, we found only six distributors (five retailers, one eBay auction) who warned against aquarium dumping. This limited amount of warning on improper disposal of unwanted marine organisms indicates that more and better outreach is needed. A new website, www.habitattitude.net, was recently created for just this reason. This national initiative has been developed by the ANS Task Force and the aquarium, pet, nursery, and landscape industries to raise consumer awareness about invasive species and alternatives to release of unwanted organisms into the wild. A number of other partners are also involved, including US and state-level Fish and Wildlife Services and the National Sea Grant College Program. By engaging and receiving support from the industries that distribute non-native flora and fauna for the first time, this outreach program has a much greater chance of success than previous federal and state-level efforts that operated on a more confrontational level. To date, only a limited number of retail outlets and suppliers have shown interest, but expectations are high that this campaign will help reduce the number of releases of invasive species in terrestrial, fresh, and marine systems.

■ Acknowledgements

We thank P Sacks, C Glardon, M Black, and all the searchers. For funding, we thank the National and Florida Sea Grant College Programs, Pinellas County Environmental Fund, Tampa Bay Estuary Program, Florida Department of Agriculture, University of Groningen, and the University of Central Florida. Suggestions by P Windle substantially improved this manuscript.

■ References

Belsher T and Meinesz A. 1995. Deep water dispersal of the tropical alga *Caulerpa* taxifolia introduced into the Mediterranean. *Aquat Bot* **51**: 163–69.

Davis A, Roberts D, and Cummins S. 1997. Rapid invasion of a sponge-dominated deep-reef by *Caulerpa scalpelliformis* (Chlorophyta) in Botany Bay. *Aust J Ecol* **22**: 146–50.

de Villèle X and Verlaque M. 1995. Changes and degradation in a *Posidonia oceanica* bed invaded by the introduced tropical alga *Caulerpa taxifolia* in the north western Mediterranean. *Bot Mar* **38**: 79–87.

Jacoby C, Lapointe B, and Creswell L. 2004. Are native and non-indigenous seaweeds overgrowing Florida's east coast reefs? Gainesville, FL: Florida Sea Grant College Program SGEF-156.

Jousson O, Pawlowksi J, Zaninetti L, *et al.* 1998. Molecular evidence for the aquarium origin of the green alga *Caulerpa taxifo-*

lia introduced to the Mediterranean Sea. *Mar Ecol Prog Ser* **172**: 275–80.

Jousson O, Pawlowski J, Zaninetti L, *et al.* 2000. Invasive alga reaches California. *Nature* **408**: 157–58.

Littler D and Littler M. 2000. Caribbean reef plants. Washington, DC: OffShore Graphics, Inc.

Meinesz A. 1999. Killer algae. Chicago, IL: University of Chicago Press.

Meinesz A, Belsher T, Thibault T, *et al.* 2001. The introduced green alga *Caulerpa taxifolia* continues to spread in the Mediterranean. *Biol Invas* **3**: 201–10.

Meusnier I, Valero M, Destombe C, *et al.* 2002. Polymerase chain reaction-single strand conformation polymorphism analyses of nuclear and chloroplast DNA provide evidence for recombination, multiple introductions and nascent speciation in the *Caulerpa taxifolia* complex. *Mol Ecol* **11**: 2317–25.

Millar A. 2004. New records of marine benthic algae from New South Wales, eastern Australia. *Phycol Res* **52**: 117–28.

Padilla D and Williams S. 2004. Beyond ballast water: aquarium and ornamental trades as sources of invasive species in aquatic ecosystems. *Front Ecol Environ* **2**: 131–38.

Schaffelke B, Murphy N, and Uthicke S. 2002. Using genetic techniques to investigate the sources of the invasive alga *Caulerpa taxifolia* in three new locations in Australia. *Mar Pollut Bull* **44**: 204–10.

Semmens B, Buhle E, Salomon A, and Pattengill-Semmens C. 2004. A hotspot of non-native marine fishes: evidence for the aquarium trade as an invasion pathway. *Mar Ecol Prog Ser* **266**: 239–44.

Smith C and Walters L. 1999. Fragmentation as a strategy for *Caulerpa* species: fates of fragments and implications for management of an invasive weed. *PSZN I: Mar Ecol* **20**: 307–19.

Verlaque M, Afonso-Carrillo J, Candelaria Gil-Rodríguez M, *et al.* 2004. Blitzkrieg in a marine invasion: *Caulerpa racemosa* var. *cylindracea* (Bryopsidales, Chlorophyta) reaches the Canary Islands (north-east Atlantic). *Biol Invas* **6**: 269–81.

Verlaque M, Durand C, Huisman J, *et al.* 2003. On the identity and origin of the Mediterranean invasive *Caulerpa racemosa* (Caulerpales, Chlorophyta). *Eur J Phycol* **38**: 325–39.

Whitfield P, Gardner T, Vives S, *et al.* 2002. Biological invasions of the Indo-Pacific lionfish (*Pterois volitans*) along the Atlantic coast of North America. *Mar Ecol Prog Ser* **235**: 289–97.

Wiedenmann J, Baumstark A, Pillen TL, *et al.* 2001. DNA fingerprints of *Caulerpa taxifolia* provide evidence for the introduction of an aquarium strain into the Mediterranean Sea and its close relationship to an Australian population. *Mar Biol* **138**: 229–34.

Williams E and Grosholz E. 2002a. International *Caulerpa taxifolia* Conference Proceedings. California Sea Grant College Program, University of California, La Jolla, Pub No T-047.

Williams S and Grosholz E. 2002b. Preliminary reports from the *Caulerpa taxifolia* invasion in southern California. *Mar Ecol Prog Ser* **233**: 307–10.

Williams S and Schroeder S. 2004. Eradication of the invasive seaweed *Caulerpa taxifolia* by chlorine bleach. *Mar Ecol Prog Ser* **272**: 69–76.

Zaleski S and Murray S. Taxonomic diversity, geographic distribution, and commercial availability of aquarium-traded species of *Caulerpa* (Chlorophyta, Caulerpaceae) in southern California, USA. *Mar Ecol Prog Ser.* In press.

Bridging the pathway from instruction to research

Janet M Batzli[1], Diane Ebert-May[2], and Janet Hodder[3]

The Pathways articles to date were intended to engage faculty in teaching, learning, and assessment, especially in large enrollment courses. The challenge for many faculty who have changed their courses is to determine if the innovations actually improve student learning. This leads some faculty towards research models that require empirical evidence based on student assessment data.

Here we describe a framework for research on scientific teaching. Articles in subsequent months will provide practical advice for faculty who are interested in classroom research. We will use constructivist theories of how people learn (ie existing knowledge is used to build new knowledge; Bransford *et al.* 1999) to explore questions about how students actively gain meaningful understanding (Ausubel 2000). We also provide examples of research strategies and how one might gather evidence to assess changes in student learning.

■ Inquiry into students' learning

Recognizing a problem in student learning

To scientists who have committed their lives to education, research, and the pursuit of knowledge, it may take a great deal of self-reflection and bouts of frustration to arrive at the question, "Why aren't students learning in my course?" This is the first and most important step for catalyzing change.

Self-reflection

In order to understand the extent of the problem, instructors must look closely at individual student work and talk with students who show indications of low achievement in class. "What does student work tell you about their learning? What are your assumptions and the variables you need to recognize to effectively interpret student work?" Each teacher will have a different take on these questions and will approach the problem from a unique perspective. The direction taken will be a discovery process for newcomers to this type of inquiry, and questions of confidence may arise as instructors go beyond their comfort zone of disciplinary expertise. Perhaps you recognize yourself in the statement, "I was not formally trained to do this. I don't know anything about educational research".

At this point it may be helpful to think about your interest in and reasons for pursuing inquiry into learning.

How much time, energy, and support do you have to commit to classroom research? What are your goals? Is the inquiry purely for yourself and your students' benefit? Or do you plan to share your investigation with others? Perhaps you are in a position where you need to convince others about the value of your instructional strategies, course, curriculum, or program. At what stage are you in your career? Is teaching excellence recognized as the basis for promotion and tenure? From a practical point of view, Kreber (2002) provides helpful descriptions of teacher development along a continuum of inquiry into learning, starting with the *effective* or *excellent teacher*, and *expert teacher*, to those who fully engage as *teaching scholars*. Through self-reflection, energy and time, effective or excellent teachers provide the most stimulating and inspiring learning environment possible, convey concepts in an active way, and help students overcome difficulty in their learning. The expert goes an additional step, consulting literature on pedagogy, attending workshops, and entering into a discourse with colleagues about teaching and learning. Research on teaching and learning starts with self-reflection and conversations with colleagues. A growing number of educators are going even further to pursue scholarship in their teaching, seeking ways to publish their work in a peer reviewed setting. Most importantly, instructors must remind themselves explicitly that one does not have to be a teaching scholar to help students learn.

Diving deeper, doing research

As teachers undergo systematic study of their own practice and student learning, they develop greater insight into potential problems. Undoubtedly, many of the issues that arise are connected with motivating students to think critically and inspiring them to take ownership and initiative for their own learning.

Using an example from this issue of *Frontiers* (Walters *et al.* pp 75–79), we outline a general framework for moving beyond instruction to investigating a research question. In this case, we examine students' ability to demonstrate critical thinking about ill-structured problems (ie those that cannot be described with a high degree of completeness or solved with a high degree of certainty; eg overpopulation), in contrast to well-structured problems, (ie those with a high degree of completeness, certainty, and correctness; eg a puzzle; King and Kitchner 1994). We designed an ill-structured problem (Panel 1) that integrates several ecological topics, including invasion biology, weed ecology, biodiversity, community dynamics, and population growth, as a starting point to discuss a research approach

[1]*University of Wisconsin,* [2]*Michigan State University,* [3]*University of Oregon*

Panel 1. Example problem about invasive species
(species and biology are accurate; the situation is hypothetical)

San Diego Daily News
The green creep: killer algae
An environmental monitoring team associated with Southern California Caulerpa Action Team plans to release thousands of non-native tropical sea slugs (*Elysia subornata*; Mollusca) into a coastal lagoon in Southern California over the next two summers, in an effort to control the spread of an invasive green algae (*Caulerpa taxifolia*). This plant, dubbed "killer algae" by European scientists following Alexandre Meinesz's 1999 book by the same name, spreads "like cancer" and is difficult to control, given its broad environmental tolerance and few predators. The monitoring team has tried covering *Caulerpa* stands with tarps and then applying chlorine underneath the covering. They plan to test the effectiveness of the sea slugs as a biological control for the *Caulerpa*. This project follows previous laboratory and field studies with sea slugs in experimental pools, which resulted in successful eradication of *C taxifolia*. If the sea slugs fail, this invasive alga will pose a substantial threat to marine ecosystems in California, particularly to the extensive eelgrass meadows and other benthic environments that make coastal waters a rich and productive environment. Is release of *E subornata* into California coastal waters a reasonable and promising plan for control of *Caulerpa*?

Questions to consider:
• The words "invasive species" are in the news all the time. How do we know, and what is the evidence, that this species of alga is invasive?
• What is the basis for the threat of *C taxifolia* on California's marine ecosystems?
• What are the risks and benefits for release of *E subornata* into the coastal lagoon?
• What are the alternatives for controlling the spread of *Caulerpa*? Are these reasonable, good alternatives?
• On what basis would the research team make their decision about the effectiveness of *E subornata* as a biological control agent?
• What information do you need and what basic assumptions would you consider to estimate the impact of releasing *E subornata* into this coastal lagoon?

to analyze students' critical thinking. The learning objectives and instructor's research goals provided below are general enough to be customized to different courses.

Learning objectives for critical thinking

Students should be able to:
• Generate questions and identify important variables and assumptions associated with an ill-structured problem.
• Gather information and data from the literature to help generate a logical argument and inform decisions.
• Describe and explain limits of an argument based on assumptions and analysis of the strength of evidence, and present potential consequences and alternative solutions.
• Construct a model or design an experiment that informs decision making for solving a complex problem.

Research goals

• Use pre-test data to pose a specific question about student

critical thinking that can be investigated empirically (see March 2005 Pathways article for types of questions).
• Use a rubric designed to evaluate aspects of critical thinking revealed in student work.
• Develop a coding scheme to categorize student responses within the context of the rubric and to help generate evidence to explain student reasoning.
• Combine quantitative and qualitative student data to draw conclusions about the effectiveness of an instructional strategy to promote student critical thinking.

■ Process of inquiry into student learning

Before presenting students with the ill-structured problem, instructors should consider developing a pre-test to reveal preconceptions and identify learning issues or potential difficulties. Pre-tests can be developed to uncover misconceptions in multiple-choice format, using alternative concepts as strong distracters. Alternatively, short answer responses may provide information to help define the level of expectations for the assignment and to gauge the instructional pace and how to stage the activity.

Example pre-test

1. What characteristic(s) do you think make a species invasive?
2. What characteristic(s) do you think make a habitat susceptible to invasion by a non-native species?
3. Name an example of an invasive species that you know of and explain:
   • What characteristics have allowed it to invade habitats easily?
   • What are the consequences of invasion?

Implementing classroom instruction

Instructors could stage an activity based on an ill-structured problem (Panel 1) by directing students to form smaller groups through informal "turn-to-your-neighbor" clusters or use of established groups. The instructor may choose to give students some background information in the form of homework reading or mini-lectures, or have them find information entirely on their own. The activity should prompt initial questions that serve as a springboard for further investigation. The method by which students get their information in a more or less guided way is important when considering the level of student investment and ownership in their argument and proposed solution. By facilitating greater student autonomy in the classroom, instructors shift the spotlight off of themselves, helping to create a student-centered rather than instructor-centered classroom (Finkel and Monk 1983).

Evaluating student work

Instructors should design assignments that allow students to

Panel 2. Example rubric

Excerpt from Facione and Facione (1994) developed through iterative testing and validation. Criteria at each level explicitly define instructor expectations associated with critical thinking evident in student responses. Two of the four levels are described as follows:

Level 4 defines student responses that:
"Consistently do all or almost all of the following: accurately interprets evidence, statements, graphics, questions. Identifies the salient arguments (reasons and claims) pro and con. Thoughtfully analyzes and evaluates major alternative points of view. Draws warranted, judicious, non-fallacious conclusions. Justifies key results and procedures, explains assumptions and reasons. Fair-mindedly follows where evidence and reasons lead."

Level 1 defines student responses that:
"Consistently do all or almost all of the following: offers biased interpretations of evidence, statements, graphics, questions, information, or the points of views of others. Fails to identify or hastily dismisses strong, relevant counter-arguments. Ignores or superficially evaluates obvious alternative points of view. Argues, using fallacious or irrelevant reasons and unwarranted claims. Does not justify results or procedures, nor explain reasons. Regardless of the evidence or reasons, maintains or defends views based on self-interest or preconceptions. Exhibits close-mindedness or hostility to reason."

---

articulate their understanding of the problem, the variables involved, and potential solutions. The final product may be in the form of an individual or group paper, poster, oral presentation, or public debate. Regardless of the format, the assignment should require that students prepare a document that allows examination of their argument, rationale, and logic. When it comes to evaluating student work, particularly written work that is difficult to assess with an entirely objective eye, rubrics are an essential evaluation tool.

Rubrics define instructor's expectations and criteria explicitly for each level of achievement. There are many rubrics available, as well as tools to help instructors make their own (Ebert-May 1999; Taggart *et al.* 2001). Often used solely for grading, rubrics are equally useful for initial evaluation of student responses in answer to a research question. Once expectations are defined in the rubric, the instructor should share it with the students, as part of the assignment. As an example (Panel 2), an excerpt from a general rubric developed by Facione and Facione (1994) may be particularly useful to help guide evaluation of critical thinking.

As roles change from instructor to researcher, it is important to calibrate the rubric, based on the learning goals for the specific problem. The process of developing a rubric for research purposes is iterative – initial criteria are defined and, with further use, refined so that student achievement levels are clear to all evaluators. Once researchers have categorized student responses using a rubric, they can look closely within categories to classify elements of the argument or reasoning and identify patterns of student thinking.

Classifying student use of particular words or phrases, assumptions and alternative explanations often leads to further inquiry by the researcher. Questions may include

why students responded the way they did and if the response is cognitively relevant or an artifact of an ambiguous problem or instructional design. These types of questions are fuel for further investigations that may include surveys, interviews, and student self-reflection.

■ Final note

As faculty apply scientific curiosity, creativity, and reasoning skills in the classroom, they begin to pose questions such as:

- Are students achieving content objectives as well as developing higher-level thinking skills?
- Are students becoming more sophisticated in their ability to develop solutions to ill-structured problems?

Scholarly investigations about teaching and learning will contribute toward achieving excellence in undergraduate science education. When scientists critically examine and report their students' accomplishments in response to their instructional innovations, our understanding of "what works" in our courses will expand and catalyze further investigations. Ultimately, we encourage instructors to make their teaching and inquiry into students' learning visible to their colleagues and the public.

■ Acknowledgements

We thank the National Science Foundation for their long-term support of the FIRST project, Faculty Institutes for Reforming Science Teaching (DUE 0088847). All Pathways papers are peer reviewed.

■ References

Ausubel D. 2000. The acquisition and retention of knowledge: a cognitive view. Boston, MA: Kluwer Publishers.

Bransford JD, Brown AL, and Cocking RR (Eds). 1999. How people learn. Washington, DC: National Academy Press.

Ebert-May D. 1999. Scoring rubrics. National Institute for Science Education. Madison, WI: University of Wisconsin. www.flaguide.org/cat/rubrics/rubrics7.htm. Viewed 10 Feb 2006.

Ebert-May D, Batzli J, and Lim H. 2003. Disciplinary research strategies for assessment of learning. *BioScience* **53**: 1221–28.

Facione PA and Facione NC. 1994. Holistic critical thinking scoring rubric. Millbrae, CA: California Academic Press. www.insightassessment.com/pdf_files/rubric.pdf. Viewed 10 February 2006.

Finkel DL and Monk GS. 1983. Teachers and learning groups: a dissolution of the atlas complex. In: Bouton C and Garth RY (Eds). Learning in groups. New directions for teaching and learning 14. San Francisco, CA: Jossey-Bass.

King PM and Kitchner KS. 1994. Developing reflective judgement: understanding and promoting intellectual growth and critical thinking in adolescents and adults. San Francisco, CA: Jossey-Bass.

Kreber C. 2002. Teaching excellence, teaching expertise, and the scholarship of teaching. *Innov High Educ* **27**: 5–23.

Meinesz A. 1999 Killer algae. Chicago, IL: University of Chicago Press.

Taggart GL, Phifer SJ, Nixon JA, and Wood M. 2001. Rubrics: a handbook for construction and use. Lanham, MD: Scarecrow Press.

Will human-induced changes in seawater chemistry alter the distribution of deep-sea scleractinian corals?

John M Guinotte[1,2], James Orr[3], Stephen Cairns[4], Andre Freiwald[5], Lance Morgan[1], and Robert George[6]

The answer to the title question is uncertain, as very few manipulative experiments have been conducted to test how deep-sea scleractinians (stony corals) react to changes in seawater chemistry. Ocean pH and calcium carbonate saturation are decreasing due to an influx of anthropogenic CO_2 to the atmosphere. Experimental evidence has shown that declining carbonate saturation inhibits the ability of marine organisms to build calcium carbonate skeletons, shells, and tests. Here we put forward a hypothesis suggesting that the global distribution of deep-sea scleractinian corals could be limited in part by the depth of the aragonite saturation horizon (ASH) in the world's oceans. Aragonite is the metastable form of calcium carbonate used by scleractinian corals to build their skeletons and the ASH is the limit between saturated and undersaturated water. The hypothesis is tested by reviewing the distribution of deep-sea, bioherm-forming scleractinian corals with respect to the depth of the ASH. Results indicate that > 95% of 410 coral locations occurred in saturated waters during pre-industrial times. Projections indicate that about 70% of these locations will be in undersaturated waters by 2099. Lab experimentation, in situ experimentation, and monitoring efforts are needed to quantify the effects of changing seawater chemistry on deep-sea coral ecosystems.

Front Ecol Environ 2006; 4(3): 141–146

Seawater chemistry and the calcium carbonate saturation state of the world's oceans are changing as a result of the addition of fossil fuel CO_2 to the atmosphere (Kleypas *et al*. 1999; Feely *et al*. 2004; Orr *et al*. 2005). The pH of surface oceans has dropped by 0.1 units since the industrial revolution and if fossil fuel combustion continues at present rates, the pH of the world's oceans will prob-

ably drop another 0.3 to 0.4 units by 2100 (Mehrbach *et al*. 1973; Lueker *et al*. 2000; Caldeira and Wickett 2003). "This influx of anthropogenic CO_2 is causing the world's oceans to become more acidic, to the detriment of corals and other marine calcifiers, including plankton, which occupies the base of marine food webs. Corals and some species of plankton (coccolithophores and foraminiferans) use carbonate ions obtained from the surrounding water to build their skeletons and protective shells. As oceanic pH and carbonate ions decrease as a result of rising fossil fuel CO_2 levels, the calcification mechanisms and abilities of many marine organisms will be negatively impacted.

In recent decades, only half of anthropogenic CO_2 has remained in the atmosphere; the other half has been taken up by the terrestrial biosphere (20%) and the oceans (30%) (Feely *et al* 2004; Sabine *et al* 2004). This uptake initiates a series of chemical reactions, increasing the hydrogen ion concentration (H^+), lowering pH, and reducing the number of carbonate (CO_3^{2-}) ions available in seawater. All of this will make it more difficult for marine calcifying organisms to form biogenic calcium carbonate ($CaCO_3$). Although little is known about the effects of decreasing aragonite saturation state on deep-sea corals, lab experiments have conclusively shown that lowering carbonate ion concentration reduces calcification rates in tropical reef builders by 7–40% (Gattuso *et al*. 1999; Langdon *et al*. 2000, 2003; Marubini *et al*. 2003). In fact, all marine calcifying organisms tested to date have shown a similar negative response to decreasing carbonate saturation state. As the world's oceans become less saturated over time, corals are expected to build weaker

In a nutshell:

- Anthropogenic CO_2 from the combustion of fossil fuels is altering the chemistry of the world's oceans
- Seawater chemistry changes have the potential to alter the distribution and abundance of marine organisms that use calcium carbonate to build their shells and skeletons (corals, plankton, etc) and the organisms that depend on them for survival (fishes, marine mammals, etc)
- Major funding and experimentation is needed to quantify the effects of changing seawater chemistry on marine calcifiers; experimentation should be a top priority for countries with commercial industries dependent on deep-sea coral bioherms
- The transition from fossil fuels to alternative "clean" sources of energy needs to occur as soon as possible

[1]*Marine Conservation Biology Institute, 2122 112th Ave NE, Bellevue, WA, USA (john@mcbi.org)*; [2]*School of Tropical Environment Studies and Geography, James Cook University, Townsville, Australia*; [3]*Laboratoire des Sciences du Climat et de l'Environnement, Paris, France*; [4]*National Museum of Natural History, Smithsonian Institution, Washington, DC, USA*; [5]*Institute of Paleontology, University of Erlangen, Erlangen, Germany*; [6]*George Institute for Biodiversity and Sustainability, Wilmington, NC, USA*

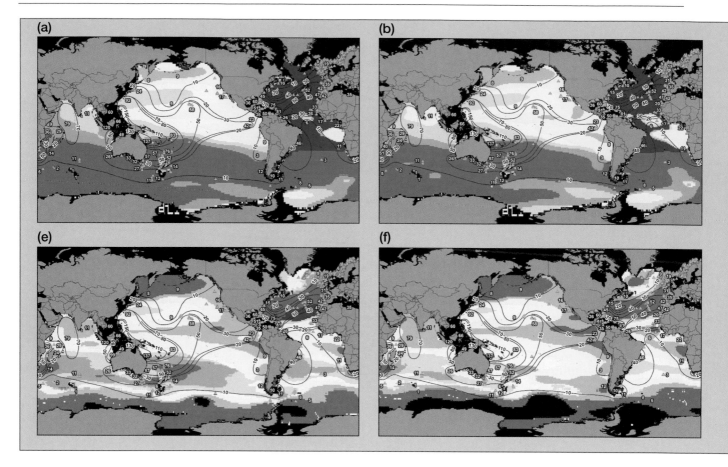

skeletons (a process similar to osteoporosis in humans) and/or experience slower growth rates (Buddemeier and Smith 1999; Gattuso *et al.* 1999; Kleypas *et al.* 1999; Guinotte *et al.* 2003). Both processes will make it more difficult for corals to withstand erosion and to retain a competitive advantage over other marine organisms.

■ Seawater chemistry: the movement of the aragonite saturation horizon (ASH)

Orr *et al.* (2005) calculated future changes in carbonate saturation state (aragonite and calcite) for the world's oceans and found that decreasing carbonate saturation state will not be limited to surface waters, but will occur in the deep sea as well. Orr's aragonite saturation horizon (ASH; the limit between saturation and undersaturation) projections were based on the Intergovernmental Panel on Climate Change (IPCC) IS92a scenario (788 ppmv in the year 2100). The IS92a scenario is generally regarded as the "business-as-usual" scenario, where nations do very little to curb emissions. These projections were incorporated in a geographic information system (GIS) with approximately 410 records of deep-sea bioherm-forming corals (*Lophelia pertusa, Madrepora oculata, Goniocorella dumosa, Oculina varicosa, Enallopsammia profunda, Solenosmilia variabilis*) provided by Andre Freiwald (Freiwald *et al.* 2004; Figure 1). Bioherm is defined as an ancient organic reef of mound-like form built by a variety of marine invertebrates, including corals, echinoderms, gastropods, mollusks, and others

(Encyclopedia Britannica 2006). Cairns' (in press) diversity contours for 706 species of azooxanthellate scleractinian corals were overlayed on ASH projections to highlight the relationship between coral diversity and ASH depth.

The projections clearly show the ASH moving shallower over time as atmospheric CO_2 concentrations increase. Aragonite projections were used because aragonite is the calcium carbonate mineral form deposited by scleractinian corals to build their skeletons. Calcite, the less soluble form of $CaCO_3$ used by octocorals (soft corals) and other marine organisms, is not included in this study. It should be noted that the sclerites of octocorals are calcitic, but the axes may be composed of calcite, aragonite, or amorphous carbonate hydroxylapatite (Bayer and Macintyre 2001). The saturation depth for calcite is considerably greater than for aragonite because calcite is less soluble than aragonite in seawater. However, calcitic marine organisms will not be immune from saturation changes in the oceans because the depth of the calcite saturation horizon is also moving progressively shallower over time.

Based on 410 known locations of deep-sea, bioherm-forming corals obtained from Freiwald *et al.* (2004) and and the estimated pre-industrial (year 1765) ASH depth, >95% of the coral locations were found in areas that were supersaturated (omega > 1) in terms of aragonite (Figure 2). The mean omega value for all coral locations in pre-industrial times was 1.98 (supersaturated). By 2099, only 30% of coral locations remain in supersaturated waters, the vast majority of which are located in the North Atlantic,

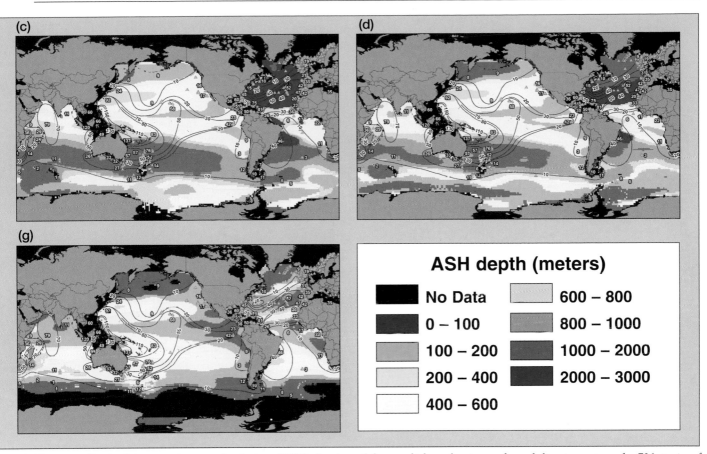

Figure 1. *Depth of the aragonite saturation horizon (ASH), locations of deep-sea bioherm-forming corals, and diversity contours for 706 species of azooxanthellate corals. (a) Projected ASH depth for year 1765; pCO₂ = 278 ppmv. (b) Estimated ASH depth for year 1995; pCO₂ = 365 ppmv. (c) Projected ASH depth for year 2020; pCO₂ = 440 ppmv. (d) Projected ASH depth for year 2040; pCO₂ = 513 ppmv. (e) Projected ASH depth for year 2060; pCO₂ = 594 ppmv. (f) Projected ASH depth for year 2080; pCO₂ = 684 ppmv. (g) Projected ASH depth for year 2099; pCO₂ = 788 ppmv. Green triangles are locations of the six deep-sea bioherm-forming coral species. Black areas appearing in the Southern Ocean in figures 1e–g and the North Pacific in Figure 1g indicate areas where ASH depth has reached the surface. Numerals not falling on diversity contours indicate number of azooxanthellate coral species.*

where the ASH remains relatively deep. Mean omega values for all coral locations in 2099 is 0.99 (undersaturated). Lab experiments performed on hermatypic, shallow-water corals in supersaturated waters have shown that relatively modest reductions in aragonite saturation state can cause substantial decreases in calcification (Langdon *et al.* 2003; Langdon and Atkinson 2005). If future experiments show the same is true for deep-sea, bioherm-forming corals, then calcification rates may decrease well before corals become undersaturated with respect to aragonite.

■ Deep-sea coral distributions in the Atlantic and Pacific

Deep-sea scleractinian corals are found in all ocean basins. Figure 1 shows that the center of species diversity for azooxanthellate corals are the waters surrounding the Philippines (~160 species), followed by New Caledonia (~140 species), and the Caribbean Sea (~80 species) (Cairns in press). The majority of deep-sea, bioherm-forming scleractinians have been discovered in the North Atlantic, which is probably a function of sampling bias, but may also be connected to the ASH depth. Extensive deep

water surveys in the North Pacific (Aleutian and Hawaiian Islands; Baco pers comm; Stone pers comm) have not documented deep-sea scleractinian bioherms like those found in the North Atlantic, although some records of small pieces exist from collections (Rogers 1999). One possible reason for their absence in the North Pacific might be the shallow depth of the ASH throughout much of the region.

The ASH in the North Atlantic is very deep (>2000 m) and many of the deep-sea scleractinians found in these waters are bioherm-forming, robust, and cover areas several kilometers in size. The *Lophelia pertusa* bioherms off the coasts of Norway and Sweden are prime examples of such corals; they cover large areas and occur at relatively shallow depths (Fosså *et al.* 2002). Deep-sea scleractinian accretion in the North Atlantic produces structures several meters in height, due to the corals' ability to grow on top of the dead skeletons (coral rubble) of their predecessors. Bioherm accretion in the deep sea is a slow process; the age of North Atlantic corals vary, but recent estimates indicate they are less than 10 000 years old (Schröder-Ritzrau *et al.* 2005).

North Pacific deep-sea coral ecosystems are quite unlike those found in the North Atlantic. Present-day ASH depth in the North Pacific is relatively shallow

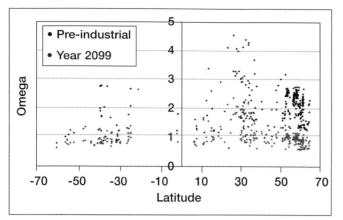

Figure 2. *Projected ASH values for deep-sea coral locations in pre-industrial times (year 1765; black dots) and in the year 2099 (red dots). ASH (saturation boundary) is omega = 1; n = 410.*

(50–600 m) and scleractinian corals found there do not form bioherms. North Pacific scleractinians tend to be found in solitary colonies and the region is dominated by octocorals (soft corals, stoloniferans, sea fans, gorgonians, sea pens) and stylasterids. Octocorals and a small percentage (about 10%) of stylasterid species use calcite to build their spicules and skeletons (Carins and Macintyre 1992). Cairns and Macintyre (1992) studied 71 stylasterid species, seven of which were from the temperate North Pacific. Remarkably, six of the seven species had calcitic skeletons (the less soluble polymorph), even though calcite is rare among the stylasterids. These calcitic stylasterids were found in abundance at depths of 50–500 m. The Aleutian Islands, a region where the approximate depth of the ASH is < 150 m, is one example of an area dominated by octocorals, stylasterids, and sponges.

The depth at which many azooxanthellate corals are found in the waters surrounding the Galápagos Islands lends further credence to the hypothesized ASH–scleractinian relationship. Figure 1 shows global diversity contours for 706 species of azooxanthellate corals, regardless of depth. Across all ocean basins, 91 of the 706 species (13%) occur exclusively in shallow water (0–50 m). However, 19 of the 42 species (45%) found in the waters off the Galápagos Islands are found in less than 50 m of water. This is interesting, given the fact that present-day ASH depth in the waters surrounding the Galápagos is quite shallow (< 300 m) due to upwelling.

Stony corals in the North Pacific are found in close proximity to, or at slightly shallower depths than, the ASH, suggesting that corals may be surviving in a marginal aragonite saturation state environment. Coral rubble fields are nonexistent in the North Pacific, where aragonite dissolution rates in the upper 1000 m are twice as high as the dissolution rates of the North Atlantic (Feely *et al.* 2004). The shallow depth of the ASH and the high dissolution rates in North Pacific waters could work synergistically to make bioherm accretion unlikely, if not impossible. Corals may have biophysical mechanisms which allow them to survive in close proximity to the ASH, but not to flourish and form accumu-

lated structures such as those found in the North Atlantic, where the ASH is much deeper and dissolution rates are low.

The North Atlantic is not the only region where deep-sea scleractinians form bioherms. Such structures are also found in several ocean basins, where the ASH is deep and dissolution rates are low (eg the South Pacific and South Atlantic). Scleractinians are not known to form deep bioherms in the North Pacific or northern Indian Ocean, where the ASH is shallow and dissolution rates are high. A strong qualitative correlation exists between areas of low azooxanthellate coral diversity and areas where the present-day ASH is relatively shallow (Figure 1b). These areas include the temperate North Pacific, off the west coast of South America, the northern Indian Ocean, and off the southwest coast of Africa.

The exception to the low scleractinian diversity–shallow ASH relationship is the Southern Ocean, where scleractinian diversity is low (< 10 species) and the present-day ASH depth is relatively deep (> 800 m) for much of the region. Low species diversity in the Southern Ocean is not due to lack of exploration in the region and it is generally accepted that the taxonomy of Antarctic scleractinians is fairly well known (Cairns pers comm). The reason(s) for this exception are not known, but possibilities include past and present barriers to coral recruitment and/or the extent of sea ice throughout geologic history.

■ Food availability

There is warranted concern that changing seawater chemistry could have an indirect, detrimental effect on deep-sea corals, by limiting the amount of food and nutrients available to deep-sea coral ecosystems. Very little information exists on the food sources of these organisms, but it is probable that they depend on suspended organic matter and zooplankton for nourishment (Kiriakoulakis *et al.* 2005). Since corals are sessile filter feeders, they can obtain nourishment either from organic matter falling from the surface or via currents that bring organic matter and zooplankton to the coral. Deep-sea corals are found in waters that have above-average surface primary productivity, indicating that food falling from the surface is important to their survival (Figures 3 and 4). There is also a strong correlation between chlorophyll-a concentration and particulate organic carbon (POC) in the world's oceans (Legendre and Michaud 1999; Gardner unpublished).

Many species of plankton (eg coccolithophores and foraminiferans) and pteropods (small gastropod mollusks), which form the base of marine food webs, use carbonate ions to build their $CaCO_3$ shells/tests and are sensitive to the seawater chemistry changes previously noted (Riebesell *et al.* 2000; Riebesell 2004; Orr *et al.* 2005). If changing seawater chemistry causes a reduction in phytoplankton and zooplankton production in surface waters, the feedback to deep-sea coral ecosystems will probably be negative, as deep-sea corals may not be able to attain their nutritional requirements.

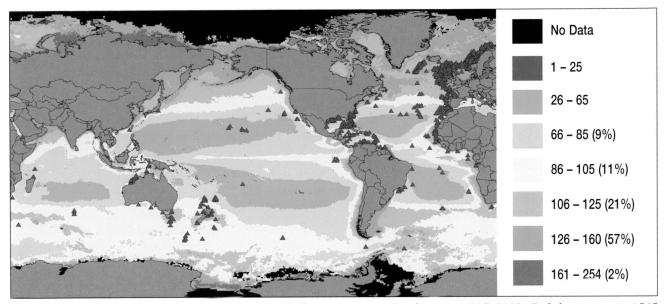

Figure 3. *Coral locations and global average chlorophyll-a concentration for the years 1997–2000. Red dots represent 1565 locations of the six deep-sea bioherm-forming coral species. Note: legend values for chlorophyll-a concentration range from 0–255; Data used was converted from mg/m³ to a color unit scale, with 0 indicating no chlorophyll and 255 the highest chlorophyll concentration found in the oceans for this time period. Figures in parentheses indicate the percentage of total coral records within each concentration range. (Source: SeaWiFS Project, NASA/Goddard Space Flight Center.)*

■ Other factors

Changing seawater chemistry is not the only threat deep-sea corals face in the age of global climate change. These organisms have evolved in steady-state, cold, dark, nutrient-rich environments and it is possible that changes in temperature, salinity, or water motion may also have negative consequences. Model projections for these variables vary considerably, uncertainties are high, and the biological feedbacks to changes in these factors are poorly understood in terms of their effects on deep-sea corals. Nevertheless, worrisome physical changes are taking place in the world's oceans. Global sea temperatures are rising in the deep-sea, due to increasing amounts of anthropogenic CO_2 in the atmosphere (Barnett *et al.* 2005). Rising sea temperatures will probably influence deep-sea coral calcification rates, physiology, and biochemistry, even though specific ranges and thresholds are not yet known.

Climate change is also altering the salinity of the world's oceans (Curry *et al.* 2003). Increased evaporation in tropical waters has led to more saline conditions at lower latitudes, whereas glacial ice melt in polar waters has produced less saline conditions at higher latitudes. Freshwater inputs to high latitude waters are expected to increase as global temperatures continue to rise and the influx of freshwater may slow down water circulation, reduce upwelling, and/or alter the trajectory of present-day current patterns (Curry *et al.* 2003). Since deep-sea corals are sessile organisms that

depend on currents to bring them food, any change in the direction and/or velocity of currents could have a serious impact on their distribution.

■ Summary

The oceans are changing both chemically and physically as a result of the uptake of anthropogenic CO_2. Shallow-water corals and other marine calcifiers react negatively when

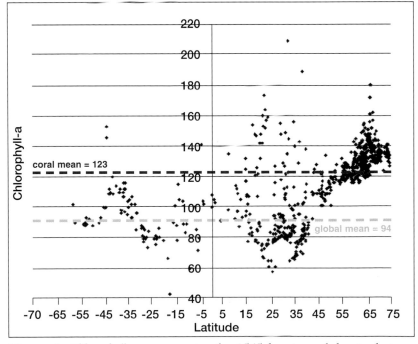

Figure 4. *Chlorophyll-a concentration for 1565 locations of the six deep-sea bioherm-forming coral species plotted with latitude.*

exposed to reduced carbonate saturation state conditions. Biological feedbacks and the reactions of marine organisms to these changes will be complex and will probably affect all trophic levels of the world's oceans. Deep-sea coral ecosystems will not be immune from these changes and probably have not experienced the combination of chemical and physical stresses described for a very long time. The synergistic effects of these stresses occurring in concert are uncertain, but these changes will probably have serious implications for deep-sea coral ecosystems.

The effects of decreasing aragonite saturation state on deep-sea, bioherm-forming scleractinians are not well understood and further experimentation is warranted. Lab and in situ monitoring experiments are needed to help us understand and quantify how chemical changes might affect deep-sea coral ecosystems in the future. If (a) aragonite saturation state is as important to deep-sea scleractinians as it is to shallow-water hermatypic corals and (b) the depth of the ASH moves progressively into shallower waters as projected, then over time, deep-sea, bioherm-forming corals will be exposed to an increasingly marginal environment. If the hypothesis presented is valid and the shallow depth of the ASH in certain regions of the oceans (eg the North Pacific) is limiting deep-sea scleractinians from forming bioherms, then we can expect substantial changes in the distribution of deep-sea corals and the structures they form within this century. The upward migration of the ASH has the potential to alter the global distribution of deep-sea scleractinian bioherms and the organisms that depend on them.

■ Acknowledgements

We are grateful for early comments and advice from R Buddemeier, J Kleypas, and R Feely. The TESAG department of James Cook University provided scholarships and stipends for J Guinotte's PhD research. Special thanks to the Marine Conservation Biology Institute for allocating time to work on this research.

■ References:

Barnett TP, Pierce DW, AchutaRao K, *et al.* 2005. Penetration of human-induced warming into the world's oceans. *Science* **309**: 284–87.

Bayer FM and Macintyre IG. 2001. The mineral composition of the axis and holdfast of some gorgonacean octocorals (Coelenterata: Anthozoa), with special reference to the family Gorgoniidae. *Proc Biol Soc Wash* **114**: 309–45.

Buddemeier RW and Smith SV. 1999. Coral adaptation and acclimatization: a most ingenious paradox. *Am Zool* **39**: 1–9.

Caldeira K and Wickett ME. 2003. Anthropogenic carbon and ocean pH. *Nature* **425**: 365.

Cairns SD and Macintyre IG. 1992. Phylogenetic implications of calcium carbonate mineralogy in the Stylasteridae (Cnidaria: Hydrozoa). *Palaios* **7**: 96–107.

Cairns SD. Deep-water corals: a primer. *Bull Mar Sci*. In press.

Curry R, Dickson B, and Yashayaev I. 2003. A change in the freshwater balance of the Atlantic Ocean over the past four decades. *Nature* **426**: 826–29.

Encyclopedia Britannica. 2006. Bioherm. Encyclopedia Britannica Premium Service. www.britannica.com/eb/article-9079259. Viewed 15 February 2006.

Feely R, Sabine C, Lee K, *et al.* 2004. Impact of anthropogenic CO_2 on the $CaCO_3$ system in the oceans. *Science* **305**: 362–66.

Fosså JH, Mortensen PB, and Furevik DM. 2002. The deep-water coral *Lophelia pertusa* in Norwegian waters: distribution and fishery impacts. *Hydrobiologia* **471**: 1–12.

Freiwald A, Fosså JH, Grehan A, *et al.* 2004. Cold-water coral reefs. Cambridge, UK: UNEP–WCMC.

Gardner WD, Mishonov AV, and Richardson MJ. Global POC concentrations from in-situ and satellite data. Unpublished.

Gattuso J-P, Allemand D, and Frankignoulle M. 1999. Photosynthesis and calcification at cellular, organismal and community levels in coral reefs: a review on interactions and control by carbonate chemistry. *Am Zool* **39**: 160–83.

Guinotte JM, Buddemeier RW, and Kleypas JA. 2003. Future coral reef habitat marginality: temporal and spatial effects of climate change in the Pacific basin. *Coral Reefs* **22**: 551–58.

Kiriakoulakis K, Harper E, Wolff GA, *et al.* 2005. Lipids and nitrogen isotopes of two deep-water corals from the North-East Atlantic: initial results and implications for their nutrition. In: Freiwald A and Roberts JM (Eds). Cold-water corals and ecosystems. Heidelberg, Germany: Springer Verlag.

Kleypas JA, Buddemeier RW, Archer D, *et al.* 1999. Geochemical consequences of increased atmospheric carbon dioxide on coral reefs. *Science* **284**: 118–20.

Langdon C and Atkinson MJ. 2005. Effect of elevated pCO_2 on photosynthesis and calcification of corals and interactions with seasonal change in temperature/irradiance and nutrient enrichment. *J Geophys Res* **110**: C09S07. doi:10.1029/2004JC002576.

Langdon C, Broecker W, Hammond D, *et al.* 2003. Effect of elevated CO_2 on the community metabolism of an experimental coral reef. *Global Biogeochem Cy* **17**: 1–14.

Langdon C, Takahashi T, Sweeney C, *et al.* 2000. Effect of calcium carbonate saturation state on the calcification rate of an experimental coral reef. *Global Biogeochem Cy* **14**: 639–54.

Legendre L and Michaud J. 1999. Chlorophyll-a to estimate the particulate organic carbon available as food to large zooplankton in the euphotic zone of oceans. *J Plankton Res* **21**: 2067–83.

Lueker TJ, Dickson AG, and Keeling CD. 2000. Ocean pCO_2 calculated from dissolved inorganic carbon, alkalinity, and equations for K1 and K2: validation based on laboratory measurements of CO_2 in gas and seawater at equilibrium. *Mar Chem* **70**: 105–19.

Marubini F, Ferrier-Pages C, and Cuif JP. 2003. Suppression of skeletal growth in scleractinian corals by decreasing ambient carbonate-ion concentration: a cross-family comparison. *Proc R Soc Lond B* **270**: 179–84.

Mehrbach C, Culberson CH, Hawley JE, and Pytkowicz RM. 1973. Measurement of the apparent dissociation constants of carbonic acid in seawater at atmospheric pressue. *Limnol Ocenaogr* **18**: 897–907.

Orr JC, Fabry VJ, Aumont O, *et al.* 2005. Anthropogenic ocean acidification over the twenty-first century and its impact on calcifying organisms. *Nature* **437**: 681–86.

Riebesell U. 2004. Effects of CO_2 enrichment on marine phytoplankton. *J Oceanogr* **60**: 719–29.

Riebesell U, Zondervan I, Rost B, *et al.* 2000. Reduced calcification of marine plankton in response to increased atmospheric CO_2. *Nature* **407**: 364–67.

Rogers AD. 1999. The biology of *Lophelia pertusa* (Linnaeus 1758) and other deep-water reef-forming corals and impacts from human activities. *Internat Rev Hydrobiol* **84**: 315–406.

Sabine CL, Feely RA, Gruber N, *et al.* 2004. The oceanic sink for anthropogenic CO_2. *Science* **305**: 367–71.

Schröder-Ritzrau A, Freiwald A, and Mangini A. 2005. U/Th-dating of deep-water corals from the eastern North Atlantic and the western Mediterranean Sea. In: Freiwald A and Roberts JM (Eds). Cold-water corals and ecosystems. Heidelberg, Germany: Springer Verlag.

Coding to analyze students' critical thinking

Janet Hodder[1], Diane Ebert-May[2], and Janet Batzli[3]

Using a problem developed from Guinotte et al. (pp 141–146), we illustrate a research approach to determine the effectiveness of inquiry-based instruction on students' understanding. Two research studies, one in biology (Udovic et al. 2002) and one in chemistry (Wright et al. 1998), influenced our thinking about how to proceed. Both are exemplary studies that examined the impact of active learning and cooperative groups on student learning by comparing reformed courses to traditional existing courses. The studies coded and analyzed students' written and oral responses to determine their understanding. Udovic et al. (2002) concluded that students in the reformed course showed significant gains in conceptual learning, scientific reasoning, and attitudes about science; Wright et al. (1998) concluded that students in the reformed course demonstrated higher-level critical thinking skills in oral assessments given by faculty external to the course.

Human-induced changes in seawater chemistry, as illustrated in Guinotte et al., is a newly emerging topic in biology and is connected to larger issues surrounding global climate change. The main concept of the paper is appropriate for a unit on carbon cycling designed to expand students' understanding of carbon fluxes in both marine and terrestrial systems. For students not familiar with marine systems, it may be counterintuitive to relate addition of carbon to oceans with degradation of calcium carbonate-based skeletal structures such as corals. A common preconception among students is that as more carbon goes into the ocean, more calcium carbonate becomes available to build the skeletons of corals and other marine organisms.

■ Faculty research outcomes

- Classify student responses for comprehension and critical thinking.
- Code assessment data to provide a basis for asking questions about students' understanding.

■ Student goals

- Demonstrate critical thinking by connecting ideas and principles in the context of a problem.
- Illustrate understanding of scientific concepts and processes.

■ Inquiry into learning

Engage students with a pictorial introduction to ocean organisms that build skeletal structures of calcium car-

[1]University of Oregon, [2]Michigan State University, [3]University of Wisconsin

bonate, and provide the following problem to solve:

"As humans increase the levels of anthropogenic gases in the atmosphere, why will it be more difficult for corals and other organisms with calcium carbonate skeletons to grow?"

Students read the introduction to the paper and draw a box model or diagram that illustrates how the influx of anthropogenic CO_2 affects coral growth. The model can be derived directly from the reading and should include arrows that represent pathways and processes between components of the model. As students develop their model, they should make a list of what else they need to know to solve the problem. Lists are shared among group members for purposes of comparison.

Groups report their "need to know" list to the class as the instructor refines a master list that includes these five key questions:

- What is the source of anthropogenic carbon?
- What happens to CO_2 molecules when they enter the ocean?
- Why are the oceans becoming more acidic?
- Why does more CO_2 decrease the amount of carbonate available to corals?
- How does coral use carbonate?

For homework, students find answers to these questions and revise their original model so that it includes and interconnects all of the components necessary to address the problem. After the students turn in their model at the beginning of the next class, ask them to write a paragraph that explains the solution to the problem and includes all of the concepts and processes illustrated in their model.

■ Searching for patterns: coding responses

The instructor codes both the students' revised model and extended response. The term "coding", in a research context, refers to a classification scheme that allows an instructor to search for patterns in student work based on the rubric derived from learning objectives (Bogdan and Biklen 1998; Ebert-May et al. 2003). Coding is an iterative process: an instructor sets the criteria for coding in a rubric, but as the criteria are applied to an initial set of student responses, it may become evident that certain criteria need to be modified based on those responses. The initial set of student responses is therefore recoded accordingly. The process changes slightly when coding responses with a certain research question in mind. Once the researcher has categorized student responses using a rubric, s/he can look closely within a category to classify elements of the students responses and their reasoning to identify patterns of thinking. This may reveal common patterns related to gaps in student understanding or their lack of clarity or capacity to make connections, as well as ambiguity in the question (prompting the rewriting of the original question).

The rubric (Table 1) for this problem is used to code students' understanding of pathways and processes that result in coral skeleton dissolution. After models and extended responses are coded, the investigator looks for differences in the frequencies of each component for each assessment. For example, if students frequently did not accurately and logically explain the chemical reactions with CO_2 in the seawater, they may lack fundamental understanding of acid/base chemistry. The instructor uses the data to decide if further instruction is warranted. Clarifying why students do not understand pH in the context of this problem can lead to further inquiry by the instructor.

A final exam question could focus on the concept of carbon sequestration in the deep oceans as a mitigation measure for fossil fuel use. By coding it the same way, the instructor has a third assessment and data point to compare students' improved understanding during the course.

■ Next steps for analysis

Coding student assessments provides a systematic method for identifying patterns of critical thinking among students. The next step is to connect each of the categories in Table 1 with student understanding. Use the coded data to explore research questions about why students do not understand particular concepts, in this case by examining the permutations of student responses for each category in Table 1 to see if patterns and hierarchy in the responses can be detected. For example, if students are missing the concept that CO_2 dissolves in water, resulting in carbonic acid, did that influence their subsequent thinking about the main ideas embedded in the original question? Or are students missing many isolated bits of informa-

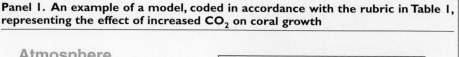

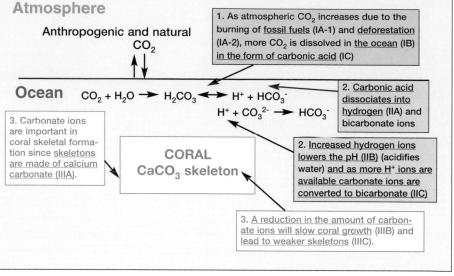

Panel 1. An example of a model, coded in accordance with the rubric in Table 1, representing the effect of increased CO_2 on coral growth

tion, thus preventing them from understanding the big picture? If there is hierarchy, what are the key concepts that are critical to understanding subordinate concepts? This is an iterative research process that drives questions and hypotheses about student understanding.

■ References

Bogdan RC and Biklen SK. 1998. Qualitative research for education. Boston, MA: Allyn and Bacon.

Ebert-May D, Batzli J, and Lim H. 2003. Disciplinary research strategies for assessment of learning. *BioScience* **53**: 1221–28.

Udovic D, Morris D, Dickman A, *et al.* 2002. Workshop biology: demonstrating the effectiveness of active learning in an introductory biology course. *BioScience* **52**: 272–85.

Wright JC, Millar SB, Koscuik SA, *et al.* 1998. A novel strategy for assessing the effects of curriculum reform on student competence. *J Chem Ed* **75**: 986–92.

Table 1. Rubric for coral problem

Concept	Component of model	Code	Pathways and processes
1	Ocean carbon input		Source of CO_2
		IA	IA-1: fossil fuels
			IA-2: deforestation
		IB	Dissolved in ocean
		IC	As carbonic acid
2	Chemical reactions in seawater	IIA	Carbonic acid dissociates into hydrogen
		IIB	Increased hydrogen ions lowers pH
		IIC	Carbonate ions converted to bicarbonate
3	Coral	IIIA	Skeletons made of calcium carbonate
		IIIB	Reduced carbonate ions slows coral growth
		IIIC	Leads to weaker skeletons

Environmental cleanup using plants: biotechnological advances and ecological considerations

Elizabeth AH Pilon-Smits[*] and John L Freeman

Plants and their associated microbes can be used in the cleanup and prevention of environmental pollution. This relatively new and growing technology uses natural processes to break down, stabilize, or accumulate pollutants. Knowledge of the biochemical processes involved may lead to the development of more efficient plants and better management practices. One approach for improving the efficiency of phytoremediation includes developing transgenic plants. Here, we give an overview of phytoremediation methods and their associated biological processes, and discuss approaches that have been used successfully to breed transgenic plants with advanced phytoremediation properties. Much is still unknown about the ecological implications of phytoremediation, especially when using transgenic plants. Phytoremediation-related processes can change the location or chemical makeup of contaminants; the question is how those processes will affect the interactions among organisms in the ecosystem, and how transgenic plants might influence these relationships. Continued multidisciplinary studies will result in a better understanding of the ecological interactions that contribute to phytoremediation, the effects of phytoremediation on ecological relationships, and the movement of pollutants through ecosystems.

Front Ecol Environ 2006; 4(4): 203–210

Our planet is becoming increasingly polluted with inorganic and organic compounds, primarily as a result of human activities. While inorganic pollutants occur as natural elements in the Earth's crust and atmosphere, human activities such as industry, mining, motorized traffic, agriculture, logging, and military actions promote their release and concentration in the environment, leading to toxicity (Nriagu 1979). Organic pollutants in the environment are mostly man-made and xenobiotic (ie not normally produced or expected to be present in organisms). Many of them are toxic and/or carcinogenic. Sources of organic pollutants in the environment include accidental releases (eg fuels, solvents), industrial activities

(eg chemical, petrochemical), agriculture (eg pesticides, herbicides), and military activities (eg explosives, chemical weapons), among others. Moreover, polluted sites often contain a mixture of both organic and inorganic pollutants (Ensley 2000). Currently $6–8 billion a year is spent on environmental cleanup in the US, and $25–50 billion per year worldwide (Glass 1999; Tsao 2003). Most remediation activity still makes use of conventional methods such as excavation and reburial, capping, and soil washing and burning. However, newly emerging biological cleanup methods, such as phytoremediation, are often simpler in design and cheaper to implement.

Phytoremediation incorporates a range of technologies that use plants to remove, reduce, degrade, or immobilize environmental pollutants from soil and water, thus restoring contaminated sites to a relatively clean, non-toxic environment. Phytoremediation depends on naturally occurring processes, in which plants detoxify inorganic and organic pollutants, via degradation, sequestration, or transformation. The different uses of plants and their associated microbes for environmental cleanup are summarized below (for reviews, see also Salt *et al.* 1998; Meagher 2000; Pilon-Smits 2005).

Phytoextraction is the removal of pollutants by the roots of plants, followed by translocation to aboveground plant tissues, which are subsequently harvested. Continuous phytoextraction uses plants that accumulate high levels of pollutants over their entire lifetime. Induced phytoextraction enhances pollutant accumulation towards the end of the plant's lifetime, when they attain their maxi-

In a nutshell:

- Phytoremediation, the use of plants and their associated microbes, is an emerging technology in the cleanup and prevention of environmental pollution
- We present an overview of what is known about phytoremediation processes and the transgenic approaches used to breed plants with better phytoremediation properties
- The ecological interactions influencing phytoremediation and the implications of the use of phytoremediation, including transgenics, are discussed
- Better knowledge of the ecological implications of these techniques will help improve risk assessment during remediation design, as well as minimizing the associated risks

Biology Department, Colorado State University, Fort Collins, CO 80523 *(epsmits@lamar.colostate.edu)

Courtesy of G Bañuelos, USDA-ARS

Figure 1. *Canola, a cultivar of rapeseed* (Brassica napus), *being used to remediate seleniferous (selenium-contaminated) soils in the San Joaquin Valley, CA. Canola holds great potential as a phytoremediator of sites with high concentrations of selenium because of its flexibility, as it is able to remove the element through both phytoextraction (ie accumulation in harvestable tissue) and phytovolatilization (ie emission of dimethylselenide, a volatile form of selenium).*

selenium, can be transformed enzymatically into volatile forms during the process of plant uptake and release (Figure 1).

Rhizofiltration uses plant roots to filter contaminants directly out of waste streams, in either a hydroponic or a constructed wetland setting. Rhizofiltration is also suitable for inorganics, as the plant material can be replaced periodically.

Erosion and leaching often mobilize soil contaminants, resulting in additional aerial or waterborne pollution. *Phytostabilization* through accumulation by plant roots or precipitation in the soil by root exudates immobilizes and reduces the availability of soil pollutants. As an added benefit, plants growing on polluted sites also stabilize the soil and serve as groundcover, thereby reducing both wind and water erosion.

Inorganics are generally dealt with by phytoextraction and/or phytostabilization, while organics are most commonly treated by phytodegradation and phytostimulation. Phytoremediation in general may involve a combination of the technologies described above. At the same time, pollutants may be stabilized, degraded, sequestered, and/or volatilized. In fact, an advantage of phytoremediation over conventional remediation is the ability to remove a variety of organic and inorganic contaminants from a site concurrently. The complete phytoremediation of contaminated soils to fully functioning soils is called *phytorestoration*.

Phytoremediation is being used successfully to deal with a wide range of solid, liquid, and gaseous substrates (Raskin and Ensley 2000; McCutcheon and Schnoor 2003). Appropriate locations for phytoremediation include military sites (trinitrotoluene [TNT], metals, organics); agricultural fields (herbicides, pesticides, metals, selenium); industrial sites (organics, metals, arsenic); mine tailings (metals); wood treatment sites (polycyclic aromatic hydrocarbons); sewage and municipal wastewater (nutrients, metals); agricultural runoff/drainage water (fertilizer nutrients, metals, arsenic, selenium, boron, organic pesticides, and herbicides); industrial wastewater (metals, selenium); coal pile runoff (metals); landfill leachate; mine drainage (metals); groundwater plumes (organics, metals); and outdoor and indoor air (NO_x, SO_2, ozone, CO_2, nerve gases, dust or soot particles, and halogenated volatile hydrocarbons).

Depending on the fate of the pollutant, vegetation used in phytoremediation may require further processing. In the case of phytoextraction, typically used for inorganics such as metals, the plant material can be further concentrated by composting or ashing (producing bioenergy), and either disposed of in a landfill or used to recycle the element. The latter process, termed *phytomining*, is currently being used for nickel (Chaney *et al.* 2000). In cases involving phy-

mal biomass, by adding chelators to the soil that reversibly bind the pollutant (usually a metal), releasing it from the soil and making it available for plant uptake. Phytoextraction is especially useful when dealing with toxic pollutants that cannot be biodegraded, such as metals, metalloids, and radionuclides. One category of plants that shows potential for phytoextraction, either as a gene source or for direct use, are the so-called hyperaccumulators, plants that accumulate toxic elements to levels that are at least 100-fold higher than non-accumulator species (Baker and Brooks 1989; Peer *et al.* 2005). Hyperaccumulator plants tend to grow relatively slowly, which limits their usefulness for phytoremediation. Nevertheless, their growth rate may be improved through selective breeding (Chaney *et al.* 2000), and the transfer of metal hyperaccumulation genes to high-biomass, fast-growing species may also help to circumvent the problem (LeDuc *et al.* 2004).

Phytodegradation involves the partial or complete degradation of contaminants by internal or secreted plant enzymes. As in phytodegradation, *phytostimulation* also involves enzymatic breakdown, but through microbial activity. Plants can stimulate microbial biodegradation in several ways. Since most organic pollutants can be broken down enzymatically, phytodegradation and phytostimulation are particularly effective for this class of pollutants.

Phytovolatilization depends on the uptake of contaminants by plant roots, followed by their release as volatile chemicals by either the root or the shoot. While some pollutants are volatile to begin with, and are simply dispersed unaffected into the atmosphere, others, such as inorganic

Table 1. Cost comparison of two popular phytoremediation technologies (shown in bold) with alternative remediation methods for soils contaminated with organics (Schnoor 1997) or inorganics (Glass 1999)

Type of treatment	Range of costs ($/ton soil)
Organics	
Rhizosphere degradation	**$10–$35**
In situ bioremediation	$50–$150
Soil washing	$80–$200
Soil venting	$20–$220
Solidification/stabilization	$240–$340
Solvent extraction	$360–$440
Incineration	$200–$1500
Inorganics	
Phytoextraction	**$25–$100**
Soil washing	$50–$150
Solidification/stabilization	$75–$205
Soil flushing	$75–$210
Electrokinetics	$50–$300
Acid leaching/extraction	$150–$400
Landfilling	$100–$500
Vitrification	$40–$600

todegradation or phytostimulation, no further processing may be needed, depending on the toxicity of the end products. However, this must be evaluated on a case by case basis. In instances of volatilization, the volatile product is dispersed and diluted, decreasing its toxicity. This makes volatilization an attractive remediation process, as it is not believed to pose a significant health or environmental hazard, even when used for the absorption of mercury (Meagher *et al*. 2000).

■ Advantages and limitations of phytoremediation

A big advantage of phytoremediation over more traditional remediation methods is that in most cases it is less expensive. Depending on the pollutant, substrate, and alternative remediation methods available, phytoremediation is typically 2–10-fold cheaper than conventional remediation methods (Table 1; Schnoor 1997; Glass 1999). It is also less invasive and more aesthetically pleasing compared to excavation and removal, chemical stabilization, or soil washing or incineration (EPA 1998, 1999). The ability to use plants in various capacities for different synergistic processes, resulting not only in environmental cleanup but also in ecosystem restoration, is the biggest advantage. Tailoring the phytoremediation technique to the specifics of a polluted environment will become more feasible as more information becomes available; for example, in the future it may be possible to select a combination of plant species with different remediation capabilities to clean up sites containing a mix of contaminants. Preferentially, native plant species will be used in order to promote ecosystem restoration during the cleanup process.

A limitation of phytoremediation is that the plant roots have to be able to reach the pollutant and act on it. Thus, the soil characteristics, toxicity level, and climate have to be amenable to plant growth, while the pollutant must not only be within physical reach of the roots, it must be bioavailable for absorption as well. Phytoremediation also usually takes longer than conventional methods. Flow-through filtration systems and plant degradation of pollutants generally work fairly fast (from days for filtration up to several years for degradation), but soil cleanup via plant accumulation may takes years to decades. Some of these limitations may be circumvented by deep planting and by amending the soil with substances that either make it more amenable to plant growth (eg lime, compost), or that make the pollutant more bioavailable (eg chelators, surfactants).

Mechanical remediation technologies and phytoremediation can be used in conjunction. Pollutant distribution and concentration are heterogeneous at many sites, so the most efficient remediation solution may be a combination of different approaches, eg excavation of the most contaminated spots, followed by phytoremediation.

■ Developing transgenic plants for phytoremediation

Transgenic plants are genetically modified organisms. In genetic engineering, plants are induced to take up a piece of DNA containing one or a few genes originating from either the same plant species or from any different species, including bacteria or animals. The foreign piece of DNA is usually integrated into the nuclear genome, but can also be engineered into the genome of the chloroplast. Foreign DNA may cause an existing enzymatic activity to become up-regulated (overexpression) or down-regulated (knockout/knockdown), or may introduce an entirely new enzymatic activity altogether. The expression of the introduced gene can be regulated by using different promoters. The gene product, a protein, may be present at all times, in all tissues (constitutive expression), or only in certain tissues (eg only in roots) or at certain times (eg only in the presence of light or a chemical inducer). Moreover, using different targeting sequences, which function as "address labels", the protein may be directed to different cellular compartments, such as the chloroplast, the vacuole, or the cell wall. In addition to the gene of interest, a marker gene is usually included in the gene construct so that transgenics can be selected for after the transformation event. Usually these marker genes confer herbicide or antibiotic resistance. The introduced genes integrate into the host DNA and are inherited by the offspring like any other gene.

In the context of phytoremediation, it is desirable to engineer high-biomass producing, fast-growing plants with an enhanced capacity to tolerate pollutants. In addition, if a pollutant is remediated via accumulation, as is often the case for inorganics, transgenics may be engineered to possess improved pollutant uptake and root–shoot translocation abilities. If the pollutant is remediated by degradation, as organics often are, enzymes that facilitate degradation in either the plant tissue or the rhizosphere (the region just outside of the root) may be overexpressed. In cases where pollutants are volatilized, enzymes involved in the volatilization process may be overexpressed.

If a transgenic approach is to be used to breed plants with superior phytoremediation properties, it is necessary to understand the underlying mechanisms involved. Once potential rate-limiting steps have been identified by means of physiological and biochemical experiments, the specific membrane transporters or enzymes responsible can be singled out for overexpression. If the genes encoding these proteins are available from any organism, they can be introduced into the plant and the transgenics can be compared with the wild type (non-transgenic) with respect to pollutant remediation. This will provide information about fundamental plant biology and may lead to the development of plants that can be used for environmental cleanup.

A great deal of research has been carried out to investigate mechanisms involved in plant uptake of inorganic and organic pollutants and their fate in the plant (for reviews see Meagher 2000; Burken 2003). Generally, inorganics are taken up by transporters for essential elements, advertently if they are indeed essential, or inadvertently if they are chemically similar to essential elements. Once inside the plant they may be detoxified by chelation and by compartmentation in a safe place such as the vacuole. Organics can move passively across plant membranes if they have the right degree of hydrophobicity, corresponding to a log K_{ow} (octanol:water partition coefficient) of 0.5–3. More hydrophilic organics cannot pass the hydrophobic interior of membranes passively, and there is usually no suitable transporter if they are foreign to the plant. More hydrophobic organics tend to stick to soil particles, thereby reducing their bioavailability, or they become stuck inside root membranes and are prevented from moving into the cell's interior. Organic pollutants that do make it into the plant can be detoxified by enzymatic degradation. They may also be stored in the vacuole or cell wall, after enzymatic modification and conjugation to glutathione or glucose, the latter referred to as the "green liver model" (Burken 2003).

■ Advances in breeding transgenics for environmental cleanup

Plants have already been engineered to better tolerate and/or accumulate various organic and inorganic pollutants, making use of our current knowledge of plant mechanisms involved in pollutant tolerance and accumulation (for reviews see

Meagher 2000; Kramer and Chardonnens 2001; Pilon-Smits 2005).

Generally, plant species that are easy to transform and have a short generation time, such as *Arabidopsis*, tobacco (*Nicotiana tabacum*), or Indian mustard (*Brassica juncea*), are used for testing transgenic approaches in initial lab and greenhouse experiments. *B juncea* is also a popular species for phytoremediation, as it is an efficient accumulator of inorganics, grows quickly, and attains a high biomass. Hybrid poplar (*Populus* sp), a perennial, fast-growing, and environmentally tolerant tree with a high transpiration rate which aids in the translocation of pollutants to the shoot, is another favored species for phytoremediation. Another tree species that is being tested in remediation studies is yellow poplar (*Liriodendron* sp). Both *Populus* and *Liriodendron* can be genetically engineered. Genetic engineering programs for phytoremediation are also underway for the development of transgenic wetland species, such as *Spartina* spp, reeds, and *Typha* spp (Czako *et al.* 2005).

A variety of genes have been used in genetic engineering for phytoremediation. For instance, bacterial enzymes involved in degradation of the explosive TNT were expressed in plants, resulting in enhanced plant TNT tolerance and degradation (French *et al.* 1999). Furthermore, expression of a mammalian cytochrome P450 in plants resulted in enhanced ability to metabolize the organic solvent trichloroethylene (Doty *et al.* 2000). Various transgenic plants were created with augmented inorganic pollutant tolerance and accumulation properties, either by overexpression of membrane transporter proteins (Hirshi *et al.* 2000; Song *et al.* 2003; Van der Zaal *et al.* 1990) or by overproduction of chelator molecules (Goto *et al.* 1999; Zhu *et al.* 1999a,b; Dhankher *et al.* 2002). Plant volatilization has also been enhanced through genetic engineering. Overexpression of two key enzymes – cystathionine-gamma-synthase and selenocysteine methyltransferase – was shown to promote the con-

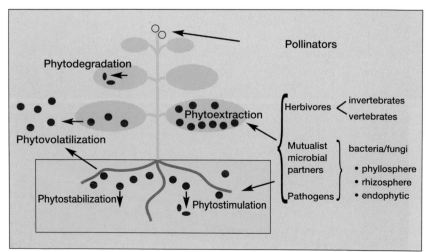

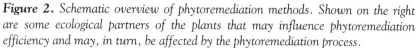

Figure 2. *Schematic overview of phytoremediation methods. Shown on the right are some ecological partners of the plants that may influence phytoremediation efficiency and may, in turn, be affected by the phytoremediation process.*

version of selenocysteine to volatile selenium (van Huysen *et al.* 2003; LeDuc *et al.* 2004). Volatilization of mercury by plants was achieved through the introduction of a bacterial mercury reductase (MerA); the resulting plants volatilized elemental mercury and were significantly more mercury-tolerant (Rugh *et al.* 1996).

While most of the testing of transgenics for phytoremediation has been done in the laboratory and greenhouse, a few studies have been undertaken using polluted soil taken from contaminated sites, and one study has been done in the field directly. These studies have confirmed results obtained in laboratory experiments. Transgenics engineered to have higher levels of metal chelators showed enhanced cadmium and zinc accumulation in greenhouse experiments using polluted soil (Bennett *et al.* 2003). Also, transgenic plants engineered to have enhanced sulfate/selenate reduction showed 5-fold higher selenium accumulation in the field (Bañuelos *et al.* 2005). A field experiment testing mercury-volatilizing poplar trees is presently underway (D Glass pers comm).

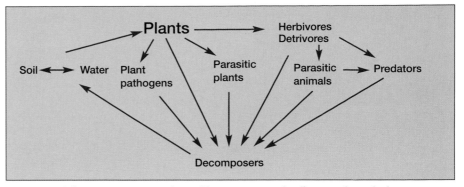

Figure 3. *Schematic overview of possible movement of pollutants through the ecosystem. The paths taken and the relative fluxes for each path will depend on the pollutant, the plant species involved, and local conditions.*

■ Ecological considerations

Many ecological issues need to be evaluated when developing a remediation strategy for a polluted site. In particular, one has to consider how the phytoremediation efforts might affect local ecological relationships. As described above and shown in Figure 2, phytoremediation-related processes can change the location or chemical makeup of contaminants in the polluted area. The question is, how do those processes affect the ecological interactions among organisms in the ecosystem? The choice of plant species for remediation will, of course, greatly influence which ecological partners and interactions will be present at the site, and consequently the fate of the pollutant. The direct ecological partners of phytoremediator plants include bacteria, fungi, animals, and other plants, all occurring inside, on, or in the vicinity of the roots and shoots of the phytoremediator plants (Figure 2). These partners may be affected positively or negatively by the ongoing phytoremediation process. If the plants stabilize or degrade the pollutant, thereby limiting its bioavailability and concentration, the phytoremediation process will probably benefit other organisms in the area. If, on the other hand, the plants accumulate the pollutant or its degradation products in their tissues, this may adversely affect microorganisms that live on or inside the plant (Angle and Heckman 1986), as well as root and shoot herbivores, and pollinators. Volatilization of a pollutant will simultaneously dilute and disperse the pollutant, which may affect ecosystems both on and off the site.

In addition to the direct ecological partners of the phytoremediator plants, the phytoremediation processes may also affect other trophic levels. If a pollutant is accumulated by the plant, this may facilitate its entry into the food chain, as depicted in Figure 3. Conversely, these ecological partners may affect the remediation process positively or negatively, by interacting with the pollutant directly or with the plants. Herbivores or pathogens may hamper plant growth and thus the phytoremediation efficiency. On the other hand, rhizosphere or endophytic microorganisms may make pollutants more bioavailable for plant uptake, or may assist in the biodegradation process. While it is known that plant–microbe consortia often work together in remediation of organic pollutants (Olson *et al.* 2001; Barac *et al.* 2004; Van Aken *et al.* 2004; Taghavi *et al.* 2005), much still remains to be discovered about the nature of the interactions and the molecular mechanisms involved (eg signal molecules, genes induced).

■ Ecological studies

Relatively little is known at this point about the ecological effects of the use of plants in phytoremediation. The study of the ecology of metal hyperaccumulator plants may give some insight into the effects toxic elements in plant tissues may have on the plant's ecological partners. Nickel or zinc hyperaccumulating plants have been shown to be protected against herbivory, due to the toxicity of the metal in their tissues (Boyd *et al.* 1994, 2002; Pollard and Baker 1997). In selenium hyperaccumulator plants such as *Stanleya pinnata* (Figure 4), selenium toxicity also reduces herbivory by generalist invertebrate and vertebrate herbivores (Freeman and Pilon-Smits unpublished). On the other hand, certain herbivores appear to have evolved nickel or selenium tolerance. These species are found predominantly on nickel- or selenium-containing plants and accumulate levels of nickel or selenium that are considered toxic to most generalists (Boyd 2002; Freeman and Pilon-Smits unpublished). Such specialist herbivores may affect ecosystem-level processes by mobilizing toxic elements into food webs, as was shown for selenium (Bañuelos *et al.* 2002) and nickel (Peterson *et al.*

Figure 4. *(a) The selenium hyperaccumulator* Stanleya pinnata *(prince's plume) growing in its native habitat (here, Fort Collins, CO) and some of its ecological partners: (b) honey bee; (c) diamondback moth larva; (d) prairie dog; (e) golden rod spider; (f) ladybug; and (g) white rust.*

2003). Metal accumulation in specialist herbivores may affect their ecological interactions at higher trophic levels via predator deterrence and toxicity, as suggested for selenium in a study by Vickerman *et al.* (2003), and as was found for a nickel-accumulating specialist herbivore (Boyd 2002).

These results from hyperaccumulator plant studies may give some insight into the potential ecological effects of the use of metal accumulating phytoremediator plants. Not much is known about the effects of phytoremediation on the movement of pollutants in the food chain when compared to alternative remediation methods or to no remediation. However, some studies have shown that herbivores were less likely to feed on agricultural plants with elevated levels of selenium, even when concentrations were well below those of hyperaccumulator plants (Trumble *et al.* 1998; Vickerman and Trumble 1999; Vickerman *et al.* 2002; Hanson *et al.* 2003, 2004). It is therefore feasible that long-term phytoextraction projects using plants with high tissue levels of inorganic pollutants will alter the local invertebrate species composition, and perhaps even lead to evolution of metal tolerance in certain fast-evolving invertebrates.

■ How may transgenic plants influence ecological relationships?

In addition to the primary question addressed above (ie what influence phytoremediation may have on ecological relationships), we can ask a secondary question: how might transgenic plants influence these ecological relationships?

Potentially, the escape of transgenic plants or genes could

result in a competitive advantage under local conditions. These risks may be alleviated by careful choice of plant material and management practices that minimize risks (Wolfenbarger and Phifer 2000). Escape of the transgene via pollen can be avoided by choosing species that do not have wild relatives. Also, genes may be incorporated into transgenics that prevent them from producing viable pollen or seed. Genes may also be inserted into the chloroplast genome rather than the nuclear genome, so that they can be dispersed only via the maternal line and not in pollen (Ruiz *et al.* 2003). Gene flow via pollen or seeds can also be controlled through management practices such as clipping before flowering, and by planting a non-transgenic buffer zone around the transgenics, as is currently done with such crops. The plants may also be contained in enclosed spaces such as large greenhouses or underground structures. An example is shown in Figure 5, where transgenics are being tested for the cleanup of metal-contaminated mine drainage water in an existing mine drainage tunnel. Large enclosed spaces have also been used for rhizofiltration of radionuclide-contaminated water (Dushenkov and Kapulnik 2000). When assessing the risk of transgene escape, one should not only take into account the probability of escape, but also the potential consequences: will the transgenics have any selective advantage, and if so, in which environments (Wolfenbarger and Phifer 2000)? Insect-resistant transgenics, such as those currently being used in agriculture, will have a clear selective advantage in any environment, and will probably affect herbivore reproduction. Plants engineered to be more tolerant to pollutants may have an advantage in polluted areas, but not in pristine conditions.

Although the use of transgenics for phytoremediation brings with it the added potential risk of escape, it may reduce other risks. If the transgenics are more efficient at detoxifying the pollutant they will reduce exposure of other organisms to that pollutant. Also, more efficient phytoextraction will reduce the time needed for cleanup, and thus pollutant exposure time. Of course, if transgenics have enhanced accumulation of pollutants, they may pose more of a threat to ecological partners if they are consumed. During this time, entry into the food chain may be minimized by fencing, netting, and wildlife repellents (eg scarecrows, periodic noise). Pollutant entry into the food chain may also be prevented in part by the herbivore deterrence effect of the pollutant itself, as was observed for a variety of inorganic elements such as cadmium, zinc, nickel, and selenium (Boyd and Martens 1994; Pollard and Baker 1997; Boyd *et al.* 1999; Hanson *et al.* 2003, 2004).

■ Conclusions

A polluted site poses a risk to the environment. This risk is correlated with the toxicity and concentration of the pollutant, the likeliness of its mobilization and spread by water and wind, and the proximity of sensitive ecosystems. The remediation strategies available for site cleanup will vary in their effectiveness in alleviating the existing risks and in the characteristics of their associated risks, and will also have different timelines and price tags. For each individual site, these initial risks will need to be evaluated in order to design an optimal remediation approach. Once the remediation strategy is decided, steps must be taken to lessen the associated risks. In the case of phytoremediation, careful choice of plant species and management practices are key to promoting ecological restoration and preventing pollutant dispersal. Where possible, native plant species with effective remediation properties and that provide natural hydraulic control (eg trees) and soil stabilization (eg grasses) should be selected. Drip irrigation can be used to prevent leaching, and fencing will minimize pollutant entry into the food chain.

Figure 5. *Transgenic* Brassica juncea *(Indian mustard) grown in a contained hydroponic setup (a mine drainage tunnel in Leadville, CO) to test the altered plants' capacity to remove metals from polluted water.*

Phytoremediation is an interdisciplinary technology that will benefit from research in many different areas. Much still remains to be discovered about the biological processes that underlie a plant's ability to detoxify and accumulate pollutants. Better knowledge of the biochemical mechanisms involved may lead to: (1) the identification of novel genes and the subsequent development of transgenic plants with superior remediation capacities; (2) a better understanding of the ecological interactions involved (eg plant–microbe interactions); (3) the effect of the remediation process on the existing ecological interactions; and (4) the entry and movement of the pollutant in the ecosystem. In addition to being desirable from a fundamental biological perspective, this knowledge will help improve risk assessment during the design of remediation plans (including the additional risks of transgenic plants) as well as alleviation of the associated risks during remediation.

■ References

Angle JS and Heckman JR. 1986. Effect of soil pH and sewage sludge on VA mycorrhizal infection of soybeans. *Plant Soil* **93**: 437–41.

Baker AJM and Brooks RR. 1989. Terrestrial higher plants which hyperaccumulate metallic elements – a review of their distribution, ecology and phytochemistry. *Biorecovery* **1**: 81–126.

Bañuelos G, Vickerman DB, Trumble JT, et al. 2002. Biotransfer possibilities of selenium from plants used in phytoremediation. *Int J Phytoremediat* **4**: 315–31.

Bañuelos G, Terry N, LeDuc DL, et al. 2005. Field trial of transgenic Indian mustard plants shows enhanced phytoremediation of selenium-contaminated sediment. *Environ Sci Technol* **39**: 1771–77.

Barac T, Taghavi S, Borremans B, et al. 2004. Engineered endophytic bacteria improve phytoremediation of water-soluble, volatile, organic pollutants. *Nat Biotechnol* **22**: 583–88.

Bennett LE, Burkhead JL, Hale KL, et al. 2003. Analysis of transgenic Indian mustard plants for phytoremediation of metal-contaminated mine tailings. *J Environ Qual* **32**: 432–40.

Boyd RS. 2002. Does elevated body Ni concentration protect insects against pathogens? A test using *Melanotrichus boydi* (Heteroptera: Miridae). *Am Midl Nat* **147**: 225–36.

Boyd RS and Martens SN. 1994. Nickel hyperaccumulated by *Thlaspi montanum* var *montanum* is acutely toxic to an insect herbivore. *Oikos* **70**: 21–25.

Boyd RS, Shaw JJ, and Martens SN. 1994. Nickel hyperaccumulation defends *Streptanthus polygaloides* (Brassicaceae) against pathogens. *Am J Bot* **81**: 294–300.

Boyd RS, Davis MA, Wall MA, and Balkwill K. 2002. Nickel defends the South African hyperaccumulator *Senecio coronatus* (Asteraceae) against *Helix aspersa* (Mollusca: Pulmonidae). *Chemoecology* **12**: 91–97.

Burken JG. 2003. Uptake and metabolism of organic compounds: green-liver model. In: McCutcheon SC and Schnoor JL (Eds). Phytoremediation: transformation and control of contaminants. New York, NY: Wiley.

Chaney RL, Li YM, Brown SL, et al. 2000. Improving metal hyperaccumulator wild plants to develop commercial phytoextraction systems: approaches and progress. In: Terry N and Bañuelos G (Eds). Phytoremediation of contaminated soil and water. Boca Raton, FL: Lewis.

Czako M, Feng X, He Y, et al. 2005. Genetic modification of wetland grasses for phytoremediation. *Z Naturforsch C* **60**: 285–91.

Dhankher OP, Li Y, Rosen BP, et al. 2002. Engineering tolerance and hyperaccumulation of arsenic in plants by combining arsenate reductase and gamma-glutamylcysteine synthetase expression. *Nat Biotechnol* **20**: 1140–45.

Doty SL, Shang TQ, Wilson AM, et al. 2000. Enhanced metabolism of halogenated hydrocarbons in transgenic plants containing mammalian cytochrome P450 2E1. *P Natl Acad Sci USA* **97**: 6287–91.

Dushenkov S, and Kapulnik Y. 2000. Phytofiltration of metals. In: Raskin I and Ensley BD (Eds). Phytoremediation of toxic metals: using plants to clean up the environment. New York, NY: Wiley.

Ensley BD. 2000. Rationale for use of phytoremediation. In: Raskin I and Ensley BD (Eds). Phytoremediation of toxic metals: using plants to clean up the environment. New York, NY: Wiley.

EPA (Environmental Protection Agency). 1998. A citizen's guide to phytoremediation. Washington, DC: EPA. Publication 542-F-98-011.

EPA (Environmental Protection Agency). 1999. Phytoremediation resource guide. Washington, DC: EPA. Publication 542-B-99-003.

French CE, Rosser SJ, Davies GJ, *et al*. 1999. Biodegradation of explosives by transgenic plants expressing pentaerythritol tetranitrate reductase. *Nat Biotechnol* **17**: 491–94.

Glass DJ. 1999. US and international markets for phytoremediation, 1999–2000. Needham, MA: D Glass Associates.

Goto F, Yoshihara T, Shigemoto N, *et al*. 1999. Iron fortification of rice seed by the soybean ferritin gene. *Nat Biotechnol* **17**: 282–86.

Hanson B, Lindblom SD, Garifullina GF, *et al*. 2003. Selenium accumulation affects *Brassica juncea* susceptibility to invertebrate herbivory and fungal infection. *New Phytol* **159**: 461–69.

Hanson BR, Lindblom SD, Loeffler ML, *et al*. 2004. Selenium protects plants from phloem-feeding aphids due to both deterrence and toxicity. *New Phytol* **162**: 655–62.

Hirschi KD, Korenkov VD, Wilganowski NL, and Wagner GJ. 2000. Expression of *Arabidopsis* CAX2 in tobacco. Altered metal accumulation and increased manganese tolerance. *Plant Physiol* **124**: 125–33.

Krämer U and Chardonnens AN. 2001. The use of transgenic plants in the bioremediation of soils contaminated with trace elements. *Appl Microbiol Biotechnol* **55**: 661–72.

LeDuc DL, Tarun AS, Montes-Bayon M, *et al*. 2004. Overexpression of selenocysteine methyltransferase in *Arabidopsis* and Indian mustard increases selenium tolerance and accumulation. *Plant Physiol* **135**: 377–83.

McCutcheon SC and Schnoor JL (Eds). 2003. Phytoremediation: transformation and control of contaminants. New York, NY: Wiley.

Meagher RB. 2000. Phytoremediation of toxic elemental and organic pollutants. *Curr Opin Plant Biol* **3**: 153–62.

Meagher RB, Rugh CL, Kandasamy MK, *et al*. 2000. Engineered phytoremediation of mercury pollution in soil and water using bacterial genes. In: Terry N and Bañuelos G (Eds). Phytoremediation of contaminated soil and water. Boca Raton, FL: CRC Press/Lewis.

Nriagu JO. 1979. Global inventory of natural and anthropogenic emissions of trace metals to the atmosphere. *Nature* **279**: 409–11.

Olson PE, Reardon KF, and Pilon-Smits EAH. 2003. Ecology of rhizosphere bioremediation. In: McCutcheon SC and Schnoor JL (Eds). Phytoremediation: transformation and control of contaminants. New York, NY: Wiley.

Peer WA, Baxter IR, Richards EL, *et al*. 2005. Phytoremediation and hyperaccumulator plants. In: Klomp LWJ, Martinoia E, and Tamás MJ (Eds). Molecular biology of metal homeostasis and detoxification: from microbes to man. Topics in current genetics. New York, NY: Springer-Verlag.

Peterson LR, Trivett V, Baker AJM, *et al*. 2003. Spread of metals through an invertebrate food chain as influenced by a plant that hyperaccumulates nickel. *Chemoecology* **13**: 103–08.

Pilon-Smits EAH. 2005. Phytoremediation. *Annu Rev Plant Biol* **56**: 15–39.

Pilon-Smits EAH, and Pilon M. 2002. Phytoremediation of metals using transgenic plants. *Crit Rev Plant Sci* **21**: 439–56.

Pollard AJ, and Baker AJM. 1997. Deterrence of herbivory by zinc hyperaccumulation in *Thlaspi caerulescens* (Brassicaceae). *New Phytol* **135**: 655–58.

Raskin I and Ensley BD (Eds). 2000. Phytoremediation of toxic metals: using plants to clean up the environment. New York, NY: Wiley.

Rugh CL, Wilde HD, Stack NM, *et al*. 1996. Mercuric ion reduction and resistance in transgenic *Arabidopsis thaliana* plants expressing a modified bacterial merA gene. *P Natl Acad Sci USA* **93**: 3182–87.

Ruiz ON, Hussein HS, Terry N, and Daniell H. 2003. Phytoremediation of organomercurial compounds via chloroplast genetic engineering. *Plant Physiol* **132**: 1344–52.

Taghavi S, Barac T, Greenberg B, *et al*. 2005. Horizontal gene transfer to endogenous endophytic bacteria from poplar improves phytoremediation of toluene. *Appl Environ Microbiol* **71**: 8500–05.

Salt DE, Smith RD, and Raskin I. 1998. Phytoremediation. *Annu Rev Plant Physiol Plant Mol Biol* **49**: 643–68.

Schnoor JL. 1997. Phytoremediation. Pittsburgh, PA: National Environmental Technology Applications Center and the University of Pittsburgh. www.gwrtac.org/pdf/phyto-e.pdf. Viewed 23 March 2006. Technology evaluation report TE-98-01.

Schnoor JL, Licht LA, McCutcheon SC, *et al*. 1995. Phytoremediation of organic and nutrient contaminants. *Environ Sci Technol* **29**: 318A–23A.

Song W, Sohn EJ, Martinoia E, *et al*. 2003. Engineering tolerance and accumulation of lead and cadmium in transgenic plants. *Nat Biotechnol* **21**: 914–19.

Trumble JT, Kund GS, and White KK. 1998. Influence of form and quantity of selenium on the development and survival of an insect herbivore. *Environ Pollut* **101**: 175–82.

Tsao DT. 2003. Overview of phytotechnologies. *Adv Biochem Engin Biotechnol* **78**: 1–50.

Van Aken B, Yoon JM, and Schnoor JL. 2004. Biodegradation of nitro-substituted explosives 2,4,6-trinitrotoluene, hexahydro-1,3,5-trinitro-1,3,5-triazine, and octahydro-1,3,5,7-tetranitro-1,3,5-tetrazocine by a phytosymbiotic *Methylobacterium* sp associated with poplar tissues (*Populus deltoides* x *nigra* DN34). *Appl Environ Microbiol* **70**: 508–17.

Van der Zaal BJ, Neuteboom LW, Pinas JE, *et al*. 1999. Overexpression of a novel *Arabidopsis* gene related to putative zinc-transporter genes from animals can lead to enhanced zinc resistance and accumulation. *Plant Physiol* **119**: 1047–55.

Van Huysen T, Abdel-Ghany S, Hale KL, *et al*. 2003. Overexpression of cystathionine-gamma-synthase enhances selenium volatilization in *Brassica juncea*. *Planta* **218**: 71–78.

Vickerman DB and Trumble JT. 1999. Feeding preferences of *Spodoptera exigua* in response to form and concentration of selenium. *Arch Insect Biochem Physiol* **42**: 64–73.

Vickerman DB and Trumble JT. 2003. Biotransfer of selenium: effects on an insect predator, *Podisus maculliventris*. *Ecotoxicology* **12**: 497–504.

Vickerman DB, Shannon MC, Banuelos GS, *et al*. 2002. Evaluation of *Atriplex* lines for selenium accumulation, salt tolerance and suitability for a key agricultural insect pest. *Environ Pollut* **120**: 463–73.

Wolfenbarger LL and Phifer PR. 2000. The ecological risks and benefits of genetically engineered plants. *Science* **290**: 2088–93.

Zhu Y, Pilon-Smits EAH, Jouanin L, and Terry N. 1999a. Overexpression of glutathione synthetase in *Brassica juncea* enhances cadmium tolerance and accumulation. *Plant Physiol* **119**: 73–79.

Zhu Y, Pilon-Smits EAH, Tarun A, *et al*. 1999b. Cadmium tolerance and accumulation in Indian mustard is enhanced by overexpressing γ-glutamylcysteine synthetase. *Plant Physiol* **121**: 1169–77.

Designing research to investigate student learning

Diane Ebert-May[1], Janet M Batzli[2], and Everett P Weber[1]

The call for evidence-based research in education has accelerated in recent years, accompanied by the need to examine the nature of inquiry into student learning. Donovan and Pellegrino (2003) make a strong appeal to improve the quality of classroom research, stating that "education needs high-quality research if the results are to be reliable for the purposes of improving practice". The challenge for a researcher in the classroom is, how can one generate valid and reliable data to address a hypothesis when the research venue is variable and data are messy? In order to address this question, educators must establish standard methods and experimental designs for research that can be applied in many classroom settings.

Our goal in this article is to analyze several different experimental designs and evaluate the validity of each approach in the context of an example research question. We build on the series of recent *Pathways* articles, which provided standard methods to assess student understanding and practical advice for implementation. In March, we demonstrated how instructors can search for patterns in students' thinking by using validated rubrics. In April, we extended these ideas by providing examples of how to code students' work. In this article, we will explain how we would design a research study to analyze how students approach an ill-structured problem (one with multiple approaches and solutions). We propose the following research question: "How can guiding questions associated with an ill-structured problem help students scaffold their knowledge and promote critical thinking and analysis?"

■ Faculty research goal

- Use both observational and empirical approaches to answer a question about student learning.

■ Student goals

- Use effective and repeatable processes to address ill-structured problems.
- Demonstrate critical thinking (refer to March *Pathways* article for student learning objectives for critical thinking).

■ Research design

We designed an ill-structured problem (Panel 1) focusing on the topic of phytoremediation, as inspired by Pilon-Smits and Freeman (pp 203–10 in this issue). This problem integrates ecological and evolutionary topics, including plant–microbe interactions; herbivore interactions and competition; biomagnification and environmental characteristics of toxins, natural selection, and evolution of pollution tolerance; and (depending on the instructor's expectations) transgenic plants and gene flow. Central to the research question is the construction of guiding questions used to facilitate students' engagement with this problem, and to provide instructors with insight into students' current and prior knowledge.

■ Systematic observation

Students address the guiding questions in groups during a large class or in smaller discussion or laboratory sections. Ideally, a research colleague is present to monitor students as they attempt to approach the problem, while the instructor continues to provide guidance. The observer moves through the room, making notes on, for example, the types of questions students are asking (confirmatory/clarification *or* probing/analytical), and how they are answering guiding questions (connecting knowledge from other situations, courses, and their personal experience, *or* quickly moving to text, computers, and classroom resources).

Systematic observation allows instructors to identify elements of the problem that students find difficult, helps illuminate misconceptions, or identifies gaps in students' knowledge. Both students and instructor need to practice using the guiding questions with different problems throughout the course, in order to make this problem-solving approach transparent and automatic. Student responses are further evaluated using a critical thinking scoring rubric (Facione and Facione 1994) given to students at the same time as the assignment. Systematic evaluation of responses helps instructors refine their understanding of students' abilities to draw upon prior knowledge to formulate salient hypotheses, draw warranted, judicious conclusions from their expected results, and explain their assumptions and reasons. This information becomes the basis for the next phase of the study, which is focused on comparison.

■ Comparison studies

We propose two (of many possible) experimental frameworks for investigating the effectiveness of guiding questions on problem-solving approaches to address ill-structured problems: multiple-group comparison and split-group comparison. Without doubt, the classroom research we are modeling takes place in messy settings, is situation dependent, and includes multiple variables that are difficult to

[1]*Michigan State University*, [2]*University of Wisconsin*

Panel 1. Example problem and activity about phyto-remediation
(note: species and biology are accurate, but situation is hypothetical)

The City of Grand Junction, CO, has received a grant from the Environmental Protection Agency (EPA) for an innovative effort to reduce selenium (Se) pollution in a 3500-ha area of the Colorado River Basin, specifically the Uncompahgre and Lower Gunnison River. Selenium is a naturally occurring element that often attains abnormally high concentrations in soils and water contaminated by the waste matter from agriculture, urban development, and other human activities. High levels of Se have been shown to cause reproductive failure and deformities in fish and aquatic birds. Current concentrations of Se within the area are 15–400 parts per billion (ppb) in water and 40–70 ppb in soil, levels far in excess of the EPA criterion of 5 ppb for protection of aquatic life.

Scientists plan to establish a phytoremediation program based on the planting of a genetically modified variety of Indian mustard (*Brassica juncea*) that absorbs high levels of Se throughout the affected floodplain area. This variety has been tested in the laboratory and in greenhouses, but not in the field. Although this seems to be a promising initiative, there are still many questions about the scale of the *B juncea* planting and the environmental/ecological impact of long-term use of *B juncea* as compared to conventional remediation methods. What is the efficacy of this phytoremediation plan and what are the potential effects for the local ecology?

Part 1 (Guiding questions – written response)
1. What things do you know or think you know about this problem?
2. What things do you not know?
3. What things are not known in the scientific community studying similar problems?
4. What things can you find out, given available review papers, primary scientific literature, and data?

Part 2
1. Develop a testable hypothesis focusing on one aspect of the ecological impact of phytoremediation of Se with *B juncea*.
2. Develop a well-supported rationale for your hypothesis.
3. Design an experiment to test your hypothesis.
4. Create a figure showing your expected results.
5. Describe your assumptions that are intrinsic to your expected results.
6. Discuss how your assumptions may lead to alternative results.

control (Suter and Frechtling 2000); in short, a type of situation that is similar to a field ecologist's research setting.

An important aspect of this research is determining the internal and external validity of the study design. Internal validity addresses the fundamental question, "Does the experimental design allow the researcher to truly test the hypothesis? Or will other variables confound results?" External validity asks the question of generalizability, that is, "To what other populations and classroom settings do the results of this study pertain?" (Shadish *et al.* 2002).

Multiple-group comparison is used when an instructional intervention is implemented in multiple sections of a course, or in a single course taught by the same instructor over multiple years (Knight and Wood 2005). Students are not selected randomly for class sections, which may jeopardize internal validity. For example, students who chose the 8 AM section might be different than students who chose the 2 PM section, and this difference cannot be separated from the treatment effect. In one section, students receive homework that includes guiding questions requiring a written response (Panel 1); in another section, students receive the same homework without the guiding questions. Student responses are coded (see March *Pathways* article).

Split-group comparison is designed to statistically remove differences caused by non-random sampling. All students receive both treatments; this design therefore has higher

internal and external validity than the multiple-group comparison, and is an effective design in large enrollment courses (Ruiz-Primo *et al.* 2002; Shadish *et al.* 2002). In this case, half of the students experience the intervention being tested, while the other half completes a comparable activity concurrently. The intervention is done at least twice during the course, in different contexts; groups switch activities. Student responses are coded as in the multiple-group comparison above. The split-group design is commonly called a split-plot design in agricultural studies. The counterbalancing in this design allows the researcher to remove variation in student performance due to external factors, such as previous coursework, by comparing the same student's performance in both treatments.

The class is randomly divided into two groups and both complete the problem as homework. One group writes responses to the guiding questions, while the other group does not receive or address the guiding questions. Key to the split-group design is another comparable problem that is assigned later in the semester, in which the treatments are reversed. The applicability of experimental results is dependent upon the course type, size, students' experience, and classroom environment. Other factors that may be important include institution type (community college, liberal arts college, or research university), and student demographics.

■ **Final note**

In this article, we describe the use of systematic observations of students' thinking that guided our selection of effective research designs for classroom studies. In the next and final article of this series, we will address the analysis and reliability of data collected using these types of designs as well as human subjects research approval. We will identify key questions about teaching and learning in undergraduate science that merit investigation and challenge our community of ecologists to become change agents who elevate the standards for this research.

■ **References**

Donovan MS and Pellegrino JW. 2003. Learning and instruction: a SERP research agenda. Washington, DC: National Academies Press.

Facione PA and Facione NC. 1994. Holistic critical thinking scoring rubric. Millbrae, CA: California Academic Press. http://www.insightassessment.com/pdf_files/rubric.pdf. Viewed 1 April 2006.

Knight JK and Wood WB. 2005. Teaching more by lecturing less. *Cell Biol Educ* **4**: 298–310.

Ruiz-Primo MA, Shavelson RJ, Hamilton L, and Klein S. 2002. On the evaluation of systemic science education reform: Searching for instructional sensitivity. *J Res Sci Teach* **39**: 369–93.

Shadish WR, Cook TD, and Campbell DT. 2002. Experimental and quasi-experimental designs for generalized causal inference. New York, NY: Houghton Mifflin Company.

Suter L and Frechtling J. 2000. Guiding principles for mathematics and science education research methods: report of a workshop. Washington, DC: National Science Foundation. Report 00-113.

Analyzing results: the tip of the iceberg

Diane Ebert-May[1], Everett P Weber[1], Janet Hodder[2], and Janet M Batzli[3]

As faculty dive deeper into educational research, accountability, reliability, and validation will push them to analyze their classroom data in more objective ways. In the May issue of *Frontiers*, we described two research designs appropriate for classroom research – multiple group and split-group comparisons. We used an example to analyze how students approach an ill-structured problem (Ebert-May *et al.* 2006). Here, in the final article in this series, we use assessment data from a single course in which we conducted a pilot study to illustrate an approach to research design and analysis. We begin by describing the human subject approval for research and then show the initial analysis of results from the study that led to further investigation. As a final note, we offer ideas about the needs and directions of future ecological education research.

■ Human subject approval of research

Reasons for pursuing research into undergraduate learning depend on faculty goals, time, energy, and support (Batzli *et al.* 2006). Regardless of the reason, faculty are responsible for becoming knowledgeable about conducting research on human subjects and abiding by federal regulations and policies, as implemented by their institutions. At universities and colleges, institutional review boards protect the rights, welfare, and privacy of human subjects who participate in research conducted by students and/or faculty.

■ Question

In previous *Pathways* articles (see pages 115, 133, and 158 in this volume) we used concept maps to show how students can visualize their thinking by building models that enable them to arrange concepts hierarchically and connect new concepts to those based on prior knowledge (Novak 1998). Concept maps are useful tools that enhance meaningful learning and retention by allowing students to practice making connections among concepts (Ausubel 2000). We designed this pilot study to test whether students who practiced using concept maps performed better on assessments designed to detect their ability to make connections than students who used another instructional tool. We implemented the use of these tools in units on evolution, invasive species/ecosystem services.

■ Research design

We chose the split-group design, randomly dividing the class into two groups (A and B). For treatments, we asked students to perform multiple representations (MRs) of concepts, a task similar to concept maps. In MRs, students define each concept and then provide an example, an analogy, and a drawing or equation illustrating the concept. Students are not asked to make connections among concepts in MRs, whereas students that constructed concept maps specifically focused on making such connections. We believe that both concept maps and MRs are ways to illustrate "model-based reasoning" skills, a term referring to everything from mental models to expert consensus models (Clement 2000). Assigned homework provided both groups with comparable tasks that required about the same time to complete.

Following a unit of instruction on evolution, all students were given concepts and randomly assigned to make either concept maps (Group A) or multiple representations (Group B) for homework (Panel 1). Each assignment was graded and returned to the student, with the option of revising. The first mid-term exam included questions about evolution. Topics during the next unit of instruction included invasive species and ecosystem services. Again, all students were given concepts to make models, and this time the groups' tasks were switched: Group A made MRs while Group B made concept maps. Students then received feedback and had the option of revising their models. The second mid-term exam included questions about invasive species and ecosystem services.

■ Results and analysis

Since the number of questions differed between Exams 1 and 2, we standardized exam scores by converting each to percent correct. In addition to the dependent variable (standardized exam score) and the treatment (concept map versus MR), the design includes trial (Exam 1 vs Exam 2) as a nuisance variable (an undesired source of variation).

The statistical model for the split-group design incorporated trial as a repeated measure crossed with treatment. The resulting ANOVA table has three effects: treatment (concept maps versus MRs), trial (Exam 1 or Exam 2), and the interaction of treatment by trial. If treatment was significant and the interaction was not significant, concept maps made a substantial difference in student performance on exam questions. If the trial was significant but treatment was not, students performed better on one test than the other. If the interaction was significant, regardless of the significance of treatment and trial alone, there may be a more complicated pattern to explain and further analysis is required. The results indicated "no difference" between the effect of concept maps or MRs in terms of students' understanding of evolution, invasive species/ecosystem services, as indicated by their scores on assessment questions (Panel 1). Based on our results, we rejected the hypothesis

[1]*Michigan State University*, [2]*University of Oregon*, [3]*University of Wisconsin*

Panel 1. Split-group study design and results

The split-plot repeated measures ANOVA (df = 1, 38) showed no significant effect for treatment (f = 0, P = 0.95), trial (f = 0.21, P = 0.65), or the interaction of treatment by trial (f = 3.0, P = 0.58). SAS proc mixed was used for analysis.

Instructional unit	Group A (n = 18)	Group B (n = 21)	Assessment	# Questions
Evolution[1]	Concept map 76 (± 2.5)[3]	MR[4] 77 (± 2.4)	Exam 1	14 MC[5] 12 ER[6]
Invasive species[2]/ Ecosystem services	MR 75 (± 3.0)	Concept map 77 (± 2.8)	Exam 2	1 MC 8 ER

[1]First unit of instruction, homework, and exam (time = 1); [2]Second unit of instruction, homework, and exam (time = 2); [3]Mean percent correct on exam (± standard error); [4]MR = multiple representations; [5]MC = multiple choice questions; [6]ER = extended response questions (written short answer)

that concept maps help students perform better on contextual assessments than MRs.

Next steps

Both concept maps and MRs require critical thinking, and assessments suggest that both tools affect student learning in similar ways and have value in active learning classrooms. Given that we found no difference in the pilot study, what is the added value of these instructional tools? The next steps in our research include using discriminate analysis to see if concept maps or MRs help students answer some types of questions better than others, and refining the rubrics for the extended response questions to identify where students made connections. Building on this information, we will balance the number of questions for each treatment with respect to format, conceptual level, and number of questions, and increase power and external validity by performing the study in numerous semesters of the course. Experimental designs cannot tease out the effect of multiple factors that play into an *individual* students' conceptual change, but experimental designs that take into consideration the context of the classroom, instructional design, students' prior knowledge, and how students use multiple learning strategies *can* provide insight about how a *population* of students learn science best.

Final note

This article touched only the tip of the iceberg of possible questions to investigate how students learn science best. One avenue for research in science education is model-based learning that stems from the emerging theory of conceptual change (Strike and Posner 1992; Clement 2000). The use of inquiry-based, active learning strategies in classrooms leads to questions about students' conceptual models that promote "conceptual understanding" in science at a level that goes beyond memorization of facts, equations, or procedures. Investigation of questions such as, "What is the role of mental models in science learning?", "What learning processes are involved in constructing them, and what teaching strategies can promote these learning processes?", could make important contributions to theories of instruction and provide practical applications.

Studies conducted about teaching and learning using large sample sizes and quantitative study designs will enable scientists to critically examine and report their students' achievements in response to innovations in their courses. During this process, studies on faculty professional development (including graduate and postdoctoral students) will contribute to our understanding of how and why people, departments, and institutions change. Seymour *et al.* (2005) addressed the role teaching assistants (TAs) play as partners in innovation and provided an analysis of TAs responses to new pedagogies and their need for professional development. Moving ecology education research forward requires a community of investigators who collaborate to solve complex problems (D'Avanzo 2003).

Beginning in August 2004, our intent was to provide examples of how to use active, inquiry-based teaching in large (and small) enrollment courses, how to assess the impact of teaching innovations on student learning, and how assessment data could drive subsequent decisions about instruction. Beginning in March 2006, we have attempted to bridge the pathway from instruction to research and to encourage instructors to make their teaching and inquiry into students' learning visible. The *Pathways* series engaged the expertise of faculty from throughout the US in the development, writing, and peer review of these articles. Without their contributions, this series would have ended long before now. As we contemplate and implement future research on scientific teaching, we note that successful people are the ones who take advantage of those around them to ultimately benefit students.

Acknowledgements

We thank the National Science Foundation for their long-term support of the FIRST project, Faculty Institutes for Reforming Science Teaching (DUE 0088847) and all faculty and graduate students who contributed to these papers. All *Pathways* papers are peer reviewed.

References

Ausubel DP. 2000. The acquisition and retention of knowledge: a cognitive view. Boston, MA: Kluwer Academic Publishers.

Batzli, JM, Ebert-May D, and Hodder J. 2006. Bridging the pathway from instruction to research. *Front Ecol Environ* **4**: 105–07.

Clement J. 2000. Model based learning as a key research area for science education. *Int J Sci Educ* **22**: 1041–53.

D'Avanzo C. 2003. Research on learning: potential for improving college ecology teaching. *Front Ecol Environ* **1**: 533–40.

Ebert-May D, Batzli JM, and Weber EP. 2006. Designing research to investigate student learning. *Front Ecol Environ* **4**: 218–19.

Novak JD. 1998. Learning, creating, and using knowledge: concept maps as facilitative tools in schools and corporations. Mahwah, NJ: Lawrence Erlbaum Associates, Inc.

Seymour E, Melton G, Wiese DJ, and Pedersen-Gallegos L. 2005. Partners in innovation: teaching assistants in college science courses. Lanham, MD: Rowan and Littlefield Publishers, Inc.

Strike KA and Posner GJ. 1992. A revisionist theory of conceptual change. Albany, NY: State University of New York Press.

Chapter 8

Faculty: A Community of Researchers

Ideas from this book represent a pathway, advocated by John Dewey (1916) nearly a century ago, for teaching science in a way that truly is embodied in the nature and practice of science. We encourage you to try ideas from the articles in this book and collect assessment data to determine how well scientific teaching enhances students' abilities. Use your scientific expertise to help you address and answer questions about student learning in a systematic way and make your findings visible via discussions with your colleagues and scholarly forums.

> *My conversations about scientific teaching made me realize that I needed to think about teaching in the same manner that I did about my research. I finally starting asking questions like: What evidence would I accept that my students understood a particular concept? What questions can I formulate that will allow me to get this evidence? What methods can I use to help students develop a conceptual, well-connected understanding of chemistry? An unexpected benefit of this was that I started thinking about my research specifically along these lines. This improved my proposal and paper writing because I was able to be very clear in what I was doing, how I would do it, and how I would analyze the data.*

Holly Bevsek, Assistant Professor, Department of Chemistry, The Citadel

Frequently Asked Questions

As one designs or "renovates" a course, the following questions are commonly asked.

Do I have to change everything all at once?

It depends. If you want to begin with "one thing," stop lecturing for a few minutes and let students do an active-learning activity about the topic. A break in the lecture will allow students time to process new information (from the previous minutes in lecture) and connect it to what they know. Before you design the activity, determine a clearly defined learning goal and make certain the assessment measures students' achievement of the goal. This makes students accountable and helps you avoid the trap of creating activities that are fun, but purposeless and not a meaningful learning experience. As the instructor walks around listening to students and serving as a resource person, she/he automatically gathers formative assessment data about students' progress and understanding. Students practice cooperative interactions and learning from each other. After several groups report out, resume with a mini-lecture, and then, after 10–15 minutes, repeat the process.

How will I find time to do all this stuff?

Think for a minute. How long does it take an instructor to write a new lecture? Responses from faculty across the country indicate 3–8 hours, plus or minus. In order to not spend any additional time creating an active-learning class, we recommend cutting the material you plan to address in a given class by 25%, and spend the time you would have used to write that portion of the lecture by planning an active-learning activity that addresses one of the critical learning goals for that day. Keep in mind, coverage does not equal learning. Use student feedback, either written or reported out to the class, to gather formative assessments about the impact of the activity. If the activity helped students accomplish a learning goal, then assessment questions on exams should reveal their level of achievement and provide you feedback about the instructional design.

What if this active learning doesn't work? (I.e., "I tried this once and it didn't work.")

Without question, establishing functioning collaborative groups, getting students to share in the power and responsibility of a course, and developing active-learning instructional designs takes time. The good news is that scientific teaching is based on rock-solid principles, so often the issue is merely practice—just as in science. Trying an intervention in a course just once often yields "no difference" or even unintended consequences. Students and instructors both need time and practice to grow into the instructional designs associated with scientific teaching. Organization of the class matters (see Chapter 1). In any given course, depending on enrollment size, count on several weeks for everyone (including yourself) to get into the patterns of scientific teaching—a short-term investment for long-term gains in learning.

What if the students don't like this kind of teaching?

"Just give me the notes and tell me what to study for the test." We have all heard that chant and students know when they are in a spit-back mode. In general, students in our introductory science courses are rewarded as passive learners. A scientific teaching classroom can initially shock students because their day-to-day responsibilities change as they think like scientists to learn science. Over time, as students' capacity to perform at a higher level and actually learn how to learn science increases, their willingness to undertake more complex tasks also increases—the bar is raised. You may, however, encounter a student who is adamantly opposed to taking responsibility for his or her own learning and is not willing to participate in the class. In these cases, we advise the student to enroll in another section of the course or in an alternative course.

What if I don't cover everything?

Predictably, the amount of material covered in a course will decrease, but the trade-off is increased student learning. Pick and choose the topics for the course that are challenging for students to learn; they are quite capable of learning easy concepts during their own time. Ask yourself and colleagues, what do we want the students to know and be able to do after completing this course? What learning is important to meet the goals of subsequent courses (if majors) or of general education (if non-majors). The key is collaborating with your peers in determining big picture learning outcomes for programs—this is not a trivial step.

Am I really teaching them?

Scientific teaching does not remove you from the classroom, it just shifts the focus from instructor to students. You are an expert, students are novices. Active learning provides opportunities for them to interact with the material and make connections to prior knowledge, with you as the guide and facilitator. You still give lectures, but they become mini-lectures with time in between when students actually work with the material to build understanding. The shift from "I" to "them" in an environment where power is shared evokes striking changes in students' motivation and responsibility.

Community of Researchers

What do you do when you encounter a question in scientific research? Often you contact colleagues in your own department, from other departments, in specialized research centers at your university, or at other schools. Networks of experts with similar or cross-disciplinary interests are key to helping you advance your scholarly work. So too in scientific teaching—we do not do this alone, as a matter of fact, we cannot do it alone—collaborations matter.

In science, communities of experts with common interests help each other advance scholarly work. Different levels of support are available both within and outside institutions. At the individual level, mentoring matters, because the maxim "we teach the way we were taught" still rings true. Mentors who model scientific teaching are critical to this network and directly influence future and early career faculty.

The thing that made the biggest difference in my career direction was the support and respect of the instructor for whom I was a T.A....He was not faculty, rather an academic professional that taught me the value of active learning and development of learning objectives. He was very innovative, using lots of technology, assessment and active learning in a monstrous, awful, 500-student classroom. He was an outstanding model for me, and when he saw my interest in teaching...he nurtured it.

Janet Batzli, Associate Director, Biocore, University of Wisconsin, Madison

The pathway to change for many instructors is often stimulated when they realize their students are not learning. Once they embrace and practice scientific teaching, the support by their mentor *and* the department and scientific community matters.

I think of my years with my mentor as a "teaching apprenticeship" where I learned the craft of scientific teaching. Just as I had worked with my Ph.D. advisor to learn the methods of ecology research, I worked with my mentor to learn how to design meaningful learning experiences for students. Scientific teaching perfectly captures the essence of how she approaches teaching, what she has trained me to do, and the basis of all of my lesson designs. I never made much progress in improving my courses until I started using this approach. For any concept I want to teach, I can start with my "hypothesis" of the best way to teach it, implement my "experiment" in the classroom, and collect "data"

to see how well it worked. Not only has this approach helped me improve student learning in my classes, but it has given my efforts greater respectability among my science colleagues and helped me find a place for myself in two different institutions.

Debra Linton, Assistant Professor, Department of Biology, Central Michigan University

At a broader level, there are increasing numbers of individuals in science departments at colleges and universities who have expertise in science and education. They conduct research on teaching and learning and generate funding to support their scholarly work. These faculty are a source of ideas and collaborations. Likewise, many colleges and universities have teaching and learning centers where faculty can learn about research on scientific teaching and connect with others who have a strong interest in student learning. Initially, find one or two people to contact for immediate support about teaching and learning when you need it—that person may be from within your college or from another. Join education sections of scientific professional societies and participate in their formal activities at annual meetings. Consider opportunities for external funding for both curricular and research ideas in undergraduate science education from agencies such as the National Science Foundation, Howard Hughes Medical Institute, or state and local sources. Finally, as you contemplate changing one class meeting, a course, or the entire curriculum, we encourage you to remember that "successful people are the ones who take advantage of those around them to ultimately benefit students."

Reprint Citations

Banks, J. E. 2004. Divided culture: integrating agriculture and conservation biology. *Frontiers in Ecology and the Environment* 2(10): 537–545.

Batzli, J. M., D. Ebert-May, and J. Hodder. 2006. Bridging the pathway from instruction to research. *Frontiers in Ecology and the* Environment 4(2): 105–107.

Beedlow, P. A., D. T. Tingey, D. L. Phillips, W. E. Hogsett, and D. M. Olszyk. 2004. Rising atmospheric CO_2 and carbon sequestration in forests. *Frontiers in Ecology and the Environment* 2(6): 315–322.

Callaway, R. M., and W. M. Ridenour. 2004. Novel weapons: invasive success and the evolution of increased competitive ability. *Frontiers in Ecology and the Environment* 2(8): 436–443.

Derting, T. L., D. Ebert-May, J. Hodder, and E. P. Weber. 2005. Determining confidence: sex and statistics. *Frontiers in Ecology and the Environment* 3(6): 338–339.

Ebert-May, D., J. M. Batzli, and E. P. Weber. 2006. Designing research to investigate student learning. *Frontiers in Ecology and the Environment* 4(4): 218–219.

Ebert-May, D., J. Hodder, E. Weber, and D. Luckie. 2005. Unleashing problem solvers: from assessment to designing research. *Frontiers in Ecology and the Environment* 3(2): 101–102.

Ebert-May, D., D. L. Linton, J. Hodder, and T. Long. 2005. Active Homework—preparation for active classes. *Frontiers in Ecology and the Environment* 3(5): 283–284.

Ebert-May, D., E. P. Weber, J. Hodder, and J. M. Batzli. 2006. Analyzing results: the tip of the iceberg. *Frontiers in Ecology and the Environment* 4(5): 274–275.

Ebert-May, D., K. Williams, D. Luckie, and J. Hodder. 2004. Climate change: confronting student ideas. *Frontiers in Ecology and the Environment* 2(6): 324–325.

Ebert-May, D., K. S. Williams, E. P. Weber, J. Hodder, and D. Luckie. 2004. Practicing scientific inquiry: what are the rules? *Frontiers in Ecology and the Environment* 2(9): 492–493.

Ellison, A. M., M. S. Bank, B. D. Clinton, E. A. Colburn, K. Elliott, C. R. Ford, D. R. Foster, B. D. Kloeppel, J. D. Knoepp, G. M. Lovett, J. Mohan, D. A. Orwig, N. L. Rodenhouse, W. V. Sobczak, K. A. Stinson, J. K. Stone, C. M. Swan, J. Thompson, B. Von Holle, and J. R. Webster. 2005. Loss of foundation species: consequences for the structure and dynamics of forested ecosystems. *Frontiers in Ecology and the Environment* 3(9): 479–486.

Fang, J., S. Rao, and S. Zhao. 2005. Human-induced long-term changes in the lakes of the Jianghan Plain, Central Yangtze. *Frontiers in Ecology and the Environment* 3(4): 186–192.

Finelli, C., D. Ebert-May, and J. Hodder. 2005. Collaborative learning—a jigsaw. *Frontiers in Ecology and the Environment* 3(4): 220–221.

Gaiser, E., K. Rosenfeld, D. Ebert-May, E. P. Weber, and A. McConney. 2005. Here today, not gone tomorrow? *Frontiers in Ecology and the Environment* 3(8): 452–453.

Guinotte, J. M., J. Orr, S. Cairns, A. Freiwald, L. Morgan, and R. George. 2006. Will human-induced changes in seawater chemistry alter the distribution of deep-sea scleractinian corals? *Frontiers in Ecology and the Environment* 4(3): 141–146.

Gurnell, A., K. Tockner, P. Edwards, and G. Petts. 2005. Effects of deposited wood on biocomplexity of river corridors. *Frontiers in Ecology and the Environment* 3(7): 377–382.

Harvel, D., R. Aronson, N. Baron, J. Connell, A. Dobson, S. Ellner, L. Gerber, K. Kim, A. Kuris, H. McCallum, K. Lafferty, B. McKay, J. Porter, M. Pascual, G. Smith, K. Sutherland, and J. Ward. 2004. The rising tide of ocean diseases: unsolved problems and research priorities. *Frontiers in Ecology and the Environment* 2(7): 375–382.

Hodder, J., D. Ebert-May, and J. Batzli. 2006. Coding to analyze students' critical thinking. *Frontiers in Ecology and the Environment* 4(3): 162–163.

Hodder, J., D. Ebert-May, and K. S. Williams. 2005. Unraveling complexity: building an understanding of Everglades restoration. *Frontiers in Ecology and the Environment* 3(3): 170–171.

Hodder, J., D. Ebert-May, K. Williams, and D. Luckie. 2004. Marine Pathology: revealing the ocean's etiology to earthbound students. *Frontiers in Ecology and the Environment* 2(7): 383–384.

Hodder, J., G. Middendorf, and D. Ebert-May. 2005. Problem solving: a foundation for modeling. *Frontiers in Ecology and the* Environment 3(9): 501–502.

Kappel, C. V. 2005. Losing pieces of the puzzle: threats to marine, estuarine, and diadromous species. *Frontiers in Ecology and the Environment* 3(5): 275–282.

Knapp, A. K., M. D. Smith, S. L. Collins, N. Zambatis, M. Peel, S. Emery, J. Wodjak, M. C. Horner-Devine, H. Biggs, J. Kruger, and S. J. Andelman. 2005. Generality in ecology: testing North American grassland rules in South African savannas. *Frontiers in Ecology and the Environment* 2(9): 483–491.

Kremen, C., and R. S. Ostfeld. 2005. A call to ecologists: measuring, analyzing, and managing ecosystem services. *Frontiers in Ecology and the Environment* 3(10): 540–548.

Marvier, M., and R. C. Van Acker. 2005. Can crop transgenes be kept on a leash? *Frontiers in Ecology and the Environment* 3(2): 99–106.

Nagel, L. M., D. Ebert-May, E. P. Weber, and J. Hodder. 2005. Learning through peer assessment. *Frontiers in Ecology and the Environment* 3(7): 390–391.

Pilon-Smits, E. A. H., and J. L. Freeman. 2006. Environmental cleanup using plants: Biotechnological advances and ecological considerations. *Frontiers in Ecology and the Environment* 4(4): 203–210.

Richmond, C., D. Ebert-May, and J. Hodder. 2005. Lyme disease: a case about ecosystem services. *Frontiers in Ecology and the Environment* 3(10): 557–558.

Sklar, F. H., M. J. Chimney, S. Newman, P. McCormick, D. Gawlik, S. Miao, C. McVoy, W. Said, J. Newman, C. Coronado, G. Crozier, M. Korvela, and K. Rutchey. 2005. The ecological-societal underpinnings of Everglades restoration. *Frontiers in Ecology and the Environment* 3(3): 161–169.

Walters, L. J., K. R. Brown, W. T. Stam, and J. L. Olsen. 2006. E-commerce and *Caulerpa*: unregulated dispersal of invasive species. *Frontiers in Ecology and the Environment* 4(2): 75–79.

Wilcove, D. S., and L. L. Master. 2005. How many endangered species are there in the United States? *Frontiers in Ecology and the Environment* 3(8): 414–420.

Williams, K. S., D. Ebert-May, D. Luckie, and J. Hodder. 2004. Ecological controversy: analysis to synthesis. *Frontiers in Ecology and the Environment* 2(10): 546–547.

Williams, K. S., D. Ebert-May, D. Luckie, J. Hodder, and S. Koptur. 2004. Novel assessments: detecting success in student learning. *Frontiers in Ecology and the Environment* 2(8): 444–445.

Willingham, E. J. 2005. The effects of atrazine and temperature on turtle hatchling size and sex ratios. *Frontiers in Ecology and the Environment* 3(6): 309–313.

References

Angelo, T. A., and K. P. Cross. 1993. *Classroom assessment techniques: A Handbook for College Teachers*, 2nd ed. San Francisco, CA: Jossey-Bass, Inc.

Ausubel, D. P. 2000. *The acquisition and retention of knowledge: a cognitive view*. Boston: Kluwer Academic Publishers.

Baldwin, J., D. Ebert-May, and D. J. Burns. 1999. The development of a college biology self-efficacy instrument for non-majors. *Science Education* 83: 397–408.

Beichner, R. L., L. Bernold, E. Burniston, P. Dail, R. Felder, J. Gastineau, M. Gjertsen, and J. Risley. 1999. Case study of the physics component of an integrated curriculum. *Physics Education Research* 67: S16–S24.

(BSCS) Biological Sciences Curriculum Study. 1993. *Developing biological literacy: A guide to developing secondary and post-secondary biology curricula*. Colorado Springs, CO: BSCS.

Bransford, J. D., A. L. Brown, and R. R. Cocking. 2000. *How People Learn: Brain, Mind, Experience, and School*. Washington DC: National Academies Press.

Dewey, J. 1916. *Democracy and education: an introduction to the philosophy of education*. New York: Macmillan.

Etkina, E., J. P. Mestre, and A. O'Donnell. 2005. The impact of the cognitive revolution on science learning and teaching. In: J. M. Royer, ed. *The impact of the cognitive revolution on educational psychology*. Greenwich, CT: Information Age Publishing. pp. 119–164.

Fosnot, C. E. 1996. *Constructivism: theory, perspectives, and practice*. New York: Teachers College Press.

Freire, P. 1993. *Pedagogy of the oppressed*. New York: Continuum Press.

Freeman, S., E. O'Conner, J. W. Parks, D. H. Cunningham, D. Haak, C.Dirks, and M. P. Wenderoth. 2007. Prescribed active learning increases performance in introductory biology. *CBE Life Science Education* 6: 132–139.

Handelsman, J., D. Ebert-May, R. Beichner, P. Bruins, A. Chang, R. DeHaan, J. Gentile, S. Lauffer, J. Steward, S. Tilghman, and W. Wood. 2004. Scientific teaching. *Science* 304: 521–522.

Handelsman, J., S. Miller, and C. Pfund. 2007. *Scientific teaching*. New York: Freeman and Co.

Johnson, D. W., R. T. Johnson, and L. Scott 1978. The effects of cooperative and individualized instruction on student attitudes and achievement. *Journal of Social Psychology* 104: 207–216.

Johnson, D. W., R. T. Johnson, and K. A. Smith. 1998. *Active Learning: Cooperation in the College Classroom*. Edina, MN: Interaction Book Company.

Lawson, A. E., M. R. Abraham, and J. W. Renner. 1989. *A Theory of Instruction: Using the Learning Cycle to Teach Science Concepts and Thinking Skills*. Cincinnati, OH: National Association for Research in Science Teaching.

Mazur, E. 1996. *Peer Instruction: A User's Manual*. Upper Saddle River, NJ: Prentice Hall.

Smith, K. A., S. D. Sheppard, D. W. Johnson, and R. T. Johnson. 2005. Pedagogies of engagement: classroom-based practices. *Journal of Engineering Education* 94(1):87–101.

Springer, L., M. E. Stanne, and S. Donovan. 1999. Effects of small-group learning on undergraduates in science, mathematics, engineering, and technology: a meta-analysis. *Review of Educational Research* 69(1): 21–51.

Weimer, M. 2002. *Learner-centered Teaching: Five Key Changes to Practice*. San Francisco, CA: Jossey-Bass, Inc.

Wiggins, G., and J. McTighe. 1998. *Understanding by Design*. Alexandria, VA: Association for Supervision and Curriculum Development.

Wright, R. and J. Boggs. 2002. Learning cell biology as a team: a project-based approach to upper-division cell biology. *Cell Biology Education* 1(Winter): 145–153.

Index